KT-528-308

Published by: Travel Publishing Ltd, 7a Apollo House, Calleva Park, Aldermaston, Berks, RG7 8TN

ISBN 1·902·00791·3

© Travel Publishing Ltd

First published 1989, second edition 1993, third edition 1994, fourth edition 1996, fifth edition 1999, sixth edition 2001, seventh edition 2003

Printing by: Scotprint, Haddington

Maps by: © Maps in Minutes ™ (2003)
© Crown Copyright, Ordnance Survey 2003

Editor: Barbara Vesey

Cover Design: Lines & Words, Aldermaston

Cover Photograph: Windmill, Cley-next-the-Sea, Norfolk
© www.britainonview.com

Text Photographs: © www.britainonview.com

THE HIDDEN PLACES OF

EAST ANGLIA

Including Essex, Suffolk, Norfolk and Cambridgeshire

By Barbara Vesey

Foreword

The *Hidden Places* is a collection of easy to use travel guides taking you in this instance on a relaxed but informative tour of Essex, Suffolk, Norfolk and Cambridgeshire. These East Anglian counties offer plenty for the visitor to explore in real *Hidden Places* country. *Norfolk* is rightly famous for the Norfolk Broads, but also possesses gentle rolling hills, delightful pastoral scenes and a beautiful coastline rich in wildlife. *Suffolk* is blessed with incomparable rural beauty. Meandering tidal rivers and numerous streams, brooks and gullies intersect a land blended with low hills and vast open spaces. Suffolk was made famous by the brush of John Constable and his paintings reflect the sheer beauty and tranquility of this attractive county. *Essex* with its large estuaries and fishing communities, has a rich maritime tradition going back as far as Roman times. The county is equally well endowed with pretty stone-built villlages and contains the oldest recorded town in England namely Colchester. *Cambridgeshire* is most famous for its ancient university as well as being the birthplace of Oliver Cromwell and Samuel Pepys. The county offers a wealth of peaceful and attractive countryside with many towns and villages steeped in history and tradition.

The covers and pages of the *Hidden Places* series have been comprehensively redesigned and this edition of *The Hidden Places of East Anglia* is the fourth title to be published in the new format. All *Hidden Places* titles will now be published in this new style which ensures that readers can properly appreciate the attractive scenery and impressive places of interest in East Anglia and, of course, throughout the rest of the British Isles.

Our books contain a wealth of interesting information on the history, the countryside, the towns and villages and the more established places of interest. But they also promote the more secluded and little known visitor attractions and places to stay, eat and drink many of which are easy to miss unless you know exactly where you are going.

We include hotels, inns, restaurants, public houses, teashops, various types of accommodation, historic houses, museums, gardens, and many other attractions throughout the area, all of which are comprehensively indexed. Most places are accompanied by an attractive photograph and are easily located by using the map at the beginning of each chapter. We do not award merit marks or rankings but concentrate on describing the more interesting, unusual or unique features of each place with the aim of making the reader's stay in the local area an enjoyable and stimulating experience.

Whether you are visiting the area for business or pleasure or in fact are living in the counties we do hope that you enjoy reading and using this book. We are always interested in what readers think of places covered (or not covered) in our guides so please do not hesitate to use the reader reaction forms provided to give us your considered comments. We also welcome any general comments which will help us improve the guides themselves. Finally if you are planning to visit any other corner of the British Isles we would like to refer you to the list of other *Hidden Places* titles to be found at the rear of the book and to the Travel Publishing website at **www.travelpublishing.co.uk.**

Travel Publishing

Contents

PLACES TO STAY, EAT AND DRINK

● Denotes entries in other chapters

1 South and West Essex

The small northwest Essex towns of Saffron Walden, Thaxted, Great Dunmow and Stansted Mountfichet are some of the most beautiful and interesting in the country. This area is also home to a wealth of picturesque villages boasting weather-boarded houses and pargetting. The quiet country lanes are perfect for walking, cycling or just exploring. This area also retains three beautiful and historic windmills, at Stansted Mountfichet, Aythorpe Roding and Thaxted.

Visitors to southwest Essex and the Epping Forest may associate it solely with its larger towns, some of the most populous in the county, including Harlow and Brentwood. All offer excellent shopping and a variety of very

Hunting Lodge, Epping Forest

PLACES TO STAY, EAT AND DRINK

● Denotes entries in other chapters

Dawn at Westcliffe

good entertainment venues, but focusing on these towns is to overlook the region's wealth of woodland, nature reserves, superb gardens and rural delights.

The Epping Forest dominates much of the far western corner, but all of this part of Essex is rich in countryside, forests and parks, including the magnificent Lee Valley Regional Park, Thorndon Country Park at Brentwood, and Weald Country Park at South Weald. Many of these parks arrange special events during the year. Southwest Essex is also home to the famous Waltham Abbey.

Bordering the north bank of the Thames, the southern Essex borough of Thurrock also boasts a good number of fine towns and villages, with attractions ranging from superb heritage sites and museums to family-run specialist shops as these communities continue to go from strength to strength. Henry VIII built riverside Block Houses at East and West Tilbury, which later became Coalhouse Fort and Tilbury Fort. It was at West Tilbury that Queen Elizabeth I

gave her famous speech to her troops, gathered to meet the Spanish Armada threat. Both forts also played an important defensive role during the two World Wars.

At the extreme southeast of the county, Southend is a popular and friendly seaside resort with a wealth of sites and amenities. There are also smaller seaside communities that repay a visit.

The area surrounding the Blackwater and Crouch estuaries boasts one of the county's principal towns, Chelmsford, and a wealth of ancient woodland and other natural beauties, particularly along the estuaries and the Chelmer and Blackwater Canal. This corner of Essex is ideal for those who enjoy any kind of watersports activities. The island of Northey near Maldon is owned by the National Trust and is a haven for wildlife.

This is also the region of Essex dominated by hundreds of acres of ancient woodland, much of it coppiced - the traditional woodland management technique which encourages a vast array of natural flora and fauna.

Saffron Walden

Named after the Saffron crocus - grown in the area to make dyestuffs and fulfil a variety of other uses in the Middle Ages - Saffron Walden has retained much of its original street plan, as well as hundreds of fine old buildings, many of which are timbered and have overhanging upper floors and decorative plastering (also known as pargetting). Gog and Magog (or, in some versions, folk-hero Tom Hickathrift and the Wisbech Giant) battle forever in plaster on the gable of the **Old Sun Inn**, where, legend has it, Oliver Cromwell and General Fairfax both lodged during the Civil War.

A typical market town, Saffron Walden's centrepiece is its magnificent church. At the **Saffron Walden**

Saffron Walden Parish Church

Museum, as well as a glove worn by Mary Queen of Scots on the day she died is what was once believed to be a piece of human skin which coated the church door at Hadstock. The museum first opened to the public at its present location in 1835, and was founded 'to gratify the inclination of all who value natural history'. It remains faithful to this credo, while widening the museum's scope in the ensuing years. The museum has won numerous awards, including

joint winner of the Museum of the Year Award for best museum of Industrial or Social History in 1997. At this friendly, family-sized museum visitors can try their hand at corn grinding with a Romano-British quern, see how a medieval timber house would have been built, admire the displays of Native American and West African embroidery, and come face to face with Wallace the Lion, the museum's faithful guardian. Over two floors, exhibits focus on town and country, with furniture and woodwork, costumes, ancient Egyptian and Roman artefacts, geology exhibits, and ceramics and glass. In the 'ages of man' gallery, the history of northwest Essex is traced from the Ice Age to the Middle Ages. The ruins of historic Walden Castle are also on-site.

On the local **Common**, once

Saffron Walden

known as Castle Green, is the largest surviving Turf Maze in England. Only eight ancient turf mazes survive in England: though there were many more in the Middle Ages, if they are not looked after they soon become overgrown and are lost. This one is believed to be some 800 years old.

Henry Winstanley - inventor, engineer and engraver, and builder of the first Eddystone Lighthouse at Plymouth - was born in the town in 1644. His design for the lighthouse drew heavily on his previously constructed wooden 'lantern' which then crowned the 16th century parish church. The Lighthouse, and Winstanley with it, were swept away in a fierce storm in 1703.

To the north of the town are the **Bridge End Gardens**, a wonderfully restored example of early Victorian gardens, complete with the wonderful Hedge Maze, which is open only by appointment (which can be made at the TIC). A viewing platform was reinstated in 2000 to enhance visitors' enjoyment of these lovely gardens.

Next to the gardens is the **Fry Public Art Gallery**, with a unique collection of work by 20th century artists and designers such as Edward Bawden, Michael Rothenstein, Eric Ravilious, John Aldridge and Sheila Robinson. It also exhibits work by contemporary artists working in Essex today, demonstrating the area's

continuing artistic tradition. The gallery was purpose-designed and opened in 1856 to house the collection of Francis Gibson. The gallery also houses the Lewis George Fry RBA, RWA (1860-1933) Collection, which is exhibited each summer, along with works by Robert Fry (1866-1934) and Anthony Fry.

Close to Bridge End is the **Anglo-American War Memorial** dedicated by Field Marshal the Viscount Montgomery of Alamein in 1953 to the memory of all the American flyers of the 65th Fighter Wing who lost their lives in the Second World War.

Audley End House was built by the first Earl of Suffolk, and was at one time owned by Charles II. The original early 17th century house, with its two large courtyards, had a magnificence claimed to match that of Hampton Court. Remodelled in the 18th century by Robert Adam, unfortunately the subsequent earls lacked their forebears' financial resources, and much of the house was demolished as it fell into

Audley End House

THE BELL INN

Royston Road, Wendons Ambo, Saffron
Walden, Essex CB11 4JY
Tel: 01799 540382

Painted an eye-catching deep red, **The Bell
Inn** is an impressive listed building dating to
the 16th century and set in 5 acres which
includes a 'wilderness walk' within the
grounds. Inside, all is cosy and welcoming:
oak beams, huge log fire, quaint and
crammed with character. All the food at this
superb pub (served every day 12.00-14.30,
and Tues-Sat 18.30-21.30) is home-cooked
to order, with a range of traditional favourites
to accompany the excellent range of drinks
on offer.

disrepair. Nevertheless it remains today
one of England's most impressive
Jacobean mansions; its distinguished
stone facade set off perfectly by
Capability Brown's lake. The remaining
state rooms retain their palatial
magnificence and the exquisite state bed
in the Howard Room is hung with the
original embroidered drapes. The silver,
the Doll's House, the Jacobean Screen
and Robert Adam's painted Drawing
Room are among the many sights to
marvel at. The natural history collection
features more than 1,000 stuffed animals
and birds. To complement this, there are
paintings by Holbein, Lely and
Canaletto. Fascinating introductory talks
help visitors get the most from any visit
to this, one of the most magnificent
houses in England. This jewel also has a
kitchen garden and grounds landscaped
by Capability Brown, including the
'Temple of Concord' dedicated to
George III. There is a lovely parterre,
lake and Pond Garden. Circular walks
help visitors make the most of all there
is to see. The organic kitchen garden
was recently opened to the public for the

first time in 250 years. The gardens are
managed by the Henry Doubleday
Research Association, who grow and sell
a wide range of organic produce in the
shop. The Audley End Miniature
Railway (separate admission charge) is
1.5 miles long and takes visitors along
Lord Braybrooke's private 10¼-inch
gauge railway through the beautiful
private woods of the house.

Within the rolling parkland of the
grounds there are several elegant
outbuildings, some of which were
designed by Robert Adam. Among these
are an icehouse, a circular temple and a
Springwood Column.

Around Saffron Walden

Radwinter

*4 miles E of Saffron Walden off the
B1053*

Radwinter boasts a fine church, which
was largely renovated and rebuilt in the
19th century by architect William Eden
Nesfield and has a fine 14th century

THE PLOUGH INN

Sampford Road, Radwinter, Saffron Walden,
Essex CB10 2TL
Tel: 01799 599222 Fax: 01799 599161

Just east of the unspoilt village of Radwinter,
and at the crossroads of the B1053/B1054,
The Plough Inn is a large and handsome pub
and restaurant dating back to the 17th
century. Landlord Derek Clarke is also the
chef, and the emphasis here is on quality
home-cooked food, served at lunch (12.00-

14.00 daily) and dinner (18.30-21.00 Mon-
Thurs; 18.30-21.30 Fri-Sat).

porch. The village also has cottages and
almshouses designed by Eden Nesfield.

Hempstead

*5 miles E of Saffron Walden off the
B1054*

The highwayman, Dick Turpin, was born
here in 1705. His parents kept the Bell
Inn, later renamed the Bluebell and
more recently known by the sobriquet
'Turpin's Tavern'. Gilt letters announce
that *'It is the Landlord's great desire that
no one stands before the fire'* over the
wide hearth where logs still burn;
pictures all around celebrate the infamy
of the former innkeeper's son.

Inside the 14th to 15th century village
church, an impressively life-like bust

carved by Edward Marshall recalls the
town's rather worthier son, William
Harvey (1578-1657), who is buried in
the crypt. Harvey was chief physician to
Charles I and the discoverer of the
circulation of blood, as recorded in his
De Motu Cordis of 1628.

Like many other villages, Hempstead
once boasted a village cockpit; its faint
outline can still be traced, though the
steep banks are now crowned with trees.

Widdington

*4 miles S of Saffron Walden off the
B1383*

Covering over 20 acres, **Mole Hall
Wildlife Park** offers visitors the chance
to come close to a range of wild and

STOW FARMHOUSE

High Street, Great Sampford, Saffron Walden,
Essex CB10 2RG
Tel/Fax: 01799 586060
e-mail: joanne.barratt@lineone.net

At this five hundred year old farmhouse, set in
stunning countryside, guests can enjoy log
fires in winter, 1 acre of manicured grounds
with croquet lawn in summer and a separate
leisure suite in the annexe with steam and
sauna room. Owner Joanne Barratt is a
holistic and beauty therapist providing

Aromatherapy, reflexology and a range of
beauty treatments. Three-course evening meal
is available-in fact the perfect relaxing break.

domesticated animals. With the private fully-moated 13th century manor house as a backdrop, the wide variety of animals in this excellent park include South American llamas, flamingos, Formosa Sika deer (which are extinct in the wild), chimpanzees, muntjac, Arctic fox, wallabies, red squirrels and much more. Mole Hall is also home to two species of otters: Short-clawed and North American. Domesticated animals such as guinea pigs, rabbits, goats, pigs and sheep can also be seen. The Butterfly Pavilion offers a tropical experience where brilliantly coloured butterflies flit about freely. Within the tropical pavilion you can also find lovebirds and small monkeys, along with a variety of snakes, spiders and insects (safe behind glass). The pools are home to goldfish, toads and terrapins.

Widdington is also home to **Priors Hall Barn**, one of the finest surviving medieval 'aisled' barns in all of southeast England, and owned by English Heritage.

Stansted Mountfichet
8 miles SW of Saffron Walden off the B1383

Though rather close to Stansted Airport, there are plenty of reasons to visit this small town. Certainly pilots approaching the airport may be surprised at the sight of a **Norman Village**, complete with domestic animals, and the reconstructed motte-and-bailey **Mountfichet Castle**, standing just two miles from the runway. The original castle was built after 1066 by the Duke of Boulogne, a cousin of the Conqueror. Siege weapons on show include two giant catapults. Voted Essex attraction of the year in 2002 by the Good Britain Guide, visitors can take a trip to the top of the siege tower and tiptoe into the baron's bed chamber while he sleeps!

Next door to the castle is **The House on the Hill Museum Adventure**, where there are three museums for the price of one. The Toy Museum is the largest of its kind in the world, and here children of every age are treated to a unique and nostalgic trip back to their childhood. There is every toy imaginable here, many of them now highly prized collectors' items. There is a shop selling new toys and a collectors' shop with many old toys and books to choose from. The Rock 'n' Roll, Film and Theatre Experience and the End-of-the-pier Amusement machine displays also contribute to a grand day out here in Stansted Mountfichet.

Stansted Windmill is one of the best-preserved tower mills in the country. Dating back to 1787 and in use until 1910, most of the original machinery has survived. It is open on the first Sunday of each month from April to October every Sunday in August, and on Bank Holiday Mondays.

Hadstock
4 miles N of Saffron Walden off the B1052

As well as claiming to have the oldest church door in England, at the parish

Church of St Botolph, Hadstock also has a macabre tale to tell. The church's north door was once covered with a piece of skin, now to be seen in Saffron Walden Museum. Local legend says it is a 'Daneskin', from a Viking flayed alive, but recent DNA analysis has disproved this legend. Lining doors with animal leather was common in the Middle Ages, and many so-called 'Daneskins' are just that.

The door itself is Saxon, as are the 11th century carvings, windows and arches, rare survivors that predate the Norman Conquest.

Linton Zoo near the village is a privately owned collection of wild animals set in 10½ acres of gardens. There is a free car park, children's play area, picnic areas and a cafe on site.

Bartlow
5 miles NE of Saffron Walden off the B1052

Bartlow Hills are reputed to be the largest burial mounds in Europe dating from Roman times, one 15 metres high. They date back to the 2nd century.

Thaxted
7 miles SE of Saffron Walden on the B184

This small country town has a recorded history that dates back to before the *Domesday Book.* Originally a Saxon settlement, it developed around a Roman road. The town's many beautiful old buildings contribute to its unique character and charm. To its credit Thaxted has no need of artificial tourist attractions, and is today what is has been for the last ten centuries: a thriving and beautiful town.

Thaxted has numerous attractively pargetted and timber-framed houses, and a magnificent **Guildhall,** built as a meeting-place for cutlers around 1390. The demise of the cutlery industry in this part of Essex in the 1500s led it to becoming the administrative centre of the town. Restored in Georgian times, it became the town's Grammar School, as well as remaining a centre of administration. Once more restored in 1975, the Parish council still holds its meetings here.

The town's famous **Tower Windmill**

THE THREE HORSESHOES

Helions Bumpstead, Saffron Walden,
Essex CB9 7AL
Tel: 01440 730298

Here in this lovely little village that straddles three counties – Essex, Cambridgeshire and Suffolk – **The Three Horseshoes** is an attractive and welcome pub dating back to the 17th century. The cosy interior has recently been refurbished and is beautifully decorated and comfortably furnished. The menu of traditional favourites features freshly prepared

home-made dishes served at lunch (12.00-14.30) Tues-Sun and dinner (19.00-21.30) Weds-Sat. The wine list is very good.

Morris Dancers, Thaxted

flag in the church. Incensed Cambridge students tore them down and substituted the Union Jack; Noel in turn ripped that down, and his friends are said to have slashed the tyres of the students' cars and motorbikes. A fine bronze in the church celebrates this adventurous man of the cloth.

Conrad Noel's wife is remembered for encouraging Morris dancing in the town. Today, the famous Morris Ring is held annually (usually on the Spring Bank Holiday), attracting over 300 dancers from all over the country, who dance through the streets. Dancing can also be seen around the town on most Bank Holiday Mondays, usually in the vicinity of a pub!

Gustav Holst, composer of, amongst other pieces, the renowned 'Planets' Suite', lived in Thaxted from 1914-1925, and often played the church organ. To celebrate his connection with the town there is a music festival in late June/early July which attracts performers of international repute.

In Park Street, at Aldborough Lodge, the Thaxted Garden for Butterflies is an ordinary garden that has been developed with a view to pleasing birds, butterflies and other wildlife species - including humans. Displays depict the 22 native wild butterfly species that have visited the garden since its inception in 1988.

was built in 1804 by John Webb. In working order until 1907, it had fallen into disuse and disrepair but work is in progress to restore it to full working order. It contains a rural life museum, well worth a visit. Close to the windmill are the town's **Almshouses**, which continued to provide homes for the elderly even 250 years after they were built for that purpose.

Thaxted Church stands on a hill and soars cathedral-like over the town's streets. It has been described as the finest Parish church in the country and, though many towns may protest long and loud at this claim, it certainly is magnificent. It was also the somewhat unlikely setting for a pitched battle in 1921. The rather colourful vicar and secretary of the Church Socialist League, the Revd Conrad Noel, displayed the red flag of communism and the Sinn Fein

THE SWAN

Great Easton, Dunmow, Essex CM6 2HG
Tel: 01371 870359
e-mail: theswangreateaston@talk21.com

Looking more like a charming house than a pub, **The Swan** is a cosy little pub dating back to the 16th century. Whitewashed and pristine, this excellent village inn boasts traditional features such as exposed oak beams and large open log fire.

To drink, there's a good choice of real ales, lagers, wines, spirits and soft drinks. The food is all home-cooked and good value for money, served at lunch every day and at dinner Mon-Sat, served in the bar or in the separate restaurant/function suite.

Great Easton
3 miles S of Thaxted off the B184

Great Easton boasts a wealth of cottages and farmhouses with ornamental plasterwork, clustered Tudor chimneys and half-timbering. Great Easton's well-known and very popular Green Man pub occupies a handsome building dating back to the 15th century.

Little Easton
5 miles S of Thaxted off the B184

The charming 12th century **Church** in this small village is rich in historic features. Its Maynard Chapel features some outstanding marble monuments of the family that gives the chapel its name, as well as some famous brasses. The church's oldest treasures are, however, a well-preserved and priceless 12th century wall painting and several 15th century frescoes. Two more recent additions, a pair of stained glass windows, were unveiled in 1990. The 'Window of the Crusaders' and the 'Window of Friendship and Peace' are a lasting memorial to the American 386th

Bomb Group. Known as 'The Crusaders', they were stationed nearby for 13 months and lost over 200 of their number in battle overseas during that short time. They flew from an airstrip created in the park of **Easton Lodge**, the favourite home of Frances, Countess of Warwick – Edward VII's 'Darling Daisy'. The gardens have recently been restored (see panel opposite).

The Barn Theatre at Little Easton Manor is situated in one of the finest and oldest tithe barns in the country, with magnificent oak timbers and ancient tiled roof. It was visited by some of the most distinguished actors and impresarios of the early 20th century, including Ellen Terry, Hermione Baddeley, Charlie Chaplin, George Formby, Basil Dean (who married Daisy's daughter) and George Bernard Shaw. The sympathetic restoration of the facilities has meant its continued use as a setting for special events.

Both the Barn Theatre and the Turkey Barn within the grounds are available for private hire. Day-ticket angling can also be arranged.

THE GARDENS OF EASTON LODGE

Easton Lodge, Great Dunmow, Essex CM6 2BB
Tel: 01371 876979
e-mail: enquiries@eastonlodge.co.uk
website: www.eastonlodge.co.uk

The Gardens of Easton Lodge comprise 23 romantic acres designed in 1902 by Harold Peto for Daisy, Countess of Warwick. Abandoned in 1950, they have been gradually restored from 1995. Highlights of a visit include the sunken Italian garden - a delightful suntrap with a 100' balustraded pool; the Glade, formerly Peto's Japanese Garden; the Peto Pavilion; the ruined Shelley Pavilion; the skeleton of the Tree House; and the living sundial with a border featuring every plant mentioned in Shakespeare's plays and sonnets. The 17th century dovecote now houses an exhibition of photography, prints and writings showing the history of Easton Lodge since 1950.

Broxted
3 miles SW of Thaxted off the B1051

The parish **Church of St Mary the Virgin** here in the handsome village of Broxted has two remarkably lovely stained glass windows commemorating the captivity and release of John McCarthy and the other Beirut hostages, dedicated in January 1993. Though just a few minutes drive from Stansted Airport off the M11, it is a welcoming haven of rural tranquillity.

Church Hall Farm Antique and Craft Centre in Broxted is housed in a magnificent Grade II listed barn flanked by a willow-lined pond with its own resident ducks! The building itself is a miracle of medieval craftsmanship, located just a few yards from Broxted parish church.

Great Dunmow
13 miles SE of Saffron Walden on the A120

The town is famous for the 'Flitch of Bacon', an ancient ceremony which dates back as far as the early 12th century. A prize of a flitch, or side, of bacon was awarded to the local man who *'does not repent of his marriage nor quarrel, differ or dispute with his wife within a year and a day after the marriage'*.

Amidst great ceremony, the winning couple would be seated and presented with their prize. The custom lapsed on the Dissolution of the Monasteries, was briefly revived in the 18th century, and became established again after 1885. 'Trials' to test the truth are all in good fun, and carried out every leap year. The successful couple are carried through the streets on chairs and then presented with the Flitch. The original 'bacon chair' can be seen in Little Dunmow parish church.

Other places of historical interest include the parish church of St Mary at Church End, Great Dunmow, dating back to 1322. The Clock House, a private residence built in 1589, was the

THE LION & LAMB

Stortford Road, Little Canfield, nr Takeley, Dunmow, Essex CM6 1SR
Tel: 01279 870257 Fax: 01279 870423
e-mail: info@lionandlambtakeley.co.uk
website: www.lionandlambtakeley.co.uk

Hospitality is in generous supply at **The Lion & Lamb**, situated on the B1256 (the old A120) at Little Canfield, which is easily found leaving the new A120 at Dunmow West Junction and travelling one mile toward Takeley, the pub will be found on your right hand side. A coaching inn dating from the 18th century, this lovely old hostelry is run by Mike Shields, who's belief in traditional pub values has made the place a great success.

Inside, the spacious bars have a delightful old-world appeal, with masses of oak beams, open fires, red brick and rustic furniture. In this cosy, comfortable ambience, Essex-brewed Ridleys ales come from the pump in perfect condition, and an outstanding international selection of wines can be enjoyed on their own or to complement the food, the full menu is served throughout the day from 11am to 10pm, seven days a week.

The Kitchen offers quality restaurant and bar meals at pub prices. The menu provide a nice variety of prime fresh produce used wherever possible. Salads and quiches provide light wholesome meals, whilst the main menu provides more substantial items such as peppered sirloin steak with Stilton cheese, a large selection of fresh fish or chicken supreme filled with sun-dried tomatoes and spinach, served with a lobster sauce. There are also some unusual items on the menu including char-grilled kangaroo fillet. The popular Sunday menu proposes a good choice of starters framing the main courses, which always include two roasts, a fish dish and a vegetarian option. There are smoking and non-smoking areas in the restaurant, whilst the conservatory doors lead out to a patio and gardens which makes an ideal venue for private parties. The inn has a large car park, and there are plenty of seats in the beer garden for summer supping. Great Dunmow, a village full of history, is a short drive along the B1256, and The Lion & Lamb is also close to Stansted Airport and the M11 (junction 8).

THE THREE HORSESHOES

Mole Hill Green, Takeley, Bishops Stortford,
Essex CM22 6PQ
Tel: 01279 870313
e-mail: trevor@threehorseshoes.info
website: www.threehorseshoes.info

Dating from the 15th century, **The Three
Horseshoes** is a beautiful thatched inn that is
one of Essex's oldest hostelries. This
charming pub has been extended over the
years, but retains a stunning 'old section' that
was the original pub. Rustic and characterful,
this excellent inn is well worth seeking out,
not just for its relaxed and cosy ambience but
for the great food and drink on offer. Home-
cooked dishes include steak and ale pie and a
range of curries.

home of St Anne Line, martyred for
sheltering a Jesuit priest. Clock House
was subsequently occupied by Sir George
Beaumont. He used it to store and
display his extensive art collection,
which he bequeathed to the nation and
which forms the nucleus of the National
Gallery collection in London.

The **Great Dunmow Maltings**,
opened to the public in 2000 after
restoration costing £750,000, is the most
complete example of a medieval timber-
framed building of its type in the United
Kingdom, and a focal point for local
history in the shape of Great Dunmow
Museum, with changing displays
illustrating the history of the town from
Roman times to the present day.

H G Wells lived at Brick House in
Great Dunmow, overlooking the
Doctor's Pond, where in 1784 Lionel
Lukin is reputed to have tested the first
unsinkable lifeboat.

The Flitch Way is a 15-mile country
walk along the former Bishop's
Stortford-to-Braintree railway, taking in
Victorian stations, impressive views, and
a wealth of woodland wildlife.

Takeley
*4 miles W of Great Dunmow off the
A120*

The village is built on the line of the
old Roman **Stane Street**. There are
plenty of pretty 17th century timbered
houses and barns to be seen in the
village, and the church still has many of
its original Norman features along with
some Roman masonry. Rather unusually,
it has a modern font that is surmounted
by a six-foot-high medieval cover.

Hatfield Broad Oak
*3 miles SW of Great Dunmow off
the B184*

This very pretty village has many
notable buildings for visitors to enjoy,
including a church dating from Norman
times, some delightful 18th century
almshouses and several distinctive
Georgian houses.

Nearby **Hatfield Forest** is a rare
surviving example of a medieval Royal
hunting forest. It has wonderful 400-
year-old pollarded trees, two ornamental
lakes and an 18th century shell house.
Guided tours can be arranged. Once

covering a great deal more land, the remaining 400 hectares are now protected by the National Trust and offer splendid woodland walks along with good chases and rides.

Aythorpe Roding
4 miles SW of Great Dunmow off the B184

Aythorpe Roding Windmill is the largest remaining post mill in Essex. Four storeys high, it was built around 1760 and remained in use up until 1935. It was fitted in the 1800s with a fantail which kept the sails pointing into the wind. It is open to the public on the last Sunday of each month from April to September, 2-5 p.m.

Pleshey
5 miles SE of Great Dunmow off the A130

Pleshey, midway between Chelmsford and Great Dunmow, is surrounded by a mile-long earthen rampart, protecting its castle, of which only the motte with its moat and two baileys survive. There are good views from the mound, which although only 60 feet high, is nonetheless one of the highest points in Essex. The village is truly delightful, with a number of thatched cottages, and the area is excellent for walkers and ramblers.

Sawbridgeworth
6 miles SW of Great Dunmow off the A1184

Quite a number of fine old buildings, many of which are Georgian, survive in this small town. To the south is **Pishiobury**, built by James Wyatt in 1782, now a school. In St Mary's Church there are 15 wonderful ancient and beautifully preserved brasses.

Waltham Abbey

The town of Waltham began as a small Roman settlement on the site of the present-day Market Square. The early Saxon kings maintained a hunting lodge here; a town formed round this, and the first church was built in the 6th century. By the 8th, during the reign of Cnut, the town had a stone minster church with a great stone crucifix that had been brought from Somerset, where it had been found buried in land owned by Tovi, a trusted servant of the king. This cross became the focus of pilgrims seeking healing. One of those cured of a serious illness, Harold Godwinsson, built a new church, the third on the site, which was dedicated in 1060 - and it was this self-same Harold who became king and was killed in the battle of Hastings six years on. Harold's body was

The Denny Tomb, Waltham Abbey

Waltham Abbey

brought back to Waltham to be buried in his church. The church that exists today was built in the first quarter of the 12th century. It was once three times its present length, and incorporated an Augustinian Abbey, built in 1177 by Henry II. The town became known for the Abbey, which was one of the largest in the country and the last to be the victim of Henry VIII's Dissolution of the Monasteries, in 1540.

The Abbey's Crypt Centre houses an interesting exhibition explaining the history of both the Abbey and the town, highlighting the religious significance of the site. Some visible remains of the Augustinian Abbey include the chapter house and precinct walls, cloister entry and gateway in the surrounding Abbey Gardens. The Abbey Gardens are also host to a Sensory Trail exploring the highlights of hundreds of years of the site's history; there's also a delightful Rose Garden.

Along the Cornhill Stream, crossed by the impressive stone bridge, the town's **Dragonfly Sanctuary** is home to over half the native British species of dragonflies and damselflies. It is noted as the best single site for seeing these species in Greater London, Essex and Hertfordshire.

A Tudor timber-framed house forms part of the **Epping Forest District Museum** in Sun Street. The wide range of displays includes exhibits covering the history of the Epping Forest District from the Stone Age to the 20th century. Tudor and Victorian times are particularly well represented, with some magnificent oak panelling dating from the reign of Henry VIII, and re-creations of Victorian rooms and shops. There is also an archaeological display and temporary exhibitions covering such subjects as contemporary arts and crafts. The museum has several hands-on displays which help to bring history to life, and features special events and adult workshops throughout the year.

Sun Street is the town's main thoroughfare, and it is pedestrianised. It contains many buildings from the 16th century onwards. The Greenwich Meridian (0 degrees longitude) runs through the street, marked out on the pavement and through the Abbey Gardens.

In spite of its proximity to London and more recent development, the town retains a peaceful, traditional character, with its timber-framed buildings and small traditional market which has been held here since the early 12th century (now every Tuesday and Saturday – there is also a Farmers' Market held

ROYAL GUNPOWDER MILLS

Powdermill Lane, Waltham Abbey,
Essex EN9 1BN
Tel: 01992 767022 Fax: 01992 710341
website: www.royalgunpowdermills.com

In spring 2001 the **Royal Gunpowder Mills** in Waltham Abbey opened its doors to the general public for the first time in its 300 year history. Thanks to funding from the Heritage Lottery Fund and Ministry of Defence, this secret site which was home to gunpowder and explosive production and research for more than three centuries, has been developed to offer visitors a truly unique day out.

Gunpowder production began at Waltham Abbey in the mid 1660's on the site of a late medieval fulling mill. The gunpowder Mills remained in private hands until 1787, when they were purchased by the crown. From this date, the Royal Gunpowder Mills developed into the pre-eminent powder works in Britain and one of the most important in Europe.

Set in 175 acres of natural parkland and boasting 21 important historic buildings the regenerated site will offer visitors a unique mixture of fascinating history, exciting science and beautiful surroundings. Approximately 70 acres of the site, containing some of the oldest buildings and much of the canal network, will be open for visitors to explore freely. The remaining area of the site including the largest heronry in Essex has been designated as a Site of Special Scientific Interest and will be accessible to the public by way of special guided tours.

every third Thursday of the month, when farm-fresh produce is the order of the day). The whole of the town centre has been designated a conservation area. The Market Square boasts many fine and interesting buildings such as the Lych-gate and The Welsh Harp, dating from the 17th and 16th centuries respectively.

The **Town Hall** offers a fine example of Art Nouveau design, and houses the Waltham Abbey Town Council Offices and Epping Forest District Council Information Desk. The Tourist Information Centre is in Highbridge Street, opposite the entrance to the Abbey Church.

To the west of town, the **Lee Navigation Canal** offers opportunities for anglers, walkers, birdwatching and pleasure craft. Once used for transporting corn and other commercial goods to the growing City of London, and having associations with the town's important gunpowder industry for centuries, the canal remains a vital part of town life.

Gunpowder production became established in Waltham as early as the 1660s; by the 19th century the **Royal Gunpowder Mills** employed 500 workers, and production did not cease until 1943, after which time the factory became a research facility. In the spring of 2000, however, all this changed and the site was opened to the public (see panel opposite).

Lee Valley Regional Park is a leisure area stretching for 26 miles along the River Lea (sometimes also spelled Lee) from East India Dock Basin, on the north bank of the River Thames in East London, to Hertfordshire. There's a range of facilities ideal for anglers, walkers and birdwatchers. The Lee Valley is an important area of high biodiversity, sustaining a large range of wildlife and birds. Two hundred species of birds, including internationally important populations of Gadwall and Shoveler ducks, can be seen each year on the wetlands and water bodies along the Lea. The Information Centre in the Abbey Gardens provides displays and information on a range of countryside pursuits and interests, sport, leisure and heritage facilities and special events. Of national importance for over-wintering waterbirds including rare species of bittern and smew, this fine park makes an ideal place for a picnic. Guided tours by appointment.

At the southern end of Lee Valley Park, **The House Mill**, one of two tidal mills still standing at this site, has been restored by the River Lea Tidal Mill Trust. It was built in 1776 in the Dutch style, and was used to grind grain for gin distilling.

Lee Valley Park Farms, along Stubbins Hall Lane, boasts two farms on site: Hayes Hill and Holyfield Hall. At Hayes Hill Farm, visitors can interact with the animals and enjoy a picnic or the children's adventure playground. This traditional farm also boasts old-fashioned tools and equipment, an exhibition in the medieval barn and occasional craft demonstrations. The entry fee to Hayes Hill Farm also covers a visit to Holyfield

Hall Farm, a working farm and dairy where visitors can see milking and learn about modern farming methods. Seasonal events such as sheep-shearing and harvesting are held, and there's an attractive farm tea room and a toy shop. A farm trail is another of the site's attractions, offering wonderful views of the Lee Valley, an expanse of open countryside dotted with lakes and wildflower meadows attracting a wide range of wildlife including otters, bats, dragonfly, kingfisher, great-crested grebe and little-ringed plover. The area is ideal for walking or fishing, and the bird hides are open to all at weekends; permits available for daily access. Guided tours by arrangement.

Myddleton House Gardens within Lee Valley Park is the place to see the work of the famous plantsman who created them - E.A. Bowles, the greatest amateur gardener of his time. Breathtaking colours and interesting plantings - such as the National Collection of award-winning bearded iris, the Tulip Terrace and the Lunatic Asylum (home to unusual plants) - are offset by a beautiful carp lake, two conservatories and a rock garden.

Around Waltham Abbey

Loughton
5 miles SE of Waltham Abbey off the A121

Corbett Theatre in Rectory Lane in Loughton is a beautiful Grade I listed converted medieval tithe barn, where

Epping Forest

classical, modern and musical theatre productions are performed. The theatre is set in a five-acre site with lovely gardens.

Loughton borders **Epping Forest**, a magnificent and expansive tract of ancient hornbeam coppice, mainly tucked between the M25 and London. There are miles of leafy walks and rides (horses can be hired locally), with some rough grazing and occasional distant views.

Abridge
7 miles SE of Waltham Abbey off the A113

The **BBC Essex Garden** at Crowther Nurseries, Ongar Road, is a working garden consisting of a vegetable plot, two small greenhouses, lawns and herbaceous and shrub borders. Sheila Chapman, clematis expert, is also on site, as the garden boasts 600 varieties of clematis. The garden is also home to a range of farmyard animals which visitors are welcome to see and interact with, and there's a delightful tea shop filled with homemade cakes.

Chigwell
8 miles SE of Waltham Abbey off the A113

Hainault Forest Country Park is an ancient woodland covering 600 acres, with a lake and rare breeds farm, managed by the London Borough of Redbridge and the Woodland Trust for Essex County Council.

Chingford
6 miles S of Waltham Abbey off the A11

Queen Elizabeth Hunting Lodge in Ranger's Road, Chingford, is a timber-framed hunting grandstand first built for Henry VIII. This unique Tudor-era survivor boasts exceptional carpentry, and is situated in a beautiful part of Epping Forest with ancient oaks and fine views. The Visitor Centre can be found at High Beach, Epping.

Hoddesdon
6 miles NW of Waltham Abbey off the A10

Rye House Gatehouse in Rye Road was built by Sir Andre Ogard, a Danish nobleman, in 1443. It is a moated building and a fine example of early English brickwork. Now restored, visitors can climb up to the battlements. A permanent exhibition covers the architecture and history of the Rye House Plot to assassinate Charles II in 1683. Guided tours by prior arrangement. The building lies adjacent to a Royal Society for the Protection of Birds reserve. Other features include an information centre, shop, and circular walks around the site.

Harlow

The 'New Town' of Harlow sometimes gets short shrift, but it is in fact a lively and vibrant place with a great deal more than excellent shopping facilities. There are some very good museums and several sites of historic interest. The **Gibberd Collection** in Harlow Town Hall offers a delightful collection of British watercolours featuring works by Blackadder, Sutherland, Frink, Nash and Sir Frederick Gibberd, Harlow's master planner and the founder of the collection.

Harlow Museum in Passmores House, Third Avenue, occupies a Georgian manor house set in picturesque gardens which includes a lovely pond and is home to several species of butterfly. The museum has extensive and important Roman, post-medieval and early 20th century collections, as well as a full programme of temporary exhibitions.

Mark Hall Cycle Museum and Gardens in Muskham Road offers a unique collection of cycles and cycling accessories illustrating the history of the bicycle from 1818 to the present day, including one made of plastic, one that folds, and one where the seat tips forward and throws its rider over the handlebars if the brakes are applied too hard. The museum is housed in a converted stable block within Mark Hall manor. Adjacent to the museum are three period walled gardens.

Gibberd Gardens, on the eastern outskirts of Harlow in Marsh Lane, Gilden Way, is well worth a visit, reflecting as it does the taste of Sir Frederick Gibberd, the famous architect. This 7-acre garden was designed by Sir Frederick on the side of a small valley, with terraces, wild garden, landscaped vistas, pools and streams and some 80 sculptures. Marsh Lane is a turning off the B183.

Harlow Study and Visitors Centre in Netteswellbury Farm is set in a medieval tithe barn and 13th century church. The site has displays outlining the story of Harlow New Town.

Parndon Wood Nature Reserve, Parndon Wood Road, is an ancient woodland with a fine variety of birds, mammals and insects. Facilities include two nature trails with hides for observing wildlife, and a study centre.

Around Harlow

Roydon
3 miles W of Harlow off the A414

Preserved in this handsome village are the old parish cage, stocks and a whipping post. Just about 1 mile southwest of Roydon are the ruins of Tudor **Nether Hall**, a manor house that once belonged to the Coates family. Here Thomas More came to woo and win the elder daughter of John Coates.

Chipping Ongar
8 miles SE of Harlow on the A414

Today firmly gripped in the commuter belt of London, Chipping Ongar began as a Saxon market town protected beneath the walls of a Norman castle. The motte and bailey were built by Richard de Lucy in 1155. Indeed, the town's name comes from 'cheaping', meaning market. Only the mound and moat of the castle remain, but the contemporary **Church of St Martin of Tours** still stands. Built in 1080, it has fine Norman flint walls and an anchorite's recess.

Explorer David Livingstone was a pupil pastor of the town's United Reform Church, and lived in what are now called **Livingstone Cottages** before his missionary work in Africa began.

Bobbingworth
2 miles NW of Chipping Ongar off the A414

Blake Hall Gardens at Bobbingworth near Chipping Ongar incorporates a Tropical House, an Ice House, Bog garden, wild gardens, herbaceous borders, rose garden, sunken garden, duck pond and an ornamental wood. The south wing of Blake Hall itself houses the **Airscene Aviation Museum** run by local RAF enthusiasts.

Willingale
3 miles NE of Chipping Ongar off the B184

St Christopher's and **St Andrew's**, churches of the respective parishes of Willingale Doe and Willingale Spain, stand side by side in the same churchyard in the heart of this lovely village. St Andrew's is the older, dating back to the 12th century.

Fyfield
2 miles N of Chipping Ongar off the B184

The name 'Fyfield' means five river meadows. Originally a Saxon enclave, the village church of St Nicholas is Norman. There's a beautiful mill house with flood gates in the village. **Fyfield Hall**, opposite the church, is said to be the oldest inhabited timber frame building in England (it dates from AD 870).

Beauchamp Roding
3 miles NE of Chipping Ongar off the B184

One of the eight Rodings, it was at Beauchamp Roding that a local farm labourer, Isaac Mead, worked and saved enough to become a farmer himself in 1882. To show his gratitude to the land that made him his fortune, he had a corner of the field consecrated as an eternal resting place for himself and his family. Their graves can still be seen in the undergrowth.

Beauchamp's **Church of St Botolph** stands alone in the fields, marked by a tall 15th century tower and reached by a track off the B184. Inside, the raised pews at the west end have clever space-saving wooden steps, pulled out of slots by means of iron rings.

GARNISH HALL

Margaret Roding, on the A1060,
Essex CM6 1QL
Tel: 01245 231209 Fax: 01245 231224
e-mail: peter@garnishhall.fsnet.co.uk

A true rural retreat, **Garnish Hall** stands amid 7 acres of lovely grounds including a large duck pond, tennis court and walled garden. Once home to the Earl de Vere, this marvellous 15th century manor house has three comfortable and beautiful guest bedrooms, all period decorated and with exquisite views. With a lecture room and dining room that can accommodate up to a dozen guests, this superior hall also makes an excellent location for small functions, seminars and business meetings.

Good Easter and High Easter
5 miles NE of Chipping Ongar off the B184

A quiet farming village, now in the commuter belt for London, Good Easter's claim to fame is the making of a world-record daisy chain (6,980 ft 7 inches) in 1985. The village's interesting name is probably derived from 'Easter', the Old English for 'sheepfolds' and 'Good' from a Saxon lady named Godiva.

Close to Good Easter, and thus named because it stands on higher ground than its neighbour, High Easter is a quiet and very picturesque village not far from the impressive **Aythorpe Post Mill**.

Blackmore
3 miles E of Chipping Ongar off the A414

The plague almost totally destroyed the village of Blackmore. Red Rose Lane was so-named because a red rose had to be given at the toll to indicate clear health from the dreaded disease. Henry VIII's mistress Bessie Blount lived in Jericho Priory in the village. Her son by Henry, the Earl of Rochford, also made his home here.

ACRELAND GREEN

Pleshey, Chelmsford,
Essex CM3 1HP
Tel/Fax: 01245 231277

Bed and breakfast with a difference awaits guests at **Acreland Green**. This charming rural retreat, formerly two cottages dating back to 1590, offers three attractive and comfortable en suite guest bedrooms, delicious breakfasts and beautiful gardens. Open all year round, this excellent establishment is conveniently located for Braintree, Great Dunmow, Chelmsford,

Stansted Airport and all the sights and attractions of the region. ETC 4 Diamonds. No smoking.

THE WHITE HART INN

Swan Lane, Margaretting Tye, Ingatestone,
Essex CM4 9JX
Tel: 01277 840478 Fax: 01277 841178
website: www.thewhitehart.co.uk

An excellent public house serving real ales and great food, **The White Hart Inn** in Margaretting Tye is well worth seeking out. Its rural setting lends itself to a number of excellent walks, which makes it a firm favourite with Ramblers, Cyclists and other

clubs as a meeting place. Fresh home-cooked food awaits all guests at this popular pub, which dates back in parts to the 1600s. Swan Lane is a Grade II listed street, and inside the pub, the snug bar is over 200 years old and the heavily beamed vaulted ceiling and open fires add to the traditional and cosy ambience.

Classic favourites abound on the menu, together with more innovative dishes. There are also special children's, vegetarian and 'evening snacks' menus. Owner Liz Haines and her staff offer a very warm welcome, and the atmosphere in this superior pub is always friendly and comfortable.

Real ale enthusiasts will find at least three permanent ales on tap – including Adnams and Mighty Oak IPA – along with four to six regularly changing guest ales from local breweries and those further afield. An annual beer festival is held in June (Ascot week) within the grounds. At this time there's a selection of 30-40 real ales, champagne and Pimm's on offer, together with live entertainment and a barbecue. Liz also holds a "Village Day" in August, with live Jazz on the green and numeruos stalls, BBQ and games for all of the family. All funds raised are donated to "Essex Air Ambulance".

The attractive new conservatory dining area is tastefully decorated in lemon yellow

and green. More delights await the visitor outside, with a safe children's play area with interesting pets' corner featuring goats and other farm animals, Aviary, and a large duck pond with waterfall. Plans are afoot to convert the former stable into conference facilities offering very competitive delegate packages. Liz also holds the licence at the Village Hall in Margaretting and caters for much larger gatherings including weddings.

For more information on menus and special events, please do visit the pub's very helpful website.

Ingatestone

6 miles E of Chipping Ongar off the B1002

Ingatestone Hall on Hall Lane is a 16th century mansion set in 11 acres of grounds. It was built by Sir William Petre, Secretary of State to four monarchs, whose family continue to reside here. Open to the public in summer, the Hall contains family portraits, furniture and memorabilia accumulated over the centuries. Guided tours by prior arrangement.

Margaretting Tye

6 miles E of Chipping Ongar off the A12/B1007

The nickname of this town is 'Tigers Island'. Legend has it that in bygone days, bare-knuckle fights known as 'Tigers' would take place on Fridays, and the 'island' part of its soubriquet derives from the fact that in ancient times the area was subject to flooding all round the village.

Mountnessing

6 miles SE of Chipping Ongar off the A12

This village has a beautifully restored early 19th century windmill as its main landmark, though the isolated church also has a massive beamed belfry. **Mountnessing Post Mill** in Roman Road is open to the public. This traditional weather-boarded post mill was built in

---

THE NAGS HEAD

Moreton, nr Ongar, Essex CM5 9RQ
Tel: 01277 890239

Here in the centre of the Conservation Area of this peaceful village, **The Nags Head** dates from the late 16th century and is a charming example of a traditional country pub. This fine inn has it all: a warm and welcoming atmosphere, real ales including Ridleys IPA, Old Bob, Prospect and Rumpus, and chef-prepared, delicious traditional and modern

British cuisine using the freshest locally sourced ingredients.

THE CRICKETERS

Mill Green, Ingatestone, Chelmsford, Essex CM4 0JD
Tel: 01277 352400
e-mail: thecricketers@tiscali.co.uk

The accent is on great food at **The Cricketers**, a fine little village pub dating back to the early 1800s. Picturesque and elegant throughout, this inn is tastefully furnished and decorated, comfortable and relaxed. The superb cuisine includes fresh seafood and game in a menu and blackboard specials changed daily and is

served at lunch every day (12.00-14.00) and Tues-Sat at dinner (19.00-21.00). The service and quality is second to none.

1807 and restored to working order in 1983. Visitors can see the huge wooden and iron gears; one pair of stones have been opened up for viewing.

Kelvedon Hatch
4 miles S of Chipping Ongar off the A128

A simple bungalow in the rural Essex village of Kelvedon Hatch is the deceptively simple exterior for the **Kelvedon Secret Nuclear Bunker**. Built in 1952, 40,000 tons of concrete were used to create a base some 80 feet underground for up to 600 top Government and civilian personnel in the event of nuclear war. Visitors can explore room after room to see communications equipment, a BBC studio, sick bay, massive kitchens and dormitories, power and filtration plant, government administration room and the scientists' room, where nuclear fallout patterns would have been measured.

Greensted
1½ miles SW of Chipping Ongar off the A414

St Andrew's in Greensted is the world's oldest wooden church, dating from the 9th-11th centuries, with a later Tudor chancel. It is famous as the only surviving example of a Saxon log church extant in the world, built from split oak logs held together with dowells. Over the centuries the church has been enlarged and restored; later additions

Kelvedon Secret Nuclear Bunker

include the simple weather-boarded tower, Norman flint walls, the Tudor tiled roof, Victorian stone coping, porch and stained glass windows. The body of King Edmund (later canonised a saint) is believed to have rested here in 1013.

The village also has associations with the Tolpuddle Martyrs - six Dorset farm labourers who were taken to court on a legal technicality because they agitated for better conditions and wages, and formed a Trades Union. After their conviction in 1834 they were condemned to transportation to Australia for seven years. There was a public outcry for their release, and their sentences were commuted in 1837. Unable to return to Dorset, they were granted tenancies in Greensted and High Laver. One of the martyrs, James Brine, of New House Farm (now Tudor Cottage, on Greensted Green), married Elizabeth Standfield, daughter of one of his fellow victims - the record of their marriage in 1839 can be seen in the parish register.

North Weald
3 miles W of Chipping Ongar off the A414

North Weald Airfield Museum and Memorial at Ad Astra House, Hurricane Way, North Weald Bassett is a small, meticulously detailed 'House of Memories' displaying the history of the famous airfield and all who served at RAF North Weald from 1916 to the present. Collections of photos and artefacts such as uniforms and the detailed records of all flying operations are on display. There is also a video exhibit recounting a day-to-day account of North Weald history. Guided tours of the airfield can be arranged for large groups.

Brentwood

Brentwood is a very pleasant shopping and entertainment centre, with quite a distinguished past. The town was on the old pilgrim and coaching routes to and from London. Mainly post-war in character, the town is the setting for the UK headquarters of Ford Motors.

Brentwood Cathedral on Ingrave Road was built in 1991. This classically-styled church incorporates the original Victorian church that stood on this spot. It was designed by the much-admired architect Quinlan Terry, with roundels by Raphael Maklouf (who also created the relief of the Queen's head used on current coins).

Brentwood Centre on Doddinghurst Road is one of the top entertainment venues in the UK, with an extensive programme of concerts, shows, bands and top comedy names. Sport and fitness facilities include pool, health suite and sunbeds.

Brentwood Museum at Cemetery Lode in Lorne Road, in the Warley Hill area of Brentwood, is a small and picturesque cottage museum concentrating on local and social interests during the late 19th and early 20th centuries. It is set in an attractive disused cemetery, which is in itself of unique interest and is open on the first Sunday of every month from 2.30-4.30 p.m. and throughout the summer months.

Thorndon Country Park boasts historic parkland, lakes and woods. The site, formerly a Royal deer park, also features a wildlife exhibition and attractive gift shop. Fishing is also available.

Around Brentwood

Billericay
6 miles E of Brentwood off the A129

There was a settlement here as far back as the Bronze Age, though there is to date no conclusive explanation of Billericay's name. There is no question about the attraction of the High Street, though, with its timber weather-boarding and Georgian brick. **The Chantry House**, built in 1510, was the home of Christopher Martin, treasurer to the Pilgrim Fathers.

The Peasants' Revolt of 1381 saw the massacre of hundreds of rebels just northeast of the town, at **Norsey Wood**. Today this area of ancient woodland is a country park, managed by coppicing (the traditional way of ensuring the timber supply), which also encourages plant and birdlife.

Barleylands Farm Museum and Visitors' Centre features a glass-blowing studio, blacksmith's and other craft shops, a wealth of farm animals, chick hatchery, duck pond and one of the largest collections of vintage farm machinery in the country, together with a play area, picnic area and, on Sunday afternoons, a steam railway.

Great Warley
1 mile S of Brentwood on the B186

Warley Place was formerly home to one of the most famous women gardeners, Ellen Willmott, who died in 1934. She introduced to Warley - and to Britain - many exotic plants. A trail takes visitors through what is now Warley Place Nature Reserve, with 16 acres of what was once domesticated garden but has now reverted to woodland. A fascinating selection of trees, shrubs and wildlife make this well worth a visit.

South Weald
2 miles W of Brentwood off the A12

This very attractive village has, at its outskirts, **Weald Country Park**, a former estate with medieval deer park, partially landscaped in the 1700s. Featuring lake and woodland, visitors' centre, landscapes exhbition and gift shop, with facilities for fishing and horse-riding, there are guided events and activities programmes held throughout the year.

Another good day out in the open air can be had at **Old Macdonald's Educational Farm Park**, where visitors can see the largest selection of pure-bred British farm animals and poultry in the southeast of England. Specialising in native rare-breeds, with nine breeds of pig, 23 of sheep, six of cattle, 30 of poultry and 30 of rabbit to see and learn about, as well as shire horses, deer, owls, otters, goats, ferrets, red squirrels and much more. The farm boasts informative breed labelling and excellent facilities.

The North Thames Corridor

Bordering the north bank of the Thames, the borough of **Thurrock** has long been a gateway to London but also affords easy access to southwest Essex and to Kent. This thriving borough encompasses huge swathes of green belt country, and along its 18 miles of Thames frontage there are many important marshland wildlife habitats. This stretch of Essex affords some marvellous walking, cycling, birdwatching and other nature pursuits. The area has many bridleways, footpaths and country parks, including Davy Down within the Mardyke Valley. The river's flood plain is a broad tract of grassland which is an important feature of the landscape of the area.

Grays
4 miles S of Brentwood off the M25

Thurrock Museum is in the Thameside Complex in Grays. It collects, conserves and displays items of archaeology and local history from prehistoric times to the end of the 20th century. The archaeological items include flint and metal tools of people who lived in prehistoric Thurrock and pottery, jewellery and coins from the Roman and Saxon period.

Thameside Theatre in Grays town centre offers a good range of productions throughout the year, with a popular pantomime now 24 years strong.

West Thurrock
1½ miles SW of Grays off the A13

Immortalised by the film *Four Weddings and a Funeral*, little **St Clement's church** occupies a striking location and is one of a number of picturesque ancient churches in the borough. Although this 12th century church is now deconsecrated, it was in its day a stopping point for pilgrims; visitors can see the remains of its original round tower. There is also a mass grave to the boys of the reformatory ship *Cornwall* who were drowned in an accident off Purfleet.

Arena Essex Raceway is the chief venue for motorsports in the area. Regular 'banger racing' takes place at the track in West Thurrock, near **Lakeside Shopping Centre** and Retail Park. The Centre attracts many millions of visitors

a year, and boasts over 300 shops, a food court and multiplex cinema. The Retail Park features more shops, as well as restaurants, a cinema, a leisure bingo complex and a watersports centre at the lake.

Purfleet
3 miles W of Grays off the M25/ A13

Fans of Bram Stoker's novel *Dracula* will know that in this book the famous vampire buys a house called 'Carfax' in Purfleet. The town's esteemed **Royal Hotel**, by the Thames, is said to have played host to Edward VII, while still Prince of Wales in the 1880s and 1890s, at which time the hotel was called Wingrove's.

The **Purfleet Heritage and Military Centre** is a heritage and military museum featuring displays of many items of interest and memorabilia in the setting of the No 5 Gunpowder Magazine on Centurion Way. This remaining magazine was built in the 1770s for testing and issuing gun powder to the army and navy.

Purfleet Conservation Area includes several buildings which were part of a planned village built by the one-time owners of the chalk quarry, the Whitbread family.

Aveley
3 miles NW of Grays off the A13

Mardyke Valley is an important wildlife corridor running from Ship Lane in Aveley to Orsett Fen. Many pleasant views can be had along the seven-mile stretch of footpaths and bridleways. Davy Down within Mardyke Valley consists of riverside meadows, ponds and wetland. The Visitors' Centre is in the well-preserved water pumping station on the B186 near South Ockendon.

Aveley's 12th century **St Michael's Church** features many Flemish brasses and other items of historical interest.

South Ockendon
3 miles N of Grays off the A13/ A1306

Belhus Woods Country Park covers approximately 250 acres and contains an interesting variety of habitats, including woodland, two lakes and the remains of a pond designed by 'Capability' Brown. The Visitors' Centre to this superb park can be found at the main entrance off Romford Road. Belhus Park Golf Course is a well-established 18-hole course set within this beautiful parkland.

Grangewaters Country Park, also in South Ockendon, has two lakes. Managed by Thurrock Environmental and Outdoor Education Centre, it offers watersports such as windsurfing, sailing and canoeing, as well as off-road biking, climbing and other outdoor pursuits. **Brannetts Wood** is one of the oldest recorded ancient woodlands in South Essex. It can be reached from the Mardyke Way, or from South Road here in South Ockendon.

The village **Church of St Nicholas** has one of only six round church towers in Essex. This one was built in the 13th

century and used to have a spire, which was sadly destroyed by lightning in the 17th century.

Horndon-on-the Hill
6 miles NE of Grays off the B1007/A13

Listed in the *Domesday Book* as *Horninduna*, a name which also appears on a Saxon coin of Edward the Confessor (1042-1066), it is said to have once been the site of a Royal Anglo-Saxon mint. The town's 16th century **Woolmarket** indicates the importance of the wool trade to the region, and is one of the area's historical treasures. The upper room served as Horndon's manor courtroom, while the lower, open area was used for trading in woollen cloth.

The main entrance and Visitors' Centre for **Langdon Hills Conservation Centre and Nature Reserve** are located off the Lower Dunton Road north of Horndon-on-the-HIll. A bridleway and footpaths lead visitors to meadows, a pond and outstanding ancient woods. Also within the reserve is the **Plotlands Museum**, housed in an original 1930s plotland bungalow known as the Haven.

Linford
3 miles NE of Grays off the A13/ A1013

Walton Hall Museum on Walton Hall Road has a large collection of historic farm machinery in a 17th century barn. It affords visitors the opportunity to watch traditional craftsmen, such as a blacksmith, saddlemaker, printer and wheelwright, together with a printing shop, baker's, dairy and nursery.

Stanford-le-Hope
4 miles NE of Grays off the A1014

Stanford Marshes is an area to the south of Stanford-le-Hope, next to the Thames. The Marshes are home to a variety of wildlife and are an ideal location for birdwatching. **Grove House Wood** in Stanford-le-Hope is a nature reserve managed by Essex Wildlife Trust and the local Girl Guides. A footpath here leads to reed beds, a pond and a brook as well as an area of woodland.

The graveyard of St Margaret's Church has an unusual half-barrelled tomb, for one James Adams (d. 1765), that is decorated with a gruesome stone-carved symbols of death.

Canvey Island
10 miles NE of Grays off the A130

Canvey Island is a peaceful and picturesque stretch of land overlooking the Thames estuary with views to neighbouring Kent.

The island boasts two unusual museums: **Dutch Cottage Museum** is an early 17th century eight-sided cottage built by Dutch workmen for Dutch workmen and boasting many traditional Flemish features. **Castle Point Transport Museum** is housed in a 1930s bus garage. It houses an interesting collection of historic and modern buses and coaches, mainly of East Anglian origin.

The **Canvey Miniature Railway** at the Waterside Farm Centre has two steam miniature railways guaranteed to delight the child in all of us.

West Tilbury
3 miles E of Grays off the AA1089

West Tilbury was the site chosen for the Camp Royal in 1588, to prepare for the threatened Spanish invasion. Queen Elizabeth I visited the army here, and made her famous speech, *'I know I have the body but of a weak and feeble woman: but I have the heart and stomach of a king, and a king of England too.'*

Hidden away in rural tranquillity over-looking the Thames estuary, West Tilbury remains unspoilt in spite of its proximity to busy, industrial Tilbury. The former local church (now a private dwelling) in this quaint little village is a nautical landmark used for navigation. The list of Rectors of the church, dating from 1279-1978, when the church was disestablished, can be seen in The Kings Head Pub.

East Tilbury
5 miles E of Grays off the A13

Coalhouse Fort is considered to be one of the best surviving examples of a Victorian Casement fortress in the country. As such it is a protected Scheduled Ancient Monument. Built between 1861 and 1874 as a first line of defence to protect the Thames area against invasion, it stands on the site of other defensive works and fortifications dating back to around 1400. Even before the Middle Ages, this was an important site.

Part of the construction work on the Fort was overseen by Gordon of Khartoum. It was constructed to be a dedicated Artillery casement fortress, which meant that the guns were housed in large vaulted rooms with armour-plated frontages. Beneath these rooms lies an extensive magazine tunnel system to service the artillery.

Over the years many alterations were made to the Fort to accommodate new artillery. The Fort was manned during both World Wars, and is now owned by Thurrock Borough Council and administered by The Coalhouse Fort Project, a registered charity manned entirely by volunteers. Open to the public, it contains reconstructions of period guns and other displays, and also houses the **Thameside Aviation Museum**, with a large collection of local finds and other aviation material. In the two parade grounds visitors will find various artillery pieces and military vehicles. One recent addition to the many pieces of historical military equipment is a Bofor Anti-Aircraft Gun of the Second World War. The site also offers visitors the chance to handle period equipment or try on a period uniform.

During the year the Fort hosts a range of shows, including an historic artillery rally when various big guns are fired by crews in the uniforms of the period, including a Second World War crew firing a 1940 25pdr field gun. A guided tour (included in the price of admission) allows visitors to see the magazine tunnels beneath the gun casements and offers a feel for the work and conditions of a Victorian gunner. The tour also takes in the roof of the Fort, from which you will be able to judge for yourself the value of a fortification at this point along the Thames. The view from here is outstanding, taking in the two sister forts in Kent and, on a clear day, Southend.

The Fort is set in a lovely riverside park with walks and a children's play area, as well as other items of military history including a Quick Fire Battery and Minefield Control box. You can also follow the old railway tracks from the Fort to the side of the old jetty, where many of the armaments and supplies for the fort were shipped in.

It is possible that East Tilbury's **St Catherine's** church occupies the site of one of the first Christian monasteries in the 7th century. Its half-built tower was constructed by the First World War Garrison of Coalhouse Fort.

The Bata Estate is a conservation area of architectural and historical interest. Established in 1933, the British Bata Shoe Company was the creation of Czech-born Thomas Bata, who also developed a housing estate for his workforce. This range of uniform flat-roofed houses can still be seen on site.

Tilbury
3 miles SE of Grays off the A1089

Tilbury Fort is a well-preserved and unusual 17th century structure with double moat. The largest and best example of military engineering in England at that time, the fort also affords tremendous views of the Thames estuary. The most violent episode in the fort's history occurred in 1776, during a particularly vociferous cricket match which left three people dead. For a small fee visitors to the fort can fire a 1943 3.7mm anti-aircraft gun - a prospect most children and many adults find irresistible! Owned by English Heritage, the site was used for a military Block House during the reign of Henry VIII and was rebuilt in the 17th century. It remains one of Britain's finest examples of a star-shaped bastion fortress. Extensions were made in the 18th and 19th centuries, and the Fort was still being used in the Second World War.

Tilbury Festival is held every year in July in the field near the fort, and features arena events, craft and food stalls, and living history re-enactments. **Tilbury Energy and Environment Centre** at Tilbury Power Station provides a nature reserve and study centre for schools and community education. There is a flat two-mile nature trail leading to and from the Centre.

Southend-on-Sea
22 miles E of Grays on the A127

Beside the seaside in Southend-on-Sea there is always plenty to do and see, and many events throughout the year to ensure its continuing interest and popularity. The town is one of the best loved and most friendly resorts in Britain, featuring the very best ingredients for a break at the seaside. With seven miles of beaches and the only European Blue Flag award in Essex, this treasure trove boasts **Adventure Island** theme park, **Cliffs Bandstand**, **Cliffs Pavilion** (the largest purpose-built performing arts venue in Essex), a distinguished art gallery and several interesting museums.

Southend Pier and Museum brings to life the fascinating past of the longest Pleasure Pier in the world. The Pier itself is 1.33 miles long; visitors can either take a leisurely walk along its length or take advantage of the regular train service that plies up and down the pier.

Central Museum, Planetarium and Discovery Centre on Victoria Avenue is

Southend Beach

the only planetarium in the southeast outside London, and also features local history exhibits, archaeology and wildlife exhibits. **Beecroft Art Gallery** boasts the work of four centuries of artistic endeavour, with some 2,000 works including those by Lear, Molenaer, Seago and Constable.

Sealife Adventure employs the most advanced technology to bring you incredibly close to the wonders of British marine life, offering fun ways of exploring life under the waves, with concave bubble windows helping to make it seem you're actually part of the sea-creatures' environment. Another exhibit features a walk-through tunnel along a reconstructed seabed. The Shark Exhibition is not to be missed.

A floral trail guided tour around the parks and gardens will reveal why Southend has won the Britain in Bloom Awards every year since 1993, as well as medals at the Chelsea Flower Show.

The Kursaal on the Eastern Esplanade is an indoor entertainment complex, one of the largest in the country, with indoor bowling, synthetic ice and roller rink, a fun casino, children's play area, snooker and pool, arts and crafts, retail units and theme restaurants.

Boat trips in summer include occasional outings on a vintage paddle steamer. Ferry trips to Felixstowe are

Prittlewell Priory Park

also available from Southend.

The **Southchurch Hall Museum** in Park Lane is a delightful 13th to 14th century timber-framed manor house with various displays and landscaped gardens. Period room settings are among this museum's many delights.

Prittlewell Priory Museum, slightly north of Southend town centre in Priory Park, is a well-preserved 12th century Cluniac Priory set in lovely grounds and housing collections of the Priory's history, natural history and the Caten collection of radios and communications equipment.

Old Leigh
½ mile W of Southend off the A13

The unspoilt fishing village of Old Leigh has a long and distinguished history. It is picturesque, with seafront houses and narrow winding alleys. It has also earned its place in history: The pilgrim ship *The*

Mayflower restocked here en route to the New World of America back in the mid-17th century, and the Dunkirk rescue embarked from here, as commemorated in a framed poem on the wall of the local pub, The Crooked Billet.

Leigh-on-Sea
2 miles W of Southend off the A13

Leigh-on-Sea has quite a distinct character to Southend, being more intimate and serene, with wood-clad buildings and shrimp boats in the working harbour. The shellfish stall on the harbourside is justly famous. The **Leigh Heritage Centre**, housed in a former ancient blacksmith's in the waterside High Street of the Old Town, now houses historical artefacts including a photographic display of the history of Leigh-on-Sea.

Hadleigh
5 miles NW of Southend off the A13

Hadleigh Castle, built originally for Edward III, is owned by English Heritage and once belonged to Anne of Cleves, Catherine of Aragon and Katherine Parr. The ruins were also immortalised in a painting by Constable. The remains of this once impressive castle can still be seen. The curtain walls towers, which survive almost to their full height, overlook the Essex marshes and the Thames estuary.

Hadleigh Castle Country Park offers a variety of woodland and coastal walks in grounds overlooking the Thames estuary. A Guided Events programme runs throughout the year.

Hullbridge
8 miles NW of Southend off the A132

Jakapeni Rare Breed Farm at Burlington Gardens in Hullbridge is a pleasant small-holding set in 30 acres of rolling countryside. Specialising in sheep and pigs, with other pets and wildlife, there's also a fishing lake, country walk and pets corner. Snacks and light refreshments are available from the café, and there's an attractive shop.

Hockley
6 miles NW of Southend off the A129

Hockley Woods is a 280-acre ancient woodland, managed for the benefit of wildlife and for the public. Traditional coppice management encourages a diverse array of flora and fauna, including the nationally rare Heath Fritillary butterfly.

Volpaia in Woodlands Road is a lily specialist's small but beautiful woodside garden, with rare collected species and own-bred hybrid lilies, shade-loving shrubs and plants for sale.

Rayleigh
6 miles NW of Southend off the A1016

Dutch Cottage at Crown Hill in Rayleigh is a tiny traditional Flemish eight-sided cottage based on a 17th century design created by Dutch settlers.

MIAMI HOTEL & CONFERENCE CENTRE

Princes Road, Chelmsford, Essex CM2 9AJ
Tel: 01245 264848/269603
Fax: 01245 259860
e-mail: sales@miamihotel.co.uk
website: www.miamihotel.co.uk

Within five minutes of the centre of Chelmsford on the A414 (A12), **The Miami Hotel and Conference Centre** is ideally situated for exploring Chelmsford and the region, with main road links to the A12 and M25 and just minutes from Chelmsford Railway Station. Here in the heart of Essex, this gracious, modern hotel has 55 guest bedrooms – all doubles or twins, and all en suite and boasting amenities such as cable television, trouser press, hair dryer, tea/coffee facilities and direct dial phone. Each room is spacious and supremely comfortable, with tasteful furnishings and décor and every home comfort.

The five conference suites and facilities are excellent and can cater for parties and functions of all types and sizes, with TVs/video recorders, lecterns and audio-visual equipment as needed.

This excellent family-run hotel offers genuine hospitality and comfort at reasonable prices.

GLADES RESTAURANT

Princes Road, Chelmsford, Essex CM2 9AJ
Tel: 012454 264848/269603
Fax: 01245 259860
e-mail: glades@miamihotel.co.uk
website: www.miamihotel.co.uk

The **Glades Restaurant** and Retreat Bar in the Miami Hotel is an elegant place to savour a delicious meal or drink. This fully licensed restaurant boasts an international cuisine. The bright and airy décor is enhanced by a charming ornamental pond, which adds to the relaxed and pleasant ambience.

Guests at the hotel can take their breakfast in the restaurant. The restaurant is open seven days a week for lunch and dinner, including the special Saturday night dinner and dance, when diners' tables are exclusively theirs until midnight.

The menu offers a comprehensive choice of expertly prepared and presented dishes, complemented by a wide selection of wines. The Retreat Bar is a comfortable and welcoming place to enjoy hot and cold bar snacks and a quiet drink.

The restaurant can also cater for a variety of special occasions and celebrations.

Rayleigh Mount is a prominent landmark in this part of the county. Once a motte-and-bailey castle built in the 11th century, it was abandoned some 200 years later. **Rayleigh Windmill**, in Bellingham Lane close to Rayleigh Mount, was built around 1809; the tower mill houses a fascinating collection of bygones mostly used in and around Rayleigh. Refreshments are available from the coffee shop adjacent to the Mill.

Rochford
3 miles N of Southend off the B1013

The Old House, at 17 South Street, is an elegant, lovingly restored house originally built in 1270. The twisting corridors and handsome rooms of this fine structure offer a glimpse into the past; the building now houses some District Council offices, and is said to be haunted.

Chelmsford

Roman workmen cutting their great road linking London with Colchester built a fort at what is today called Chelmsford. Then called *Caesaromagus*, it stands at the confluence of the Rivers Chelmer and Can. The town has always been an important market centre and is now the bustling county town of Essex. It is also directly descended from a new town planned by the Bishop of London in 1199. At its centre are the principal inn, the **Royal Saracen's Head**, and the elegant **Shire Hall** of 1791. Three plaques situated high up on the eastern face of the Hall overlooking the High Street represent Wisdom, Justice and Mercy. The building now houses the town magistrates court.

Christianity came to Essex with the Romans and again, later, with St Cedd (AD 654); in 1914 the diocese of Chelmsford was created. **Chelmsford Cathedral** in New Street dates from the 15th century and is built on the site of a church constructed 800 years ago. The cathedral is noted for the harmony and unity of its perpendicular architecture. It was John Johnson, the distinguished local architect who designed both the Shire Hall and the 18th century **Stone Bridge** over the River Can, who also rebuilt the Parish Church of St Mary when most of its 15th century tower fell down. The church became a cathedral when the new diocese of Chelmsford was created. Since then it has been enlarged and re-organised inside. The cathedral boasts memorial windows dedicated to the USAAF airmen who were based in Essex from 1942-5.

The Marconi Company, pioneers in the manufacture of wireless equipment, set up the first radio company in the world here in Chelmsford, in 1899. Exhibits of those pioneering days of wireless can be seen in the **Chelmsford Museum** (see panel on page 38) in Oaklands Park, Moulsham Street, as can interesting displays of Roman remains and local history. Fine and decorative arts (ceramics, costume, glass), coins, natural history (live beehive, animals, geological exhibits) rub shoulders with

CHELMSFORD MUSEUM & ESSEX REGIMENT MUSEUM

Oaklands Park, Moulsham Street,
Chelmsford, Essex CVM2 9AQ
Tel: 01245 615100 Fax: 01245 611250
e-mail: oaklands@chelmsfordbc.gov.uk
website:
www.chelmsfordbc.gov.uk/leisure/museums

Regiments from 1741 to the modern Royal Anglian Regiment. Among the many items on display are a tailcoat of 1785 with Pompadour purple collar

Chelmsford Museum, founded in 1835, has since 1930 been located in a lovely Victorian mansion in a city-centre park. The history of Chelmsford and its people from prehistoric times right up to the present day is told through displays that include geology, natural history (with a live beehive!), costumes and coins. Fine and Decorative Arts are represented by works by Edward Bawden and other regionally based artists, the Tunstall Bequest of 18th century drinking glasses and flamboyant Victorian pieces from Castle Hedingham Pottery.

The Essex Regiment on the same site relates the story of the 44th and 56th

and cuffs, a French eagle standard captured in battle in 1812, the Regimental silver and silver drums presented by the people of Essex, medals won by Essex men including four Victoria Cross winners, the Colours of the 44th Foot carried for 102 years, and an Essex Home Guard display. Regularly changing temporary exhibitions supplement the permanent displays at both Museums.

Also under the aegis of Chelmsford Borough Council is a developing Science and Industry project at Sandford Mill, Chelmer Village (Tel/Fax: 01245 475498) with visits by appointment or on open days and science weeks for local schools.

THE WHITE HORSE

The Street, Pleshey, nr Chelmsford,
Essex CM3 1HA
Tel: 01245 237281
e-mail: thewhitehorse@ukonline.co.uk
website: www.thewhitehorsepleshey.co.uk

Both food and drink play prominent roles at **The White Horse**, a classic country inn with a history going back to 1483. The interior is quite amazing, with brick and tiled floors, brick or plaster walls, and ancient beams and timbers adding up to a setting that is brimming with character.

In the splendid restaurant, with linen tablecloths and gleaming crystal, there's a fine choice of traditional and modern dishes. An excellent wine list complements the food, and

there are cask ales for those who prefer the hop to the grape.

Home-made cakes and scones are served Sun-Fri for afternoon tea (14.00-17.30), and there's a charming in-house gift shop selling collectibles, antiques and second-hand books. The function suite, which can seat 90, is an ideal venue for private parties. Outside, The White Horse boasts extensive parking, a patio and a spacious lawn.

THE GREEN MAN

The oldest pub in Essex, dating back to the 14th century, at a time when ale was brewed right here in Howe Street, **The Green Man** is a wonderful and distinguished pub, heavily beamed and with other charming original features that add to the traditional and cosy ambience. Excellent home-cooked food and a

choice of real ales are more reasons to stop and enjoy yourself at this convivial and welcoming inn.

displays exploring the history of the distinguished Essex Regiment. The museum is set in a lovely park complete with children's play area.

Also in the town, at Parkway, is **Moulsham Mill Business & Craft Centre**, set in an early 18th century water mill that has been renovated and now houses a variety of craft workshops and businesses. Crafts featured include jewellery, pottery, flowers, lace-making, dolls houses and bears, and decoupage work. There is a charming picnic area nearby, and a good café.

Three modern technologies - electrical engineering, radio, and ball and roller bearings - began in Chelmsford. At the **Engine House**

Project at Sandford Mill Waterworks, museum collections from the town's unique industrial story provide a fun and fascinating insight into the science of everyday things.

Around Chelmsford

Great Baddow
1 mile S of Chelmsford off the A12/A130

Baddow Antiques Centre at The Bringy, Church Street, is one of the leading antiques centres in Essex. Here, 20 dealers offer a wide selection of silver, porcelain, glass, furniture, paintings and collectibles.

THE BEEHIVE

The Beehive is a local landmark, well-known for the quality of its food, drink and hospitality. Open 11.30-23.00 weekdays, and 12.00-22.00 Sundays, this convivial pub serves Ridleys real ales and a good range of lagers, spirits and soft drinks. The homemade food ranges from snacks to hearty steak-and-ale pie and curries. The interior is bright,

warm and comfortable, while outside the large gardens include a children's play area. There's a quiz night every Sunday and live music on Saturday night.

Sandon

2 miles SE of Chelmsford off the A414

The village green here in Sandon has produced a notable Spanish oak tree, the biggest in the country, planted in the centre of the village green. This oak tree is remarkable not so much for its height as for the tremendous horizontal spread of its branches. Around the green are a fine church and a number of attractive old houses, some dating back to the 16th century when Henry VIII's Lord Chancellor, Cardinal Wolsey, was Lord of the Manor of Sandon.

South Hanningfield

6 miles S of Chelmsford off the A130

The placid waters of nearby **Hanningfield Reservoir** were created by damming Sandford Brook, and transformed the scattered rural settlement of Hanningfield into a lakeside village. Now on the shores of the lake, the 12th century village church's belfry has been a local landmark in the flat Essex countryside for centuries. Some of the timbers in the belfry are said to have come from Spanish galleons, wrecked in the aftermath of Sir Francis Drake's defeat of the Armada.

The Visitor Centre at the Reservoir overlooks the 870-acre reservoir and the gateway to the 100-acre woodland beyond. The Centre also offers refreshments, a gift shop and toilet.

Writtle

2 miles W of Chelmsford off the A414

Hylands House was built in 1728; this beautiful neo-Classical Grade II listed villa is set in over 500 acres of parkland landscaped by Repton. Rooms that are open to the public include the Blue Room, Entrance Hall, Library, Saloon, Boudoir and Drawing Room. Host to many outdoor events, including the annual 'V' concerts (V98 was a particularly great success) and the Chelmsford Spectacular, **Hylands Park** features lawns, rhododendron bushes, woodland paths, ornamental ponds and

THE GREEN MAN

Highwood Road, Edney Common, Chelmsford, Essex   Tel: 01245 248076

Dating in parts from the 16th century, **The Green Man** is a happy marriage of traditional features and modern comforts. Inside the huge feature fireplace, beamed ceilings and oak tables add to the rustic and cosy ambience, while the separate restaurant is intimate and charming. All the food is homecooked and encompasses a range of Modern English dishes at lunch (Tues-Sat 12.00-14.30, Sun 12.00-15.00) and dinner

(Tues-Sat 18.00-21.00), complemented by an excellent wine list. The atmosphere is welcoming and relaxed.

THE DUKE OF WELLINGTON

The Street, Hatfield Peverel, Chelmsford,
Essex CM3 2EA   Tel: 01245 380246
e-mail: toftcombs@aol.com

The Duke of Wellington is a traditional coaching inn in the best sense of the words. Tasteful and welcoming, the décor and furnishings are cosy and comfortable, with charming original 18th century features that complement the excellent food, drink and ambience. The award-winning chef creates menus and specials offering up a range of fresh and delicious dishes served at lunch

(Mon-Sat 12.00-14.30, Sun 12.00-20.00) and dinner (Mon-Sat 18.00-21.30). The staff are professional, attentive and friendly.

Pleasure Gardens adjacent to the House.

From a tucked-away corner of St John's Green in this village came Britain's first regular broadcasting service; an experimental 15-minute programme beamed out nightly by Marconi's engineers. Opposite the Green, the Cock and Bell is reputed to be haunted by a young woman who committed suicide on the railway. Further along this street is the Wheatsheaf, one of the smallest pubs in the country.

Writtle's parish church of St John features a cross of charred timbers, a reminder of the fire which gutted the chancel in 1974. Ducks swim on the pond of the larger and quite idyllic main village green, which is surrounded by lovely Tudor and Georgian houses.

Witham

6 miles NE of Chelmsford off the A12/B1018

The River Brain flows through this delightful town; a continuous walk has been created along its length for a distance of about three miles. The settlement dates back to at least the 10th century; remains of a Roman temple have been found at Ivy Chimneys, off Hatfield Road. Blackwater Lane leads to Whetmead, a nature reserve of 25 acres between the rivers Blackwater and Brain.

THE CROSS KEYS

The Street, White Notley, Witham,
Essex CM8 1RQ
Tel/Fax: 01376 583297

Painted a welcoming and cheerful bright pink, **The Cross Keys** is a well-cared for and charming little inn that is comfortable and traditional. Dating back to the 18th century, this handsome village inn offers a good range of beers, wines, spirits and soft drinks, and excellent meals and bar snacks at lunch and dinner every day. A relaxed and friendly place

to enjoy a drink or meal, this convivial pub is well worth seeking out.

THE SWAN INN

The Street, Hatfield Peverel,
nr Chelmsford, Essex CM3 2DW
Tel/Fax: 01245 380238
website:
www.pickapub.co.uk/swanhatpev.htm

Located on the main street through Hatfield Peverel, **The Swan Inn** was built in the 17th century and was once an important stopping point on the coaching run between London and Norwich. Much of its old-world appeal lives on in the spotless bar and lounge, where beams and brasses help to paint a very traditional scene. In Chris Ward, the inn has a young, go-ahead landlord who is passionate about The Swan and this part of Essex, and who takes excellent care of his customers with the assistance of hard-working staff. Popular with locals, it also offers motorists the chance of a pleasant break on their journey along the nearby A12. Greene King

IPA and two other real ales head the drinks list, and straightforward, no-frills bar meals and snacks are served Tuesday to Sunday lunchtimes (12.00-14.00), with evening meals available from 6 o'clock until 8.

The Swan also offers very agreeable guest accommodation in four characterful and very comfortable bedrooms (3 Diamonds ETC) with every amenity guests could expect. Two of the four rooms have en suite facilities; the other two have private baths. Breakfast is a hearty meal to set guests up for the day. With the A12 only half a mile away, the inn is an excellent base for business people who want a peaceful place to spend the night and for tourists visiting the sights of the area.

Hatfield Peverel itself has a handsome village green and some charming architecture, and is within an easy drive of the bustling town of Chelmsford, the delightful smaller town of Witham, Whetmead Nature Reserve, Constable Country, the medieval Temple Barns at Cressing and other sights and attractions of East Anglia.

This fine inn is open Monday to Friday 11.00-15.00 and 17.30-23.00, Saturdays 11.00-23.00, and Sundays 12.00-22.30.

The **Dorothy L Sayers Centre** in Newland Street houses a collection of books by and about Sayers, the theologian, Dante scholar and novelist/ creator of the Lord Peter Wimsey mysteries, who lived in Witham for many years.

Little Braxted

6 miles NE of Chelmsford off the A12/B1018

Little Braxted has been voted the best-kept village on a regular basis since 1973. St Mary's chapel was built in 1888, and can accommodate only 12 people at a time. Services are held every Wednesday. The village church of St Nicholas is mentioned in the *Domesday Book*, and is famous for its murals.

St Nicholas Church, Little Braxted

Little Baddow

5 miles E of Chelmsford off the A414

Blakes Wood is a designated Site of Special Scientific Interest, an ancient woodland of hornbeam and sweet chestnut renowned for its bluebells. There is a good circular way-marked one-and-a-half mile walk.

Cruising along the **Chelmer and Blackwater Canal** provides the visitor with a unique view of this part of rural Essex. Chelmer Cruises & Canal Centre at Paper Mill Lock in Little Baddow offers the barge *Victoria* for group hire (seats 48). Individual day trips at weekends and bank holidays can also be arranged. There's also an island picnic area, lockside tea room, walks and fishing.

Danbury

5 miles E of Chelmsford off the A414

This village is said to take its name from the Danes who invaded this part of the country in the Dark Ages. In the fine church, under a rare 13th century carved effigy, a crusader knight was found when the tomb was opened in 1779, perfectly preserved in the pickle which filled his coffin. Fine carving is also a feature of the bench ends; the oldest among them have inspired modern craftsmen to continue the same style of carving on all the pews. In 1402, '*the devil appeared in the likeness of Firor Minor, who entered the church, raged insolently to the great terror* of the parishioners ... the top of the steeple was broken down and half the chancel scattered abroad.' And, in 1941, another harbinger of disaster, a 500-lb German bomb, reduced the east end to ruins.

At **Danbury Common**, acres of gorse flower in a blaze of golden colour for much of the year. Along with Lingwood Common, Danbury Common is at the highest point of the gravel ridge between Maldon and Chelmsford. There is evidence here of Napoleonic defences and old reservoirs. Circular nature trails make exploring the area easily accessible. To the west, **Danbury Country Park** offers another pleasant stretch of open country, boasting woodland, a lake and ornamental gardens.

Woodham Walter
6 miles E of Chelmsford off the B1010

Woodham Walter is a small village which lies two and a half miles west of the ancient market town and coastal port of Maldon. It is rumoured that Henry VIII hunted in Woodham Walter during his reign. During the troubled times after Henry's death, Mary Tudor was concealed in Woodham Walter Hall, from whence she was planning to escape from England in 1550. The church in Woodham, **St Michael's**, was constructed in April 1564 and is said to be one of the oldest still standing in the world.

Maldon
10 miles E of Chelmsford on the A414

Maldon's High Street has existed since medieval times, and the alleys and mews leading from it are full of intriguing shops, welcoming old inns and good places to eat. One of the most distinctive features of the High Street is the **Moot Hall**. Built in the 14th century for the D'Arcy family, this building passed into the hands of the town corporation and was the seat of power in Maldon for over 400 years. The original brick spiral staircase (the best-preserved of its kind in England) and the 18th century courtroom are of particular interest. Guided tours are available on Saturdays in summer and by appointment with Maldon Town Council (01621 857373) at other times.

Thames Barges at Maldon

MALDON

Town Centre Manager, Kings Head Centre, 38 High Street, Maldon, Essex CM9 5PN
Tel: 01621 843984
website: www.maldon.co.uk

Maldon is an historic town with a thousand years of history and a strong maritime tradition, and the range of shops, restaurants, cafés, services and accommodation makes it an excellent place for an extended stay. Visitors should allow plenty of time to stroll around the alleyways leading off the High Street and to see some of the town's many attractions.

The High Street is filled with interesting shops, and on Thursday and Saturday the traditional market adds to the bustle; the farmers market is held on the first Tuesday of each month. At the end of the High Street, Church Street leads down to the Hythe, where visitors can appreciate Maldon's unique setting at the head of the Blackwater Estuary, home to many of the wonderful old Thames sailing barges.

A colourful appliqued embroidery made to commemorate the 1,000th anniversary of the crucial Battle of Maldon (see Northey Island, below) is on display at the **Maeldune Heritage Centre** (Maeldune being the Saxon name for Maldon). The Centre is housed in the Grade I listed St Peter's Building, erected in the 17th century by a local benefactor when the nave of the church that had once stood on this site collapsed. It can be found at the junction of the High Street and the steep and architecturally interesting Market Hill. The benefactor, one Thomas Plume, erected the building to house his collection of 6,000 books and a school; **The Plume Library** in St Peter's Building is open to the public.

A few minutes' walk down one of the small roads leading from the High Street brings you to the waterfront, where the old wharfs and quays are still active. Moored at **Hythe Quay** are several Thames sailing barges, all over 100 years old and still boasting their traditional rigging and distinctive tan sails. The barges and Quay are overlooked by two pubs, the Queen's Head and the Jolly Sailor. Maldon, famous for its sea salt, is the only place in England still making salt from sea water. Salt production in Maldon dates from Roman times, and from its current premises on the waterfront has continued uninterrupted since 1882.

Promenade Park lies adjacent to Hythe Quay. This attractive park next to the River Blackwater opened in 1895. The Edwardian-style gardens include a marine lake where children can paddle

THE WHITE HORSE INN

26 High Street, Maldon, Essex CM9 5PJ
Tel: 01621 851708
website:
www.pickapub.co.uk/whitehorsemaldon.htm

The White Horse Inn began life in the 16th-17th century as a coaching inn. Today it maintains an enviable reputation for its great food, ales and atmosphere.

The bar area is spacious and comfortable, light and airy, making it a welcoming place in which to enjoy the range of Shepherd Neame real ales and changing guest ales. All the food is freshly prepared and cooked to order, and includes excellent fresh fish, favourites such as bubble and squeak and liver and bacon, and a good range of more modern and vegetarian dishes. There's live music weekly, and children and pets are welcome. This convivial, relaxed inn is well worth a visit, and also boasts seven comfortable guest bedrooms, making it a superb base from which to explore Maldon and the region.

and a sandy play-space by the waterside. Also in the park are an adventure playground, picnic site, amusement centre, tennis courts and mini-golf. A varied programme of events takes place in the park throughout the year, including the Mad Maldon Mud Race and the RNLI Rowing Race, both held annually over the Christmas and New Year holidays.

Housed in what was original the parkkeeper's lodge, by the park gates, **Maldon District Museum** looks back on the colourful history of the town through permanent and changing displays of exhibits and objects associated with the area and the people of Maldon.

Ruins are all that remain of the **St Giles the Leper Hospital**, founded by

King Henry II in the 12th century. As with all monastic buildings, it fell into disuse after Henry VIII's Dissolution of the Monasteries, though it retained its roof and was used as a barn until the late 19th century. Many other buildings in the town, almost as old, fortunately remain - including two fine churches.

Langford
2 miles NW of Maldon off the B1019

The **Museum of Power**, Hatfield Road, covers all aspects of power, from domestic batteries to the massive machines that powered British industry. It includes the steam-powered pumping-station machinery of the redundant waterworks in which the museum is housed.

Northey Island
1 mile SE of Maldon off the B1018

This small island, comprising mainly salt-marsh, is owned by the National Trust. Access to this nature reserve is on foot via a causeway passable at low tide. It is a Site of Special Scientific Interest, important to over-wintering birds.

The sea-walls of the Island make for an interesting walk, and were used as the camp base for the Viking army in 991, when Byrhtnoth led the Saxons against the invading army. A fierce three-day battle took place, with Byrhtnoth's head eventually being cut off and the Viking warriors retreating despite their victory, leaving the English King Ethelred the Unready to pay an annual tribute, 'danegold', to the Danes to prevent further incursions.

Goldhanger
4 miles NE of Maldon off the B1026

Maldon District Agricultural & Domestic Museum, at 47 Church Street in Goldhanger, features a large collection of vintage farm tools and machinery manufactured locally, as well as printing machinery and domestic artefacts.

Tollesbury
9 miles NE of Maldon on the B1023

Located at the mouth of the River Blackwater is the marshland village of Tollesbury. **Tollesbury Marina** has been designed as a family leisure centre for the crews and passengers of visiting yachts. The Marina, with its tennis courts, heated covered swimming pool, bar and restaurant is ideally located for exploring the Blackwater and the neighbouring estuaries of the Crouch, Colne, Stour and Orwell. Guests arriving by land are welcome to use some Cruising Club facilities.

Tolleshunt D'Arcy
7 miles NE of Maldon on the B1026

Margery Allingham, one of the 'Queens of Crime', lived in this modest but picturesque and quiet village from 1935 until her death in 1966, and it was here she wrote many of her detective stories featuring Albert Campion.

Mundon
3 miles S of Maldon off the B1018

Mundon and the surrounding area boast some excellent walking. The **St Peter's Way**, a long-distance path from Ongar to St Peter's Chapel, Bradwell-on-Sea, leads through the village and past the disused Church of St Mary. This 14th century church is maintained by the Friends of Friendless Churches and is open to the public. Tolstoy is known to have visited the village.

Althorne
6 miles SE of Maldon on the B1012

The church of **St Andrew's**, some 600 years old, has a fine flint and stone tower, built in the perpendicular style. Inside the church there's a 15th century font which retains its original carvings of saints and angels. A brass plaque dated 1508 records that William Hyklott 'Paide for the werkemanship of the wall'; an inscription over the west door remembers John Wylson and John Hyll, who probably paid for the tower.

To the south, where Station Road meets Burnham Road, stands the villagers' own **War Memorial**. This solid structure of beams and tiles lends dignity and honour to the tragic roll-call of names listed on it.

To the north of the village is the golden-thatched and white-walled Huntsman and Hounds, an alehouse since around 1700.

Steeple and St Lawrence
8 miles SE of Maldon off the B1021

Public footpaths lead down to the water from the village of Steeple; the houses of St Lawrence stand close to the water. Several sailing clubs and some waterside caravan and camping parks ensure that there is plenty of activity on the adjacent stretch of the River Blackwater. The **St Lawrence Rural Discovery Church**, on high ground further inland, overlooks the villages and the River Blackwater to the north; it also offers views over the River Crouch to the south. Exhibitions with local themes are held in the church during the summer months.

Burnham-on-Crouch
12 miles SE of Maldon on the B1012

Burnham-on-Crouch is attractively old-fashioned, and probably best known as a yachting venue. It is lively in summer, especially at the end of August when the town hosts one of England's premier regattas, Burnham Week. This week of racing and shore events attracts many visiting craft and landlubbers alike. In winter many yachts are left to ride at anchor offshore, and the sound of the wind in their rigging is ever-present.

Behind the gaily-coloured cottages along the Quay lies the High Street and the rest of the town, its streets lined with a delightful assortment of old cottages and Victorian and Georgian houses and shops.

In past times, working boats thronged the estuary where yachts now ply to and fro. Seafarers still come ashore to buy provisions, following a tradition that goes back to medieval times when Burnham was the market centre for the isolated inhabitants of Wallasea and Foulness Islands in the estuary. A ferry still links Burnham with Wallasea at weekends during the summer, and a programme of boat trips to see the seals on Foulness Sands operates from Burnham Quay. Near the Yacht Harbour, west of the town and accessible along the sea-wall path is **Burnham Country Park**.

Burnham-on-Crouch & District Museum on The Quay features agricultural, maritime and social history exhibits relating to the Dengie Hundred. There is also a small archaeological collection. Special exhibitions are mounted periodically.

Mangapps Farm Railway Museum on the edge of town offers an extensive collection of railway relics of all kinds, including steam and diesel locos, carriages and wagons, relocated railway buildings, one of the largest collections of signalling equipment open to the public, a complete country station and items of East Anglian railway history. Train rides are available when the museum is open, and Thomas the Tank Engine weekends are held several times a year.

St Mary's Church is constructed of Kentish ragstone that was transported to Burnham by sea. Construction was begun in the 12th century and was completed in the 14th, but since that time the nucleus of the town has moved closer to the waterfront. The arches and pillars are particularly fine examples of medieval craftmanship, hence the church being known as 'The Cathedral of the Dengie'.

Southminster
3 miles N of Burnham on the B1021

The old market town of Southminster was important as the economic centre for the isolated marshland communities of the Dengie Peninsula.

THE QUEENS HEAD

36 Queen Street, Southminster,
Essex CMO 7BB
Tel: 01621 772315 Fax: 01621 772505
e-mail: roger@queenshead.fsnet.co.uk

Roger and Barbara Longhurst and their friendly, conscientious staff offer a warm welcome and genuine hospitality to all their guests at **The Queens Head** in Southminster. Here in this lovely part of Essex, this 19th century inn is an unspoilt example of a traditional rural hostelry. The interior is cosy and comfortable, with a separate bright and airy dining room. Outside there's an attractive garden with patio area for summer dining, lawns and safe children's play area.

The food is freshly prepared and home-cooked, and includes a range of traditional dishes and more exotic fare such as salmon pasta Florentine and Thai green curry chicken. Meals are served at both lunch and dinner, seven days a week. Real ales include Greene King IPA and Tolly Cobbold Original, together with a good choice of lagers, cider, wines, spirits and soft drinks.

Bradwell-on-Sea/Bradwell Waterside

12 miles NE of Burnham off the B1021

A visit to Bradwell-on-Sea (the name derives from the Saxon words *brad pall*, meaning 'broad wall') is well worth the long drive for its sense of being right out on the edge of things – the timeless emptiness is if anything exaggerated by the distant views of buildings across the water on Mersea Island and the bulk of the nearby (now decomissioned) nuclear power station. A walk eastwards along the old Roman road across the marshes takes you to the site of their fort, 'Othona', on which the visitors of today will find the chapel of **St Peter's on the Wall**, built by St Cedd and his followers in AD 654 using rubble from the ruined fort. In the 14th century the chapel was abandoned as a place of worship, and over the following centuries used at various times as a barn and a shipping beacon. Restored and re-consecrated in 1920, it is well worth the half-mile walk from the car park to reach it. It is the site of a pilgrimage each July.

There is an unusual war memorial marking the site of the Bradwell Bay Secret Airfield, used during the Second World War for aircraft unable to return to their original base.

Bradwell Lodge, in the village centre, is a part-Tudor former rectory that has known some famous visitors. Gainsborough, the Suffolk artist, used rooms as a studio, while the Irish writer Erskine Childers, who was shot by the

St Peter On the Wall, Bradwell-on-Sea

Irish Free State in 1920 because he fought for the IRA, wrote *The Riddle of the Sands* here.

At Bradwell Waterside, a large marina has berths for 300 boats. The now-decommissioned nuclear power station has a visitor centre with an exhibition and high-tech audio-visual displays about electricity production and the decommissioning process. A nature trail is way-marked within the grounds of the station.

To the south of the village lie the remote marshes of the **Dengie Peninsula**, parts of which are important nature reserves. The salty tang of sea air, brought inland on easterly winds, gives an exhilarating flavour to the marshlands. Like the Cambridgeshire and Lincolnshire fens, this once-waterlogged corner of Essex was reclaimed from the sea by 17th century Dutch engineers. The views across the

THE BELL INN

The Street, Purleigh, Chelmsford,
Essex CM3 6QJ
Tel: 01621 828348 Fax: 01621 828983

Comprising of an original 14th century 'Hall House' which was extensively refurbished in the 16th century the Bell is located in the conservation area next to the Church giving extensive views over the Blackwater estuary. St Peters Ancient walk from Ongar to Bradwell runs through the pub garden and there are circular walks around the village making it a popular stop for ramblers and hikers. Great food and drink is served amid friendly, quiet and relxed surroundings. Food is cooked to order lunchtimes and evenings Wednesday-Monday. Under 14's not permitted inside.

marshes take in great sweeps of countryside inhabited only by wildfowl and seabirds.

Purleigh

5 miles SW of Maldon on the B1010

The first recorded vineyard in Purleigh was planted in the early 12th century, only 400 yards from the site of New Hall Vineyards in Chelmsford Road. It covered three acres of land next to Purleigh Church, where first US president George Washington's great-great-grandfather was the rector - until the time he was removed from this office for sampling too much of the local brew! Purleigh Vineyard became Crown property in 1163; subsequently the wines produced were taken each year to London to be presented to the monarch.

South Woodham Ferrers

5 miles SW of Maldon off the B1012

The empty marshland of the Crouch estuary, a yachtsman's paradise, was chosen by Essex County Council as the site for one of its most attractive new towns schemes. At its centre, this successful 20th century new town boasts a traditional market square surrounded by pleasant arcades and terraces built in the old Essex style with brick, tile and weather-board.

Marsh Farm Country Park in Marsh Farm Road, South Woodham Ferrers, is a working farm and country park adjoining the River Crouch. Sheep, pigs, cattle and hens roam; visitors can also partake of the adventure play area, farm trail, Visitors' Centre, gift shop and tea rooms. Guided tours are available by prior arrangement. Special events are held throughout the year.

Rettendon

6 miles SW of Maldon off the A130

The **Royal Horticultural Society Garden** at Hyde Hall (see panel on page 52) comprises eight acres of year-round hillside colour, with a woodland garden, large rose garden, ornamental ponds with lilies and fish, herbaceous borders, shrubs, trees, and national collections of malus and viburnum.

Battlesbridge
7 miles SW of Maldon off the A132

Battlesbridge Antiques Centre at Hawk Hill in Battlesbridge is the largest in Essex. Housed in five period buildings, more than 70 dealers display and sell their wares. The heart of the Centre is Cromwell House, its ground floor dedicated to specialist dealers with individual units. They will advise, value and give an expert opinion free of charge. They offer a wide variety of old and interesting pieces and collectibles.

The Centre's Haybarn Cottages were constructed as dwellings, while, alongside, The Bridgebarn began life as a barn with thatched roof and dates from the 19th century, at which time there were lime kilns nearby. It was converted to its present tiled roof in the 1930s. The building retains some fine oak beamwork, and houses a small 'penny arcade' with working model roundabout, fortune teller, and 'What the Butler Saw' as well as a large collection of antiques for sale.

There are superb views from the top floor of the River Crouch and the surrounding area.

This superb location is also the site of a **Classic Motor Cycle Museum**, with displays evoking the history of motorcycling through the ages and some interesting memorabilia. Open on Sundays or by appointment. Three classic vehicle events are held annually.

RHS GARDEN HYDE HALL

Rettendon, Chelmsford, Essex CM3 8ET
Tel: 01245 400256 Fax: 01245 402100
e-mail: hydehall@rhs.org.uk
website: www.rhs.org.uk

RHS Garden Hyde Hall is the proud and impressive result of 40 years of dedication and inspiration, created despite its hilltop setting, heavy clay soil, low rainfall and frequent strong, drying winds. Donated to the Royal Horticultural Society in 1993, a programme of development and improvement has made this delightful and imaginatively planted garden a centre of excellence. Home to the National Plant Collection of Viburnum, the garden is also well known for its superb collection of roses. The colour-themed herbaceous border and new plantings around the lower pond are also striking examples of garden design. The Farmhouse Garden features a formal design full of bold colour combinations and fascinating plant associations. The Dry Garden displays plants from a variety of arid areas. The Hilltop Garden provides year-round interest with its

naturalised spring bulbs and late-flowering tender perennials producing a blaze of autumn colour.

The Visitor Centre offers a wealth of information on many subjects. In the Hyde Hall Garden Library, visitors are welcome to browse through books, journals and CD ROMs exploring a range of topics such as problem places, garden plants, pests and diseases, pruning and more. The Barn Restaurant, Tea Yard and Shop complete this fascinating day out which will delight not just gardeners but anyone with an eye for beauty. Open: every day from 18th March to 10th November. (March to August 10 am to 6 pm and September to November 10 am to 5 pm.)

2 Colchester and North East Essex

Northeast Essex has the true feel of East Anglia, particularly around the outstanding villages of the Stour Valley - which has come to be known as Constable Country along with its near neighbour, southern Suffolk. The inland villages and small towns here are notably historic and picturesque, offering very good touring and walking opportunities.

A plethora of half-timbered medieval buildings, farms and churches mark this region out as of particular historical interest. Monuments to engineering feats past and present include Hedingham Castle, Chappel Viaduct and the postmill at Bocking Church Street. Truly lovely villages such as Finchingfield abound, rewarding any journey to this part of the county. There are also many lovely gardens to visit, and this region's principal town, Colchester, is a mine of interesting sights and experiences.

The north Essex coastal region is redolent with distinguished history and a strong maritime heritage, as exemplified in towns like Harwich, Manningtree and Mistley. Further examples are the fine Martello Towers - circular brick edifices built to provide a coastal defence against Napoleon's armies - along the Tendring coast at Walton and Clacton. Dating from 1808 to 1812, each is mounted with a gun on the roof.

The Tendring Peninsula, which takes its name from the old Tendring Hundred (a name coming from the county divisions of Saxon times, of which Tendring was a centre), has a rich and varied heritage ranging from prehistoric remains to medieval churches and elegant Victorian villas. It was settled by successive waves of invading Romans, Angles, Saxons and Vikings. Place

Clacton on Sea

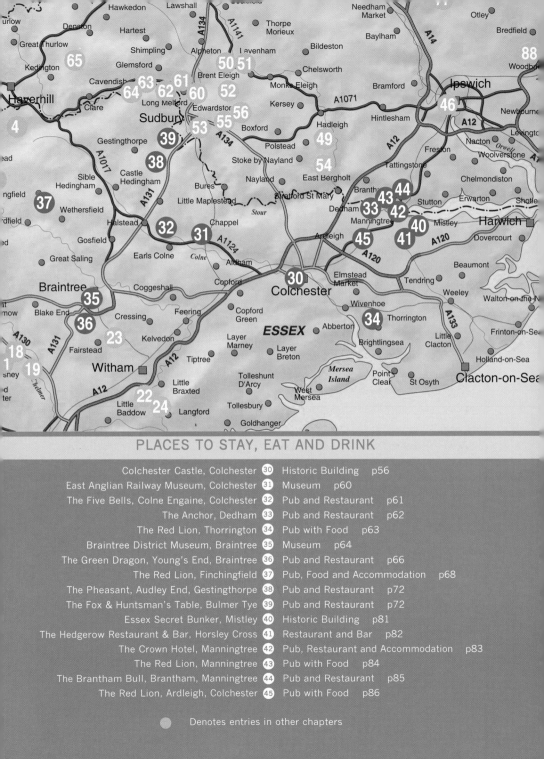

PLACES TO STAY, EAT AND DRINK

● Denotes entries in other chapters

names include the Danish ending 'by', meaning a settlement, and the Old English 'ea' and 'ey' for an island. Among the many attractive villages in the district are Thorpe-le-Soken, Kirby-le-Soken and Great Bentley - the last reputed to have the largest village green in England. The Tendring Coast contains an interesting mix of extensive tidal inlets, sandy beaches and low cliffs.

Castle Hedingham

The Stour Estuary, Hamford Water and Colne Estuary are all renowned for seabirds and other wildlife. Many areas are protected nature reserves. The Manningtree-to-Ramsey road passes through some of the best coastal scenery in Essex, with some outstanding views of the Suffolk shore.

This is, of course, also the part of the county known as 'the sunshine holiday coast'. Resorts, both boisterous and more sedate, dot the coastline here: Clacton-on-Sea, Frinton-on-Sea and Walton-on-the-Naze to name but three - and offer many opportunities for relaxation and recreation.

Colchester

This ancient market town and garrison stands in the midst of rolling East Anglian countryside. England's oldest recorded town, it has over 2,000 years of history, there to be discovered by visitors. First established during the 7th century BC, west of town there are the

remains of the massive earthworks built to protect Colchester in pre-Roman times. During the 1st century, Colchester's prime location made it an obvious target for invading Romans. The Roman Emperor Claudius accepted the surrender of 11 British Kings in Colchester. In AD60, Queen Boudica helped to establish her place in history by taking revenge on the Romans and burning the town to the ground, before going on to destroy London and St Albans. Here in this town that was once capital of Roman Britain, Roman walls - the oldest in Britain - still surround the oldest part of town. Balkerne Gate, west gate of the original Roman town, is the largest surviving Roman gateway in the country, and remains magnificent to this day.

Today the town is presided over by its lofty town hall and enormous Victorian water tower, nicknamed 'Jumbo' after London Zoo's first African elephant, an animal sold to P T Barnum (causing some controversy) in 1882. The tower has four massive pillars made up of one-and-a-quarter million bricks, 369 tons of stone and 142 tons of iron, all working to support the 230,000-gallon tank.

The town affords plenty to see and explore. There are many guided town walks available, as well as bus tours. The local Visitor Information Centre on Queen Street has details of the many places to visit. Market days in this thriving town are Friday and Saturday.

A good place to start any exploration of the town is **Colchester Castle** (see panel below) itself and its museum.

When the Normans arrived, Colchester (a name given the town by the Saxons) was an important borough. The Normans built their castle on the foundations of the Roman temple of Claudius. Having used many of the Roman bricks in its construction, it boasts the largest Norman keep ever built in Europe - the only part still left standing. The keep houses the Castle Museum, one of the most exciting hands-on historical attractions in the country. Its fascinating collection of Iron Age, Roman and medieval relics is one of the most important in the country.

COLCHESTER CASTLE

Castle Park, High Street, Colchester
Tel: 01206 282939
website: www.colchestermuseums.co.uk

Colchester Castle is undeniably one of the most important historic buildings in the country, and today, a thousand years after it was built, it is still a living, vibrant place, a potent symbol of Britain's oldest recorded town. Colchester was the first capital of Britain and beneath the Castle's foundations are the remains of one of the most renowned Roman buildings, the Temple of Claudius. To the Romans it was the symbol of their power and success, but to the native Britons it was a symbol of oppression.

The temple became a main target of the rebels led by Queen Boudica (Boadicea) who attacked the Roman town in AD60. The town's citizens barricaded themselves in the temple but after two days they were all killed. It is estimated that as many as 30,000 could have been killed during the sacking of Colchester. After the revolt had been suppressed the town and the temple were rebuilt.

Around 1076 King William I ordered a royal fortress to be built at Colchester, and the great stone base of the now ruined temple was an obvious foundation for the

central tower or keep of the new castle. The great size of the temple dictated that of the keep, which was the largest ever built in Britain.

For most of its life the Castle was used as a prison; one of the most infamous episodes in its history occurred in 1645 when Matthew Hopkins, the self-styled Witchfinder General, used the Castle to imprison and interrogate suspected witches. The Castle first opened its doors in the role of Museum in 1860 and today features many hands-on displays to help explain the town-people's experience of Colchester's varying fortunes. Visitors can slip into a toga, feel the weight of Roman armour, try on medieval hats and shoes and see treasures like the Roman bronze statue of Mercury and the Colchester Vase, one of the finest examples of Roman pottery found in Britain.

There are tombstones carved in intricate detail and exquisite examples of Roman glass and jewellery. Visitors can try on Roman togas and helmets, touch some of the 2,000-year-old pottery unearthed nearby, and experience the town's murkier past by visiting the Castle prisons, where witches were interrogated by the notorious Witchfinder General Matthew Hopkins.

Hollytrees Museum in the High Street is located in a fine Georgian home dating back to 1718. This award-winning museum, found on the edge of Castle Park, houses a wonderful collection of toys, costumes, curios and antiquities from the last two centuries. Purchased for the town by Viscount Cowdray it first opened as a museum in 1920. Also nearby, housed in the former All Saints' Church, is the **Natural History Museum**, with exhibits many hands-on displays illustrating the natural history of Essex from the Ice Age right up to the present day.

Housed in the Minories Art Gallery, **First Site** is a recent addition to Colchester's fine choice of art institutes, and features changing exhibitions of contemporary visual art, housed in a converted Georgian town house with beautiful walled garden. An arch in Trinity Street leads to **Tymperleys Clock Museum**, the 15th century timber-framed home of William Gilberd, who entertained Elizabeth I with experiments in electricity. Today this fine example of architectural splendour houses a magnificent collection of 18th and 19th century Colchester-made clocks. The **Colchester Arts Centre**, not far from Balkerne Gate, features a regular programme of visual arts, drama, music, poetry and dance; the **Mercury Theatre** is the town's premiere site for stage dramas, comedies and musical theatre.

Dutch Protestants arrived in Colchester in the 16th century, fleeing Spanish rule in the Netherlands, and revitalised the local cloth industry. The houses of these Flemish weavers in the **Dutch Quarter** to the west of the castle, and the Civil War scars on the walls of Siege House in East Street, bear testimony to their place in the town's history. The Dutch Quarter west of the castle remains a charming and relatively quiet corner of this bustling town.

Close to the railway station are the ruins of **St Botolph's Priory**, the oldest Augustinian priory in the country. Its remains are a potent reminder of the bitterness of Civil War times, as it was here that Royalists held out for 11 weeks during the siege of Colchester, before finally being starved into submission.

On Bourne Road, south of the town centre just off the B1025, there's a striking stepped-and-curved gabled building known as **Bourne Mill**, now owned by the National Trust. Built in 1591 from stone taken from the nearby St John's Abbeygate, this delightful restored building near a lovely millpond was originally a fishing lodge, later converted (in the 19th century) into a mill - and still in working order.

St Botolph's Priory

Colchester Zoo, just off the A12 outside the town, stands in the 40-acre park of Stanway Hall, with its 16th century mansion and church dating from the 14th century. Founded in 1963, the Zoo has a wide and exciting variety of attractions. The Zoo has gained a well-deserved reputation as one of the best in Europe. Its award-winning enclosures allow visitors closer to the animals and provide naturalistic environments for the 170 species. There are 15 unique daily displays including opportunities to feed an African elephant, bear, chimp or alligator, stroke a snake and watch a penguin parade.

Colchester has been famous in its time for both oysters and roses. Colchester oysters are still cultivated on beds in the lower reaches of the River Colne, which

skirts the northern edge of town. A visit to the **Oyster Fisheries** on Mersea Island is a fascinating experience, and the tour includes complimentary fresh oysters and a glass of wine.

Just north of the centre of town, **High Woods Country Park** offers 330 acres of woodland, grassland, scrub and farmland. A central lake is fed by a small tributary of the River Colne. The land originated as three ancient farms, and forms part of a Royal hunting forest. Large numbers of musket balls dating from the Civil War period have been unearthed, indicating that the woods served as a base for the Roundheads.

Around Colchester

Abberton
3 miles S of Colchester off the B1026

Two natural beauties are within reach of this village. **Abberton Reservoir Nature Reserve** is a 1,200 acre reservoir and wildlife centre, ideal for birdwatching. A site of international importance, home to 700 goldeneye, 8,000 wigeon and nearly 500 gadwall and shovellers, as well as a resting colony of cormorants, the site features a conservation room, shop, toilets and hides.

Copford Green & Copford
3½ miles SW of Colchester off the B1022

Copford is home to the wonderful Norman church of **St Michael and All**

Angels, with its magnificent, well-restored medieval wall paintings, whilst Copford Green, a lovely and peaceful village, is home to **Springfields at Copford** with 17 acres of gardens and parkland. Here visitors will find old established south gardens with roses and shrubbery, as well as a parterre planted in 1997 with 330 rose bushes. Other attractions include a rare Maidenhair Gingko tree, ancient mulberry, woodland walks, spring-fed water gardens and lake, and croquet and putting greens. The church of **St Mary the Virgin** also repays a visit.

Layer Breton
5½ miles SW of Colchester off the B1026

On the right side of Layer Breton Heath there's **Stamps and Crows**, a must for gardening enthusiasts. Two and a half acres of moated garden surrounding a 15th century farmhouse (not open to the public) boast herbaceous borders, mixed shrubs, old roses and good ground cover. There is also a recently created bog garden and dovecote.

Layer Marney
6 miles SW of Colchester off the B1022

The mansion, which was planned to rival Hampton Court, was never completed, but its massive 8-storey Tudor gatehouse, known as **Layer Marney Tower**, is very impressive. Built between 1515 and 1525, it is one of the most striking examples of 16th century

architecture in Britain. Its magnificent four red brick towers, covered in 16th century Italianate design, were built by Lord Marney, Henry VIII's Lord Privy Seal. As well as spectacular views from the top of the towers, they are surrounded by formal gardens designed at the turn of the century, with lovely roses, yew hedges and herbaceous borders. There is also on site a rare breeds farm, farm shop and tea room.

Tiptree
7 miles SW of Colchester on the B1023

As all true jam-lovers will know, Tiptree is famed as the home of the **Wilkin and Son Ltd** jam factory, a Victorian establishment which now boasts a fascinating visitors' centre in the grounds of the original factory.

Aldham
4 miles W of Colchester off the A604

This picturesque village was, for a time, home to the famous Essex historian Philip Morant, who held the post of vicar here. He is buried in the local churchyard. **Old Hill House** in Aldham is a one-acre garden with mixed shrubs, herbaceous borders and formal herb garden for year-round interest.

Chappel
5 miles W of Colchester off the A604

Here, on a 4-acre site beside Chappel and Wakes Colne Station, is the **East**

There is also a delightful miniature railway.
Special steam days and events are held
throughout the year.

Anglian Railway Museum (see panel above), a comprehensive collection spanning 150 years of railway history, with period railway architecture, engineering and memorabilia in beautifully restored station buildings. For every railway buff, young or old, this is the place to try your hand at being a signalman and admire the handsome restored engines and carriages. There is also a delightful miniature railway. Special steam days and other events are held throughout the year.

The dramatic 32-arched **Chappel Viaduct** standing 75 feet above the Colne Valley, a designated European Monument, was begun in 1846 and opened in 1849.

Earls Colne
7 miles W of Colchester off the A604

The de Veres, Earls of Oxford, and the River Colne bestowed this village with its name. Aubery de Vere founded a Benedictine priory here in the 12th century, and both he and his wife, sister of William the Conqueror, were buried

there. Today the site is marked by a redbrick Gothic mansion. Though the commuter culture has spread modern housing around the village, the cluster of timbered cottages hearkens back to this village's distinguished past.

Dedham
6 miles NE of Colchester off the A14

This is true Constable country, along the border with Suffolk, the county's prettiest area. The village has several fine old buildings, especially the 15th century flint church, its pinnacled tower familiar from so many Constable paintings. There's also the school Constable went to, and good walks through the protected riverside meadows of Dedham Vale to **Flatford**, where **Bridge Cottage** is a restored thatched 16th century building housing a display about Constable, who featured this cottage in several of his paintings (his father's mill is across the river lock in Dedham).

Dedham Vale Family Farm on Mill Street is a nicely undeveloped 16-acre

THE FIVE BELLS

7 Mill Lane, Colne Engaine, Colchester,
Essex CO6 2HY
Tel: 01787 224166
e-mail: petitfour@dlingley.freeserve.co.uk

Here in the picturesque village of Colne
Engaine, secluded and peaceful, **The Five
Bells** inn is well worth seeking out. This top-
of-the-range inn boasts an extremely
handsome interior,
with many original
features and an air
of real luxury and
comfort. The
elegance and grace
of a gentler age is
captured in this
superior inn. The
building dates back
over 500 years, and
a record of the inn's
landlords going
back to 1579 is
proudly displayed in
the bar area. The
recently refurbished
interior retains
lovely features such as the original exposed
timbers and is tastefully decorated and
furnished; outside, a lovely terrace
commands stunning views over the Colne
Valley.

Owners Darran and Caroline Lingley are

happy to uphold the inn's long and fine
tradition of hospitality, quality and service.
Affable hosts, they and their friendly staff
make all their guests feel most welcome.

Open every session weekdays, and all day
at weekends, there's a choice of real ales
available at this Free House, together with
four draught lagers, Guinness, Strongbow
and a good range of wines, spirits and soft
drinks.

The menu is a happy mix of modern food
and traditional values, and makes use of only
the freshest ingredients and local produce.
All food is home-cooked and freshly
prepared, including the delicious breads. All
meat is cured and fish smoked on the
premises. Guests choose from the

blackboard menu to
sample the range of
delicious favourites and
more innovative dishes
on offer. Food is
available between
midday and 2pm and
7pm and 9.30pm. The
dining area seats 80 (no
smoking; booking
advised at weekends),
while upstairs there's a
newly refurbished coffee
lounge.

For a real taste of
old-world charm, great
food and drink and
genuine hospitality,
look no further.

farm boasting a comprehensive collection of British farm animals, including many different breeds of livestock such as pigs, sheep, cattle, Suffolk horses, goats and poultry. Children may enter certain of the paddocks to stroke and feed the animals (bags of feed provided).

The **Art & Craft Centre** on Dedham's High Street is well worth a visit. **Marlborough Head**, a wool merchant's house dating back to 1475, is now a pub. The **Toy Museum** has a fascinating collection of dolls, teddies, toys, games, doll houses and other artefacts of childhoods past.

At Castle House, approximately three-quarters of a mile from the village centre on the corner of East Lane and Castle

Dedham Vale, Willy Lot's Cottage

Hill, The **Sir Alfred Munnings Art Museum** is housed in the former home,

THE ANCHOR

The Heath, Dedham, Essex CO7 6BU
Tel: 01206 323131
e-mail: fredericcarlot@aol.com

Enjoying an excellent reputation for its good real ales and superb food, **The Anchor** in Dedham is well worth seeking out. It is run by Fred Carlot, a Calais native who has been in England for six years and took over at this fine pub in 2002. Real ales include Greene King IPA and Adnams. Chef Dave Spruce has created a wonderful menu of both traditional favourites such as mixed grills and home-make steak and kidney pudding and dishes such as trout Normandie and an international selection of meals including Chinese, Thai, Indian and Malaysian delicacies, all cooked to perfection.

The interior is warm and welcoming, and features a bar area and separate restaurant. Heavily beamed and featuring an interesting plaster montage of the original pub on one wall, the ambience at this superior pub is always friendly and relaxed.

studios and grounds of the famous painter, who lived here between 1898 and 1920. The museum prides itself on the diversity of paintings and sculptures on view. The house itself is a mixture of Tudor and Georgian periods, carefully restored. Munnings' original furniture is still in place. The spacious grounds boast well-maintained gardens.

Wivenhoe

4 miles SE of Colchester off the A133

This riverside town on the banks of the River Colne was once renowned as a smugglers' haunt, and there is a very pretty quayside that is steeped in maritime history. There are still strong connections with the sea, with boat-building having replaced fishing as the main industry. The pretty church, with its distinctive cupola atop a sturdy tower, stands on the site of the former Saxon church and retains some impressive 16th century brasses.

The small streets lead into each other and end at the picturesque waterfront, where fishing boats and small sailing craft bob at their moorings. On the Quay visitors will find the **Nottage Institute**, the River Colne's nautical academy; classes here teach students about knots, skippering and even how to build a boat! It is open to visitors on Sundays in summer. The Wivenhoe Trail, by the river, is an interesting cycle track starting at the railway station and continuing along the river to Colchester Hythe. Wivenhoe Woods is dotted with grassy glades set with tables, the perfect place for a picnic.

East of the Quay, the public footpath takes visitors to the Tidal Surge Barrier, one of only two in the country. Volunteers run a ferry service operating across the River Colne between the Quay at Wivenhoe, Fingringhoe and Rowhedge. Nearby Wivenhoe Park has been the site of the campus for the University of Essex since 1962. Visitors are welcome to stroll around the grounds.

Braintree

This town, along with its close neighbour Bocking, are sited at the

---

crossing of two Roman roads and were brought together by the cloth industry in the 16th century. Flemish weavers settled here, followed by many Huguenots. One, Samuel Courtauld, set up a silk mill in 1816 and, by 1866, employed over 3,000 Essex inhabitants.

The magnificent former Town Hall is one of the many Courtauld legacies in the town. It was built in 1928 with panelled walls, murals by Grieffenhagen showing stirring scenes of local history, and a grand central tower with a five-belled striking clock. A smaller but no less fascinating reminder of Courtauld's

generosity is the 1930s bronze fountain, with bay, shell and fish, near St Michael's Church.

Huguenot names such as Courtauld are connected with international enterprises to this day. Their reason for coming to Britain is a fascinating and poignant tale. Formed in France in 1559 as an organised Protestant group taking direction from Calvin and the Calvinistic Reformation in Geneva, the Huguenots were at first allowed to live and worship freely. However, as political and religious rivalries grew in France, the Catholic majority started to

BRAINTREE DISTRICT MUSEUM

The Town Hall Centre, Market Place,
Braintree, Essex CM7 3YG
Tel: 01376 328868 Fax: 01376 344345
e-mail: jean@bdcmuseum.demon.co.uk
website: www.braintree.gov.uk/museum

In the historic market square (market days Wednesday and Saturday), **Braintree District Museum** is housed in a beautifully converted Victorian school. Visitors are assured of a warm welcome at this award-winning museum, whose elegant exhibition areas are in contrast to the somewhat stern Victorian facade; the exception to this is the faithfully re-created Victorian classroom, where nostalgia lovers will be in their element and where role-play lessons are provided for schools on a daily basis.

Braintree was the centre of the medieval wool trade in north Essex and gained international fame when Courtaulds evolved their revolutionary silk industry in the town. The permanent galleries tell the fascinating story of this industry and also of the development of engineering design · Braintree was also the home of Crittalls. Country crafts such as straw plaiting are featured, along with the rural artists who made their home in Great Barfield and became pivotal in the development of fine and decorative arts in the 1950s and 1960s. John Ray, often considered the father of English natural history, has a dedicated gallery to his ground-breaking research in the 17th century.

A feature of the Museum is the programme of changing exhibitions, often with a craft base such as ceramics, decorative arts and particularly textiles. Friendly staff are pleased to welcome visitors with a free Soundalive audio tour and explain the wide range of craft items available in the shop.

persecute them; a century of war, massacre and bloodshed followed. Finally in 1685 all their rights were stripped. In the chaos that ensued, many died and thousands fled. It was to turn out to be France's loss, for the Huguenots were among the most industrious and economically advanced elements in French society. Others gained at France's expense; Huguenots poured into England, and especially East Anglia, where their skills soon made them welcome and valued members of the community.

The **Braintree District Museum** (see panel opposite) on Manor Street tells the story of Braintree's diverse industrial heritage and traditions. The **Town Hall Centre** is a Grade II listed building housing the Tourist Information Centre and the Art Gallery, which boasts a continuous changing programme of exhibitions and works.

Around Braintree
Coggeshall
5 miles E of Braintree on the A120

This medieval hamlet, a pleasant old cloth and lace town, has some very fine timbered buildings. **Paycocke's House** on West Street, a delightful timber-framed medieval merchant's home dating from about 1500, boasts unusually rich panelling and wood carvings, and is owned by the National Trust. Inside there's a superb carved ceiling and a display of Coggeshall lace. Outdoors there's a lovely garden. The village also has some good antique shops and a

working pottery.

Located in Stoneham Street, **Coggeshall Heritage Centre** displays items of local interest and features changing exhibitions on themes relating to the past of this historic wool town.

The National Trust also owns the restored **Coggeshall Grange Barn**, which dates from around 1140 and is the oldest surviving timber-framed barn in Europe. Built for the monks of the nearby Cistercian Abbey, it is a magnificent example of this type of architecture.

MarksHall is an historic estate and arboretum that began life in Saxon times, and is mentioned in the *Domesday Book*. In the 15th century, then-owner Sir Thomas Honywood was a leading Parliamentarian who commanded the Essex Regiment during the Civil War. Local legend has it that the two artificial lakes on the grounds were dug by Parliamentary troops during the siege of Colchester in 1648. One of his successors, General Philip Honywood, in 1758 forbade (under the terms of his will) any of his successors to fell timber - thus his lasting legacy of avenues of mature oaks, limes and horse chestnuts, surrounded by one of the largest continuous areas of ancient woodland in the county.

The estate fell on hard times in the 19th and early 20th century, but owner Thomas Phillips Price began an association with Kew Gardens and left the estate to be held and used for 'advancement in the National interest of Agriculture, Aboriculture and Forestry'.

The Thomas Phillips Price Trust was formed and registered as a charity in 1971, and a major programme of revitalisation and restoration began. The estate now flourishes with native plants and wildlife, ornamental lakes, a 17th century walled garden, cascades, Coach House and Information Centre. This last is housed in a painstakingly refurbished 15th century barn, and features informative displays as well as a gift shop and tea room.

Plans for the on-site arboretum were first drawn up in the late 1980s, to cover 120 acres. Still being established, it will contain a collection of trees from all over the world, laid out in geographical themes - Europe, Asia, America, and the southern hemisphere.

Cressing
4 miles E of Braintree off the B1018

Cressing Temple Barns, set in the centre of an ancient farmstead, are two splendid medieval timber barns commissioned in the 12th century by the Knights Templar. They contain the timber of over 1,000 oak trees; an interpretive exhibition explains to visitors how the barns were made, as a special viewing platform brings visitors up into the roof of the magnificent Wheat Barn for a closer look. There's also a beautiful walled garden re-creating the Tudor style, with an arbour, fount and physic garden. Special events are held throughout the year.

Feering
6 miles E of Braintree off the A12

Feeringbury Manor near Feering has a fine, extensive riverside garden with ponds, streams, a little waterwheel, old-fashioned plants and bog gardens, and fascinating sculpture by artist Ben Coode-Adams.

Kelvedon
6 miles SE of Braintree off the A12

This village alongside the River Blackwater houses the **Feering and Kelvedon Museum**, which is dedicated to manorial history and houses artefacts from the Roman settlement of Canonium, agricultural tools through the ages and other interesting exhibits.

THE GREEN DRAGON

Upper London Road, Young's End, Braintree, Essex CM7 8QN
Tel: 01245 361030 Fax: 01245 362575
e-mail: green.dragon@virgin.net

Dating back to the mid-1700s, **The Green Dragon** is an elegant and attractive coaching inn offering great food and drink and warm hospitality. Furnished and decorated to a high standard, this characterful inn offers a superb range of home-cooked food served at lunch and dinner Mon-Sat and from midday to 8 p.m. on

Sundays. Discerning diners flock here to dine in the upper or lower dining areas, occupying the former stables and hayloft respectively.

Fairstead
4 miles S of Braintree off the A131

Fairstead (or Fairsted) is an undulating parish about three miles east of the A131. The **Church of St Mary and St Peter** is an ancient building of flint, in the Norman style, consisting of chancel, nave, north porch and a western tower with a lofty shingled spire with four bells, one of which dates back to before the Reformation. During restoration in the late 1800s various handsome mural paintings were discovered, including, over the chancel arch, those entitled *Our Lord's Triumphal Entry into Jerusalem, The Last Supper, The Betrayal, Our Lord being crowned with thorns, and Incidents on the way to Calvary.*

Blake End
3 miles W of Braintree off the A120

The Great Maze at Blake End is one of the most challenging in the world. Set in over 10 acres of lovely North Essex farmland, it is grown every year from over half a million individual maize and sunflower seeds, and is open every summer. Continuing innovations bring with them extra twists and turns, making this wonderful maze, with more than five miles of pathways, even more of a brain teaser. A viewing platform makes it easy to help anyone hopelessly lost! Ten per cent of all profits go to the Essex Air Ambulance service.

Blake House Craft Centre comprises carefully preserved farm buildings centred round a courtyard. Visitors will find a fine array of craft shops and a restaurant serving breakfast and morning coffee, lunch and afternoon tea.

Great Saling
4 miles NW of Braintree off the A120

Saling Hall Garden is a 12-acre garden including a walled garden dating from 1698. The small park boasts a collection of fine trees, and there are ponds, a water garden and an extensive collection of unusual plants with an emphasis on rare trees.

Wethersfield
5 miles NW of Braintree on the B1053

Boydells Dairy Farm is a working farm where visitors are welcome to join in with tasks such as milking, feeding and more. A guided tour mixes fun with education, and all questions are most welcome. From bees to llamas, just about every kind of farm animal can be found here. Goat rides and donkey cart rides, a lovely picnic area and refreshments such as 'Yoggipops' (sheep's milk yogurt ice-lollies made on site) make for a perfect family day out. Open to the public April to September.

Great Bardfield
6 miles NW of Braintree off the B1053

This old market town on a hill above the River Pant is a pleasant mixture of cottages and shops, nicely complemented

THE RED LION

6 Church Hill, Finchingfield,
Essex CM7 4NN
Tel/Fax: 01371 810400
e-mail: franktyler@excite.co.uk
website: www.red-lion-finchingfield.com

Frank and Zahra Tyler have brought their extensive hotel and catering experience to this quiet and picturesque corner of Essex and the impressive **Red Lion**. Here they have created a comfortable, cosy and convivial inn, as their enthusiasm for good food, good wine and good company is truly infectious. Here

restaurant boasts real Georgian elegance. The pub has featured several times in *The Good Beer Guide* (1995-2003). The wide-ranging menu of over 50 different dishes features generously filled traditional Essex 'Huffers' and a full a la carte selection, all making the most of locally-supplied produce wherever possible. Traditional favourites such as sausage and mash, steaks and fresh fish dishes are augmented by special themed nights featuring French cuisine and other continental menus.

The three guest bedrooms are comfortably furnished with locally-produced and hand-painted pine furnishings, and

since 1996, and now 'assisted' by their one-year-old son, Flynn, they and their friendly staff offer a warm welcome and great service to all their guests.

make an excellent base from which to explore this part of Essex and the surrounding region. Open all day every day, this fine inn has been awarded 3 Diamonds

A hub of local community activity for this and the surrounding vilages, as well as attracting a number of foreign visitors (Stansted Airport is not all that far away), this quintessentially English inn – located in what has been called the country's prettiest village, boasting a number of antiques shops, craft shops and tearooms, and located near some excellent walking country – dates back to 1520 (though it was extensively 'modernised' in 1823).

The interior of the bar is a splendid mix of oak beams, brick and brass. The

by the 14th century church of **St Mary the Virgin**. Perhaps Great Bardfield's most notable feature is, however, a restored windmill that goes by the strange name of 'Gibraltar'.

Here in one of the prettiest villages in all of Essex, the **Great Bardfield Museum** occupies a 16th century charity cottage and 19th century village lockup, and features exhibits of mainly 19th- and 20th century domestic and agricultural artefacts and some fine examples of rural crafts such as corn-dollies and straw-plaiting.

Finchingfield

Finchingfield
6 miles NW of Braintree off the B1053

This charming village is graced with thatched cottages spread generously around a sloping village green that dips to a stream and duck pond at the centre of the village. Nearby stands an attractive small 18th century Post Mill with one pair of stones and tailpole winding. Extensively restored, today's visitors can climb up the first two floors.

Just up the hill, visitors will find the Norman church of **St John the Baptist**, the **Guildhall** (mentioned in the *Domesday Book*), which has a small museum open Sundays and also houses a local heritage centre with displays of artwork, paintings, pottery, sewing and weaving.

Finchingfield is easily one of the most picturesque and most photographed villages in Essex, featured in many television programmes and the home of the series *Lovejoy*. Here visitors will also find the privately owned Tudor stately home, **Spains Hall**, which has a lovely flower garden containing a huge Cedar of Lebanon planted in 1670 and an Adams sundial. Many good roses surround the kitchen garden, which contains an ancient Paulonia tree and a bougainvillea in the greenhouse. The garden is generally open on summer Sunday afternoons.

Finchingfield also has an easily followed path along the Finchingfield Brook leading from the village to Great Bardfield, a short distance away.

Gosfield
4 miles N of Braintree off the A1017

Gosfield Lake Leisure Resort, the county's largest freshwater lake, lies in the grounds of Gosfield Hall. This Tudor mansion was remodelled in the 19th century by its owner Samuel Courtauld. He also built the attractive mock-Tudor houses in the village.

Halstead

The name 'Halstead' comes from the Anglo-Saxon for *healthy place*. Like Braintree and Coggeshall, Halstead was an important weaving centre. **Townsford Mill** is certainly the most picturesque reminder of Halstead's industrial heritage. Built in the 1700s, it remains one of the most handsome buildings in a town with a number of historic buildings. This white, weather-boarded three-storey mill across the River Colne at the Causeway was once a landmark site for the Courtauld empire, producing both the famous funerary crepe and rayon. Today the Mill is an antiques centre, one of the largest in Essex, with thousands of items of furniture, porcelain, collectibles, stamps, coins, books, dolls, postcards, costume, paintings, glass and ceramics, old lace and clocks.

There are a number of historic buildings in the shopping centre of Halstead, which is part of a designated conservation area. Markets are held every Tuesday, Friday and Saturday, and each year in March the town hosts the Grand Prix of Essex - an international cycle race through Halstead and the surrounding area. The prestigious Dynes Hall International Horse Trials are held nearby.

Though it may now seem somewhat improbable, Halstead's most famous product was once mechanical elephants. Life-sized and weighing half a ton, they were built by W Hunwicks. Each one consisted of 9,000 parts and could carry a load of eight adults and four children at speeds of up to 12 miles per hour. Rather less unusual is the Tortoise Foundry Company, remembered for its warm 'tortoise stoves'.

Around Halstead
Castle Hedingham
3 miles NW of Halstead off the B1058

This town is named for its Norman **Castle**, which dominates the landscape. One of England's strongest fortresses in the 11th century, even now it is impossible not to sense its power and strength. The impressive stone keep is one of the tallest in Europe, with four floors and rising over 100 feet, with 12-ft thick walls. The banqueting hall and minstrels' gallery can still be seen. It was

Castle Hedingham

owned by the Earls of Oxford, the powerful de Veres family, one of whom was among the barons who forced King John to accept the Magna Carta. Amongst those entertained at the castle were Henry VII and Elizabeth I.

The village itself is a maze of narrow streets radiating from Falcon Square, named after the half-timbered Falcon Inn. Attractive buildings include many Georgian and 15th century houses comfortably vying for space, and the **Church of St Nicholas**, built by the de Veres, which avoided Victorian 'restoration' and is virtually completely Norman, with grand masonry and interestingly carved choir seats. There is a working pottery in St James' Street.

At the **Colne Valley Railway and Museum**, a mile of the Colne Valley and Halstead line between Castle Hedingham and Great Yeldham has been restored and now runs steam trains operated by enthusiasts. These lovingly restored Victorian railway buildings feature a collection of vintage engines and carriages; short steam train trips are available. **Colne Valley Farm Park**, set in 30 acres of traditional river meadows, is open from April to September.

The B1058 towards Sudbury, then left through Gestingthorpe and the Belchamps, makes for a pleasant excursion.

Sible Hedingham
3 miles NW of Halstead off the A1017

Mentioned in the *Domesday Book* as the largest parish in England, Sible Hedingham was the birthplace of Sir John Hawkwood, one of the 14th century's most famous soldiers of fortune. He led a band of mercenaries to Italy, where he was paid to defend Florence and where he also died. There is a monument to him in the village church, decorated with hawks and various other beasts.

Swan Street is the main artery of this charming village, boasting several delightful establishments devoted to providing visitors and natives of the town with places to shop, dine, enjoy a quiet drink and even stay for the night.

Gestingthorpe
5 miles N of Halstead off the A131

The Church of **St Mary the Virgin** in Gestingthorpe is distinctive in many respects. Witness to centuries of Christian worship, the *Domesday Book* of 1086 tells that 'Ghestingetorp' was held by Ledmer the priest before 1066. The oldest part extant of the existing building is the blocked-up lancet window in the north wall of the chancel, which dates back to the 1200s. Apart from this, most of the chancel, nave and south aisle dates from the 14th century. The tower, constructed in about 1500, is 66 feet high. Of the six bells hung in the tower, four were cast in 1658-9 by Miles Gray, a Colchester bellfounder. The 16th century fifth and sixth bells were cast in Bury St Edmunds, and recast in 1901. The west door, set in a stepped brick arch, is the original. The unusual tracery in the East window consists of

THE PHEASANT

Audley End, Gestingthorpe, Essex CO9 3AU
Tel/Fax: 01787 461196
e-mail: ianmcrane@aol.com

Dating back some 400 years, **The Pheasant** occupies a tranquil and lovely spot. From the rear garden overlooking the beautiful Suffolk countryside, you can see 25 churches.

Popular with locals, holidaymakers and ramblers – there are many fine footpaths in the area – this fine inn is run by Ian and Kay Crane, who are friendly and welcoming hosts. They and their conscientious staff offer all their guests genuine hospitality.

The bar boasts the original heavy beamwork and other traditional features; there are also two

restaurant areas. All are tastefully furnished and decorated, and supremely comfortable.

Real ales at this excellent Free House include Greene King IPA, Morland 'Old Speckled Hen' and Adnams, together with guest ales such as Nethergate Augustinian. All the food is home-cooked and freshly prepared, and features a range of traditional favourites and tempting specialities.

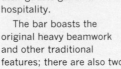

arches placed atop the apexes of the arches beneath them. The late 15th century/early 16th century nave roof is of the double hammer-beam type, and one of the finest in Essex. The font is late 14th century. One of the church's handsome memorials commemorates Captain L E G Oates, who died in an

attempt to save the lives of his companions on an ill-fated expedition to the Antarctic in 1912.

Little Maplestead
3 miles NE of Halstead off the A131

Little Maplestead has an unusual round

THE FOX & HUNTSMAN'S TABLE

Bulmer Tye, nr Sudbury, Suffolk CO10 7EB
Tel: 01787 377505 Fax: 01787 312777

Dating from the early 18th century, **The Fox & Huntsman's Table** is a large and impressive inn that has been sensitively extended and modernised. The décor is stylish and attractive in the lounge, public bar and conservatory-style restaurant. All dishes on the menu are home-cooked and use the freshest ingredients. There's a carvery every day and a good range of traditional favourites. Open Tues-Sat 11.00-15.00, 18.00-23.00; Sun

12.00-15.00, 19.00-22.30; food served Tues-Sat 12.00-14.30; Sun 12.00-14.30 and Tue-Fri 19.00-21.00; Sat-Sun 19.00-21.30. Closed all day Monday.

church, dedicated to **St John the Baptist**, modelled on the Holy Sepulchre in Jerusalem, and used as a stopping-point for pilgrims on their way there. Built more than 600 years ago by the military order of the Knights Hospitallers, their 'Perceptory' at Little Maplestead was suppressed more than 400 years ago by Henry VIII.

The North Essex Coast

Clacton-on-Sea

16 miles SE of Colchester on the A133

Clacton is a traditional sun-and-sand family resort with a south-facing, long sandy beach, lovely gardens on the seafront and a wide variety of shops and places to explore. It also boasts a wide variety of special events and entertainments taking place throughout the year.

Settled by hunters during the Stone Age - which is borne witness to by the wealth of flint implements and the fossilised bones of the cave lion, straight-tusked elephant and wild ox unearthed on the Clacton foreshore and at Lion Point - the town grew over the centuries from a small village into a prosperous seaside resort in the 1800s, when the craze for the health benefits of coastal air and bathing was at its peak. The Pier was constructed in 1871; at first paddle steamers provided the only mode of transport to the resort, the railway arriving in

1882. **The Pier** was widened from 30 to over 300 feet in the 1930s. On the pier, apart from the marvellous traditional sideshows, big wheel, restaurants and fairground rides, there is the fascinating **Seaquarium and Reptile Safari**.

Amusement centres include the arcades and **Clacton Pavilion**. The two theatres, Princes Theatre and West Cliff, are open all year. Clacton Pavilion boasts a range of attractions, including crazy golf, dodgems and a rock & roll Fun House. The **Clifftop Public Gardens** also repay a visit.

Great Clacton is the oldest part of town, comprising an attractive grouping of shops, pubs and restaurants within the shadow of the 12th century parish church.

A walk round the town rewards the visitor with some very handsome sights. There are three Martello Towers along this bit of the Essex coast. Just south of the town, **Jaywick Sands** is the ideal spot for a picnic by the sea, boasting one

Gardens, Clacton-on-Sea

of the finest natural sandy beaches in the county.

Holland-on-Sea

1½ miles NE of Clacton off the B1032

This attractive community is home to **Holland Haven Country Park**, 100

Frinton-on-Sea

acres of open space near the seashore, ideal for watching the marine birds and other wildlife of the region. Throughout the area there are a number of attractive walks which take full advantage of the varied coastal scenery

Frinton-on-Sea

3 miles NE of Clacton off the B1032

Once a quiet fishing village, this town was developed as a select resort by Sir Richard Cooper, and expanded in the 1880s to the genteel family resort it is today. Situated on a long stretch of sandy beach, Frinton remains peaceful and unspoilt. The tree-lined residential avenues sweep elegantly down to the Esplanade and extensive clifftop greensward. Along its main shopping street in Connaught Avenue, the 'Bond Street' of the East Coast, shopkeepers maintain a tradition of friendly and courteous service. Summer theatre and other open-air events take place throughout the season, and there are

also some excellent tennis and golf clubs in the town. The grace and elegance of this sophisticated resort is evidenced all round, as are hints of its distinguished past: Victorian beach huts still dot the extensive beach.

The area south of **Frinton Gates** has a unique local character, being laid out with detached houses set along broad tree-lined avenues.

The Church of Old St Mary in the town contains some panels of stained glass in the East window designed by the Pre-Raphaelite artist Burne Jones.

A good example of 20th century English vernacular architecture is The Homestead at the corner of Second Avenue and Holland Road, built in 1905 by C F Voysey.

Weeley

5 miles NW of Clacton off the A133

St Andrew's is the handsome parish church just south of the centre of this picturesque village. There is a lovely tree-lined path that passes Weeleyhall Wood and Weeley Lodge, with its beautifully kept gardens. Here visitors will also pass a navigational beacon that forms part of Aircraft Flight Operations for both civil and military flights.

A mile south, off the B1411, Weeley Heath is a small and attractive community boasting a lovely village green and stunning surrounding countryside.

Little Clacton
3 miles NW of Clacton off the A133

Though it shares its name with its near neighbour, this is a town apart. Quiet and secluded, multiple-winner of the Best Kept Village award, Little Clacton features a lovely Jubilee Oak, planted to celebrate Victoria's 50th year on the throne.

The fine church of **St James** has been described as one of the most beautiful medieval churches in Essex, and sits at the heart of the village

Oakwood Crafts Resource Centre in Little Clacton provides an environment for people with learning disabilities to learn and develop work skills, motivation, responsibility, team spirit, self-esteem and confidence through horticulture, woodwork, ceramics, crafts and catering. Set in three acres of land, it opened in 1975 and, as a horticultural centre, sells a wide range of bedding plants, shrubs and hanging baskets seasonally, along with a selection of wooden garden implements, furnishings

and other items, and ceramics. Teas and coffees are available.

Tendring
7 miles NW of Clacton off the A133

This village that gives its name to both the peninsula and the district council contains the handsome church of **St Edmund** with its elegant spire which can be seen for miles around. The church is dedicated to the last King of independent East Anglia, martyred by the Danes in the 9th century.

Walton-on-the-Naze
8 miles NE of Clacton on the B1034

Walton is all the fun of the fair. It is a traditional, singular and cheerful resort which focuses on the pier and all its attractions, including a ten-pin bowling alley. The gardens at the seafront are colourful and the beach has good sand. The Backwaters to the rear of Walton are made up of a series of small harbours and saltings, which lead into Harwich harbour.

Walton has an outstanding sandy beach. The town's seafront was developed in 1825 and provides a fine insight into the character of an early Victorian seaside resort. The charming narrow streets of the town contain numerous shops, restaurants and pubs overlooking the second longest pier in the country. **Marine Parade**, originally called The Crescent, was built in 1832. **The Pier**, first built in 1830, was originally constructed of wood and measured 330 feet long. It was extended to its present length of 2,610 feet in 1898, at the same time as the electric train service began.

Marina, Walton-on-the-Naze

The wind-blown expanse of **The Naze** just north of Walton is an extensive coastal recreation and picnic area, pleasant for walking, especially out of season when the visitor is likely to have all 150 acres virtually to him or herself, with great views out over the water. The shape of the Naze is constantly changing, eroded by wind, water and tide.

The year 1796 saw the demise of the medieval church, and somewhere beyond the 800-foot pier lies medieval Walton. The sandstone cliffs are internationally important for their shell fossil deposits. Inhabitants have been enjoying the bracing sea air at Walton since before Neolithic times: flint-shaping instruments have been found here, and the fossil teeth and the ears of sharks and whales have been discovered in the Naze's red crag cliffs. The **Naze Tower** is brickbuilt and octagonal in shape, originally built as a beacon in 1720 to warn seamen of the West Rocks off shore. A nature trail has been created nearby, and the Essex Skipper butterfly

and Emperor moth can be seen here.

The **Old Lifeboat House Museum** at East Terrace, in a building over 100 years old, houses an interpretive museum of local history and development, rural and maritime, covering Walton, Frinton and the Sokens.

Beaumont-cum-moze
4 miles NW of Walton on the Naze off the B114

This small village once had a quay originally constructed for loading and unloading the vessels plying the Walton backwaters. The disused **Trading Quay** was rebuilt in 1832 using stone from the old London Bridge.

Brightlingsea
7 miles W of Clacton on the B1029

Brightlingsea enjoys a long tradition of shipbuilding and seafaring. In 1347, 51 men and five ships were sent to the siege of Calais. Among the crew members of Sir Francis Drake's fleet which vanquished the Spanish Armada was one

'William of Brightlingsea'. Brightlingsea has the distinction of being the only limb of the Cinque Ports outside Kent and Sussex.

The 13th century **Jacobes Hall** in the town centre is one of the oldest occupied buildings in Essex. It is timber-framed with an undulating tile roof and an external staircase. Used as a meeting hall during the reign of Henry III, its name originates from its first owner, Edmund, Vicar of Brightlingsea, who was known locally as Jacob le Clerk.

Brightlingsea

All Saints Church, which occupies the highest point of the town on a hill about a mile from the centre, is mainly 13th century. Here are to be found some Roman brickwork and a frieze of ceramic tiles commemorating local residents whose lives were lost at sea. Its 97-foot tower can be seen from 17 miles out to sea. A light was once placed in the tower to guide the town's fishermen home

The **Town Hard** is where you can see all the waterfront comings and goings, including the activities of the Colne Smack Preservation Society, which maintains a seagoing link with the past.

Brightlingsea Museum in Duke Street offers an insight into the lives, customs and traditions of the area, housing a collection of exhibits relating to the town's maritime connections and the oyster industry.

There are plenty of superb walks along Brightlingsea Creek and the River Colne, which offer a chance to watch the birdlife on the saltings and the plethora of boats on the water. Today the town is a haven for the yachting fraternity and is the home of national and international sailing championships, with one of the best stretches of sailing on the East Coast. Day and half-day sailing and canoeing sessions are held at the **Brightlingsea Outdoor Education Centre**.

Elmstead Market
6 miles N of Brightlingsea off the A120

The Church of **St Anne and St Lawrence** to the north of this village has a rare carved oak, recumbent effigy of a knight in armour.

Elmstead Market is perhaps best known as the location of **Beth Chatto Gardens**, at White Barn House, designed and still presided over by the famous gardener herself. Here visitors will find five acres of landscaped gardens including extensive water gardens, shady walks and a Mediterranean-style garden where aromatic drought-loving plants thrive. The adjoining nursery contains a wide variety of plants for sale. Close by is the **Rolts Nursery Butterfly Farm**.

Thorrington
3 miles NW of Brightlingsea off the AB1027

Thorrington Tide Mill, built in the early 19th century, is the only remaining Tide Mill in Essex, and one of very few left in East Anglia. It has been fully restored, and although no longer in use, the Wheel can be run for guided groups. There is a public footpath which runs along the creek here.

China Maroc Bonsai is a specialist nursery, part of which is devoted to a peaceful Japanese garden with a waterfall and pool, where one can enjoy the tranquil atmosphere and the many fascinating outdoor bonsai. Crossing the bridge over the pool, one enters a tropical tunnel containing hundreds of indoor bonsai, many of which are imported from the hotter regions of the world, as well as bonsai and seedlings grown and cultivated on the premises.

Point Clear
2 miles SE of Brightlingsea off the B1027

The **East Essex Aviation Society & Museum**, located in the Martello Tower at Point Clear, not only retains its original flooring and roof, but today contains interesting displays of wartime aviation, military and naval photographs, uniforms and other memorabilia with local and US Air Force connections. There are artefacts on show from the crash sites of wartime aircraft in the Tendring area, including the engine and fuselage section of a recovered P51D Mustang fighter. The museum also explores civil and military history from both World Wars. There are very good views from the tower over the Colne Estuary and Brightlingsea.

St Osyth
3 miles SE of Brightlingsea off the B1027

This pretty little village has a fascinating history and centres around its Norman church and the ancient ruins of **St Osyth Priory**, founded in the 12th century. The village and Priory were named by Augustinian Canons after St Osytha, martyred daughter of Frithenwald, first Christian King of the East Angles, who was beheaded by Diceian pirates AD 653. Little of the original Priory remains, except for the magnificent late 15th century flint gatehouse, complete with battlements.

The village is centred on a crossroads and contains an attractive group of shops and restaurants. The Church of **St Peter and St Paul** in the village centre has unusual internal red brick piers and arches. The nearby creek has a small boatyard.

Mersea Island

2 miles SW of Brightlingsea off the B1025

Much of this island is a National Nature Reserve, home to its teeming shorelife. The island is linked to the mainland by a narrow causeway which is covered over at high tide. The towns of both East and West Mersea have excellent facilities for sailing enthusiasts. East Mersea is also a haven for birdwatchers.

Cudmore Grove Country Park on Bromans Lane, East Mersea, boasts fine views across the Colne and Blackwater estuaries. Grassland adjoining a sandy beach, it's an ideal spot for shore walks and picnics. There's also a pathway on the sea wall and a birdwatching hide.

Harwich Lighthouse

Harwich

Harwich's name probably originates from the time of King Alfred, when 'hare' meant army, and 'wic' a camp. This attractive old town was built in the 13th century by the Earls of Norfolk to exploit its strategic position on the Stour and Orwell estuary; the town has an important and fascinating maritime history, the legacy of which continues into the present.

During the 14th and 15th century French campaigns, Harwich was an important naval base. The famous Elizabethan seafarers Hawkins, Frobisher and Drake sailed from Harwich on various expeditions; in 1561 Queen Elizabeth I visited the town, describing it *'a pretty place and want[ing] for nothing'*.

Christopher Newport, leader of the *Goodspeed* expedition which founded Jamestown, Virginia, in 1607, and Christopher Jones, master of the Pilgrim ship *The Mayflower*, lived in Harwich (the latter just off the quay in King's Head Street), as did Jones' kinsman John Alden, who sailed to America in 1620. The famous diarist Samuel Pepys was MP for the town in the 1660s, thus it was also during this time headquarters for the King's Navy. Charles II took the first pleasure cruise from Harwich's shores. Other notable visitors included Lord Nelson and Lady Hamilton, who are reputed to have stayed at The Three Cups in Church Street.

Harwich remains popular as a vantage point for watching incoming and outgoing shipping in the harbour and across the waters to Felixstowe. Nowadays, lightships, buoys and miles of strong chain are stored along the front, and passengers arriving on North Sea ferries at Harwich International Port see the 90-foot high, six-sided **High Lighthouse** as the first landmark. Now housing the **National Vintage Wireless and Television Museum**, it was built in 1818 along with the **Low Lighthouse**. When the two lighthouses were in line they could indicate a safe shipping channel into the harbour. Each had replaced earlier wooden structures, and were themselves replaced by cast iron structures (both of which still stand on the front in nearby Dovercourt) in 1863 when the shifting sandbanks altered the channel. Shipping now relies on light buoys to find its way. The Low lighthouse is now the town's **Maritime Museum**, with specialist displays on the Royal Navy and commercial shipping.

Two other worthwhile museums in the town are the **Lifeboat Museum** off Wellington Road, which contains the last Clacton offshore 34-foot lifeboat and a history of the lifeboat service in Harwich, and the **Ha'penny Pier Visitor Centre** on the Quay, with information on everything in Harwich and a small heritage exhibition.

The **Treadwell Crane** now stands on Harwich Green, but for over 250 years it was sited in the Naval Shipyard. It is worked by two people walking in two 16-foot diameter wheels, and is the only known British example of its kind.

Amazingly, it was operational up until the 1920s. Another fascinating piece of the town's history is the **Electric Palace Cinema**, built in 1911 and now the oldest unaltered purpose-built cinema in Britain. It was restored by a trust and re-opened in 1981.

The importance of Harwich's port during the 19th century is confirmed by **The Redoubt**, a huge grey fort built between 1808 and 1810. Its design is an enlarged version of the Martello towers which dotted the English coast, awaiting a Napoleonic invasion that never came (some of these towers, of course, still exist). Today the Harwich Society has largely restored it and opened it as a small museum.

The old town also contains many ancient buildings, including the **Guildhall**, which was rebuilt in 1769 and is located in Church Street. The Council chamber, Mayor's Parlour and other rooms may be viewed. The former gaol contains unique graffiti of ships, probably carved by prisoners, and is well worth putting aside a morning to explore (by appointment only). Documents on show include those detailing the connection of Harwich with Pepys, the Pilgrim Fathers, and the Virginia settlement.

Around Harwich

Dovercourt
1 mile S of Harwich off the A120

This residential and holiday suburb of Harwich has Market Day on Fridays. With its attractive cliffs and beach, it also boasts the **Iron Lighthouse** or 'Leading Lights' located just off lower Marine Parade. The town has been settled from prehistoric times, as attested to by the late Bronze Age axeheads found here (now in Colchester Museum). The Romans found the town a useful source of the stone 'Septaria', taken from the cliffs and used in building. The town that visitors see today developed primarily in Victorian times as a fashionable resort.

Mistley

7 miles W of Harwich off the B1352

Here at the gateway to Constable Country, local 18th century landowner and MP Richard Rigby had grand designs to develop Mistley into a fashionable spa to rival Harrogate and Bath, adopting the swan as its symbol. Sadly, all that remains of Rigby's ambitious scheme is the Swan Fountain, a small number of attractive Georgian houses and **Mistley Towers**, the remains of a church (otherwise demolished in 1870) designed by the flamboyant architect Robert Adams. From the waterfront, noted for its colony of swans, there are very pleasant views across the estuary to Suffolk.

Mistley Quay Workshops in the High Street feature a pottery workshop, lute/cello maker, harpsichord maker, wood worker, bookbinder, and stained-glass

ESSEX SECRET BUNKER

Crown Building, Shrubland Road, Mistley, Essex CO11 1HS
Tel: 01206 392271 Fax: 01206 393847
e-mail: info@essexsecretbunker.com
website: www.essexsecretbunker.com

Follow the **'Secret Bunker'** signs on the B1352 to discover a Cold War operations centre that was the emergency headquarters for the county of Essex in the event of a nuclear war. The 14,000 sq ft concrete bunker was built in 1951, half above ground and half below. The walls are constructed of two feet thick concrete strengthened every few inches with steel mesh; the roof is over three feet thick and the foundations are set in almost ten feet of concrete. Maintained and kept operational for the 40 years of the Cold War, the building lost its original purpose (for which it was thankfully never needed) when the Government decided that the threat of nuclear war had receded sufficiently for the network of bunkers to be decommissioned. In early 1995 the building was renovated and refurbished prior to being opened as a public tourist attraction in time for Easter 1996.

Many of the original equipment and fittings have been returned to the site, so the bunker is now a fully authentic exhibition, showing the HQ as it would have been in full readiness for a nuclear attack with the help of sound effects, historically accurate displays, videos and cinemas. The bunker, which is in the care of the Bunker Preservation Trust, is bright and air-conditioned, suitable for all ages, with post Cold War amenities such as a café, gift shop and play area.

Another Cold War bunker, also open to the public, is at Kelvedon Hatch (qv).

THE HEDGEROW RESTAURANT & BAR

Clacton Road, Horsley Cross,
nr Manningtree, Essex CO11 2NR
Tel/Fax: 01206 395585
e-mail: d.brosnan@virgin.net

The Hedgerow is a substantial roadside inn on the B1025, a short drive from

themed evenings feature the cuisines of Spain, Mexico and other nations.

The menu changes frequently, so any return visit – and many of the clientele return again and again – is certain to produce a new range of delights. The ingredients are, as far as possible, top-quality British, many of them locally sourced, and the distinguished food is complemented by well-priced wines and a good choice of cask ales, draught and bottled beers, lager and cider.

Horsley Cross is located at the junction of the A120 and the B1035. Manningtree and Mistley are a short drive to the north, Ramsey and Harwich to the east, and Thorpe-le-Soken, Walton and Frinton to the south. So before or after a meal in this excellent place there's plenty to do and see in the area, including walks in

Manningtree. Its appeal is twofold – it's both a village local and a top-notch dining venue. Adjoining the bar is an immaculately appointed restaurant overlooking the garden, open for food from 11.30 to 3 and from 7 to 10, with service all day Sunday (booking recommended).

the country or by the sea, sailing, craft workshops, museums, churches, country parks and all the fun of traditional seaside resorts.

This fine establishment is open Tuesday to Sunday 11.30-15.00 and 19.00-23.00.

Partners Paul Chenery and Denis Brosnan lease the catering arrangements from the pub's tenant; these two accomplished chefs take it in turns to man the ovens, and both are equally passionate about what they create for diners. Their dishes range from the simple to the more elaborate and sometimes exotic, and there are often French or Italian influences evident in the cooking. Regular

window maker and restorer. There is also a tea-shop on the premises (the key to Mistley Towers can be obtained from the Workshops).

Mistley Place Park Environmental & Animal Rescue Centre is 25 acres of parkland affording country walks, wildlife habitats, lake, farm animals and great views across the Stour Estuary. Over 2,000 rescued animals including rabbits, Vietnamese pigs and horses roam free.

Manningtree
9 miles W of Harwich off the B1352

The Walls, on the approach to Manningtree along the B1352, offer unrivalled views of the Stour estuary and the Suffolk coast, and the swans for which the area is famous. Lying on the River Stour amid beautiful rolling countryside, the scene has oft been depicted by artists over the centuries.

Back in Tudor times, Manningtree was the centre of the cloth trade, and later a port filled with barges carrying their various cargoes along the coast to London. Water still dominates today and the town is a centre of leisure sailing.

Manningtree has been a market town since 1238, and is still a busy shopping centre. It is the smallest town in Britain, and a stroll through the streets reveals the diversity of its past.

There are still traditional (and mainly Georgian) restaurants, pubs and shops,

---

THE CROWN HOTEL

51 High Street, Manningtree,
Essex CO11 1AH
Tel: 01206 396333 Fax: 01206 390320
e-mail: julie@crownhotel-manningtree.co.uk
website: www.crownhotel-manningtree.co.uk

Voted the New Millennium's Pub of the Year by Greene King Pub Partners, **The Crown Hotel** in Manningtree well deserves this accolade for its quality, service and its warm and friendly atmosphere. One of the oldest pubs in town, it dates back to the 16th century. Today it enjoys an enviable place as the most popular family venue in the area. With great food, quality beers and genuine hospitality, it's easy to see why.

Snacks and lunchtime and evening meals can be savoured in either of the two comfortable and traditional bars – the Public Bar and River Bar – or in the River Restaurant, which commands fine views of the River Stour. People come from all over the county to sample the excellent Sunday lunches.

Accommodation is also available at this fine inn, in two self-contained family flats.

THE RED LION

42 South Street, Manningtree, Essex
CO11 1BG
Tel: 01206 395052
e-mail: mmunro@aspects.net

In a narrow street just off Manningtree's busy main thoroughfare, the 16th century **Red Lion** is a great place to relax and unwind with a pint of Adnams, perhaps over a game of darts. In summer the inn is bedecked in colourful flower baskets and window boxes (the display is a regular award-winner), and inside there are two bars, the neat public bar and the elegant little lounge with a homely, inviting feel. The inn is owned and run by Chris and Myrtle Elliott, who for several years lived next to the inn. They bought it at the end of 2001 and have worked hard to create a charming, spotless little inn that is building a loyal following among the citizens of Manningtree and the surrounding area. They and their friendly staff offer genuine hospitality to all their guests. The ambience is always relaxed and genial, making this just the place to enjoy a quiet drink or meal.

The appeal lies not only in the atmosphere and the well-kept beer but also in Myrtle's very good home cooking. Her smoked salmon tart is the talk of the town, and there's always a good turn-out for the monthly theme nights, which could be Spanish one month, Tex-Mex the next. The monthly folk music night is another fixture in many local diaries, and the inn can host conferences and private gatherings of up to 80 people in the function suite, which boasts its own bar. The owners' plans include the bringing onstream of overnight accommodation for guests. This will be a considerable boon for visitors to Manningtree and a convenient base for exploring the region, which includes the world-famous sights of Constable Country.

This excellent inn is open Monday to Saturday 11.30-15.00 and 19.00-23.00, Sundays 12.00-14.30 and 19.00-22.30.

as well as handcraft and specialist outlets. The views over the river are well known to birdspotters, sailors and ramblers. The town has an intriguing past - as a river crossing, market, smugglers' haven and home of Matthew Hopkins, the reviled and self-styled Witchfinder General who struck terror into the local community during the 17th century. Some of his victims were hanged on Manningtree's small village green.

It is believed that the reference in Shakespeare's *Henry IV* to Falstaff as 'that roasted Manningtree ox' relates to the practice of roasting an entire ox, as was known at that time to be done at the town's annual fair.

Manningtree Museum in the High Street opened in the late 1980s and mounts two exhibitions a year, together with permanent photographs and pieces relating to the heritage of Manningtree, Lawford, Mistley and the district.

Ardleigh
10 miles W of Harwich off the A137

Tendring's westernmost village comprises an attractive group of 16th and 17th century cottages grouped around the fine 15th century **Butterfield Church**.

THE BRANTHAM BULL

The Street, Brantham, Manningtree,
Essex CO11 1PN
Tel: 01473 328494
e-mail: branthambull@btopenworld.com

Situated alongside the A137 – despite its postal address, a mile into Suffolk – **The Brantham Bull** is a welcoming public house dating back to the 18th century and boasts traditional features such as the open fire and heavy beamwork. Personally run by Peter and Lynne Hunter, friendly and hospitable hosts, this fine pub is open every session weekdays and all day at weekends.

The warm ambience, great food and selection of real ales – which includes Greene

King IPA and Adnams – lagers, stout, cider, wines, spirits and soft drinks, make this a justly popular place. Meals are served in the handsome and characterful restaurant, the cosy bar and the large and attractive beer garden, with panoramic views of the River Stour and surrounding countryside. All dishes – which include a good selection of vegetarian meals - are freshly prepared and make use of the best local ingredients.

THE LION INN

The Street, Ardleigh, nr Colchester,
Essex CO7 7LD
Tel: 01206 230083

The Lion Inn is a convivial and very pleasant place to enjoy a drink or meal. Located opposite the village church, this handsome establishment is believed to date back to the 16th century, and retains its original heavy beamwork. This friendly pub serves up a selection of Greene King IPA real ales, together with regularly changing guest ales and a good range of lagers, cider, wines, spirits and soft drinks. The traditional food is freshly prepared and home-cooked, and includes Saturday breakfast and Sunday lunch served all day.

Pasta is just one speciality on the lunchtime and dinner menus.

There's live music on Thursday nights and some Saturdays. This fine pub also boasts not one, not two, but three resident ghosts, one of which is fond of mischievous pranks like turning the furniture upside-down, and another who frequents the kitchen and announces her arrival by producing a distinct chill in the air!

Spring Valley Mill, a now privately owned 18th century timber-framed and weather-boarded edifice, was once a working watermill, later adapted to steam. Day and half-day canoeing and sailing lessons can be taken at the **Ardleigh Outdoor Education Centre**.

Nearby is **Ardleigh Reservoir**, offering up many opportunities for water sports and trout fishing.

3 South and West Suffolk

John Constable, England's greatest landscape painter, was born at East Bergholt in 1776 and remained at heart a Suffolk man throughout his life. He was later to declare *'I associate my careless boyhood with all that lies on the banks of the Stour. Those scenes made me a painter and I am grateful.'* He painted the occasional portrait and even attempted a couple of religious works, but he concentrated almost entirely on the scenes that he knew and loved as a boy. The Suffolk tradition of painting continues to this day, with many artists drawn particularly to Walberswick and what is known as 'Constable country'. Its beauty is not always that easy to appreciate when crowds throng the Stour valley at summer weekends, but at other times the peace and beauty are much as they were in Constable's day.

Much of Suffolk's character comes from its rivers, and in the part of the county surrounding Ipswich, the Orwell and the Stour mark the boundaries of the Shotley Peninsula. The countryside here is largely unspoilt, with wide-open spaces between scattered villages. The relative flatness of Suffolk gives every encouragement for motorists to leave their machines, and the peninsula, still relatively peaceful, is ideal for a spot of walking or cycling, or even boating. Southeast of Ipswich, the peninsula created by the River Deben and the River Orwell is one of the prettiest areas in Suffolk, its winding lanes leading through a delightful series of quiet rural villages and colourful riverside communities.

Cambridgeshire, Norfolk, the A134 and the A14 frame the northern part of West Suffolk, which includes Bury St

Willy Lotts Cottage, Flatford Mill

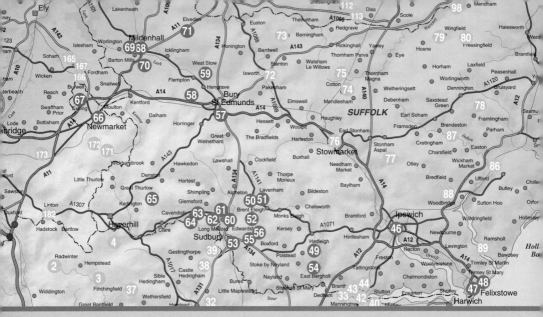

PLACES TO STAY, EAT AND DRINK

● Denotes entries in other chapters

Edmunds, a pivotal player in the country's religious history, and Newmarket, one of the major centres of the horseracing world. Between and above them are picturesque villages, bustling market towns, rich farming countryside, the fens, and the expanse of sandy heath and pine forest that is Breckland. Many of the remains of the Anglo-Saxon period are on display, notably at West Stow and in Bury St Edmunds (Abbey ruins and Moyse's Hall), in Blythburgh, Sutton Hoo and Snape, and in museums in Ipswich and Woodbridge.

The area south and west of Bury towards the Essex border contains some of Suffolk's most attractive and peaceful countryside. The visitor will come upon a succession of picturesque villages, historic churches, remarkable stately homes, heritage centres and nature reserves. In the south, along the River Stour, stand the historic wool towns of Long Melford, Cavendish and Clare.

The Ancient House, Ipswich

Ipswich

History highlights Ipswich as the birthplace of Cardinal Wolsey, but the story of Suffolk's county town starts very much earlier than that. It has been a port since the time of the Roman occupation, and by the 7th century the Anglo-Saxons had expanded it into the largest port in the country. King John granted a civic charter in 1200, confirming the townspeople's right to their own laws and administration, and for several centuries the town prospered as a port, exporting wool, textiles and agricultural products.

Thomas Wolsey arrived on the scene in 1475, the son of a wealthy butcher. Educated at Magdalen College, Oxford, he was ordained a priest in 1498 and rose quickly in influence, becoming chaplain to Henry VII and then Archbishop of York, a cardinal, and Lord Chancellor under Henry VIII. He was quite indispensable to the king and had charge of foreign policy as well as powerful sway over judicial institutions. He also managed to amass enormous wealth, enabling him to found a grammar school in Ipswich and Cardinal's College (later Christ Church) in Oxford. Wolsey had long been hated by certain nobles for his low birth and arrogance, and they were easily able to turn Henry against him when his attempts to secure an annulment from the Pope of the king's marriage to Catherine of Aragon met with failure. Stripped of most of his offices following a charge of overstepping his authority as a legate, he was later charged with treason, but died while travelling from York to London to face the king. His death put an end to his plans for the grammar school - all that remains now is a red-brick gateway.

When the cloth market fell into decline in the 17th century, a respite followed in the following century, when the town was a food-distribution port during the Napoleonic Wars. At the beginning of the 19th century the risk from silting was becoming acute at a time when trade was improving and industries were springing up. The Wet Dock, constructed in 1842, solved the silting problem and, with the railway arriving shortly after, Ipswich could once more look forward to a safe future. The Victorians were responsible for considerable development: symbols of their civic pride include the handsome **Old Custom House** by the Wet Dock, the Town Hall, and the splendid **Tolly Cobbold** brewery, rebuilt at the end of the 19th century, 150 years after brewing started on the site. Victorian enterprise depleted some of the older buildings, but a number survive, notably the house where Wolsey was born, the Ancient House with its wonderful pargetting, and the fine former Tudor merchants' houses which grace the town's historic waterfront, such as Isaac Lord's and The Neptune (the latter was once home of Thomas Eldred, who circumnavigated the world with Thomas Cavendish

St Peter's Dock, Ipswich

shortly after Drake). A dozen medieval churches remain, of which St Margaret's is the finest, boasting some very splendid flintwork and a double hammerbeam roof. Another, St Stephen's, today houses the town's Tourist Information Centre.

Christchurch Mansion is a beautiful Tudor home standing in 65 acres of attractive parkland a short walk from the town centre. Furnished as an English country house, it contains a

Christchurch Mansion

Mansion which features changing displays including touring and national exhibitions.

Ipswich Museum is in a Victorian building in the High Street. Displays include a natural history gallery, a wildlife gallery complete with a model of a mammoth, a reconstruction of a Roman villa, and replicas of Sutton Hoo treasures. A recent addition is a display of elaborately carved timbers from the homes of wealthy 17th century merchants. There is also a rolling programme of exciting temporary exhibitions, events and displays.

major collection of works by Constable and Gainsborough, as well as many other paintings, prints and sculptures by Suffolk artists from the 17th century onwards.

Wolsey Art Gallery is a purpose-built space entered through Christchurch

In a former trolleybus depot on

IPSWICH TRANSPORT MUSEUM

Old Trolleybus Depot, Cobham Road,
Ipswich, Suffolk IP3 9JD
Tel: 01473 715666
website: www.ipswichtransportmuseum.co.uk

The **Ipswich Transport Museum** is dedicated to preserving the transport and engineering heritage of the Ipswich area. The collection is believed to be the largest in the country devoted to just one area and is an entirely volunteer run and funded museum, housed in a former trolleybus depot. The building has been altered to include a gift shop, tearoom and outdoor picnic area.

Among the more unusual exhibits are a monorail for transporting spoil, a road sweeper conversion from a Morris car, a petrol roller for rolling grass runways, a horse drawn tower wagon for maintaining overhead wires, the oldest trolleybus in the world (Ipswich no. 2, built by Railless in 1923), and a collection of wheelchairs. There are additional exhibition rooms covering air, water and rail transport of the Ipswich area, with

exhibits and photographs. The Ipswich area was the hub of experimentation in the 1930's with research bases for fixed wing aircraft, seaplanes and bombing ranges. Radar was developed nearby at Bawdsey Manor.

Ipswich was an engineering town throughout the 19th and 20th centuries. The museum commemorates this heritage through its collection of Ipswich-made exhibits, which include lawnmowers, mobile cranes, fork lift trucks and factory trucks. Photographs depict the huge Walking Drag-lines built in Ipswich, weighing up to 2,000 tons.

Cobham Road is the **Ipswich Transport Museum** (see page 91) a fascinating collection of vehicles, from prams to fire engines, all made or used around Ipswich.

Ipswich's position at the head of the River Orwell has always influenced the town's fortunes; today, a stroll along the waterfront should be included in any visit. Tudor houses and medieval churches stand alongside stylish new apartments which overlook the new marinas. An art gallery and choice of eateries enhance the experience, and there are regular pub cruises, leaving the Ipswich waterfront and travelling the Orwell (recently voted one of the prettiest rivers in England) as far as Felixstowe harbour.

On the outskirts of town, signposted from Nacton Road, is **Orwell Country Park**, a 150-acre site of wood, heath and reedbeds by the Orwell estuary. At this point the river is crossed by the imposing Orwell Bridge, a graceful construction in pre-stressed concrete that was completed in 1982 and is not far short of a mile in length.

Notables from the world of the arts with Ipswich connections include Thomas Gainsborough, who got his first major commissions here to paint portraits of local people; David Garrick, the renowned actor-manager, who made his debut here in 1741 as Aboan in Thomas Southerne's *Oroonoko*; and the peripatetic Charles Dickens, who stayed at the Great White Horse while still a young reporter with the *Morning Chronicle*. Soon afterwards, he featured the tavern in *The Pickwick Papers* as the place where Mr Pickwick wanders inadvertently into a lady's bedroom. Sir V S Pritchett was born in Ipswich, while Enid Blyton trained as a kindergarten teacher at Ipswich High School.

Around Ipswich

Nacton
4 miles SE of Ipswich off the A14

South of Nacton's medieval church lies **Orwell Park House**, which was built in the 18th century by Admiral Edward Vernon, sometime Member of Parliament for Ipswich. The admiral, who had won an important victory over the Spanish in the War of Jenkins Ear, was known to his men as 'Old Grog' because of his habit of wearing a cloak of coarse grogram cloth. His nickname passed into the language when he ordered that the rum ration dished out daily to sailors should be diluted with water to combat the drunkenness that was rife in the service. That was in 1740, but this allotted ration of 'grog' was officially issued to sailors right up until 1970.

George Tomline bought Orwell Park House in 1857 and made it even more splendid, adding a conservatory, a ballroom and towers. He also changed the facade along handsome Georgian lines. The house became the setting for some of the grandest shooting parties ever seen in this part of the world, and such was the power of the Tomlines that they were able to move the village away from the house to its present site.

Nacton picnic site in Shore Lane (signposted from the village) commands wonderful views of the Orwell and is a prime spot in winter for birdwatchers. The birds feed very well off the mud flats.

Levington
5 miles SE of Ipswich off the A14

A pretty village on the banks of the Orwell. Fisons established a factory here in 1956, and developed the now famous Levington Compost. On the foreshore below the village is an extensive marina which has brought a bustling air to the area. The coastal footpath along the bank of the Orwell leads across the nature reserve of **Trimley Marshes** and on to Felixstowe.

Trimley St Mary & Trimley St Martin
6 miles SE of Ipswich off the A14

Twin villages with two churches in the same churchyard, famous Trimley residents have included the Cavendish family, whose best-known member was the adventurer Thomas Cavendish. In 1590 he became the second man to sail round the world. Two years later he died while embarked on another voyage. He is depicted on the village sign.

Trimley Marshes were created from farmland and comprise grazing marsh, reed beds and wetland that's home to an abundance of interesting plant life and many species of wildfowl, waders and migrant birds. Access is on foot from Trimley St Mary.

Newbourne
7 miles E of Ipswich off the A12

A small miracle occurred here on the night of the hurricane of October 1987. One wall of the ancient St Mary's Church was blown out, and with it the stained glass, which shattered into fragments. One piece, showing the face of Christ, was found undamaged and was later incorporated into the rebuilt wall.

Two remarkable inhabitants of Newbourne were the Page brothers, who both stood over 7 feet tall; they enjoyed a career touring the fairs, and are buried in Newbourne churchyard.

Waldringfield
7 miles E of Ipswich off the A12

Waldringfield lies on a particularly beautiful stretch of the Deben estuary, and the waterfront is largely given over to leisure boating and cruising. The quay was once busy with barges, many of them laden with coprolite. This fossilised dung, the forerunner of today's fertilisers, was found in great abundance in and around Waldringfield, and a number of exhausted pits can still be seen.

Felixstowe
12 miles SE of Ipswich off the A14

Until the early 17th century, Felixstowe was a little-known village - but it was the good Colonel Tomline of Orwell Park who put it on the map by creating a port to rival its near neighbour Harwich. He also started work on the

THE WAVERLEY HOTEL

Wolsey Gardens, Felixstowe, Suffolk IP11 7DF
Tel: 01394 282811 Fax: 01394 670185

A graceful and handsome Victorian building perched high on a clifftop in the town centre, **The Waverley Hotel** is a distinguished and relaxed place to enjoy a pleasant break. Each of the ensuite guest bedrooms is tastefully and comfortably decorated and furnished, and has its own distinct character.

All the rooms are weicloming and appointed with every facility guests could expect. The

Wolsey Restaurant and Gladstone's Bar offer excellent food, drink and hospitality.

Ipswich-Felixstowe railway (with a stop at Nacton for the guests of his grand parties), and 1887 saw the completion of both projects. Tomline also developed the resort aspects of Felixstowe, rivalling the amenities of Dovercourt, and when he died in 1887 most of his dreams had become reality. (He was, incidentally, cremated, one of the first in the county to be so disposed of in the modern era.) What he didn't live to see was the pier, opened in 1904 and still in use.

The town has suffered a number of ups and downs since that time, but continues to thrive as one of England's busiest ports, having been much extended in the 1960s. The resort is strung out round a wide, gently curving bay, where the long seafront road is made even prettier with trim lawns and gardens.

The Martello tower is a noted landmark, as is the **Pier**, which was once long enough to merit an electric tramway. It was shortened as a security measure during the Second World War. All kinds of attractions are provided for holidaymakers, including one very unusual one. This is the **Felixstowe Water Clock**, a curious piece assembled from dozens of industrial bits and pieces.

The original fishing hamlet from which the Victorian resort was developed lies beyond a golf course north of the town. This is **Felixstowe Ferry**, a cluster of holiday homes, an

THE DOOLEY

Ferry Lane, Felixstowe, Suffolk IP11 3QX
Tel: 01394 674379

Named after a famous Felixstowe vessel, **The Dooley** is a welcoming and friendly pub offering good food and drink amid relaxed surroundings. Dating back to the 16th century, this fine inn has a rustic feel and traditional features such as the low beamed ceilings, oak tables and red tiled floors. Delicious home-made food is served in the conservatory-style restaurant at lunch and dinner every day, and

there's a good range of lagers, cider, stout, wines, spirits and soft drinks to enjoy while watching Sky Sports.

Sailing at Felixstowe

inn, a boatyard, fishing sheds and a Martello tower. The sailing club is involved mainly with dinghy racing, and the whole place becomes a hive of activity during the class meetings. A ferry takes foot passengers (plus bicycles) across to Bawdsey.

At the southernmost tip of the peninsula is **Landguard Point**, where a nature reserve supports rare plants and migrating birds.

Just north on this shingle bank is **Landguard Fort**, built in 1718 (replacing an earlier construction) to protect Harwich harbour. It is now home to **Felixstowe Museum**. The museum is actually housed in the Ravelin Block (1878), which was used as a mine storage depot by the army when a mine

barrier was laid across the Orwell during the First World War. A fascinating variety of exhibits includes local history, model aircraft and model paddle steamers, Roman coins and the history of the fort itself, which was the scene of the last invasion of English soil, by the Dutch in 1667. Beyond the fort is an excellent viewing point for watching the comings and goings of the ships.

Freston
3 miles S of Ipswich off the B1080

Freston is an ancient village on the south bank of the Orwell, worth visiting for some fine old buildings and some curiosities. The most curious and best known of these buildings is the six-storey Tudor tower by the river in **Freston Park** (it's actually best viewed from across the river). This red-brick house, built around 1570, has just six rooms, one per storey. It might be a folly, but it was probably put up as a lookout tower to warn of enemies sailing up the river. The nicest theory is that it was built for Ellen, daughter of Lord Freston, to study a different subject each day, progressing floor by floor up the tower (and with Sundays off, presumably). A 4,000-year-old archaeological site at Freston was revealed by aerial photography.

Woolverstone
4 miles S of Ipswich on the B1456

Dating back to the Bronze Age, Woolverstone has a large marina along the banks of the Orwell. One of the buildings in the complex is **Cat House**, where it is said that a stuffed white cat placed in the window would be the all-clear sign for smugglers. **Woolverstone House** was originally St Peter's Home for 'Fallen Women', run by nuns. It was designed by Sir Edwin Lutyens and has its own chapel and bell tower.

Tattingstone
4 miles S of Ipswich off the A137

Tattingstone Wonder, on the road between Tattingstone and Stutton, looks like a church from the front, but it isn't. It was built by a local landowner to provide accommodation for estate workers. He presumably preferred to look at a church from his mansion than some plain little cottages. Tattingstone lies at the western edge of Alton Water, a vast man-made lake created as a reservoir in the late 1970s. A footpath runs round the perimeter, and there's a wildlife sanctuary. On the water itself all sorts of leisure activities are on offer, including angling, sailing and windsurfing.

Stutton
6 miles S of Ipswich on the B1080

The elongated village of Stutton lies on the southern edge of Alton Water. The *Domesday Book* records six manor houses standing here, and there are still some grand properties down by the

Stour. St Peter's Church stands isolated overlooking Holbrook Bay, and a footpath from the church leads all the way along the river to Shotley Gate. A little way north, on the B1080, Holbrook is a large village with a brook at the bottom of the hill. Water from the brook once powered Alton Mill, a weather-boarded edifice on a site occupied by watermills for more than 900 years. The mill is now a restaurant.

Chelmondiston
5 miles S of Ipswich on the B1456

The church here is modern, but incorporates some parts of the original, which was destroyed by a flying bomb in 1944. In the same parish is the tiny riverside community of **Pin Mill**, a well-known beauty spot and sailing centre. The river views are particularly lovely at this point, and it's also a favourite place for woodland and heathland walks. Pin Mill was once a major manufacturer of barges, and those imposing craft can still

House by the Waterside, Pin Mill

be seen, sharing the river with sailing boats and pleasure craft. Each year veteran barges gather for a race that starts here, at Buttermans Bay, and ends at Harwich. Arthur Ransome, author of *Swallows and Amazons*, stayed here and had boats built to his specifications. His *We Didn't Mean to Go to Sea* starts aboard a yacht mooring here.

The local hostelry is the 17th century Butt & Oyster, much visited, much painted and one of the best-known pubs in the county. To the east of the Quay is Cliff Plantation, an ancient coppiced wood of alder and oak.

Erwarton
6 miles S of Ipswich off the B1456

An impressive red-brick Jacobean gatehouse with a rounded arch, buttresses and pinnacles is part of **Erwarton Hall**, the family home of the Calthorpes. Anne Boleyn was the niece of Philip Calthorpe, and visited as a child and as queen. Just before her execution Anne apparently requested that her heart be buried in the family vault at St Mary's Church. A casket in the shape of a heart was found there in 1836, but when opened contained only dust that could not be positively identified. The casket was resealed and laid in the Lady Chapel.

Shotley
8 miles S of Ipswich on the B1456

Right at the end of the peninsula, with the Orwell on one side and the Stour on the other, Shotley is best known as the home of *HMS Ganges*, where generations of sailors received their training. The main feature is the 142-foot mast, up which trainees would shin at the passing-out ceremony. A small museum records the history of the establishment from 1905 to 1976, when it became a police academy. At the very tip of the peninsula is a large marina where a classic boat festival is an annual occasion.

Hintlesham
7 miles W of Ipswich on the A1071

Hintlesham's glory is a magnificent hall dating from the 1570s, when it was the home of the Timperley family. It was considerably altered during the 18th century, when it acquired its splendid Georgian facade. For some years the hall was owned by the celebrated chef Robert Carrier, who developed it into the county's leading restaurant. It still functions as a high-class hotel and restaurant.

Hadleigh
10 miles W of Ipswich on the A1071

The old and not-so-old blend harmoniously in a variety of architectural styles in Hadleigh. Timber-framed buildings, often with elaborate plasterwork, stand in the long main street as a reminder of the prosperity generated by the wool trade in the 14th to 16th centuries, and there are also some fine houses from the Regency and Victorian periods. The 15th century

Hadleigh Guild Hall

Guildhall has two overhanging storeys, and together with the Deanery Tower and the church makes for a magnificent trio of huge appeal and contrasting construction – timber for the Guildhall, brick for the tower and flint for the church.

Guthrun, the Danish leader who was captured by Alfred and pardoned on condition that he became a Christian, made Hadleigh his HQ and lived here for 12 years. He was buried in the church, then a wooden construction but subsequently twice rebuilt. In the south chapel of the present church is a 14th century bench-end carving depicting the legendary scene of the wolf guarding the head of St Edmund. The wolf is wearing a monk's habit, indicating a satirical sense of humour in the carpenter. Also of interest is the **Clock bell**, which stands outside the tower.

A famous resident of Hadleigh was the rector Dr Rowland Taylor, who was burnt at the stake on Aldham Common for refusing to hold a mass. A large stone, inscribed and dated 1555, marks the spot.

There are two good walks from Hadleigh, the first being along the Brett with access over medieval **Toppesfield Bridge**. The other is a walk along the disused railway line between Hadleigh and Raydon through peaceful, picturesque countryside. At Raydon a few buildings survive from the wartime base of the 353rd, 357th and 358th Fighter Groups of the USAAF.

Two miles east of Hadleigh is **Wolves Wood**, an RSPB reserve with woodland nature trails - and no wolves!

Kersey
12 miles W of Ipswich off the A1141

The ultimate Suffolk picture-postcard village, Kersey boasts a wonderful collection of timbered merchants' houses and weavers' cottages with paint and thatch. The main street has a **Water splash**, which, along with the 700-year-old Bell Inn, has featured in many films and travelogues. The Church of St Mary, which overlooks the village from its hilltop position, is of massive proportions, testimony to the wealth that came with the wool and cloth industry. Kersey's speciality was a coarse twill broadcloth much favoured for

Kersey Ford

greatcoats and army uniforms. Headless angels and mutilated carvings are reminders of the Puritans' visit to the church, though some treasures survive, including the ornate flintwork of the 15th century south porch.

Traditional craftsmanship can still be seen in practice at the Kersey Pottery, which sells many items of stoneware plus paintings by Suffolk artists.

Chelsworth
14 miles W of Ipswich off the A1141

Chelsworth is an unspoilt delight in the lovely valley of the River Brett, which is crossed by a little double hump-backed bridge. The timbered houses and thatched cottages look much the same as when they were built, and every year the villagers open their gardens to the public.

Monks Eleigh
16 miles W of Ipswich on the A1141

The setting of thatched cottages, a 14th century church and a pump on the village green is so traditional that Monks Eleigh was regularly used on railway posters as a lure to this wonderful part of the country.

Bildeston
14 miles W of Ipswich on the B1115

More fine old buildings here, including timber-framed cottages with overhanging upper floors. The

Timbered House, Bildeston

Church of St Mary has a superb carved door and a splendid hammerbeam roof. A tablet inside the church commemorates Captain Edward Rotherham, Commander of the *Royal Sovereign* at the Battle of Trafalgar. He died in Bildeston while staying with a friend, and is buried in the churchyard.

Brent Eleigh
17 miles W of Ipswich off the A1141

The church at Brent Eleigh, on a side road off the A1141, is remarkable for a number of quite beautiful ancient wall paintings, discovered during maintenance work as recently as 1960. The most striking and moving of the paintings is one of the Crucifixion.

Lavenham
18 miles W of Ipswich on the A1141

An absolute gem of a town, the most complete and original of the medieval 'wool towns', with crooked timbered and whitewashed buildings lining the narrow streets, from the 14th to the 16th centuries Lavenham flourished as one of the leading wool and cloth-making centres in the land. With the decline of that industry, however, the prosperous times soon came to an end. It is largely due to the fact that Lavenham found no replacement industry that so much of its medieval character remains: there was simply not enough money for the rebuilding and development programmes that changed many other towns, often for the worse. The medieval street pattern still exists, complete with market place and market cross.

More than 300 of Lavenham's buildings are officially listed as being of architectural and historical interest, and none of them is finer than the **Guildhall** (see panel opposite). This superb 16th century timbered building was originally the meeting place of the Guild of Corpus Christi, an organisation that regulated the production of wool. It now houses exhibitions of local history

Restored Medieval Houses, Lavenham

THE RED HOUSE

29 Bolton Street, Lavenham,
Suffolk CO10 9RG
Tel: 01787 248074
website: www.lavenham.co.uk/redhouse/

With three attractive and comfortable en suite guest bedrooms, **The Red House** is a handsome and welcoming Victorian house located in the heart of this wonderful medieval town. Originally the village bakery, this charming establishment features lovely south-facing gardens and guests' private lounge. At breakfast there's a superb range of delicious options. Open all year. No smoking. 4 Diamonds ETB.

THE GUILDHALL, LAVENHAM

Market Place, Lavenham, Suffolk CO10 9QZ
Tel: 01787 247646
e-mail: almjtg@smtp.ntrust.org.uk

The Guildhall, built around 1530 by the prosperous Corpus Christi religious guild, has been at the heart of village life ever since. It is a fine example of close-studded timber framing, with exuberant carvings that show off the impressive skills of the carpenters of the time. In 1547, when religious guilds were abolished as part of the Reformation, the Guildhall became parish property and in the ensuing centuries was put to various uses, including a house of correction, parish workhouse, home for WWII evacuees, Red Cross restaurant and nursery school. In 1951 it was vested in the National Trust and now houses a local history museum that includes exhibitions on the cloth industry, farming and the railway. The peaceful walled garden contains examples of plants that were used to dye cloth in medieval times.

and the wool trade, and has a walled garden with a special area devoted to dye plants. **Little Hall** is hardly less remarkable, a 15th century hall house with a superb crown post roof. It was restored by the Gayer Anderson brothers, and has a fine collection of their furniture. The Church of St Peter and St Paul dominates the town from its elevated position. It's a building of great distinction, perhaps the greatest of all the 'wool churches' and declared by the 19th century architect August Pugin to be the finest example of Late Perpendicular style in the world. It was built, with generous help from wealthy local families (notably the Spryngs and the de Veres) in the late 15th and early 16th centuries to celebrate the end of the Wars of the Roses. Its flint tower is a mighty 140 feet in height, and it's possible to climb to the top to take in the glorious views over Lavenham and the surrounding countryside. Richly carved screens and fine (Victorian) stained glass are eye-catching features within.

The Priory originated in the 13th

THE SWAN INN

The Street, Little Waldingfield, Sudbury,
Suffolk CO10 0SQ
Tel: 01787 248584 Fax: 01787 247566
e-mail: info@theswaninn.ndo.co.uk
website: www.theswaninn.ndo.co.uk

After a complete and very tasteful
refurbishment, Chris and Kim Jewell re-
opened the
delightful **Swan
Inn** in March
2003. Attracting a
loyal clientele of
locals and
holidaymakers,
this fine inn also
draws visitors who
have heard tell of
the excellent food
served here.

Built in Tudor
times (1450-
1500) and located
near the parish
church, this Grade
II listed building is
timber-framed
beneath a peg-
tiled roof, and is located in a Conservation
Area. The bar area is a happy marriage of
traditional features such as the heavy
beamwork and bright, modern paintwork.
Tastefully decorated throughout, the dining
area has walls adorned with old photos of
Little Waldingfield.

To drink, there's a range of real ales
including Greene King IPA, together with a
selection of regularly changing guest ales.

There are separate bar and dinner menus,
the former boasting a good range of
sandwiches, salads and starters as well as
tempting main courses such as chicken with
Thai green curry, fish pie, vegetable
stroganoff and Suffolk ham, while the latter
offers up a mouth-watering selection of
dishes such as pork, apple and cider

casserole, salmon fillet and sirloin steaks.
All the food is home-cooked and freshly
prepared to order, using the freshest
local ingredients.

The wine list is an impressive selection
of reds, whites, rose, champagne and
sparkling vintages.

Accommodation is
available in a separate
building that was once an
old coach house,
adjoining the pub, which
has been converted to a
high standard of quality
and comfort. There are
two twin en suite guest
bedrooms that are cosy
and comfortable and offer
every amenity.
Continental breakfast is
served direct to your
room.

Half Timbered House, Lavenham

century as a home for Benedictine monks; the beautiful timber-framed house on the site dates from about 1600. In the original hall, at the centre of the building, is an important collection of paintings and stained glass. The extensive grounds include a kitchen garden, a herb garden and a pond.

John Constable went to school in Lavenham, where one of his friends was Jane Taylor, who wrote the words to *'Twinkle Twinkle Little Star'*.

Sudbury
21 miles W of Ipswich on the A131

Sudbury is another wonderful town, the largest of the 'wool towns' and still home to a number of weaving concerns. Unlike Lavenham, Sudbury kept its industry because it was a port, and the result is a much more varied architectural picture. The surrounding countryside is some of the loveliest in Suffolk, and the River Stour is a further plus,

with launch trips and fishing available.

Sudbury boasts three medieval churches, but what most visitors make a beeline for is **Gainsborough's House** (see panel on page 104) on Gainsborough Street. The painter Thomas Gainsborough was born here in 1727 in the house built by his father John. More of the artist's work is displayed in this Georgian-fronted house than in any other gallery, and there is also assorted 18th century memorabilia and furnishings. A changing programme of contemporary art exhibitions includes fine art, photography and sculpture, highlighting East Anglian artists in particular. A bronze statue of Gainsborough stands in the square.

About those churches: All Saints dates from the 15th century and has a glorious carved tracery pulpit and

Gainsborough's House, Sudbury

GAINSBOROUGH'S HOUSE

46 Gainsborough Street, Sudbury,
Suffolk CO10 2EU
Tel: 01787 372958 Fax: 01787 376991
e-mail: mail@gainsborough.org
website: www.gainsborough.org

Gainsborough's House is the birthplace museum of Thomas Gainsborough (1727-1788), one of England's most celebrated artists. An exceptional collection of his paintings, drawings and prints is on display in this charming town house with a Georgian façade built by the artist's father. Around 25 oil paintings are on show, including a magnificent landscape of 1782 and a touching miniature of his wife, and among the Gainsborough memorabilia to be seen in the house are the artist's studio cabinet, his swordstick and his pocket watch. Two galleries and the garden showcase contemporary art and craft, and the print workshop hosts evening classes and summer courses in the techniques of etching, screenprinting, stone lithography and relief printing.

screens; 14th century St Gregory's is notable for a wonderful medieval font; and St Peter's has some marvellous painted screen panels and a piece of 15th century embroidered velvet.

Other buildings of interest are the **Victorian Corn Exchange**, now a library; **Salter's Hall**, a 15th century timbered house (sadly no longer open to the public); and the **Quay Theatre**, a thriving centre for the arts.

Constable Country

England's greatest landscape painter was born at East Bergholt in 1776 and remained at heart a Suffolk man throughout his life. His father, Golding Constable, was a wealthy man who owned both Flatford Mill and Dedham Mill, the latter on the Essex side of the Stour. The river was a major source of inspiration to the young John Constable, and his constant involvement in country matters gave him an expert knowledge of the elements and a keen eye for the details of nature. He was later to declare 'I associate my careless boyhood with all that lies on the banks of the Stour. Those scenes made me a painter and I am grateful.' His interest in painting developed early and was fostered by his friendship with John Dunthorne, a local plumber and amateur artist. Constable became a probationer at the Royal Academy Schools in 1799, and over the following years developed the technical skills to match his powers of observation. He painted the occasional portrait and even attempted a couple of religious works, but he concentrated almost entirely on the scenes that he knew and loved as a boy.

The most significant works of the earlier years were the numerous sketches in oil which were forerunners of the major paintings of Constable's mature

Artist, Flatford Mill

them, Constable's paintings were never lacking soul, and his work was much admired by the painters of the French Romantic School.

Two quotations from the man himself reveal much about his aims and philosophy:

'In a landscape I want to give one brief moment caught from fleeting time a lasting and sober existence.'

'I never saw any ugly thing in my life; in fact, whatever may be the shape of an object, light, shade or perspective can always make it beautiful.'

At the time of his death in 1837, Constable's reputation at home was relatively modest, though he had many followers and admirers in France. Awareness and understanding of his unique talent grew only in the ensuing years, so that, today, his place as England's foremost landscape painter is rarely disputed.

Suffolk has produced many other painters of distinction. Thomas Gainsborough, born in Sudbury in 1727, was an artist of great versatility, innovative and instinctive, and equally at home with portraits and landscapes. He earned his living for a while from portrait painting in Ipswich before making a real name for himself in Bath. His relations with the Royal Academy were often stormy, however, culminating in 1784 in a major dispute over the height at which a painting should be hung. He withdrew his intended hangings from the exhibition and never

years. He had exhibited at the Royal Academy every year since 1802, but it was not until 1817 that the first of his important canvases, *Flatford Mill on the River Stour*, was hung. This was succeeded by the six large paintings which became his best-known works. These were all set on a short stretch of the Stour, and all except *The Hay Wain* show barges at work. These broad, flat-bottomed craft were displayed in scenes remarkable for the realism of the colours, the effects of light and water and, above all, the beautiful depiction of clouds. His fellow-artist Fuseli declared that whenever he saw a Constable painting he felt the need to reach for his coat and umbrella. Though more realistic than anything that preceded again showed at the Royal Academy.

A man of equally indomitable spirit was Sir Alfred Munnings, born at Mendham in the north of Suffolk in 1878. The last of the great sporting painters in the tradition of Stubbs and Marshall, Munnings was outspoken in his opinions on modern art. In 1949, as outgoing President of the Royal Academy, he launched an animated attack on modern art as 'silly daubs' and 'violent blows at nothing'. The occasion was broadcast on the radio; in response many listeners complained about the 'strong language' Munnings had used. In 1956, Munnings jolted the art world again by describing that year's Summer Exhibition as 'bits of nonsense' hung on the wall.

Mary Beale, born at Barrow in 1633, was a noted portrait painter and copyist; some of her work has been attributed to Lely and Kneller, and it was rumoured that Lely was in love with her.

Philip Wilson Steer (1860-1942) was among the most distinguished of the many painters who were attracted to Walberswick. He studied in Paris and acquired the reputation of being the best of the English impressionist painters.

The Suffolk tradition of painting continues to this day, with many artists drawn to this part of the county. While nowadays crowds congregate throughout the Stour valley at summer weekends, at other times the tranquillity and loveliness are just as unmatched as they were in Constable's day.

Brantham
8 miles SW of Ipswich on the A137

Also known as 'Burnt Village' – possibly because it was sacked during a Danish invasion 1,000 years ago – Brantham's Church of St Michael owns one of the only two known religious paintings by Constable, *Christ Blessing the Children*, which he executed in the style of the American painter Benjamin West. It is kept in safety in Ipswich Museum. Just off the junction of the A137 and the B1070 is **Cattawade picnic site**, a small area on the edge of the Stour estuary. It's a good spot for birdwatching, and redshanks, lapwings and oystercatchers all breed on the well-known Cattawade Marshes. Fishing and canoeing are available, and there are public footpaths to Flatford Mill.

East Bergholt
8 miles SW of Ipswich on the B1070

Narrow lanes lead to this picturesque and much-visited little village. The **Constable Country Trail** starts here, where the painter was born, and passes through Flatford Mill and on to Dedham in Essex. The actual house where he was born no longer stands, but the site is marked by a plaque on the fence of its successor, a private house called Constables. A little further along Church Street is Moss Cottage, which Constable once used as his studio. **St Mary's** is one of the many grand churches built with the wealth brought

Georgian House, East Bergholt

children and whose early death was an enormous blow to him. His parents, to whom he was clearly devoted, and his old friend Willy Lott, whose cottage is featured famously in *The Hay Wain*, are buried in the churchyard.

East Bergholt has an interesting mix of houses, some dating back as far as the 14th century. One of the grandest is **Stour House**, once the home of Randolph Churchill. Its gardens are open to the public, as is **East Bergholt Place Garden** on the B1070.

A leafy lane leads south from the village to the Stour, where two of Constable's favourite subjects, **Flatford Mill** and **Willy Lott's cottage**, both looking much as they did when he painted them, are to be found. Neither is open to the public, and the brick

by the wool trade. This one should have been even grander, with a tower to rival that of Dedham across the river. The story goes that Cardinal Wolsey pledged the money to build the tower, but fell from grace before the funds were forthcoming. The tower got no further than did his college in Ipswich, and a bellcage constructed in the churchyard as a temporary house for the bells became their permanent home, which it remains to this day. In this unique timber-framed structure the massive bells hang upside down and are rung by hand by pulling on the wooden shoulder stocks - an arduous task, as the five bells are among the heaviest in England.

The church is naturally something of a shrine to Constable, his family and his friends. There are memorial windows to the artist and to his beloved wife Maria Bicknell, who bore him seven

Willy Lott's Cottage

watermill is run as a residential field study centre. Nearby Bridge Cottage at Flatford is a restored 16th century building housing a Constable display, a tea room and a shop. There's also a restored dry dock, and the whole area is a delight for walkers; it is easy to see how Constable drew constant inspiration from the wonderful riverside setting.

Stratford St Mary
10 miles SW of Ipswich off the A12

Another of Constable's favourite locations, Stratford St Mary is the most southerly village in Suffolk. *The Young Waltonians* and *A House in Water Lane* (the house still stands today) are the best known of his works set in this picturesque spot. The village church is typically large and imposing, with parts dating back to 1200. At the top of the village are two splendid half-timbered cottages called the **Ancient House** and the **Priest's House**. Stratford was once on the main coaching route to London, and the largest of the four pubs had stabling for 200 horses. It is claimed that Henry Williamson, author of *Tarka the Otter*, saw his first otter here.

Nayland
14 miles SW of Ipswich on the B1087

On a particularly beautiful stretch of the Stour in Dedham Vale, Nayland has charming colour-washed cottages in narrow, winding streets, as well as two very fine 15th century buildings in Alston Court and the Guildhall. Abels Bridge, originally built of wood in the

15th century by wealthy merchant John Abel, divides Suffolk from Essex. In the 16th century a hump bridge replaced it, allowing barges to pass beneath. The current bridge carries the original keystone, bearing the initial A. In the Church of St James stands an altarpiece by Constable entitled *Christ Blessing the Bread and Wine*.

One mile west of Nayland, at the end of a track off the Bures road, stands the Norman Church of St Mary at Wissington. The church has a number of remarkable features, including several 13th century wall paintings, a finely carved 12th century doorway and a tiebeam and crown post roof.

Stoke by Nayland
12 miles SW of Ipswich on the B1087

The drive from Nayland reveals quite stunning views, and the village itself has

Stoke by Nayland

a large number of listed buildings. The magnificent **Church of St Mary**, with its 120-foot tower, dominates the scene from its hilltop position. This church also dominates more than one Constable painting, the most famous showing the church lit up by a rainbow. William Dowsing destroyed 100 'superstitious pictures' here in his Puritan purges, but plenty of fine work is still to be seen, including several monumental brasses.

The Guildhall is another very fine building, now private residences but in the 16th century a busy centre of trade and commerce. When the wool trade declined, so did the importance of the Guildhall, and for a time this noble building saw service as a workhouse.

The decline of the cloth trade in East Anglia had several causes. Fierce competition came from the northern and western weaving industries, which generally had easier access to water supplies for fulling; the wars on the continent of Europe led to the closure of some trading routes and markets; and East Anglia had no supplies of the coal that was used to drive the new steam-powered machinery. In some cases, as at Sudbury, weaving or silk took over as smaller industries.

Polstead

11 miles SW of Ipswich off the B1068

Polstead is a very pretty village set in wooded, hilly countryside, with thatched, colour-washed cottages around the green and a wide duck pond at the bottom of the hill. Standing on a rise above the pond are Polstead Hall, a handsome Georgian mansion, and the

12th century Church of St Mary. The church has two features not found elsewhere in Suffolk – a stone spire and the very early bricks used in its construction. The builders used not only these bricks, but also tiles and tufa, a soft, porous stone much used in Italy. In the grounds of the hall stand the remains of a 'Gospel Oak' said to have been 1,300 years old when it collapsed in 1953. Legend has it that Saxon missionaries preached beneath it in the 7th century; an open-air service is still held here annually.

Polstead has two other claims to fame. One is for Polstead Blacks, a particularly tasty variety of cherry which was cultivated in orchards around the village and which used to be honoured with an annual fair. The other is much less agreeable, for it was here that the notorious Red Barn murder hit the headlines in 1827. A young girl called Maria Marten, daughter of the local molecatcher, disappeared with William Corder, a farmer's son who was the girl's lover and father of her child. It was at first thought that they had eloped, but Maria's stepmother dreamt three times that she had been murdered and buried in a red barn. A search of the barn soon revealed this to be true. Corder was tracked down to Middlesex, tried and found guilty of Maria's murder and hanged. His skin was used to bind a copy of the trial proceedings and this, together with his scalp, is on display at Moyse's Hall in Bury St Edmunds. The incident aroused a great deal of interest; today's visitors to the village will still find reminders of the ghastly deed: the thatched cottage where Maria lived stands, in what is now called Marten's Lane, and the farm where the murderer lived, now called Corder's Farm.

Boxford
12 miles W of Ipswich on the A1071

A gloriously unspoilt weaving village, downhill from anywhere, surrounded by the peaceful water meadows of the River Box, Boxford's St Mary's Church dates back to the 14th century. Its wooden north porch is one of the oldest of its kind in the country. In the church is a touching brass in memory of David Byrde, son of the rector, who died a baby in 1606. At the other end of the continuum is Elizabeth Hyam, four times a widow, who died in her 113th year.

Bures
17 miles W of Ipswich on the B1508

At this point the River Stour turns sharply to the east, creating a natural boundary between Suffolk and Essex. The little village of Bures straddles the river, lying partly in each county. Bures St Mary in Suffolk is where the church is, overlooked by houses of brick and half-timbering.

Bures wrote itself very early into the history books when on Christmas Day AD 855 it is thought that our old friend Edmund the Martyr, the Saxon king, was crowned at the age of 15 in the Chapel of St Stephen. For some time after that momentous occasion, Bures was the capital seat of the East Anglian kings.

Bures also has a long connection with the Waldegrave family, possibly from as far back as Chaucer's day. One of the Waldegrave memorials shows graphically the results of a visitation by Dowsing and the Puritan iconoclasts: all the figures of the kneeling children have had their hands cut off.

Edwardstone
14 miles W of Ipswich off the A1071

Just to the north of Boxford and close to Edwardstone Hall and the Temple Bar

Gate House, Edwardstone is now a 700-acre estate originally home to the Winthrop family. Winthrop was born in Edwardstone and emigrated to the New World, eventually becoming Governor of Massachusetts.

Bury St Edmunds

A gem among Suffolk towns, rich in archaeological treasures and places of religious and historical interest, Bury St Edmunds takes its name from St Edmund, who was born in Nuremberg in AD 841 and came here as a teenager to become the last King of East Anglia. He was a staunch Christian, and his refusal

THE WHITE HORSE INN

Edwardstone, Sudbury, Suffolk CO10 5PX
Tel: 01878 211211
e-mail:
holidaycottages@the-white-horse-inn.com
website: www.the-white-horse-inn.com

Full of character and a warm and friendly ambience, **The White Horse** began life as a farmhouse back in the mid-1500s. Spacious and welcoming, guests come from far and wide to enjoy real ales, home-cooked food and great hospitality. Set in over two acres where camping or caravanning is welcome, there are also two charming cottages which sleep up to six each, all making for an excellent and comfortable base from which to explore Suffolk and environs.

THE GROVE COTTAGES

Edwardstone, Lavenham, Suffolk CO10 5PP
Tel: 01787 211115
e-mail: mark@grove-cottages.co.uk
website: www.grove-cottages.co.uk

The lure of unspoilt rural living awaits visitors to **The Grove Cottages**, six charmingly converted 300-year-old farm buildings providing comfortable and superior accommodation in a beautiful countryside setting. Each of these gorgeous cottages has its own distinct personality and is a happy marriage of traditional comforts and modern amenities. Huge open fires, polished wood floors, antique farmhouse furniture and the peaceful ambience transport visitors back to more gracious times. ETC 4Star. Pets welcome and short breaks available.

St Edmundsbury Cathedral

Angel Hill, Bury St Edmunds,
Suffolk IP33 1LS
Tel: 01284 754933 Fax: 01284 768655
website: www.stedscathedral.co.uk

The site of Suffolk's Cathedral has been one of pilgrimage and worship for almost 1,000 years. One church within the precinct of a Norman Abbey was built by Abbot Anselm in the 12th century and was dedicated to St James. The nave of today's church, started in 1503, is the successor to that church, and though little remains of the abbey following the dissolution in 1539, St James' Church has continued to grow over the years and in 1914 it became the Cathedral Church of the Diocese of Saint Edmundsbury and Ipswich. The last 40 years have seen several additions to the church as well as the building of the Cathedral Centre, which houses the Song School, the refectory and meeting rooms. Outstanding features of the Cathedral include

a magnificent hammerbeam roof and a monumental bishop's throne.

to deny his faith caused him to be tortured and killed by the Danes in AD 870. Legend has it that although his body was recovered, his head (cut off by the Danes) could not be found. His men searched for it for 40 days, then heard his voice directing them to it from the depths of a wood, where they discovered it lying protected between the paws of a wolf. The head and the body were seamlessly united and, to commemorate the wolf's deed, the crest of the town's armorial bearings depicts a wolf with a man's head.

Edmund was possibly buried first at Hoxne, the site of his murder, but when he was canonised in about AD 910 his remains were moved to the monastery at Beodricsworth, which changed its name to St Edmundsbury. A shrine was built in his honour, later incorporated into

the Norman Abbey Church after the monastery was granted abbey status by King Canute in 1032. The town soon became a place of pilgrimage, and for many years St Edmund was the patron saint of England, until replaced by St George. Growing rapidly around the great abbey, which became one of the largest and most influential in the land, Bury prospered as a centre of trade and commerce, thanks notably to the cloth industry.

The next historical landmark was reached in 1214, when on St Edmund's Feast Day the then Archbishop of Canterbury, Simon Langton, met with the Barons of England at the high altar of the Abbey and swore that they would force King John to honour the proposals of the Magna Carta. The twin elements of Edmund's canonisation and the resolution of the Barons explain the motto on the town's crest: *sacrarium regis, cunabula legis* – 'shrine of a king, cradle of the law'.

Rebuilt in the 15th century, the Abbey was largely dismantled after its Dissolution by Henry VIII, but imposing ruins remain in the colourful Abbey Gardens beyond the splendid Abbey Gate and Norman Tower. **St Edmundsbury Cathedral** (see panel opposite) was originally the Church of St James, built in the 15th/16th century and

Abbey, Bury St Edmunds

accorded cathedral status (alone in Suffolk) in 1914. The original building has been much extended over the years (notably when being adapted for its role as a cathedral) and outstanding features include a magnificent hammerbeam roof, whose 38 beams are decorated with angels bearing the emblems of St James, St Edmund and St George. The monumental Bishop's throne depicts wolves guarding the crowned head of St Edmund, and there's a fascinating collection of 1,000 embroidered kneelers.

St Mary's Church, in the same complex, is also well worth a visit: an equally impressive hammerbeam roof, the detached tower standing much as Abbot Anselm built it in the 12th century, and several interesting monuments, the most important commemorating Mary Tudor, sister of

Henry VIII, Queen of France and Duchess of Suffolk. Her remains were moved here when the Abbey was suppressed; a window in the Lady Chapel recording this fact was the gift of Queen Victoria.

The **Abbey Gardens**, laid out in 1831, have as their central feature a great circle of flower beds following the pattern of the Royal Botanical Gardens in Brussels. Some of the original ornamental trees can still be seen, and other - later - features include an Old English rose garden, a water garden and a garden for the blind where fragrance counts for all. Ducks and geese live by the little River Lark, and there are tennis courts, putting and bowls greens and children's play equipment.

Bury is full of fine non-ecclesiastical buildings, many with Georgian frontages concealing medieval interiors. Among the most interesting are the handsome **Manor House Museum** with its collection of clocks, paintings, furniture, costumes and objets d'art; the **Victorian Corn Exchange** with its imposing colonnade; the Athenaeum, hub of social life since Regency times and scene of Charles Dickens's public readings; **Cupola House**, where Daniel Defoe once stayed; the **Angel Hotel**, where Dickens and his marvellous creation Mr Pickwick stayed; and the **Nutshell**, owned by Greene King Brewery and probably the smallest pub in the country. The **Theatre Royal**, now in the care of the National Trust, was built in 1819 by William Wilkins, who was also responsible for the National Gallery in London. It once staged the premiere of *Charley's Aunt*, and still operates as a working theatre.

The Nutshell

One of Bury's oldest residents and newest attractions is the **Greene King Brewery Museum and Shop**. Greene King has been brewed here in Bury since 1799; the museum's informative storyboards, artefacts, illustrations and audio displays bring the history and art of brewing to life. Brewery tours include a look round the museum and beer-tasting. The shop sells a variety of memorabilia, souvenirs, gifts and clothing – as well, of course, as bottles and cans of the frothy stuff.

The **Bury St Edmunds Art Gallery** is housed in one of Bury's noblest buildings, built to a Robert Adam design in 1774. It has filled many roles down the years, and was rescued from decline in the 1960s to be restored to Adam's original plans. It is now one of the county's premier art galleries, with eight exhibitions each year and a thriving craft shop.

Perhaps the most fascinating building of all is **Moyse's Hall Museum**, located at one end of the Buttermarket. Built of flint and limestone about 1180, it has claims to being the oldest stone domestic building in England. Originally a rich man's residence, it later saw service as a tavern, gaol, police station and railway parcels office, but since 1899 it has been a museum, and has recently undergone total refurbishment. It houses some 10,000 items, including many important archaeological collections, from a Bronze Age hoard, Roman pottery and Anglo-Saxon jewellery to a 19th century doll's house and some grisly relics of the notorious Red Barn murder. A new wing contains the Suffolk Regiment collection and education room.

Outside the Spread Eagle pub on the western edge of town is a horse trough erected to the memory of the Victorian romantic novelist 'Ouida' (Maria Louisa Ramee, 1839-1908).

Steeped though it is in history, Bury also moves with the times, and its sporting, entertainment and leisure facilities are impressive. A mile and a half outside town on the A14 (just off the East Exit) is **Nowton Park**, 172 acres of countryside landscaped in Victorian style and supporting a wealth of flora and fauna; the avenue of limes, carpeted with daffodils in the spring, is a particular delight. There's also a play area and a ranger centre.

Bury's disciplined network of streets (the layout was devised in the 11th century) provides long, alluring views. A great fire destroyed much of Bury in 1608, but it was rebuilt using traditional timber-framing techniques. Arriving here in 1698, Celia Fiennes, the inveterate traveller and architecture critic, was uncharacteristically

favourable in her remarks about Cupola House, which had just been completed at the time of her visit. William Cobbett (1763-1835), a visitor when chronicling his Rural Rides, did not disagree with the view that Bury St Edmunds was 'the nicest town in the world' - a view which would be endorsed by many of today's inhabitants and by many of the millions of visitors who have been charmed by this jewel in Suffolk's crown.

Around Bury St Edmunds

Hengrave
3 miles NW of Bury St Edmunds on the A1101

A captivating old-world village of flint and thatch, excavations and aerial photography indicate that there has been a settlement at Hengrave since Neolithic times.

Those parts of the village that are of archaeological interest are now protected. The chief attraction is **Hengrave Hall**, a rambling Tudor mansion built partly of

---

THE WHITE HORSE

Old Newmarket Road, Risby,
nr Bury St Edmunds, Suffolk IP28 6RD
Tel: 01784 810686

The White Horse is a large and impressive inn dating back to the 17th century. Relaxed and welcoming, it features an elegantly furnished restaurant and is full of character and charm. The extensive menu offers the finest beef, fish, game and other tempting dishes, all home-cooked to order and served at lunch and

dinner six days a week, and from midday to 5 p.m. on Sundays.

Northamptonshire limestone and partly of yellow brick by Sir Thomas Kytson, a wool merchant. A notable visitor in the early days was Elizabeth I, who brought her court here in 1578. Several generations of the Gage family were later the owners of Hengrave Hall - one of them, with a particular interest in horticulture, imported various kinds of plum trees from France. Most of the bundles were properly labelled with their names, but one had lost its label. When it produced its first crop of luscious green fruit, someone had the bright idea of calling it the green Gage. The name stuck, and the descendants of these trees, planted in 1724, are still at the Hall, which may be visited by appointment. In the grounds stands a lovely little church with a round Saxon tower and a wealth of interesting monuments. The church was for some time a family mausoleum; restored by Sir John Wood, it became a private chapel and now hosts services of various denominations.

Flempton
4 miles NW of Bury St Edmunds on the A1101

An interesting walk from this village just north of the A1101 follows the **Lark Valley Park** through Culford Park, providing a good view of Culford Hall, which has been a school since 1935. A handsome cast-iron bridge dating from the early 19th century - and recently brought to light from amongst the reeds - crosses a lake in the park.

West Stow
4 miles NW of Bury St Edmunds off the A1101

The villages of West Stow, Culford, Ingham, Timworth and Wordwell were for several centuries part of a single estate covering almost 10,000 acres. Half the estate was sold to the Forestry Commission in 1935 and was renamed the King's Forest in honour of King George V's Jubilee in that year.

An Anglo-Saxon cemetery was discovered in the village in 1849; subsequent years have revealed traces of Roman settlements and the actual layout of the original **Anglo-Saxon Village**. A trust was established to investigate further the Anglo-Saxon way of life and their building and farming techniques (see panel opposite). Several buildings were constructed using, as accurately as could be achieved, the tools and methods of the 5th century. The undertaking has become a major tourist attraction, with assistance from guides both human (in Anglo-Saxon costume) and in the form of taped cassettes. There are pigs and hens, growing crops, craft courses, a Saxon market at Easter, a festival in August and special events all year round. This fascinating village, which is entered through the Visitor Centre, is part of **West Stow Country Park**, a large part of which is designated a Site of Special Scientific Interest (SSSI). Over 120 species of birds and 25 species of animals have been sighted in this Breckland setting, and a well-marked 5-mile nature

WEST STOW ANGLO-SAXON VILLAGE

The Visitor Centre, Icklingham Road, West Stow, Bury St Edmunds, Suffolk IP28 6HG
Tel: 01284 728718 Fax: 01284 728277
website:
www.stedmundsbury.gov.uk/weststow.htm

Between 1965 and 1972 the low hill by the River Lark in Suffolk was excavated to reveal several periods of occupation, but in particular, over 70 buildings from an early Anglo Saxon village. There was also information from about 100 graves in the nearby cemetery. It was decided that such extensive evidence about these people should be used to carry out a practical experiment to test ideas about the buildings that formed the elements of the original village.

Part of the **Anglo Saxon Village** has been reconstructed on the site where the original (inhabited from around AD 420-650) was excavated. The reconstructions have been built over a period of more than 20 years. Each of the eight buildings is different, to test different ideas, and each has been built using the tools and techniques available to the early Anglo Saxons. Exploring the houses is an excellent way of finding out about the Anglo Saxons who lived at West Stow. Costumed "Anglo Saxons" bring the village to life at certain times, especially at Easter and during August. The new Anglo Saxon Centre is an exciting addition to the site, housing the original objects found there and at other local sites. Many of the objects have never been seen by the public before. The displays show aspects of village life and the focal point is a series of life size reconstructions of costume, based upon the grave finds.

West Stow Anglo Saxon Village lies in the middle of a beautiful 125 acre Country Park, part of which is a Site of Special Scientific Interest. The park has a number of different habitats, including woodland, heathland, a lake and a river. There is a play area, a bird feeding area and bird hides. The Park is open daily all year, from 9am-5pm in winter, 9am-8pm in summer. Entry to the park is free. Outstanding features of the Cathedral include a magnificent hammerbeam roof and a monumental bishop's throne.

trail links this nature reserve with the woods, a large lake and the River Lark.

Icklingham
8 miles NW of Bury St Edmunds on the A1101

The village of Icklingham boasts not one but two churches - the parish church of St James (mentioned in the *Domesday Book*) and the deconsecrated thatched-roofed **All Saints**, with medieval tiles on the chancels and beautiful east windows in the south aisle. At the point where the Icknield Way crosses the River Lark, Icklingham has a long history, brought to light in frequent archaeological finds, from pagan bronzes to Roman coins. The place abounds in tales of the supernatural, notably of the white rabbit who is seen at dusk in the company of a witch, causing – it is said – horses to bolt and men to die.

Great Welnetham
2 miles S of Bury St Edmunds off the A134

One of the many surviving Suffolk windmills is to be found here, just south of the village. The sails were lost in a gale 80 years ago, but the tower and a neighbouring old barn make an attractive sight.

The Bradfields
7 miles SE of Bury St Edmunds off the A134

The Bradfields - St George, St Clare and Combust - and Cockfield thread their way through a delightful part of the countryside and are well worth a little exploration, not only to see the picturesque villages themselves but for a stroll in the historic **Bradfield Woods**. These woods stand on the eastern edge of the parish of Bradfield St George and have been turned into an outstanding nature reserve, tended and coppiced in the same way for more than 700 years, and home to a wide variety of flora and fauna. They once belonged to the Abbey of St Edmundsbury, and one area is still today called Monk's Park Wood.

Coppicing involves cutting a tree back down to the ground every ten years or so. Woodlands were managed in this way to provide an annual crop of timber for local use and fast regrowth. After coppicing, as the root is already strongly established, regrowth is quick. Willow and hazel are the trees most commonly coppiced. Willow is often also pollarded, a less drastic form of coppicing where the trees are cut far enough from the ground to stop grazing animals having a free lunch.

Bradfield St Clare, the central of the three Bradfields, has a rival claim to that of Hoxne as the site of the martyrdom of St Edmund. The St Clare family arrived with the Normans and added their name to the village, and to the church, which was originally All Saints but was then rededicated to St Clare; it is the only church in England dedicated to her. Bradfield Combust, where the pretty River Lark rises, probably takes it curious name from the fact that the local hall was burnt to the ground during the 14th century riots against the Abbot of St Edmundsbury's crippling tax demands.

Cockfield
8 miles SE of Bury St Edmunds off the A1141

Cockfield is perhaps the most widely spread village in all Suffolk, its little thatched cottages scattered around and between no fewer than nine greens. Great Green is the largest, with two football pitches and other recreation areas, while Parsonage Green has a literary connection: the **Old Rectory** was once home to a Dr Babbington, whose nephew Robert Louis Stephenson was a frequent visitor and who is said to have written *Treasure Island* while staying there. Cockfield also shelters one of the last windmills to have been built in Suffolk (1891). Its working life was very short but the tower still stands, now in use as a private residence.

Thorpe Morieux
9 miles SE of Bury St Edmunds off the B1071

St Mary's Church in Thorpe Morieux is situated in as pleasant a setting as anyone could wish to find. With water meadows, ponds, a stream and a fine Tudor farmhouse to set it off, this 14th century church presents a memorable picture of old England. Look at the church, then take the time to wander round the peaceful churchyard with its profusion of springtime aconites, followed by the colourful flowering of limes and chestnuts in summer.

Lawshall
8 miles S of Bury St Edmunds off the A134

A spread-out village first documented in AD 972 but regularly giving up evidence of earlier occupation, Lawshall was the site where a Bronze Age sword dated at around 600BC was found (the sword is now in Bury Museum). The Church of All Saints, Perpendicular with some Early English features, stands on one of the highest points in Suffolk. Next to it is Lawshall Hall, whose owners once entertained Queen Elizabeth I. Another interesting site in Lawshall is the **Wishing Well**, a well-cover on the green put up in memory of Charles Tyrwhitt Drake, who worked for the Royal Geographic Society and was killed in Jerusalem.

Alpheton
10 miles S of Bury St Edmunds on the A134

There are several points of interest in this little village straddling the main road. It was first settled in AD 991 and its name means 'the farm of Aefflaed'.

That lady was the wife of Ealdorman Beorhtnoth of Essex, who was killed resisting the Danes at the Battle of Maldon and is buried in Ely Minster.

The hall, the farm and the church stand in a quiet location away from the main road and about a mile from the village. This remoteness is not unusual: some attribute it to the villagers moving during times of plague, but the more likely explanation is simply that the scattered cottages, originally in several tiny hamlets, centred on a more convenient site than that of the church. Equally possible is that the church was located here to suit the local landed family (who desired to have the church next door to their home). The main features at the church of **St Peter and St Paul** are the flintwork around the parapet (the exterior is otherwise fairly undistinguished), the carefully restored 15th century porch and some traces of an ancient wall painting of St Christopher with the Christ Child. All in all, it's a typical country church of unpretentious dignity and well worth a short detour from the busy main roads.

Back in the village, two oak trees were planted and a pump installed in 1887, to commemorate Queen Victoria's 50th year on the throne. Another of the village's claims to fame is that its American airfield was used as the setting for the classic film *Twelve o'Clock High*, in which Gregory Peck memorably plays a Second World War flight commander cracking under the strain of countless missions. Incidentally, one of the reasons for constructing the A134 was to help in the development of the airfield. The A134 continues south to Long Melford. An alternative road from Bury to Long Melford is the B1066, quieter and more scenic, with a number of pleasant places to visit en route.

Hartest
9 miles S of Bury St Edmunds on the B1066

Hartest, which has a history as long as Alpheton's, celebrated its millennium in 1990 with the erection of a village sign (the hart, or stag). It's an agreeable spot in the valley, with colour-washed houses and chestnut trees on the green. Also on the green are All Saints Church (mentioned in the *Domesday Book*) and a large glacial stone, the **Hartest Stone**, which was dragged by a team of 45 horses from where it was found in a field in neighbouring Somerton. From 1789 until the 1930s, Hartest staged a St George's Day Fair, an annual event celebrating King George III's recovery from one of his spells of illness. Just outside the village is **Gifford's Hall**, a smallholding which includes 14 acres of nearly 12,000 grapevines, as well as a winery producing white and rosé wines and fruit liqueurs. There are also organic vegetable gardens, wildflower meadows, black St Kilda sheep, black Berkshire pigs, goats and free-range fowl, together with a trailer ride ('The Grape Express') and children's play area. The Hall is particularly famous for its sweet peas and roses, and an annual festival is held on

the last weekend in June. Open from Easter to the end of October.

Shimpling
9 miles S of Bury St Edmunds off the B1066

Shimpling is a peaceful farming community whose church, St George's, is approached by a lime avenue. It is notable for Victorian stained glass and a Norman font, and in the churchyard is the **Faint House**, a small stone building where ladies overcome by the tightness of their stays could decently retreat from the service. The banker Thomas Hallifax built many of Shimpling's cottages, as well as the village school and Chadacre Hall, which Lord Iveagh later turned into an agricultural college (a role it ceased to hold in 1989 - the Hall is today again in private hands).

Glemsford
12 miles S of Bury St Edmunds off the B1066

Driving in from the north on the B1066, the old Church of St Mary makes an impressive sight on what, for Suffolk, is quite a considerable hill. Textiles and weaving have long played a prominent part in Glemsford's history, and thread from the silk factory, which opened in 1824 and is still going strong, has been woven into dresses and robes for various members of the royal family, including the late Princess Diana's wedding dress. During the last century several factories produced matting from coconut fibres, and in 1906 Glemsford was responsible for the largest carpet in the world, used to cover the floor at London's Olympia. To this day one factory processes horse hair for use in judges' wigs, sporrans and busbies.

Long Melford

13 miles S of Bury St Edmunds off the A134

Long Melford

The heart of this atmospheric wool town is its very long and, in stretches, fairly broad main street, set on an ancient Roman site in a particularly beautiful part of south Suffolk. In Roman times the Stour was a navigable river, and trade flourished. Various Roman finds have been unearthed, notably a blue glass vase which is now on display in the British Museum in London. The street is filled with antique shops, book shops and art galleries, and is a favourite place for collectors and browsers. Some of the houses are washed in the characteristic Suffolk pink, which might originally have been achieved by mixing ox blood or sloe juice into the plaster.

Holy Trinity Church, on a 14-acre green at the north end of Hall Street, is a typically exuberant manifestation of the wealth of the wool and textile trade. It's big enough to be a cathedral, but served (and still serves) comparatively few parishioners. John Clopton, grown rich in the woollen business, was largely responsible for this magnificent Perpendicular-style edifice, which has a 180-foot nave and chancel and half timbers, flint 'flushwork' (stonework) of the highest quality, and 100 large windows to give a marvellous sense of light and space. Medieval glass in the north aisle depicts religious

THE BULL INN

Melford Road, Cavendish, Suffolk CO10 8AX
Tel: 01787 280245

The interior of **The Bull Inn** is immediately welcoming and cosy, with exposed oak beams, supremely comfortable seating and friendly atmosphere. Apart from a good range of beers, wines, spirits and soft drinks, the accent here is on the superb food. Featuring speciality fish dishes and Continental cuisine, the menu offers a fine range of home-cooked meals served from midday until late. The

attractive terraced garden is another outstanding feature of this excellent inn.

traditional, with its church, thatched cottages, almshouses, Nether Hall and the **Sue Ryder Foundation Museum** spread around the green. The last, in a 16th century rectory by the pond, illustrates the work of the Sue Ryder Foundation, and was formally opened by Queen Elizabeth II in 1979. Once a refuge for concentration camp victims, it houses abundant war photographs and memorabilia. Nether Hall is a well-restored 16th century building and the headquarters of **Cavendish Vineyards**.

In the church of **St Mary**, whose tower has a pointed bellcote and a room inside complete with fireplace and shuttered windows, look for the two handsome lecterns, one with a brass eagle (15th century), the other with two chained books; and for the Flemish and Italian statues. In 1381 Wat Tyler, leader of the Peasants' Revolt, was killed at Smithfield, in London, by John Cavendish, son of Sir John Cavendish, then lord of the manor and Chief Justice of England. Sir John was then hounded by the peasants, who caught him and killed him near Bury St Edmunds. He managed en route to hide some valuables in the belfry of St Mary's here

EMBLETON HOUSE

Melford Road, Cavendish, Sudbury,
Suffolk CO10 8AA
Tel: 01787 280447 Fax: 01787 282396
e-mail: silverned@aol.com
website:
www.smoothhound.co.uk/hotels/embleton

With five excellently appointed and furnished en suite guest bedrooms, **Embleton House** is a handsome residence surrounded by well-stocked mature gardens and grounds, which include an outdoor heated pool and tennis court. An impressive and gracious home, it makes a delightful retreat or touring base. The upstairs rooms command lovely views,

while those on the ground floor are easily accessible to guests with disabilities, and two have their own private entrances. 4 Diamonds/Silver Award ETB. Which Recommended 2003.

in Cavendish, and bequeathed to the church £40, sufficient to restore the chancel. A later Cavendish – Thomas – sailed round the world in the 1580s and perished on a later voyage. In the shadow of the church, on the edge of the village green, is a cluster of immaculate thatched cottages at a spot known as Hyde Park Corner. Pink-washed and pretty as a picture, they look almost too good to be true – and they almost are, having been rebuilt twice since the Second World War due to unhappy forces that included fires and dilapidation.

Clare

6 miles W of Long Melford on the A1092

A medieval wool town of great importance, Clare repays a visit today with its fine old buildings and some distinguished old ruins. Perhaps the most renowned tourist attraction is **Ancient House**, a timber-framed building dated 1473 and remarkable for its pargetting. This is the decorative treatment of external plasterwork, usually by dividing the surface into rectangles and decorating each panel. It was very much a Suffolk speciality, particularly in the 16th and 17th centuries, with some examples also being found in Cambridgeshire and Essex. The decoration could be simple brushes of a comb, scrolls or squiggles, or more elaborate, with religious motifs, guild signs or family crests. Some pargetting is incised, but the best is in relief – pressing moulds into wet plaster or shaping it by hand. Ancient House sports some

splendid entwined flowers and branches, and a representation of two figures holding a shield. The best-known workers in this unique skill had their own distinctive styles, and the expert eye could spot the particular 'trademarks' of each man (the same is the case with the master thatchers). Ancient House is now a museum, open during the summer months and housing an exhibition on local history.

Another place of historical significance is **Nethergate House**, once the workplace of dyers, weavers and spinners. The Swan Inn, in the High Street, has a sign which lays claim to being the oldest in the land. Ten feet in length and carved from a solid piece of wood, it portrays the arms of England and France. **Clare Castle** was a motte-and-bailey fortress that sheltered a household of 250. **Clare Castle Country Park**, with a visitor centre in the goods shed of a disused railway line, contains the remains of the castle and the moat, the latter now a series of ponds and home to varied wild life. At the Prior's House, the original cellar and infirmary are still in use. Established in 1248 by Augustine friars and used by them until the Dissolution of 1538, the priory was handed back to that order in 1953 and remains their property.

A mile or so west of Clare on the A1092 lies **Stoke-by-Clare**, a pretty village on one of the region's most picturesque routes. It once housed a Benedictine priory, whose remains are now in the grounds of a school. There's a fine 15th century church and a vineyard:

Boyton Vineyards at Hill Farm, Boyton End, is open early April to the end of October for a tour, a talk and a taste.

Horringer
3 miles SW of Bury St Edmunds on the A143

Approach to Ickworth House

Rejoining the A143 by Chedburgh, the motorist will soon arrive at Horringer, whose village green is dominated by the flintstone Church of St Leonard. Beside the church are the gates of one of the country's most extraordinary and fascinating houses, now run by the National Trust. **Ickworth House** was the brainchild of the eccentric 4th Earl of Bristol and Bishop of Derry, a collector of art treasures and an inveterate traveller (witness the many Bristol Hotels scattered around Europe). His inspiration was Belle Isle, a house built on an island in Lake Windermere, and the massive structure is a central rotunda linking two semi-circular wings. It was designed as a treasure house for his art collection, and work started in 1795. Sadly, the first collection of the Earl's treasures was seized by Napoleon in 1798, so never reached England.

Derry died in 1803 and his son, after some hesitation, saw the work through to completion in 1829. Its chief glories are some marvellous paintings by Titian, Gainsborough, Hogarth, Velasquez, Reynolds and Kauffman, but there's a great deal more to enthral the visitor: late Regency and 18th century French furniture, a notable collection of Georgian silver, friezes and sculptures by John Flaxman, frescoes copied from wall paintings discovered at the Villa Negroni in Rome in 1777. The Italian garden, where Mediterranean species have been bred to withstand a distinctly non-Mediterranean climate, should not be missed, with its hidden glades, orangery and temple rose garden, and in the park landscaped by Capability Brown there are designated walks and cycle routes, bird hides, a deer enclosure and play areas. More recent attractions include the vineyard and plant centre. The House is open from Easter until the end of October, while the park and gardens are open throughout the year.

Arable land surrounds Horringer, with a large annual crop of sugar beet grown for processing at the factory in Bury, the largest of its kind in Europe.

Haverhill
18 miles SW of Bury St Edmunds on the A604

Notable for its fine Victorian architecture, Haverhill also boasts one fine Tudor gem. Although many of

Haverhill's buildings were destroyed by fire in 1665, the **Anne of Cleves House** was restored and is well worth a visit. Anne was the fourth wife of Henry VIII and, after a brief political marriage, she was given an allowance and spent the remainder of her days at Haverhill and Richmond.

Haverhill Local History Centre, in the Town Hall, has an interesting collection of memorabilia, photographs and archive material.

East Town Park is an attractive and relatively new country park on the east side of Haverhill.

Kedington

2 miles N of Haverhill on the B1061

Haverhill intrudes somewhat, but the heart of the old village of Kedington gains in appeal by the presence of the River Stour. Known to many as the 'Cathedral of West Suffolk', the church of **St Peter and St Paul** is the village's chief attraction. Almost 150 feet in length, it stands on a ridge overlooking the Stour Valley. It has several interesting features, including a 15th century font, a Saxon cross in the chancel window, a triple-decker pulpit (with a clerk's desk and a reading desk) and a sermon-timer, looking rather like a grand egg-timer. The foundations of a Roman building have been found beneath the floorboards.

The Bardiston family, one of the oldest in Suffolk, had strong links with the village and many of the family tombs are in the church. In the church grounds is a row of ten elm trees, each, the legend says, with a knight buried beneath its roots.

Following the Stour along the B1061, the visitor will find a number of interesting little villages. In Little Wratting, Holy Trinity Church has a shingled oak-framed steeple (a feature more usually associated with Essex churches). John Sainsbury was a local resident, while in Great Wratting another magnate, W H Smith, financed the restoration of St Mary's Church in 1887. This church boasts some diverting topiary in the shape of a church, a cross and – somewhat comically - an armchair.

THE PLOUGH INN

Brockley Green, Hundon, Suffolk
Tel/Fax: 01440 786789
e-mail: ploughdave@aol.com

The Plough Inn is an impressive Free House offering home-cooked food, real ales and accommodation. This pub, restaurant and country house hotel dates back to the early 1800s and is filled with traditional features like exposed oak beams and log fires. The menus offer a range of English cuisine, served at lunch and dinner every day. Each of the

eight guest bedrooms is comfortable, cosy and attractive.

Great and Little Thurlow
3 miles N of Haverhill on the B1061

Great and Little Thurlow form a continuous village on the west bank of the River Stour a few miles north of Haverhill. Largely undamaged thanks to being in a conservation area, together they boast many 17th century cottages and a Georgian manor house. In the main street is a schoolhouse built in 1614 by Sir Stephen Soame, one-time Lord Mayor of London, whose family are commemorated in the village church.

A short distance further up the B1061 stands the village of **Great Bradley**, divided in two by the River Stour, which rises just outside the village boundary. Chief points of note in the tranquil parish church are a fine Norman doorway sheltering a Tudor brick porch and some beautiful stained glass poignantly depicting a soldier in the trenches during the First World War. The three bells in the tower include one cast in the 14th century, among the oldest in Suffolk.

Denston
6 miles NE of Haverhill just off the A143

Denston lies just east of the A143 on the River Glem, and is notable chiefly for its magnificent Perpendicular church, one of 18 dedicated to St Nicholas, patron saint of sailors. Stop and admire the fan vaulting in the roof (a comparative rarity in Suffolk), the outstanding brasses and the wide variety of carved animals.

Also on the Glem is the neighbouring village of Stansfield, where stand the ruins of another mill, this one a tower mill but sadly dilapidated and lacking its cap.

Hawkedon
7 miles NE of Haverhill off the A143

Hawkedon is designated a place of outstanding natural beauty. Here the Church of St Mary is located atypically in the middle of the village green. The pews and intricately carved bench-ends take the eye here, along with a canopied stoup (a recess for holding holy water) and a Norman font. There is a wide variety of carved animals, many on the bench-ends but some also on the roof cornice. One of the stalls is decorated with the carving of a crane holding a stone in its claw: legend has it that if the crane were on watch and should fell asleep, the stone would drop and the noise would wake it.

Wickhambrook
8 miles NE of Haverhill on the B1063

Wickhambrook is a series of tiny hamlets with no fewer than 11 greens and three manor houses. The greens have unusual names - Genesis, Nunnery, Meeting, Coltsfoot - whose origins keep local historians busy. One of the two pubs has the distinction of being officially half in Wickhambrook and half in Denston.

Newmarket

On the western edge of Suffolk, Newmarket is home to some 16,000 human and 3,000 equine inhabitants. The historic centre of British racing lives and breathes horses, with 60 training establishments, 50 stud farms, the top annual thoroughbred sales and two racecourses (the only two in Suffolk). Thousands of the population are involved in the trade, and racing art and artefacts fill the shops, galleries and museums; one of the oldest established saddlers even has a preserved horse on display - 'Robert the Devil', runner-up in the Derby in 1880.

History records that Queen Boudica of the Iceni, to whom the six-mile Devil's Dyke stands as a memorial, thundered around these parts in her lethal chariot behind her shaggy-haired horses. She is said to have established the first stud here. In medieval times the chalk heathland was a popular arena for riders to display their skills. In 1605, James I paused on a journey northwards to enjoy a spot of hare coursing. He enjoyed the place and said he would be back. By moving the royal court to his Newmarket headquarters, he began the royal patronage which has remained strong throughout the years. James' son, Charles I, maintained the royal connection, but it was Charles II who really put the place on the map when he, too, moved the Royal court here in the spring and autumn of each year. He initiated the Town Plate, a race which he himself won twice as a rider and which, in a modified form, still exists.

One of the racecourses, the **Rowley Mile**, takes its name from Old Rowley, a favourite horse of the Merry Monarch. Here the first two classics of the season, the 1,000 and 2,000 Guineas, are run, together with important autumn events including the Cambridgeshire and the Cesarewich. There are some 18 race days at this track, while on the leafy July course, with its delightful garden-party atmosphere, a similar number of race days take in all the important summer fixtures.

The visitor to Newmarket can learn almost all there is to know about flat racing and racehorses by making the grand tour of the several establishments open to the public (sometimes by

Newmarket Racecourse

NATIONAL HORSERACING MUSEUM

99 High Street, Newmarket, Suffolk CB8 8JL
Tel: 01638 667333 Fax: 01638 665600
website: www.nationalstud.co.uk

"The Newmarket Experience" comprises two separate attractions: **The National Horseracing Museum** and **The National Stud**. The story of racing throughout the ages is told through the Museum's permanent collections, featuring the horses, people, events and scandals that make the sport so colourful.

Highlights include the head of Persimmon, a great Royal Derby winner in 1896; a special display about Fred Archer, the Victorian jockey who committed suicide after losing the struggle to keep his weight down; the skeleton of Eclipse, ancestor of 90 per cent of modern

thoroughbreds; items associated with Red Rum, Lester Piggott, Frankie Dettori and other heroes of the Turf. In the Practical Gallery, visitors can learn everything there is to know about the horse and jockey, and experience the thrill of riding on the horse simulator. The Gallery is staffed by retired jockeys and trainers, who make the world of racing come alive. Special exhibitions have included *"Why* did you get that hat?", a display of Gertrude Shilling's outrageous Ascot outfits. Mrs Shilling (1910-1999) was one of the most colourful and eccentric personalities ever to grace the sport.

The Museum also boasts a range of exciting temporary exhibitions, including paintings and other works of art with a racing theme. The daily minibus tours of working establishments in Newmarket are another treat, offering visitors a chance to see horses at close quarters and meet stable staff in a two-hour tour, as well as horses training on the gallops, the horses' swimming pool and a training yard, together with the historic town itself.

The National Stud extends a warm welcome to all its visitors. Breeding top-class thoroughbreds, the 500-acre site has 12 yards, 9 miles of roads and tracks, 60 miles of post and rail fencing, 21 houses, a feedmill and storage for 50 tons of hay and straw - all purpose built between 1963 and 1967. The Stud year follows a set pattern, with the breeding season officially beginning on 15th February, and ending with the annual National Stud Fair and Stallion Parade held over the first week in December. Any tour, which will vary depending on the season, takes in the superb Stallion Unit, along with the stallions in residence, Nursery Yards and mares and foals in their paddocks. The helpful, informative tour guides offer a full insight into the workings of a modern stud.

The Stud provides training courses on horse husbandry and stud management for students who wish to make their careers in the thoroughbred breeding industry.

appointment only). **The Jockey Club**, which was the first governing body of the sport and, until recently, its ultimate authority, was formed in the mid-18th century and occupies an imposing building which was restored and rebuilt in Georgian style in the 1930s. Originally a social club for rich gentlemen with an interest in the turf, it soon became the all-powerful regulator of British racing, owning all the racing and training land. When holding an enquiry the stewards sit round a horseshoe-shaped table while the jockey or trainer under scrutiny faces them on a strip of carpet by the door - hence the expression 'on the mat'.

Next to the Jockey Club in the High Street is the **National Horseracing Museum** (see panel opposite). Opened by the Queen in 1983, its five galleries chronicle the history of the Sport of Kings from its royal beginnings through to the top trainers and jockeys of today. Visitors can ride a mechanical horse, try on racing silks, record a race commentary, ask questions and enjoy a snack in the café, whose walls are hung with murals of racing personalities.

A few steps away is **Palace House**, which contains the remains of Charles II's palace and which, as funds allow, has been restored over the years for use as a visitor centre and museum. In the same street is **Nell Gwynn's House**, which some say was connected by an underground passage beneath the street to the palace. The diarist John Evelyn spent a night in (or on?) the town during a royal visit, and declared the occasion to be 'more resembling a luxurious and abandoned rout than a Christian court'.

Other must-sees on the racing enthusiast's tour are **Tattersalls**, where leading thoroughbred sales take place from April to December; the **British Racing School**, where top jockeys are taught the ropes; the **National Stud**, open from March till the end of September (plus race days in October - booking essential); and the **Animal Health Trust** based at Lanwades Hall, where there's an informative Visitor Centre. The National Stud at one time housed no fewer than 3 Derby winners - Blakeney, Mill Reef, and Grundy.

Horses aren't all about racing, however. One type of horse you won't see in Newmarket is the wonderful Suffolk Punch, a massive yet elegant working horse which can still be seen at work at Rede Hall Park Farm near Bury St Edmunds and at Kentwell Hall in Long Melford. All Punches descend from Crisp's horse, foaled in 1768. The Punch is part of the Hallowed Trinity of animals at the very centre of Suffolk's agricultural history; the others being the Suffolk Sheep and the Red Poll Cow. It is entirely appropriate that the last railway station to employ a horse for shunting wagons should have been at Newmarket. That hardworking one-horse-power shunter retired in 1967.

Newmarket also has things to offer the tourist outside the equine world, including the churches of **St Mary and**

All Saints, and **St Agnes**, and a landmark at each end of the High Street - a Memorial Fountain in honour of Sir Daniel Cooper and the Jubilee Clock Tower commemorating Queen Victoria's Golden Jubilee.

Around Newmarket

Exning

2 miles NW of Newmarket on the A14

A pause is certainly in order at this ancient village, whether on your way from Newmarket or arriving from Cambridgeshire on the A14. Anglo-Saxons, Romans, the Iceni and the Normans were all here, and the *Domesday Book* records the village under the name of Esselinga. The village was stricken by plague during the Iceni occupation, so its market was moved to the next village along - thus Newmarket acquired its name.

Exning's written history begins when Henry II granted the manor to the Count of Boulogne, who divided it between four of his knights. References to them and to subsequent Lords of the Manor are to be found in the little church of **St Martin**, which might well have been founded by the Burgundian Christian missionary monk St Felix in the 7th century. Water from the well used by that saint to baptise members of the Saxon royal family is still used for baptisms by the current vicar. The A14 is a busy main road, but pulling away from the traffic and spending time in and around this village will be rewarded by some quiet, pleasant walks.

Kentford

5 miles E of Newmarket by the A14

At the old junction of the Newmarket-to-Bury road stands the grave of a young boy who hanged himself after being accused of sheep-stealing. It was a well-established superstition that suicides should be buried at a crossroads to

THE WHEATSHEAF

Chapel Street, Exning, Newmarket,
Suffolk CB8 7HA
Tel: 01638 577239

Set back from the street in a quiet location, **The Wheatsheaf** is a large and very pleasant inn dating back to the 1800s. Cosy, clean and spacious, this charming inn offers great food, good value and convivial surroundings.

Traditional and welcoming, there's a range of real ales, lagers, cider, stout, wines, spirits and soft drinks, and food is served at lunch Tues-Sun and dinner Tues-Sat. Meals can be taken in the bar or in the lovely conservatory. There is also a no smoking area for up to 18 people.

prevent their spirits from wandering. Flowers are still sometimes laid at the **Gypsy Boy's Grave**, sometimes by punters hoping for good luck at Newmarket races.

Moulton

4 miles E of Newmarket on the B1085

This most delightful village lies in wonderful countryside on chalky downland in farming country; its proximity to Newmarket is apparent from the racehorses which are often to be seen on the large green. The River Kennett flows through the green before running north to the Lark, a tributary of the Ouse. Flint walls are a feature of many of the buildings, but the main point of interest is the 15th century **Four-arch packhorse bridge** on the way to the church.

Dalham

5 miles E of Newmarket on the B1063

Eighty per cent of the buildings in Dalham are thatched (the highest proportion in Suffolk) and there are many other attractions in this pretty village. Above the village on one of the county's highest spots stands **St Mary's** church, which dates from the 14th century. Its spire toppled over during the gales which swept the land on the night that Cromwell died, and was replaced by a tower in 1627. Sir Martin Stutteville was the leading light behind this reconstruction; an inscription at the

back of the church notes that the cost was £400. That worthy's grandfather was Thomas Stutteville, whose memorial near the altar declares that 'he saw the New World with Francis Drake.' (Drake did not survive that journey - his third to South America.) Thomas' grandson died in the fullness of his years (62 wasn't bad for those times) while hosting a jolly evening at The Angel Hotel in Bury St Edmunds.

Dalham Hall was constructed in the first years of the 18th century at the order of the Bishop of Ely, who decreed that it should be built up until Ely Cathedral could be seen across the fens on a clear day. That view was sadly cut off in 1957 when a fire shortened the hall to only two storeys high. Wellington lived here for some years, and much later it was bought by Cecil Rhodes, who unfortunately died before taking up residence. His brother Francis erected the village hall in the adventurer's memory, and he himself is buried in the churchyard.

All in all, Dalham is a place of charm and interest - clearly no longer resembling the place described in *The Times* in the 1880s as full of ruffians and drunks, where the vicar felt obliged to give all the village children boxing lessons to increase their chances of survival.

Mildenhall

8 miles NE of Newmarket off the A11

On the edge of the Fens and Breckland,

Mildenhall is a town which has many links with the past. It was once a port for the hinterlands of West Suffolk, though the River Lark has long ceased to be a trade route. Most of the town's heritage is recorded in the excellent **Mildenhall & District Museum** in King Street. Here will be found exhibits of local history (including the distinguished RAF and USAAF base), crafts and domestic skills, the natural history of the Fens and Breckland and, perhaps most famously, the chronicle of the 'Mildenhall Treasure'. This was a cache of 34 pieces of 4th century Roman silverware - dishes, goblets and spoons - found by a ploughman in 1946 at Thistley Green and now on display in the British Museum in London, while a replica makes its home here where it was found. There is evidence of much earlier occupation than the Roman era, with flint tools and other artefacts being unearthed in 1988 on the site of an ancient lake.

The parish of Mildenhall is the largest in Suffolk, so it is perhaps fitting that it should boast so magnificent a parish church as **St Mary's**, built of Barnack stone; it dominates the heart of the town and indeed its west tower commands the flat surrounding countryside. Above the splendid north porch (the largest in Suffolk) are the arms of Edward the Confessor and of St Edmund. The chancel, dating back to the 13th century, is a marvellous work of architecture, but pride of place goes to the east window, divided into seven vertical lights. Off the south aisle is the Chapel of St Margaret, whose altar, itself modern, contains a medieval altar stone. At the west end, the font, dating from the 15th century, bears the arms of Sir Henry Barton, who was twice Lord Mayor of London and whose tomb is located on the south side of the tower. Above the nave and aisles is a particularly fine hammerbeam roof whose outstanding feature is the carved angels. Efforts of the Puritans to destroy the angels failed, though traces of

ORCHARD HOUSE

23 North Terrace, Mildenhall,
Suffolk IP28 7AA
Tel: 01638 711237
e-mail: orchardhouse23@aol.com
website: www.mildenhallorchardhouse.com

With four recently refurbished and redecorated guest bedrooms, **Orchard House** provides attractive and comfortable accommodation for guests. Open all year round, this welcoming and gracious home has, in addition to the four spacious bedrooms, a lovely dining room with views over the beautiful garden. There is a well-appointed lounge. Two self-catering units are being created in the coach house. Owners Anne and Richard Greenfield offer their guests a delicious breakfast and the best in hospitality.

THE COBBLES

Market Place, Mildenhall, Suffolk
Tel: 01638 717022

A restaurant with rooms, **The Cobbles** is located in the heart of Mildenhall and has been welcoming weary travellers since the 16th century. This traditional coaching inn has been renovated over the years to provide a smart and modern exterior while retaining the interior low oak-beamed ceilings and other original features. All the delicious food is home-cooked and offers the best in traditional

English cuisine; the wine list is excellent. The three en suite guest bedrooms are comfortable and attractive.

buckshot and arrowheads remain and have been found embedded in the woodwork.

Sir Henry North built a manor house on the north side of the church in the 17th century. His successors included a dynasty of the Bunbury family, who were Lords of the Manor from 1747 to 1933. Sir Henry Edward Bunbury was the man chosen to let Napoleon Bonaparte know of his exile to St Helena, but the best-known member of the family is Sir Thomas, who in 1780 tossed a coin with Lord Derby to see whose name should be borne by a race to be inaugurated at Epsom. Lord Derby won, but Sir Thomas had the satisfaction of winning the first running of the race

with his colt, Diomed.

The other focal point in Mildenhall is the Market Place, with its 16th century timbered cross.

Barton Mills
1 mile S of Mildenhall off the A11

Known as Barton Parva (Little Barton) in Saxon times, this village changed its name during the 18th century. St Mary's Church can trace its origins back to at least 1150, and one of its early rectors had the Pope as his patron. Sir Alexander Fleming had a country house in the village, and it is possible that he worked on the invention of penicillin in a shed in the garden.

THE WHITE HART

High Street, Tuddenham, Suffolk IP28 6SQ
Tel: 01638 713061

Dating back to the 18th century and tastefully added to over the years, **The White Hart** in the quiet village of Tuddenham is a cosy and traditional pub with great food, drink and hospitality. In winter there's an open fire; in summer guests can make use of the attractive gardens. Breakfast is served every day from 10, lunch and dinner Thurs-Sun. There's a good choice of daily specials and home-made

pies and other tempting dishes, as well as bar snacks at other times of the day.

Worlington
2 miles W of Mildenhall on the B1102

Worlington is a small village near the River Lark, known chiefly as the location of **Wamil Hall**, an Elizabethan mansion which stands on the riverbank. Popular lore has it that a person called Lady Rainbow haunts the place, though the spot she once favoured for appearances, a flight of stairs, was destroyed in one of the many fires the mansion has suffered. Cricket is very much part of the village scene (there's a splendid village green), and has been since the early days of the 19th century.

Brandon
9 miles NE of Mildenhall on the A1065

On the edge of **Thetford Forest** by the Little Ouse, Brandon was long ago a thriving port, but flint is what really put it on the map. The town itself is built mainly of flint, and flint was mined from early Neolithic times to make arrowheads and other implements and weapons of war. The gun flint industry brought with it substantial wealth, and a good flint-knapper could produce up to 300 gun flints in an hour. The invention of the percussion cap killed off much of the need for this type of work, however, so they turned to shaping flints for church buildings and ornamental purposes. **Brandon Heritage Centre**, in a former fire station in George Street, provides visitors with a splendid insight

into this industry, while for an even more tangible feel, a visit to **Grime's Graves**, just over the Norfolk border, reveals an amazing site covering 35 acres and 300 pits (one of the shafts is open to visitors). With the close proximity of numerous warrens and their rabbit population, the fur trade also flourished here, and that, too, along with forestry, is brought to life in the Heritage Centre.

The whole of this northwestern corner of Suffolk, know as **Breckland**, offers almost unlimited opportunities for touring by car, cycling or walking. A mile south of town on the B1106 is **Brandon Country Park**, a 30-acre landscaped site with a tree trail, forest walks, a walled garden and a visitor centre. There's also an orienteering route leading on into Thetford Forest, Britain's largest lowland pine forest. The **High Lodge Forest Centre**, near Santon Downham (off the B1107), also attracts with walks, cycle trails and adventure facilities.

Elveden
5 miles S of Brandon on the A11

The road from Brandon leads south through the forest to a historic estate village with some unusual architectural features. Where the three parishes of Elveden, Eriswell and Icklingham meet, a tall war memorial in the form of a Corinthian column is a landmark.

Elveden Hall became more remarkable than its builders intended when Prince Duleep Singh, the last Maharajah of Punjab and a noted

GLEBE HOUSE

34 London Road, Elveden, Thetford,
Norfolk IP24 3TL
Tel/Fax: 01842 890027
e-mail: deirdre@jrudderham.freeserve.co.uk
website: www.glebecountryhouse.co.uk

Part of the 23,000-acre estate owned by the Earl of Iveagh, **Glebe House** is a gracious manor house in its own extensive grounds with three absolutely stunning, spacious and elegant guest bedrooms, each of which is tastefully decorated and furnished. Offering exceptionally comfortable accommodation in

a relaxed atmosphere, this distinctive country house is just 15 minutes from Newmarket. Open all year round. 4 Diamonds ETC.

sportsman, crack shot and the man who handed over the Koh-I-Noor diamond to Queen Victoria, arrived on the scene. Exiled to England with a handsome pension, he bought the Georgian house in 1863 and commissioned John Norton to transform it into a palace modelled on those in Lahore and Delhi. Although it is stated that in private Duleep Singh referred to Queen Victoria as 'Mrs Fagin … receiver of stolen goods', he kept close contact with the royal household and the Queen became his son's godmother. The Guinness family (Lord Iveagh) later took the Hall over and joined in the fun, adding even more exotic adornments including a replica Taj Mahal, while at the same time creating the largest arable farm in the whole of the country. In recent times, Stanley Kubrick's last film, *Eyes Wide Shut*, was shot here, as was *Tomb Raider*.

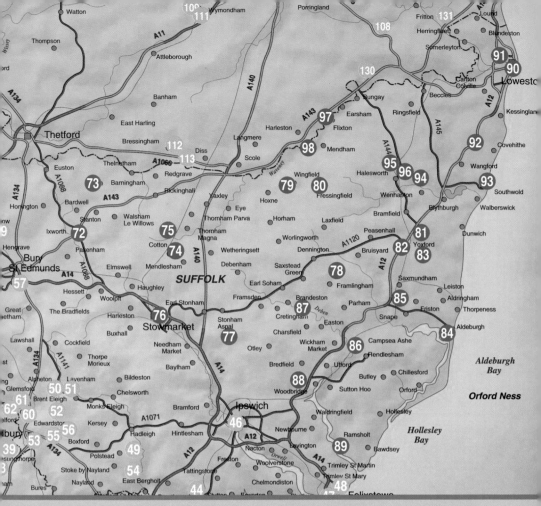

PLACES TO STAY, EAT AND DRINK

● Denotes entries in other chapters

4 Central and Eastern Suffolk

The heart of Suffolk is *the* place in the county to get away from it all. Lying between the county's heathland and coastal area, many of its villages are little changed from olden days. The Rivers Deben and Gipping run through much of the region, which naturally has its fair share of churches, museums, fayres and festivals. The little market towns of Stowmarket and Needham Market are full of interest, and in this part of Suffolk some of the best-preserved windmills and watermills are to be found. Several examples of both types of mills survive, and the village of Pakenham is lucky in having a splendid example of each.

The sea brings its own dangers, even in human form, and it was against the threat of a Napoleonic invasion that Martello Towers were built in southeastern Suffolk, in the tradition of Saxon and Tudor forts and the precursors

Sunset, Snape Maltings

of concrete pillboxes. Starting just before the end of the 18th century, over 100 of these sturdy circular fortified towers were built along the coast from Suffolk to Sussex. Aldeburgh's at Slaughden is the most northerly (and the largest), while the tower at Shoreham in Sussex the southernmost.

Aldeburgh Beach

The marshes by the coast have traditionally been a source of reeds, the raw material for the thatch that is such a pretty sight on so many Suffolk buildings. Reed-cutting happens between December and February, the beds being drained in preparation and reflooded after the crop has been gathered. Thatching itself is a highly skilled craft, but 10 weeks of work can give a thatched roof 50 years of life. Organised walks of the reed beds take place from time to time – wellies essential.

While inland Suffolk has few peers in terms of picturesque countryside and villages, Suffolk is also very much a maritime county, with over 50 miles of coastline. The whole coast is a conservation area, which the 50-mile Suffolk Coastal Path makes walkable throughout. With all the miles of meandering rivers and superb stretches of coastline, it is only natural that watery pursuits are a popular pastime, and everything from sailing to scuba diving, angling to powerboat racing, is available. Many of the local museums also have a nautical theme, and the Suffolk coast has

been a source of inspiration for many of the nation's most distinguished artists, writers and composers.

North and East of Bury St Edmunds

Pakenham

4 mile NE of Bury St Edmunds off the A143

On a side road just off the A143 (turn right just north of Great Barton) lies the village of Pakenham, whose long history has been unearthed in the shape of a Bronze Age barrow and kiln, and another kiln from Roman times.

Elsewhere in Pakenham are the 17th century **Nether Hall**, from whose lake in the park the village stream flows through the fen into the millpond. From the same period dates **Newe House**, a handsome Jacobean building with Dutch gables and a two-storey porch. The Church of St Mary has an impressive carved Perpendicular font, and in its adjacent vicarage is the famous Whistler Window - a painting by Rex Whistler of an 18th century parish priest. The fens were an important source of reeds, and many of Pakenham's buildings show off the thatcher's art.

Pakenham's current unique claim to fame is in being the last parish in England to have a working watermill *and* windmill, a fact proclaimed on the village sign. The **watermill** was built around 1814 on a site mentioned in the *Domesday Book* (the Roman excavations suggest that there could have been a mill here as far back as the 1st century AD). The mill, which is fed from Pakenham fen, has many interesting features, including the Blackstone oil engine, dating from around 1900, and the Tattersall Midget rollermill from 1913, a brave but ultimately unsuccessful attempt to compete with the larger roller mills in the production of flour. The mill and the neighbouring recreation park are well worth a visit.

No less remarkable is the **Windmill**, one of the most famous in Suffolk. The black-tarred tower was built in 1831 and was in regular use until the 1950s. One of the best preserved mills in the county, it survived a lightning strike in 1971.

Both mills lie on the village's circular walks, and fresh flour is available from both.

Ixworth

5 miles NE of Bury St Edmunds on the A143

Ixworth played its part as one of the Iceni tribe's major settlements, with important Roman connections and, in the 12th century, the site of an Augustinian priory. The remains of the priory were incorporated into a Georgian house known as Ixworth Abbey, which stands among trees by the River Blackbourne. The village has many 14th century timber-framed dwellings, and the Church of St Mary dates from the same period, though with many later additions.

A variety of circular walks take in lovely parts of the village, which is also the staring point of the Miller's Trail cycle route.

A little way north of the village, on the A1088, are a nature trail and bird reserve at Ixworth Thorpe Farm. At this point a brief diversion northwards up the A1088 is very worth while.

THE GREYHOUND

High Street, Ixworth, Suffolk IP31 2HJ
Tel: 01359 230887

The Greyhound is a classic village pub dating back to the early 1800s. Handsome and beautifully maintained, everything gleams in this welcoming and comfortable inn. Decorated in 1950s style, it is open Mon-Sat 11.00-14.30 and 18.00-23.00; Sun 12.00-15.00 and 19.00-22.30. Popular with locals and visitors alike, there's a great choice of beers, wines and spirits, and the menu offers

delicious and hearty home-cooked dishes at lunch (12.00-14.00) and dinner (18.00-20.00) every day.

Bardwell

7 miles NE of Bury St Edmunds just off the A1088

Bardwell offers another tower windmill. This one dates from the 1820s and was worked by wind for 100 years, then by an oil engine until 1941. It was restored in the 1980s, only to suffer severe damage in the great storm of October 1987, when its sails were torn off. Stoneground flour is still produced by an auxiliary engine, and there's an on-site bakery. Also in this delightful village are a 16th century inn and the Church of St Peter and St Paul, known particularly for its medieval stained glass.

Honington

7 miles NE of Bury St Edmunds on the A1088

Back on the A1088, the little village of Honington was the birthplace of the pastoral poet Robert Bloomfield (1766-1823), whose best known work is *The Farmer's Boy*. The house where he was born is now divided, one part called Bloomfield Cottage, the other Bloomfield Farmhouse. A brass plaque to his memory can be seen in All Saints Church, in the graveyard of which his parents are buried.

Euston

9 miles N of Bury St Edmunds on the A1088

Euston Hall, on the A1088, has been the seat of the Dukes of Grafton for 300 years. It's open to the public on Thursday afternoons and is well worth a visit, not least for its portraits of Charles II and its paintings by Van Dyck, Lely and Stubbs. In the colourful landscaped grounds is an ice-house disguised as an Italianate temple, the distinguished work of John Evelyn and William Kent.

Euston's church, in the grounds of the Hall, is the only one in the county dedicated to St Genevieve. It's also one of only two Classical designs in the county, being rebuilt in 1676 on part of the original structure. The interior is richly decorated, with beautiful carving on the hexagonal pulpit, panelling around the walls and a carved panel of the Last Supper. Parts of this lovely wood carving are attributed by some to Grinling Gibbons. Behind the family pew is a marble memorial to Lord Arlington, who built the church.

Euston's watermill was built in the 1670s and rebuilt in 1730 as a Gothic church.

Stanton

7 miles NE of Bury St Edmunds on the A143

Stanton is mentioned in the *Domesday Book*; before that, the Romans were here. A double ration of medieval churches - All Saints and St John the Baptist - will satisfy the ecclesiastical scholar, while for more worldly indulgences **Wyken Vineyards** will have a strong appeal. Four acres of gardens - herb, knot, rose, kitchen and woodland - are on the same site, and the complex also includes an Elizabethan manor house, a 16th century barn, a country shop and a café as well as a splendid woodland walk.

THE ROYAL GEORGE

Church Road, Barningham, Suffolk IP31 1DD
Tel: 01359 221246
e-mail: killydufc@aol.com

More like a cosy and charming home than a pub, **The Royal George** is a delightful thatched inn where good food and drink and a warm welcome are guaranteed. This stunning little village pub really is as good as it looks – surrounded by beautiful gardens and with an expertly designed interior that combines the best of the old world and new. The superb restaurant offers delicious freshly prepared home-cooked dishes at lunch (Mon-Sat 12.00-14.30; Sun 12.00-16.00) and dinner (Mon-Thurs 18.00-21.00; Fri-Sat 18.00-21.30)

Barningham

8 miles NE of Bury St Edmunds on the B1111

Near the Norfolk border, Barningham was the first home of the firm of Fisons, which started in the late 18th century. Starting with a couple of windmills, they later installed one of the earliest steam mills in existence. The engine saw service for nearly 100 years and is now in an American museum; the mill building exists to this day, supplying animal feed.

This is marvellous walking country, and **Knettishall Heath Country Park**, on 400 acres of prime Breckland terrain, is the official starting place of the Peddars Way National Trail to Holme-next-Sea and of the Angles Way Regional Path that stretches 77 miles to Great Yarmouth by way of the Little Ouse and Waveney valleys.

Walsham-le-Willows

9 miles NE of Bury St Edmunds off the A143

A pretty name for a pretty village, with weather-boarded and timber-framed cottages along the willow-banked river which flows throughout its length. **St Mary's** church is no less pleasing to the eye, with its sturdy western tower and handsome windows in the Perpendicular style. Of particular interest inside is the superb tie and hammerbeam roof of the nave, and (unique in Suffolk, and very rare elsewhere) a tiny circular medallion which hangs suspended from the nave wall, known as a 'Maiden's Garland' or 'Virgin's Crant'. These marked the pew seats of unmarried girls who had passed away, and the old custom was for the young men of the village to hang garlands of flowers from them on the anniversary of a girl's death. This particular example celebrates the virginity of one Mary Boyce, who died (so the inscription says) of a broken heart in 1685, just 20 years old. There is also a carving on the rood screen which looks rather like the face of a wolf: this may well be a reference to the benevolent creature that plays such an important role in the legend of St Edmund. A museum by the church has changing exhibitions of local history.

Rickinghall

*12 miles NE of Bury St Edmunds
on the A143*

More timber-framed buildings, some
thatched, are dotted along the streets of
the two villages, Superior and Inferior,
which follow an underground stream
running right through them. Each has a
church dedicated to St Mary and
featuring fine flintwork and tracery. The
upper church, now closed, was used as a
school for London evacuees during the
Second World War.

Redgrave

*13 miles NE of Bury St Edmunds
on the B1113*

Arachnophobes beware! Redgrave and
Lopham Fens form a 360-acre reserve of
reed and sedge beds where one of the
most interesting inhabitants is the Great
Raft Spider. The village is the source of
the Little Ouse and Waveney rivers,
which rise on either side of the B1113
and set off on their seaward journeys in
opposite directions.

Half Moon Street, Redgrave

Thelnetham

*12 miles NE of Bury St Edmunds
off the B111*

West of Redgrave between the B1113
and the B1111 lies Thelnetham – which
boasts a windmill of its own. This one is
a tower mill, built in 1819 to replace a
post mill on the same site, and worked
for 100 years. It has now been lovingly
restored. Stoneground flour is produced
and sold at the mill. If you wish to visit
you should set sail on a summer Sunday
or Bank Holiday Monday; other times
by appointment.

Cotton

*16 miles E of Bury St Edmunds off
the B1113*

South of Finningham, where Yew Tree
House displays some fine pargetting, and
just by Bacton, a lovely village originally
built round seven greens, lies the village
of Cotton, which should be visited for
several reasons, one of which is to see
the splendid 14th century flint church of
St Andrew, impressive in its dimensions
and notable for its double hammerbeam
roof with carved angels.

**Cotton's Mechanical Music Museum
& Bygones** (see panel opposite) has an
extensive collection that includes
gramophones, music boxes, street pianos,
fairground organs and polyphons, as well
as the marvellous Wurlitzer Theatre
pipe organ.

Hessett

*4 miles E of Bury St Edmunds off
the A14*

Dedicated to St Ethelbert, King of East

MECHANICAL MUSIC MUSEUM & BYGONES

Blacksmith Road, Cotton, Nr. Stowmarket,
Suffolk IP14 4QN
Tel: 01449 613876

There are musical treasures aplenty at the **Mechanical Music Museum & Bygones**, which houses a unique collection of music boxes, polyphons, street pianos, pianolas and organs. Stars of the show include a Limonaire fairground organ dating from around 1850 and a mighty Wurlitzer theatre organ originally installed in the Stilwell Theatre, Brooklyn, in 1926. It was later shipped to England and for many years graced London's Luxury Theatre (later the Leicester Square Theatre), which was built by the great star Jack Buchanan. The Mechanical Museum acquired the Wurlitzer in the early 1980s. The Museum, which also boasts a large collection of teapots and musical memorabilia, is open on Sunday afternoons from June to September, and for an annual fair organ enthusiasts day on the first Sunday in October.

Anglia, Hessett's church has many remarkable features, particularly some beautiful 16th century glass and wall paintings, both of which somehow escaped the Puritan wave of destruction. Ethelbert was unlucky enough to get on the wrong side of the mighty Offa, King of the Mercians, and was killed by him at Hereford in 794.

Woolpit

6 miles E of Bury St Edmunds on the A14

The church of St Mary the Virgin is Woolpit's crowning glory, with a marvellous porch and one of the most magnificent double hammerbeam roofs in the county. Voted winner of Suffolk Village of the Year in 2000, the village was long famous for its brick industry, and the majority of the old buildings are faced with 'Woolpit Whites'. This yellowish-white brick looked very much like more expensive stone, and for several centuries was widely exported. Some was used in the building of the Senate wing of the Capitol Building in Washington DC. Red bricks were also

THE WHITE HORSE

Station Road, Finningham, Stowmarket,
Suffolk IP14 4 TL
Tel: 01449 781250

Set in several acres in a prime location in the small village of Finningham, **The White Horse** is a distinctive Grade II listed traditional coaching inn dating back to the mid-16th century. Brightly painted outside, the interior is charming and welcoming, divided into cosy areas where guests can enjoy the excellent home-cooked food, well-kept drink and convivial hospitality on offer.

produced, and the village **Museum**, open in summer, has a brick-making display and also tells the story of the evolution of the village. Woolpit also hosts an annual music festival.

Nearby is a moated site known as **Lady's Well**, a place of pilgrimage in the Middle Ages. The water from the spring was reputed to have healing properties, most efficacious in curing eye troubles.

A favourite Woolpit legend concerns the *Green Children*, a brother and sister with green complexions who appeared one day in a field, apparently attracted by the church bells. Though hungry, they would eat nothing until some green beans were produced. Given shelter by the lord of the manor, they learned to speak English and said that they came from a place called St Martin. The boy survived for only a short time, but the girl thrived, lost her green colour, was baptised and married a man from King's Lynn – no doubt leaving many a Suffolk man green with envy!

Elmswell
7 miles E of Bury St Edmunds off the A14

Clearly visible from the A14, the impressive church of St John the Baptist with its massive flint tower stands at the entrance to the village, facing Woolpit across the valley. A short drive north of Elmswell lies **Great Ashfield**, an unspoilt village whose now disused airfield played a key role in both World Wars. In the churchyard of the 13th century All Saints is a memorial to the Americans who died during the Second World War, as attested

to by the commemorative altar. Some accounts say that Edmund was buried here in AD 903 after dying at the hands of the Danes; a cross was put up in his memory. The cross was replaced in the 19th century and now stands in the garden of Ashfield House.

Haughley
12 miles E of Bury St Edmunds off the A14

On the run into Stowmarket, Haughley once had the largest motte-and-bailey castle in Suffolk. All that now remains is a mound behind the church. **Haughley Park** is a handsome Jacobean redbrick manor house set in eight acres of gardens and surrounding woodland featuring ancient oaks and splendid magnolias. Woodland paths take the visitor past a half-mile stretch of rhododendrons, and in springtime the bluebells and lilies of the valley are a magical sight. The gardens are open on Tuesdays between May and September, the house by appointment only.

Harleston
9 miles E of Bury St Edmunds off the A14

The churches of Shelland and Harleston lie in close proximity on a minor road between Woolpit and Haughley picnic site. At Shelland, the tiny church of King Charles the Martyr is one of only four in England to be dedicated to King Charles I. The brick floor is laid in a herringbone pattern, there are high box pews and a triple-decker pulpit, but the most unusual feature is a working barrel organ dating from the early 19th century.

The church of St Augustine at Harleston stands all alone among pine trees and is reached by a track across a field. It has a thatched roof, Early English windows and a tower with a single bell.

Stowmarket

The largest town in the heart of Suffolk, Stowmarket enjoyed a period of rapid growth when the River Gipping was still navigable to Ipswich and when the railway arrived.

Much of the town's history and legacy are brought vividly to life in the splendid **Museum of East Anglian Life** (see panel opposite), situated in the centre of town to the west of the marketplace (where markets are held twice a week), in a 70-acre meadowland site on the old Abbot's Hall Estate (the aisled original barn dates from the 13th century). Part of the open-air section features several historic buildings that have been moved from elsewhere in the region and carefully re-erected on site. These include an engineering workshop from the 1870s, part of a 14th century farmhouse, a watermill from Alton and a wind pump which was rescued in a collapsed state at Minsmere in 1977. There's also a collection of working steam engines, farm animals and year-round demonstrations of all manner of local arts and crafts, from coopering to chandlery, from sheep shearing to saddlery.

Stowmarket's church of St Peter and St Mary acquired a new spire in 1994, replacing the 1715 version (itself a replacement) which was dismantled on

MUSEUM OF EAST ANGLIAN LIFE

Stowmarket, Suffolk IP14 1DL
Tel: 01449 612229 Fax: 01449 672307
website: www.suffolkcc.gov.uk/central/meal

The Museum of East Anglian Life occupies a 70-acre site in the heart of Stowmarket. Its rich collections of social, rural and industrial history include a number of historic buildings such as a working watermill, a smithy, a chapel and a 13th century farmhouse. There is something for the whole family to enjoy with a variety of farm animals, adventure playground, picnic sites, café and gift shop. Throughout the year the Museum holds special events as well as demonstrations of crafts and engines in steam. The Museum is open from April to October.

safety grounds in 1975.

The town certainly merits a leisurely stroll, while for a peaceful picnic the riverbank beckons. Serious scenic walkers should make for the **Gipping Valley River Park** walk, which follows the former towpath all the way to Ipswich.

Around Stowmarket

Buxhall

3 miles W of Stowmarket just off the B1115

The village church here is notable for its six heavy bells, but the best-known landmark in this quiet village is undoubtedly the majestic tower mill, without sails since a gale removed them in 1929 but still standing as a silent, sturdy reminder of its working days. This is good walking country, with an ancient wood and many signposted footpaths.

Needham Market

4 miles SE of Stowmarket off the A14

A thriving village whose greatest glory is the wonderful carvings on the ceiling of the church of **St John the Baptist**. The church's ornate double hammerbeam roof is nothing short of remarkable, especially when bathed in light from the strategically placed skylight. The roof is massive, as high as the walls of the church itself; the renowned authority on Suffolk churches, H Munro Cautley, described the work at Needham as 'the culminating achievement of the English carpenter'. The village also boasts some excellent examples of Tudor architecture.

The River Gipping flows to the east of the High Street and its banks provide miles of walks: the towpath is a public right of way walkable all the way from Stowmarket to Ipswich. On the riverbank at Needham is a 25-acre picnic site and a nature reserve.

Monthly farmers' markets are held at Alder Carr Farm, where there is also a pottery, crafts centre and farm shop.

Nearby **Barking**, on the B1018 south of Needham, was once more important than its neighbour, being described in 1874 as 'a pleasant village ... including the hamlet of Needham Market'. This explains the fact that Barking's church is exceptionally large for a village house of worship: it was the mother church to Needham Market and was used for Needham's burials when Needham had no burial ground of its own.

Baylham

7 miles SE of Stowmarket off the B11130

The Roman site of Combretrovium is home to **Baylham House Rare Breeds Farm**, and visitors (April-early October) will find displays and information relating to both Rome and rare animals. The farm's chief concern is the survival of rare breeds, and there are breeding groups of cattle, sheep, pigs, goats and poultry.

Bramford

11 miles SE of Stowmarket off the A14

Bramford has a pretty little church, St Mary's, with a 13th century stone screen. It was once an important spot on the river route, when barges from Ipswich stopped to unload corn; the walls of the old lock are still visible. In the vicinity is **Suffolk Water Park**, where the lake welcomes canoeists and windsurfers.

Earl Stonham

6 miles E of Stowmarket on the A1120

A scattered village set around three greens in farming land, Earl Stonham's church of St Mary the Virgin boasts one of Suffolk's finest single hammerbeam roofs, and is also notable for its Bible scene murals, the 'Doom' (Last Judgement scene) over the chancel arch and a triple hour-glass, presumably to record just how protracted were some of the sermons.

Stonham Aspal

7 miles E of Stowmarket on the A1120

On the other side of the A140 lies Stonham Aspal, where in 1962 the remains of a Roman bath-house were unearthed. The parish church has an unusual wooden top to its tower, a necessary addition to house the ten bells that a keen campanologist insisted on installing. At Stonham Barns, the **British Birds of Prey and Nature Centre** is home to every British owl, together with raptors from Britain and around the world. These wonderful birds flap their wings in regular flying displays, and in the Pets Paradise area children can meet and greet hamsters and horses, mice and meerkats, parrots and piglets.

Earl Soham

12 miles E of Stowmarket on the A1120

Earl Soham comprises a long, winding street that was once part of a Roman road. It lies in a valley, and on the largest of its three greens the village sign is a carved wooden statue of a falconer given as a gift by the Women's Institute in 1953. The 13th century church of St Mary is well worth a visit.

Saxtead Green

14 miles E of Stowmarket off the A1120

One of the prettiest sights in Suffolk is the white **18th century mill** that stands on the marshy green in Saxtead. This is a wonderful example of a post mill, perhaps the best in the world, dating back to 1796 and first renovated in the 19th century. It worked until 1947 and has since been kept in working order, with the sails turning even though the mill no longer grinds. In summer, visitors can climb into the buck (body) of this elegant weather-boarded

THE ROSE

Debenham Road, Crowfield, Suffolk IP6 9TE
Tel: 01473 890368

Dating from the early 19th century, **The Rose** is an attractive little country pub with a long and happy history of providing great food, drink and hospitality to all its guests. Inside the décor and furnishings are simple and comfortable – all is cosy and warm here, making it the perfect setting for enjoying a quiet drink or meal. The separate restaurant has well-chosen menus offering a good range of delicious meals at lunch and dinner Tues-Sun, all expertly prepared and presented.

construction and explore its machinery.

Framlingham

18 miles NE of Stowmarket on the B1119

The marvellous **Castle**, brooding on a hilltop, dominates this agreeable market town, as it has since

Framlingham Castle

Roger Bigod, 2nd Earl of Norfolk, built it in the 12th century (his grandfather built the first a century earlier, but this wooden construction was soon demolished). The Earls and Dukes of Norfolk, the Howards, were here for many generations before moving to Arundel in 1635. The castle is in remarkably good condition, partly because it was rarely attacked – though King John put it under siege in 1215. Its most famous occupant was Mary Tudor, who was in residence when proclaimed Queen in 1553. During the reign of Elizabeth I it was used as a prison for defiant priests and, in the 17th century after being bequeathed to Pembroke

College, Cambridge, it saw service as a home and school for local paupers. Nine of the castle's 13 towers are accessible - the climb up the spiral staircase and walk round the battlements are well worth the effort. On one side the view is of the Meres, a bird sanctuary. In the north wing is the **Lanman Museum**, devoted to agricultural, craftsman's tools and domestic memorabilia.

The castle brought considerable prestige and prosperity to Framlingham, evidence of which can be found in the splendid church of **St Michael**, which has two wonderful works of art. One is the tomb of Henry Fitzroy, bastard son of Henry VIII, beautifully adorned with

---

HIGH HOUSE FARM

Cransford, Framlingham, Suffolk IP13 9PO
Tel: 01728 663461 Fax: 01728 663409
e-mail: info@highhousefarm.co.uk
website: www.highhousefarm.co.uk

Hidden away from the hustle and bustle, **High House Farm** is a gracious and elegant 16th century farmhouse offering excellent bed and breakfast and self-catering accommodation. Open all year round, this charming place is decorated and furnished tastefully, with an accent on traditional comforts. Set alongside 250 acres of rolling farmland, this relaxed and peaceful place is well worth finding.

scenes from Genesis and Exodus and in a superb state of repair. The other is the tomb of the 3rd Duke, with carvings of the apostles in shell niches. Also of note is the Carolean organ of 1674, a gift of Sir Robert Hitcham, to whom the Howards sold the estate. Cromwell and the Puritans were not in favour of organs in churches, so this instrument was lucky to have escaped the mass destruction of organs at the time of the Commonwealth. Sir Robert is buried in the church.

Dennington
2 miles N of Framlingham on the B1116

The pretty little village of Dennington boasts one of the oldest post offices in the country, this one having occupied the same site since 1830. The village church has some very unusual features, none more so than the hanging 'pyx' canopy above the altar. A pyx served as a receptacle for the Reserved Sacrament, which would be kept under a canopy attached to weights and pulleys so that the whole thing could be lowered when the sacrament was required for the sick and the dying.

The church also has many interesting carvings, the most remarkable being that of a skiapod, the only known representation in this county of a mythical creature of the African desert, humanoid but with a huge boat-shaped foot with which it could cover itself against the sun.

This curious beast was 'known' to Herodotus and to Pliny, who remarked that it had 'great pertinacity in leaping'. In the chapel at the top of the south aisle stands the tomb of Lord Bardolph, who fought at Agincourt, and of his wife, their effigies carved in alabaster.

Charsfield
5 miles S of Framlington off the B1078

A minor road runs from Framlingham through picturesque Kettleburgh and Hoo to Charsfield, best known as the inspiration for Ronald Blyth's book *Akenfield*, later memorably filmed by Sir Peter Hall. A cottage garden in the village displays the Akenfield village sign and is open to visitors in the summer.

Otley
7 miles SW of Framlingham on the B1079

The 15th century **Moated Hall** in Otley is open to the public at certain times of the year. Standing in ten acres of gardens that include a canal, a nuttery

Otley Hall

and a knot garden, the hall was long associated with the Gosnold family, whose coat of arms is also that of the village. The best-known member of that family was Bartholomew Gosnold, who sailed to the New World, coined the named 'Martha's Vineyard' for the island off the coast of Massachusetts, discovered Cape Cod and founded the settlement of Jamestown, Virginia. The 13th century church of St Mary has a remarkable baptistry font measuring 6 feet in length and 2 feet 8 inches in depth. Though filled with water, the font is not used and was only discovered in 1950 when the vestry floor was raised. It may have been used for adult baptisms.

Framsden
7 miles SW of Framlingham on the B1077

The scenery in these parts is real picture-postcard stuff, and in the village of Framsden the picture is completed by a fine **Post Mill**, built high on a hill in 1760, refitted and raised in 1836 and in commercial use until 1934. The milling machinery is still in place and the mill is open for visits (at weekends, by appointment only).

Cretingham
4 miles SW of Framlingham off the A1120

The village sign is the unusual item here, in that it has two different panels: one shows an everyday Anglo-Saxon farming scene, the other a group (of Danes?) sailing up the River Deben, with the locals fleeing. The signs are made from mosaic tiles.

Brandeston
3 miles SW of Framlingham off the A1120

A further mile to the east, through some charming countryside, Brandeston is another delightful spot, with a row of beautiful thatched cottages and the parish **Church of All Saints** with its 13th century font. The best-known vicar of Brandeston was John Lowes (1572-1646) who was accused of witchcraft by the villagers, interrogated by Witchfinder General Matthew Hopkins and hanged at Bury St Edmunds. His sad end was made even sadder by the fact that before being strung up he had to read out the burial service of a condemned witch himself, as no priest was allowed to conduct the service. Hopkins made a handsome living out of this bizarre business, preying on the superstitions of the times and using the foulest means to obtain confessions. One account of Hopkins' end is that he himself was accused of being a witch and hanged. The less satisfactory alternative is that he died of tuberculosis.

Debenham
10 miles E of Stowmarket on the B1077

Debenham is a sizable village of architectural distinction, with a profusion of attractive timber-framed buildings dating from the 14th to the 17th centuries. The River Deben flows beside and beneath the main street and, near one of the little bridges, weavers still practise their craft. There is also a pottery centre. St Mary's Church is unusual in having an original Saxon tower, and the roof alternates hammerbeams with crested tie beams.

Mendlesham

6 miles NE of Stowmarket off the A140

On the green in Old Market Street, Mendlesham, lies an enormous stone which is said to have been used as a preaching stone, mounted by itinerant Wesleyan preachers. In the Church of St Mary there is a collection of parish armour assembled some 400 years ago, and also some fine carvings. The least hidden local landmark is a 1,000-ft TV mast put up by the IBA in 1959.

Wetheringsett

7 miles NE of Stowmarket off the A140

On the other side of the A140, Wetheringsett is where visitors will find **Mid-Suffolk Light Railway Museum**, open on summer Sundays and during school holidays.

Wetheringsett has had two well-known rectors, famous for very different reasons. Richard Hakluyt, incumbent from 1590 to 1616, is remembered for his major work *Voyages* (full title *Principal Navigation, Voiages, Traffiques and Discoveries of the English Nation*). The rector between 1858 and 1883 was a certain George Wilfrid Ellis, sometime

tailor and butler, and finally a bogus clergyman. After he was unmasked as a sham, a special Act of Parliament was needed to validate the marriage ceremonies he had illegally performed, and to legitimise the issue of those marriages.

Thornham Magna & Parva

10 miles N of Stowmarket off the A140

The **Thornham Walks and Field Centre**, with 12 miles of walks and a herb garden and nursery, cater admirably for hikers, horticulturists and lovers of the countryside. The tiny thatched church of St Mary at Thornham Parva houses a considerable treasure in the shape of an exquisite medieval altar painting, known as a *retable*, with a central panel depicting the Crucifixion and four saints on each side panel. Its origins are uncertain, but it was possibly the work of the Royal Workshops at Westminster Abbey and made for Thetford Priory, or for a nearby Dominican monastery. Also to be admired is the 14th century octagonal font and a series of fascinating wall paintings. In the churchyard is a monument to Sir Basil Spence (1907-76), architect of Coventry Cathedral.

Yaxley

12 miles N of Stowmarket on the A140

Yaxley's church of **St Mary** offers up more treasures. One is an extremely rare sexton's wheel, which hangs above the south door and was used in medieval times to select fast days in honour of the Virgin. When a pair of iron wheels were spun on their axle, strings attached to the outer wheel would catch on the inner, stopping both and indicating the chosen day. The 17th century pulpit is one of the finest in the country, with the most glorious, sumptuous carvings.

Eye
13 miles NE of Stowmarket on the B1117

The name of this excellent little town is derived from the Saxon for an island, as Eye was once surrounded by water and marshes. The church of **St Peter and St Paul** stands in the shadow of a mound on which a castle once stood (the remains are worth a look and the mound offers a panoramic view of the town – almost a bird's eye view, in fact). The church's 100-foot tower was described by Pevsner as 'one of the wonders of Suffolk' and the interior is a masterpiece of restoration, with all the essential medieval features in place. The rood screen, with painted panels depicting St Edmund, St Ursula, Edward the Confessor and Henry VI, is particularly fine.

Other interesting Eye sights are the ornate redbrick **Town Hall**; the timbered **Guildhall**, with the archangel Gabriel carved on a corner post; a 'crinkle-crankle' (serpentine) wall fronting Chandos Lodge, where Sir Frederick Ashton once lived; and a thriving theatre, one of the smallest professional theatres in the country.

Hoxne
4 miles NE of Eye on the B1118

Palaeolithic remains indicate the exceptionally long history of Hoxne (pronounced Hoxon), which stands along the banks of the River Waveney near the Norfolk border. It is best known for its links with King Edmund, who was reputedly killed here, though Bradfield St Clare and Shottisham have rival claims to this distinction. The Hoxne legend is that Edmund was betrayed to the Danes by a newlywed couple who were crossing the Goldbrook bridge and spotted his golden spurs reflected from his hiding place below the bridge. Edmund put a curse on all newlyweds crossing the bridge, and to this day some brides take care to avoid it.

The story continues that Edmund was tied to an oak tree and killed with arrows. That same oak mysteriously fell down in 1848 while apparently in good health, and a monument at the site is a popular tourist attraction. In the church of St Peter and St Paul an oak screen (perhaps that very same oak?) depicts scenes from the martyr's life. A more cheerful event is the Harvest Breakfast on the village green that follows the annual service.

Horham
6 miles E of Eye on the B1117

Three distinct musical connections distinguish this dapper little village. The Norman church has had its tower strengthened for the rehanging of the peal of eight bells, which is believed to be the oldest in the world. Benjamin Britten, later associated with the Aldeburgh Festival, lived and composed in Horham for a time, and on a famous day during the Second World War, Glenn Miller brought his band here to celebrate the 200th flying mission to set out from the American aerodrome.

Worlingworth

8 miles SE of Eye off the B1118

It's well worth taking the country road to Worlingworth, a long, straggling village whose church of St Mary has a remarkable font cover reaching up about 30 feet. It is brilliantly coloured and intricately carved, and near the top is an inscription in Greek which translates as 'wash my sin and not my body only.' Note, too, the Carolean box pews, the carved pulpit and an oil painting of Worlingworth's Great Feast of 1810 to celebrate George III's jubilee.

Wingfield

6 miles E of Eye off the B1118

Wingfield College is one of the country's most historic seats of learning, founded in 1362 as a college for priests with a bequest from Sir John de Wingfield, Chief Staff Officer to the Black Prince. Sir John's wealth came from ransoming a French nobleman at the Battle of Poitiers in 1356. Surrendered to Henry VIII at the time of the Dissolution, the college became a farmhouse and is now in private hands. The facade is now Georgian, but the original medieval Great Hall still stands, and the college and its three acres of gardens are open to the public at weekends in summer. Attractions include regular artistic events and printing demonstrations.

The church of St Andrew was built as the collegiate church and has an extra-large chancel to accommodate the college choir. The church contains three really fine monuments: to Sir John (in stone); to Michael de la Pole, 2nd Earl of Suffolk (in wood); and to John de la Pole, Duke of Suffolk (in alabaster). In the churchyard there is a 'hudd' – a shelter for the priest for use at the graveside in bad weather.

On a hill outside the village are the imposing remains of a castle built by the 1st Earl.

traditional 16th century farmhouse boasts three lovely and comfortable guest bedrooms.

Fressingfield
10 miles E of Eye on the B1116

Heveningham Hall

Fressingfield's first spiritual centre was the **Church of St Peter and St Paul**. It has a superb hammerbeam roof and a lovely stone bell tower that was built in the 14th century. On one of the pews the initials A P are carved. These are believed to be the work of Alice de la Pole, Duchess of Norfolk and grand-daughter of Geoffrey Chaucer. Was this a work of art or a bout of vandalism brought on by a dull sermon?

At nearby **Ufford Hall** lived the Sancroft family, one of whom became Archbishop of Canterbury. He led the revolt of the bishops against James II and was imprisoned in the Tower of London. Released by William IV and sacked for refusing to swear the oath of allegiance, he returned home and is entombed by the south porch of the church.

The village sign is a pilgrim and a donkey, recording that Fressingfield was a stopping place on the pilgrim route from Dunwich to Bury St Edmunds.

Laxfield
12 miles E of Eye on the B1117

Laxfield & District Museum, in the 16th century Guildhall, gives a fine insight into bygone ages with geology and natural history exhibits, agricultural and domestic tools, a Victorian kitchen, a village shop and a costume room. The museum is open on Saturday and Sunday afternoons in summer.

The Fox & Goose Inn

Fressingfield, Suffolk IP21 5PB
Tel: 01379 586247 Fax: 01379 586106
e-mail: foxandgoose@uk2.net
website: www.foxandgoose.net

The Fox & Goose Inn was once a Guild Hall, built in about 1509. Divided into several elegant rooms, the accent here is on great food, with menus offering up a broad range of Modern English and French dishes making use of the freshest seafood, game, produce and more, all home-cooked to order. To

complement the food there is an excellent wine list, together with real ales, lagers, spirits and soft drinks.

All Saints Church is distinguished by some wonderful flint 'flushwork' (stonework) on its tower, roof and nave. In the 1808 Baptist church is a plaque remembering John Noyes, burnt at the stake in 1557 for refusing to take Catholic vows. History relates that the villagers - with a single exception - dowsed their fires in protest. The one remaining fire, however, was all that was needed to light the stake.

A couple of miles east of Laxfield, **Heveningham Hall** is a fine Georgian mansion, a model of classical elegance designed by James Wyatt with lovely grounds by Capability Brown. As it runs through the grounds, the River Blyth widens into a lake.

Along the Coast

Dunwich

4 miles SW of Southwold off the B1105

Surely the hidden place of all hidden places, Dunwich was once the capital of East Anglia, founded by the Burgundian Christian missionary St Felix and for several centuries a major trading port (wool and grain out; wine, timber and cloth in) and a centre of fishing and shipbuilding. The records show that in 1241 no fewer than 80 ships were built here for the king. By the middle of the next century, however, the sea attacked from the east and a vast bank of sand and shingle silted up the harbour. The course of the river was diverted, the town was cut off from the sea and the

town's trade was effectively killed off. For the next 700 years the relentless forces of nature continued to take their toll, and all that remains now of ancient Dunwich are the ruins of a Norman leper hospital, the archways of a medieval friary and a buttress of one of the nine churches which once served the community.

Today's village comprises a 19th century church and a row of Victorian cottages, one of which houses the **Dunwich Museum**. Local residents set up the museum in 1972 to tell the Dunwich story; the historical section has displays and exhibits from Roman, Saxon and medieval times, the centrepiece being a large model of the town at its 12th century peak. There are also sections devoted to natural history, social history and the arts.

Experts have calculated that the main part of old Dunwich extended up to seven miles beyond its present boundaries, and the vengeance of the sea has thrown up inevitable stories of drama and mystery. The locals say that when a storm is threatening, the sound of submerged church bells can still be heard tolling under the waves as they shift in the currents. Other tales tell of strange lights in the ruined priory and the eerie chanting of long-gone monks.

Dunwich Forest, immediately inland from the village, is one of three – the others are further south at Tunstall and Rendlesham – named by the Forestry Commission as Aldewood Forest. Work started on these in 1920 with the planting of Scots pine, Corsican pine and some Douglas fir; oak and poplar were tried but did not thrive in the sandy soil. The three forests, which between them cover nearly 9,000 acres, were almost completely devastated in the hurricane of October 1987, Rendlesham alone losing more than a million trees. Replanting will take many years to be established.

South of the village lies **Dunwich Heath**, one of Suffolk's most important conservation areas, comprising the beach, splendid heather, a field study centre, a public hide and an information centre and restaurant in converted coastguard cottages. 1998 marked the 30th anniversary of the heath being in the care of the National Trust.

Around Dunwich Heath are the attractive villages of Westleton, Middleton, Theberton and Eastbridge.

In **Westleton**, the 14th century thatched church of St Peter, built by the monks of Sibton Abbey, has twice seen the collapse of its tower. The first fell down in a hurricane in 1776; its smaller wooden replacement collapsed when a bomb fell during the Second World War.

The village is also the main route of access to the RSPB-managed **Minsmere Bird Sanctuary**, the most important sanctuary for wading birds in eastern England. The marshland was flooded during the Second World War, and nature and this wartime emergency measure created the perfect habitat for innumerable birds. More than 100 species nest here, and a similar number of birds visit throughout the year. It is thus a birdwatcher's paradise, with many hides, and the **Suffolk Coastal Path** runs along the foreshore.

A little way inland from Westleton lies **Darsham**, where another nature reserve is home to many varieties of birds and flowers.

Yoxford

10 miles SW of Southwold on the A12

Once an important stop on the London-to-Yarmouth coaching route, Yoxford now attracts visitors with its pink-washed cottages and its arts and crafts, antiques and food shops. Look for the cast-iron signpost outside the church, with hands pointing to London,

THE FOX INN

Fox Lane, Darsham, Saxmundham, Suffolk, IP17 3QE
Tel: 01728 668436

Modern amenities and old-fashioned traditional charm meet at **The Fox Inn**, a delightful rural pub that offers great food and drink. The menus are put together with flair and passion, to provide diners with a range of fresh fish, steaks and many other tempting, home-made dishes and light snacks. Meals are served every day at lunch (12.00-14.30)

and dinner (19.00-21.00). The atmosphere at this excellent inn is always friendly and welcoming.

THE BLOIS ARMS

High Street, Yoxford, Suffolk IP17 3EP
Tel: 01728 668238
e-mail: nigel.trapp@btopenworld.com

Occupying a corner site in the village high street, **The Blois Arms** is a large and handsome pub. Pleasant, clean and bright with a genuinely warm and welcoming atmosphere, there's a good range of food and drink every day and two guest bedrooms. Whether looking for a quiet drink, a home-cooked meal or comfortable accommodation, all provided with a friendly smile and real hospitality, look no further.

THE BELL INN

Middleton, Yoxford, Suffolk
Tel: 01728 648286

The Bell Inn is a charming, part-thatched traditional pub that draws customers from far and wide. This well-kept secret boasts a delightful small public bar with wood floors, solid wood tables and chairs, low ceilings with oak beams and open fires, together with an exquisite little restaurant with feature fireplace. All food is home-cooked and delicious (served daily 12.00-14.00 and 19.00-21.00), and the range of beers, wines, spirits and soft drinks has something to quench every thirst.

Yarmouth and Framlingham set high enough to be seen by the driver of a stagecoach.

Saxmundham

12 miles SW of Southwold off the A12

A little town that was granted its market charter in 1272. On the font of the church in Saxmundham is the carving of a 'woodwose' - a tree spirit or green man. He, and others like him, have given their name to a large number of pubs in Suffolk and elsewhere.

Bruisyard

4 miles NW of Saxmundham off the B1119

Just west of this village is the **Bruisyard** **Vineyard, Winery and Herb Centre**, a complex of a 10-acre vineyard with 13,000 Müller Thurgau grape vines, a wine-production centre, herb and water gardens, a tea shop and a picnic site.

Peasenhall

6 miles NW of Saxmundham on the A1120

A little stream runs along the side of the main street in Peasenhall, whose buildings present several styles and ages. Most distinguished is the old timbered **Woolhall**, splendidly restored to its 15th century grandeur. The oddest is certainly a hall in the style of a Swiss chalet, built for his workers by James Josiah Smyth, grandson of the founder of James Smyth & Sons. This company, renowned for its agricultural drills, was for more than two centuries the dominant industrial presence in Peasenhall. On the south side of St Michael's churchyard stands the 1805 drill-mill where James Smyth manufactured his Nonpareil seed drills, one of which is on display in Stowmarket's museum.

Leiston
4 miles E of Saxmundham off the B1119

The first **Leiston Abbey** was built on Nunsmere marshes in 1182, but in 1363 the Earl of Suffolk rebuilt it on its present site. It became one of the largest and most prestigious monasteries in the country, and its wealth probably spelled its ruin, as it fell within Henry VIII's plan for the Dissolution of the Monasteries. A new abbey was built near the ruins of the old, and the restored old hall is used as a base for PROCORDA, a group promoting musical excellence.

For 200 years the biggest name in Leiston was that of Richard Garrett, who founded an engineering works here in 1778 after starting a business in Woodbridge. In the early years ploughs, threshers, seed drills and other agricultural machinery were the main products, but the company later started one of the country's first production lines for steam machines. The Garrett works are now the **Long Shop Museum**, the factory buildings having been lovingly restored, and many of the Garrett machines are now on display, including traction engines, a steam-driven tractor

and a road roller. There's also a section where the history and workings of steam engines are explained. A small area of the museum recalls the USAAF's 357th fighter group, who flew from an airfield outside Leiston during the Second World War. One of their number, a Captain Chuck Yeager, was the first man to fly faster than the speed of sound

The Garrett works closed in 1980, but what could have been a disastrous unemployment situation was alleviated to some extent by the nuclear power station at **Sizewell**. The coast road in the centre of Leiston leads to this establishment, where visitors can take tours - on foot with access to buildings at Sizewell A or by minibus, with a guide and videos, round Sizewell B.

Aldringham
4 miles E of Saxmundham on the B1122

Aldringham's church is notable for its superb 15th century font, and the village inn was once a haunt of smugglers. It now helps to refresh the visitors who flock to the **Aldringham Craft Market**, founded in 1958 and extending over three galleries, with a serious selection of arts and crafts, clothes and gifts, pottery, basketry, books and cards.

Thorpeness
6 miles E of Saxmundham on the B1353

Thorpeness is a unique holiday village with mock-Tudor houses and the general look of a series of eccentric film sets.

House in the Clouds, Thorpeness

House in the Clouds, it is now available to rent as a holiday home. The neighbouring mill, moved lock, stock and millstones from Aldringham, stopped pumping in 1940 but has been restored and now houses a visitor centre. Every August, in the week following the Aldeburgh Carnival, a regatta is held on the Meare, culminating in a splendid fireworks show. Thorpeness is very much a one-off, not at all typical Suffolk but with a droll charm that is all its own.

Buying up a considerable packet of land called the Sizewell estate in 1910, the architect, barrister and playwright Glencairn Stuart Ogilvie created what he hoped would be a fashionable resort with cottages, some larger houses and a shallow boating and pleasure lake called the Meare. The 85-foot water tower, built to aid in the lake's construction, looked out of place, so Ogilvie disguised it as a house. Known ever since as the

Aldeburgh
6 miles SE of Saxmundham on the A1094

And so down the coast road to Aldeburgh, another coastal town that once prospered as a port with major

MARSHWINDS

32 Saxmundham Road, Aldeburgh,
Suffolk IP15 5JE
Tel: 01728 452695
website: www.marshwinds.co.uk

Marshwinds is an elegant and charming seaside retreat with two spacious, modern and attractive en suite guest bedrooms, each of which has been decorated and furnished to the highest standards of comfort and quality. Just a 15-minute walk from the front door to the seafront, this wonderful place enjoys a warm and relaxed ambience. Contemporary prints, photographs, modern ceramics and

wooden artefacts enhance the appeal of this attractive and welcoming home.

fishing and shipbuilding industries. Drake's *Greyhound* and *Pelican* were built at Slaughden, now taken by the sea, and during the 16th century some 1,500 people were engaged in fishing. Both industries declined as shipbuilding moved

Beach, Aldeburgh

elsewhere and the fishing boats became too large to be hauled up the shingle.

Suffolk's best-known poet, George Crabbe, was born at Slaughden in 1754 and lived through the village's hard times. He reflected the melancholy of those days when he wrote of his fellow townsmen:

Here joyless roam a wild amphibious race,
With sullen woe displayed in every face;
Who far from civil arts and social fly,
And scowl at strangers with suspicious eye.

He was equally evocative concerning the sea and the river, and the following lines written about the River Alde could apply to several others in the county:

With ceaseless motion comes and goes the tide
Flowing, it fills the channel vast and wide;
Then back to sea, with strong majestic sweep
It- rolls, in ebb yet terrible and deep;
Here samphire-banks and salt-wort bound the flood
There stakes and seaweed withering on the mud;
And higher up, a ridge of all things base,
Which some strong tide has rolled upon the place.

It was Crabbe who created the character of the solitary fisherman Peter Grimes, later the subject of an opera composed by another Aldeburgh resident, Benjamin Britten.

Aldeburgh's role gradually changed into that of a holiday resort, and the Marquess of Salisbury, visiting early in the 19th century, was one of the first to be attracted by the idea of sea-bathing without the crowds. By the middle of the century the grand houses that had sprung up were joined by smaller residences, the railway had arrived, a handsome water tower was put up (1860) and Aldeburgh prospered once more. There were even plans for a pier, and construction started in 1878, but the project proved too difficult or too expensive and was halted, the rusting girders being removed some time later.

One of the town's major benefactors was Newson Garrett, a wealthy businessman who was the first mayor under the charter of the Local Government Act of 1875. This colourful character also developed the **Maltings at**

Snape, but is perhaps best remembered through his remarkable daughter Elizabeth, who was the first woman doctor in England (having qualified in Paris at a time when women could not qualify here) and the first woman mayor (of Aldeburgh, in 1908). This lady married the shipowner James Skelton Anderson, who established the golf club in 1884.

Aldeburgh

If Crabbe were alive today he would have a rather less cantankerous opinion of his fellows, especially at carnival time on a Monday in August when the town celebrates with a colourful procession of floats and marchers, a fireworks display and numerous other events.

As for the arts, there is, of course, the **Aldeburgh Festival**, started in 1948 by Britten and others; the festival's main venue is Snape Maltings, but many performances take place in Aldeburgh itself.

The town's maritime connections remain very strong. There has been a lifeboat here since 1851, and down the years many acts of great heroism have been recorded. The very modern lifeboat station is one of the town's chief attractions for visitors, and there are regular practice launches from the shingle beach. A handful of fishermen still put out to sea from the beach, selling their catch from their little wooden huts, while a thriving yacht club is the base for sailing on the Orde and, sometimes, on the sea.

At the very southern tip of the town, the Martello tower serves as a reminder of the power of the sea: old pictures show it standing well back from the waves, but now the seaward side of the moat has disappeared and the shingle is constantly being shored up to protect it. Beyond it, a long strip of marsh and shingle stretches right down to the mouth of the river at Shingle Street.

Back in town there are several interesting buildings, notably the **Moot Hall** and the parish church of **St Peter and St Paul**. The Moot Hall is a 16th century timber-framed building that was built in what was once the centre of town. It hasn't moved, but the sea long ago took away several houses and streets. Inside the Hall is a museum of town history and finds from the nearby Snape burial ship. Britten set the first scene of Peter Grimes in the Moot Hall. A sundial on the south face of the Hall proclaims, in Latin, that it only tells the time when the sun shines.

The church, which stands above the town as a very visible landmark for mariners, contains a memorial to George Crabbe and a beautiful stained-glass window, the work of John Piper, depicting three Britten parables: *Curlew River*, *The Burning Fiery Furnace* and *The Prodigal Son*. Britten is buried in the churchyard, part of which is set aside for the benefit of wildlife.

Friston

3 miles SE of Saxmundham off the A1094

Friston's **Post Mill**, the tallest in England, is a prominent sight on the Aldeburgh-Snape road, moved from Woodbridge in 1812 just after its construction. It worked by wind until 1956, then by engine until 1972.

Snape

3 miles S of Saxmundham on the A1094

This 'boggy place' has a long and interesting history. In 1862 the remains of an Anglo-Saxon ship were discovered here, and since that time regular finds have been made, with some remarkable cases of almost perfect preservation. Snape, like Aldeburgh, has benefited over the years from the philanthropy of the Garrett family, one of whose members built the primary school and set up the Maltings, centre of the Aldeburgh Music Festival.

The last 30-odd years have seen the development of the **Snape Maltings Riverside Centre**, a group of shops and galleries located in a complex of restored Victorian granaries and malthouses that is also the setting for the renowned Aldeburgh festival. The Maltings began their designated task of converting grain into malt in the 1840s, and continued thus until 1965, when the pressure of modern techniques brought them to a halt. There was a real risk of the buildings being demolished, but George Gooderham, a local farmer, bought the site to expand his animal feeds business and soon saw the potential of the redundant buildings (his son Jonathan is the current owner of the site).

The Concert Hall came first, in 1967,

HONEYPOT LODGE

Aldecar Lane, Benhall Green, Saxmundham,
Suffolk IP17 1HN
Tel/Fax: 01728 602449
e-mail: honeypot@freeuk.com

In a secluded spot tucked away off the main thoroughfare, **Honeypot Lodge** is a delightful place to stay, with two attractive and comfortable en suite guest bedrooms. Tastefully furnished and decorated, with extensive grounds and heated swimming pool, it makes a relaxing and welcoming place to

enjoy a break or use as a base from which to explore this part of Suffolk. 4 Diamonds ETB.

The Maltings, Snape

and in 1971 the Craft Shop was established as the first conversion of the old buildings for retail premises. Conversion and expansion continue to this day, and in the numerous outlets visitors can buy anything from fudge to country-style clothing, from herbs to household furniture, silver buttons to top hats. Plants and garden accessories are also sold, and art galleries feature the work of local painters, potters and sculptors. The Centre hosts regular painting, craft and decorative art courses, and more recent expansion saw the creation of an impressive country-style store.

A short distance west of Snape, off the B1069, lies Blaxhall, famed for its growing stone. The **Blaxhall Stone**, which lies in the yard of Stone Farm, is reputed to have grown to its present size (5 tons) from a comparative pebble the size of a football, when it first came to local attention 100 years ago. Could there be more 'Blarney' than Blaxhall at work here?

Campsea Ashe
6 miles NE of Woodbridge on the B1078

On towards Wickham Market the road passes through Campsea Ashe in the parish of Campsey Ashe. The 14th century church of St John the Baptist has an interesting brass showing one of its first rectors in full priestly garb.

DOG & DUCK

Station Road, Campsea Ashe, Ipswich, Suffolk IP13 0PS
Tel: 01728 748439

A large and welcoming pub, **Dog & Duck** is an inviting and relaxed place where great food and drink, fine accommodation and warm hospitality are guaranteed. There's a good range of ales, wines, spirits and soft drinks to quench your thirst, and steak pie is just one house speciality in a menu of hearty traditional favourites, served at lunch and dinner Thurs-Tues. The excellent

accommodation comprises five comfortable en suite guest bedrooms.

Wickham Market

5 miles N of Woodbridge off the A12

Places to see in this straggling village are the picturesque watermill by the River Deben and All Saints Church, whose 137-foot octagonal tower has a little roof to shelter the bell. At Boulge, a couple of miles southwest of Wickham Market, is the grave of Edward Fitzgerald, whose free translation of *The Rubaiyat of Omar Khayyam* is an English masterpiece. Tradition has it that on his grave is a rose bush grown from one found on Omar Khayyam's grave in Iran.

Easton

5 miles N of Woodbridge off the B1078

A scenic drive leads to the lovely village of Easton, one of the most colourful, flower-bedecked places in the county. A remarkable sight to the west of the village is the two-mile-long **Crinkle-Crankle Wall** that surrounds Easton Park. This extraordinary type of wall, also known as a ribbon wall, weaves snake-like in and out and is much stronger than if it were straight. This particular wall, said to be the world's longest, was built by Lord of the Manor, the Earl of Rochford, in the 1820s.

Tucked away three miles off the A12 in the beautiful Deben Valley, **Easton Park Farm** is one of Suffolk's greatest attractions. 2003 sees its 30th year, and in that time more than a million visitors have passed through the gates to have a great day out; they leave knowing a lot more about the ways of the countryside than when they arrived. It's a marvellous place to bring the family, as the children can have endless fun feeding and making friends with the animals in Pets Paddock, riding ponies or simply running around in the adventure playground. The showpiece of the park is the Victorian dairy, an ornate octagonal building, while the Dairy Centre is contrastingly modern, with walkways over the top of the stalls and a viewing gallery over the milking parlour.

Parham

8 miles N of Woodbridge on the B1116

Parham Airfield is now agricultural

THE CHEQUERS INN

The Street, Kettleburgh, Suffolk IP13 7JS
Tel/Fax: 01728 723760
e-mail: info@thechequers.net

The River Deben runs along the rear garden of **The Chequers**, an impressive 19th century pub that is well worth seeking out. Open 12.00-15.00 and 18.00-23.00 six days a week, and 12.00-15.00 and 19.00-22.30 Sundays, there's an excellent range of drinks on offer, good food served at lunch and dinner every day, and the atmosphere is always welcoming

and relaxed. Elegant and traditional, the décor and furnishings are comfortable and attractive.

land, but in the control tower and an adjacent hut can be found memorabilia of the 390th Bomb Group of the USAAF.

Ufford
4 miles N of Woodbridge off the A12

Pride of place in a village that takes its name from Uffa (or Wuffa), the founder of the leading Anglo-Saxon dynasty, goes to the 13th century **Church of the Assumption**. The font cover, which telescopes from 5 feet to 18 feet in height, is a masterpiece of craftsmanship, its elaborate carving crowned by a pelican. Many 15th century benches have survived, but Dowsing smashed the organ and most of the stained glass – what's there now is mainly Victorian, some of it a copy of 15th century work at All Souls College, Oxford. Ufford is where the Suffolk Punch originated, Crisp's 404 being, in 1768, the progenitor of this distinguished breed of horses.

Bredfield
3 miles N of Woodbridge off the A12

There's a plaque on the wall of the village pub in Bredfield commemorating a day in 1742 on which nothing at all happened. On a day in 1809, however, something *did* happen: Edward Fitzgerald was born.

Something else happened in 1953: a wrought-iron canopy with a golden crown, made at the village forge, was put on the crossroads pump to celebrate Queen Elizabeth II's coronation.

Woodbridge
Udebyge, Wiebryge, Wodebryge, Wudebrige ... just some of the ways of spelling this splendid old market town since it was first mentioned in writing back in AD 970. As to what the name means, it could simply be 'wooden bridge' or 'bridge by the wood', but the most likely and most interesting explanation is that it is derived from Anglo-Saxon words meaning 'Woden's (or Odin's) town'. Standing at the head of the Deben estuary, it is a place of considerable charm with a wealth of handsome, often historic buildings and a considerable sense of history, as both a market town and a port.

River Deben, Woodbridge

The shipbuilding and allied industries flourished here, as at most towns on the Suffolk coast, and it is recorded that both Edward III, in the 14th century, and Drake in the 16th sailed in Woodbridge ships. There's still plenty of activity on and by the river, though nowadays it is all leisure-orientated. The town's greatest benefactor was Thomas Seckford, who rebuilt the abbey, paid for the chapel in the north aisle of St Mary's Church and founded the original almshouses in Seckford Street. In 1575 he gave the town the splendid Shire Hall on Market Hill. Originally used as a corn exchange, it now houses the **Suffolk Punch Heavy Horse Museum**, with an exhibition devoted to the Suffolk Punch breed of heavy working horse, the oldest such breed in the world. The history of the breed and its rescue from near-extinction in the 1960s is covered in fascinating detail, and there's a section dealing with the other famous Suffolk breeds – the Red Poll cattle, the Suffolk sheep and the Large Black pigs. Opposite the Shire Hall is **Woodbridge Museum**, a treasure trove of information on the history of the

town and its more notable residents; from here it is a short stroll down the cobbled alleyway to the magnificent parish church of St Mary, where Seckford was buried in 1587.

Seckford naturally features prominently in the museum, along with the painter Thomas Churchyard, the map-maker Isaac Johnson and the poet Edward Fitzgerald. 'Old Fitz' was something of an eccentric and, for the most part, fairly reclusive. He loved Woodbridge and particularly the River Deben, where he often sailed in his little boat *Scandal*.

Woodbridge is lucky enough to have two marvellous mills, both in working order, and both great attractions for the visitor. The **Tide Mill**, on the quayside close to the town centre, dates from the late 18th century (though the site was mentioned 600 years previously) and worked by the power of the tide until 1957. It has been meticulously restored and the waterwheel still turns, fed by a recently created pond which replaced the original huge mill pond when it was turned into a marina. **Buttrum's Mill**, named after the last miller, is a tower

TURKS HEAD

Low Road, Hasketon, Woodbridge,
Suffolk IP13 6JG
Tel: 01394 382584

More like a charming family home than a pub, **Turks Head** is a charming little brickbuilt 16th century low house that is welcoming inside and out. This traditional rural pub is a relaxed and cosy place to enjoy the excellent range of food and drink on offer. All the meals are home-made and make use of fresh local beef, fish and other ingredients, served at lunch and

dinner. Well worth seeking out, this lovely pub also has camping facilities on-site.

mill standing just off the A12 bypass a mile west of the town centre. A marvellous sight, its six storeys make it the tallest surviving tower mill in Suffolk. There is a ground-floor display of the history and workings of the mill.

Many of the town's streets are traffic-free, so shopping is a real pleasure. If you should catch the Fitzgerald mood and feel like 'a jug of wine and a loaf of bread', Woodbridge can oblige with a good variety of pubs and restaurants.

Around Woodbridge

Sutton Hoo
1 mile E of Woodbridge off the B1083

A mile or so east of Woodbridge on the opposite bank of the Deben is the **Sutton Hoo Burial Site**, a group of a dozen grassy barrows which hit the headlines in 1939. Excavations brought to light the outline of an 80-foot long Anglo-Saxon ship, filled with one of the greatest hoards of treasure ever discovered in Britain. The priceless find includes gold coins and ornaments, silverware, weapons and armoury, drinking horns and leather cups; it is housed in the British Museum in London, but there are exhibitions, replicas and plenty of other items of interest at the site. Research continues, and it is now believed that the ship was the burial place of Raedwald, of the Wuffinga dynasty, King of East Anglia from about AD 610 to AD 625. Access to the site is on foot from the B1083.

Rendlesham
5 miles NE of Woodbridge on the A1152

The church of **St Gregory the Great** dates from the 14th century, but there is evidence (not physical, unfortunately) of an earlier Christian presence in the shape of Raedwald's palace.

Rendlesham Forest, part of the Forest of Aldewood, was ravaged by the great hurricane of October 1987. Seven years before that, on Christmas night, another visitation had occurred. Security guards at RAF Woodbridge, at that time a front line NATO base, spotted strange lights in the forest and went to investigate. They came upon a nine-foot high triangular object with a series of lights around it. As they approached, it did what all good UFOs do and flew off before it could be photographed. The next day the guards returned to the spot where it had landed and found three depressions in the ground. The UFO was apparently sighted again two days later, and security in the area was heightened. No explanation has ever been forthcoming about the incident, but interest in it continues and from time to time guided walks to the landing site are arranged.

Butley
5 miles NE of Woodbridge on the B1084

At the northern edge of Rendlesham Forest, the village of Butley has a splendid 14th century gatehouse, all that remains of **Butley Priory**, an

Augustinian priory founded by Ranulf de Glanville in 1171. The gatehouse is, by itself, a fairly imposing building, with some interesting flintwork on the north facade (1320) and baronial carvings. Butley still has a working mill, remarkable for its fine Regency porch, and the parish church is Norman, with a 14th century tower.

There are some splendid country walks here, notably by **Staverton Thicks**, which has a deer park and woods of oak and holly. The oldest trees date back more than 400 years. Butley Clumps is an avenue of beech trees planted in fours, with a pine tree at the centre of each clump – the technical term for such an arrangement is a *quincunx*. Butley was long renowned for its oysters, and the beds have recently been revived.

Chillesford
6 miles E of Woodbridge on the B1084

Brick was once big business here, and while digging for clay the locals made many finds, including hundreds of varieties of molluscs and the skeleton of an enormous whale. Chillesford supplies some of the clay for Aldeburgh brickworks.

Orford
12 miles E of Woodbridge at the end of the B1084

Without doubt one of the most charming and interesting of all the places in Suffolk, Orford has something to please everyone. The ruins of the **Castle**, one of the most important in medieval England, are a most impressive sight, even though the keep is all that remains of the original building commissioned by Henry II in 1165. The walls of the keep are 90 foot high and 10 foot deep, and behind them are many rooms and passages in a remarkable state of preservation. A climb up the spiral staircase to the top provides splendid views over the surrounding countryside and to the sea.

St Bartholomew's Church was built at the same time, though the present church dates from the 14th century. A wonderful sight at night when floodlit, the church is regularly used for the performance of concerts and recitals, and many of Benjamin Britten's works were first heard here. At the east end lie the still-splendid Norman remains, all that is left of the original chancel.

These two grand buildings indicate that Orford was a very important town at one time. Indeed it was once a thriving port, but the steadily growing shingle bank of Orford Ness gradually cut it off from the sea, and down the years its appeal has changed. The sea may have gone but the river is still there, and in summer the quayside is alive with yachts and pleasure craft. On the other side of the river is **Orford Ness**, the largest vegetated shingle spit in England which is home to a variety of rare flora and fauna. The lighthouse marks the most easterly point (jointly with Lowestoft) in Britain.

Access to the spit, which is in the

St Bartholomew's Church, Orford

fair quota of smuggling tales, a well-loved restaurant serving Butley oysters and a smokehouse where kippers, salmon, trout, ham, sausages, chicken and even garlic are smoked over Suffolk oak.

Bawdsey

7 miles SE of Woodbridge on the B1083

The B1083 runs from Woodbridge through farming country and several attractive villages (Sutton, Shottisham, Alderton) to Bawdsey, beyond which lies the mouth of the River Deben, the end of the Sussex Coastal Path, and the ferry to Felixstowe. The late-Victorian Bawdsey Manor was taken over by the Government and became the centre for radar development when Orford Ness was deemed unsuitable. By the beginning of the Second World War there were two dozen secret radar stations in Britain, and radar HQ moved from Bawdsey to Dundee. The manor is now a leisure centre.

Ramsholt

7 miles SE of Woodbridge off the B1083

Ramsholt is a tiny community on the north bank of the Deben a little way up

hands of the National Trust, is by ferry from Orford quay. For many years the Ness was out of bounds to the public, being used for various military purposes, including pre-war radar research under Sir Robert Watson-Watt. Boat trips also leave Orford quay for the RSPB reserve at **Havergate Island**, haunt of avocet and tern (the former returned in 1947 after being long absent).

The Dunwich Underwater Exploration Exhibition in Front Street features exhibits on marine archaeology, coastal erosion and more, gleaned from the exploration of the ruins of the former town of Dunwich, now largely claimed by the sea.

Back in the market square are a handsome town hall, two pubs with a

THE RAMSHOLT ARMS

Dock Road, Ramsholt, Woodbridge,
Suffolk IP12 3AB
Tel: 01394 411229 Fax: 01394 411818
e-mail: ramsholtarms@tinyworld.co.uk
website: www.ramsholtarms.co.uk

Situated on the tidal estuary of the River Deben, **The Ramsholt Arms** is a wonderful inn voted one of the top ten pubs in the country by *The Independent*, popular with locals, holidaymakers, sea-farers and other

visitors from near and far, drawn to the fine views over the river, the excellent choice of local walks and footpaths, and the inn's reputation for its fine food, drink, accommodation and hospitality. Owners Patrick Levy and Elizabeth Bell have a wealth of experience in the trade, and own two other pubs in East Anglia – The White Swan in Stow-cum-Quy, Cambridgeshire, and The Dog Inn at Luddon Bridge, on the Norfolk Broads.

Thought originally to be ferrymen's cottages, this impressive inn has a large terrace overlooking the river, with a sandy beach and grassy area leading down to the riverbank. To the rear there's a large garden. The interior is equally charming, with its blend of original, traditional features such as the exposed beamwork and tasteful décor and furnishings, all adding up to a cosy and relaxed ambience.

Real ales served at this Free House include Adnams Best and Broadside, together with changing guest ales. There's also a good selection of lagers, cider, stout, wines, spirits and soft drinks.

The menu highlights fresh locally-caught fish and game, and the three chefs maintain a constantly changing and mouthwatering selection of home-cooked and freshly prepared meals. The delicious puddings are well worth leaving room for!

The marvellous accommodation comprises three double bedrooms with private baths, handsomely and comfortably decorated and furnished, and commanding wonderful views of the river.

For a delightful retreat that is within easy reach of the many sights and attractions of this part of the county and further afield, The Ramsholt Arms is an excellent choice.

from Bawdsey. The pub is a popular port of call for yachtsmen, and half a mile from the quay, in quiet isolation, stands the Church of All Saints with its round tower. Road access to Ramsholt is from the B1083 just south of Shottisham.

Fishing Boats, Lowestoft

Hollesley

5 miles SE of Woodbridge off the B1083

The Deben and the Ore turn this part of Suffolk almost into a peninsula, and on the seaward side lie Hollesley and Shingle Street. The latter stands upon a shingle bank at the entrance to the Ore and comprises a row of little houses, a coastguard cottage and a Martello tower. Its very isolation is an attraction, and the sight of the sea rushing into and out of the river is worth the journey.

Brendan Behan did not enjoy his visit. Brought here on a swimming outing from the Borstal at Hollesley, he declared that the waves had 'no limit but the rim of the world'. Looking out to the bleak North Sea, it is easy to see what he meant.

Lowestoft

The most easterly town in Britain had its heyday as a major fishing port during the late 19th and early 20th centuries, when it was a mighty rival to Great Yarmouth in the herring industry. That industry has been in major decline since the First World War, but Lowestoft is still a fishing port and the trawlers still chug into the harbour in the early morning with the catches of the night. Guided tours of the **Fish Market** and the **Harbour** are available.

Lowestoft is also a popular holiday resort, the star attraction being the lovely South Beach with its golden sands, safe swimming, two piers and all the expected seaside amusements and entertainments. **Claremont Pier**, over 600 feet in length, was built in 1902, ready to receive day-trippers on the famous Belle steamers. The buildings in this part of town were developed in mid-Victorian times by the company of Sir Samuel Morton Peto, also responsible for Nelson's Column, the statues in the Houses of Parliament, the Reform Club and Somerleyton Hall.

At the heart of the town is the old harbour, home to the **Royal Norfolk & Suffolk Yacht Club** and the **Lifeboat Station**. Further upriver is the commercial part of the port, used chiefly by ships carrying grain and timber. The history of Lowestoft is naturally tied up with the sea, and much of that history is recorded in fascinating detail in the **Lowestoft & East Suffolk Maritime Museum** with model boats, fishing gear, a lifeboat cockpit, paintings and shipwrights' tools. The setting is a flint-built fisherman's cottage in Sparrow's Nest Gardens. The

Fishing at Lowestoft

Royal Naval Patrol Museum nearby remembers the minesweeping service in models, photographs, documents and uniforms.

Lowestoft had England's first lighthouse, installed in 1609. The present one dates from 1874. Also in Sparrow's Nest Gardens is the **War Memorial Museum**, dedicated to those who served during the Second World War. There's a chronological photographic collection of the bombing of the town, aircraft models and a chapel of remembrance.

St Margaret's Church, notable for its decorated ceiling and copper-covered spire, is a memorial to seafarers, and the north aisle has panels recording the names of fishermen lost at sea from 1865 to 1923.

Lowestoft also has some interesting literary and musical connections. The Elizabethan playwright, poet and pamphleteer Thomas Nash was born here in 1567. His last work, *Lenten Stuffe*, was a eulogy to the herring trade and specifically to Great Yarmouth.

Joseph Conrad (Jozef Teodor Konrad Korzeniowski), working as a deckhand on a British freighter bound for Constantinople, jumped ship here in 1878, speaking only a few words of the language in which he was to become one of the modern masters. Benjamin Britten, the greatest English composer of the 20th century, is associated with several places in Suffolk, but Lowestoft has the earliest claim, for it is here that he was born in 1913.

Just north of town, with access from the B1385, **Pleasurewood Hill** is the largest theme park in East Anglia.

Oulton Broad, on the western edge of Lowestoft, is a major centre of amusements afloat, with boats for hire and cruises on the Waveney. It also attracts visitors to Nicholas Everitt Park to look around **Lowestoft Museum**, housed in historic Broad House. Opened by the Queen and Prince Philip in 1985, the museum displays archaeological finds from local sites, some now lost to the sea, costumes, toys, domestic bygones and a fine collection of Lowestoft porcelain. (The porcelain industry lasted from about 1760 to 1800, using clay from the nearby Gunton Hall Estate. The soft-paste ware, resembling Bow porcelain, was usually decorated in white and blue.)

Lowestoft's **ISCA Maritime Museum** (see panel below) has a unique collection of ethnic working boats, including coracles, gondolas, junks, dhows, sampans and proas.

Around Lowestoft
Carlton Colville
3 miles SW of Lowestoft on the B1384

Many a transport enthusiast has enjoyed a grand day out at the **East Anglia Transport Museum**, where children young and old (and very old) can climb aboard to enjoy rides on buses, trams and trolleybuses (one of the resident

---

LOWESTOFT MARITIME MUSEUM

Sparrows Nest Park, Whapload Road,
Lowestoft, Suffolk NR32 1XG
Tel: 01502 561963

Anyone with an interest in the sea and ships should steer a steady course for Britain's most easterly museum under the lighthouse on Whapload Road. Open daily from May to September, **Lowestoft Maritime Museum** specialises in the history of the Lowestoft fishing fleet, from early sail to steam and through to the modern diesel-powered vessels. Methods of fishing are recorded, including trawling and the no longer practised driftnet fishing for herring, and

other displays depict the evolution of lifeboats and the town's association with the Royal Navy.

A replica of the aft cabin of a steam drifter and a fine picture gallery are other attractions of this fascinating museum, where the attendants are ex-seamen and others interested in the port of Lowestoft. They are all delighted to answer any questions visitors

have about the Museum and its exhibits. School parties are particularly welcome, with takeaway educational packs available, and out-of-season parties can be catered for with notice.

The Museum, which is maintained by members of the Lowestoft and East Suffolk Maritime Society, was established in 1968 and extended in 1978, when the Duke of Edinburgh was guest of honour. The objects of the Society are to educate the public in shipping, old and modern, in Lowestoft and the County of Suffolk, and in trades and crafts associated with shipping lore in general and in particular to maintain the Museum.

trolleybuses was built at the Garrett works in Leiston). The East Suffolk narrow-gauge railway winds its way around the site, and there's a 1930s street with all the authentic accessories, plus lorries, vans and steamrollers.

Carlton Marshes is Oulton Broad's nature reserve, with grazing marsh and fen, reached by the Waveney Way footpath.

Blundeston

4 miles N of Lowestoft off the A12

Known chiefly as the village used by Charles Dickens as the birthplace of that writer's 'favourite child', David Copperfield, the morning light shining on the sundial of Blundeston's church – which has the tallest, narrowest Saxon round tower of any in East Anglia – greeted young David as he looked out of his bedroom window in the nearby Rookery. He said of the churchyard: *"There is nothing half so green that I know anywhere, as the grass of that churchyard, nothing half so shady as its trees; nothing half so quiet as its tombstones."*

Blundeston has another notable literary connection: Blundeston Lodge was once the home of Norton Nichols, whose friend the poet Gray is reputed to have taken his inspiration for *An Elegy Written in a Country Church Yard* while staying there.

Lound

5 miles N of Lowestoft off the A12

Lound's parish church of **St John the Baptist**, in the very north of the county,

is sometimes known as the 'golden church'. This epithet is the result of the handiwork of designer/architect Sir Ninian Comper, seen most memorably in the gilded organ-case with two trumpeting angels, the font cover and the rood screen. The last is a very elaborate affair, with several heraldic arms displayed. The surprise package here is the modern St Christopher mural on the north wall. It includes Sir Ninian at the wheel of his Rolls Royce – and in 1976 an aeroplane was added to the scene!

Somerleyton

5 miles NW of Lowestoft on the B1074

Somerleyton Hall (see panel opposite), one of the grandest and most distinctive of stately homes, is a splendid Victorian mansion built in Anglo-Italian style by Samuel Morton Peto. The grounds include a renowned yew-hedge maze, where people have been going round in circles since 1846, walled and sunken gardens, and a 300-foot pergola. There's also a sweet little miniature railway, and **Fritton Lake Countryworld**, part of the Somerleyton Estate, is a 10-minute drive away. The Hall is open to the public on most days in summer.

Samuel Morton Peto learned his skills as a civil engineer and businessman from his uncle, and was still a young man when he put the Reform Club and Nelson's Column into his CV. The Somerleyton Hall he bought in 1843 was a Tudor and Jacobean mansion. He and his architect virtually rebuilt the place,

SOMERLEYTON HALL & GARDENS

Lowestoft, Suffolk NR32 5QQ
Tel: 01502 730224 Fax: 01502 732143
website: www.somerleyton.co.uk

The stately home of Lord and Lady Somerleyton is a splendid early Victorian mansion virtually rebuilt from the Tudor and Jacobean house that stood on the site. The Victorian building was designed by Sir Morton Peto and his architect John Thomas in elaborate Anglo-Italian style, and the facade has many lavish features and magnificent carved stonework. The house was bought from Sir Morton in 1863 by the carpet manufacturer Sir Francis Crossley, whose descendants have occupied it ever since; the present Lord Somerleyton is the great-grandson of Sir Francis.

The Oak Room, with 17th century panelling from the original Jacobean house, some outstanding wood carvings and an exquisite silver and gilt mirror made for the Doge's Palace in Venice, is one of several superb

rooms in this grandest of houses; others include the elegant Library, its walls lined with over 3,500 books; the Dining Room, adorned by some of the Hall's best paintings and some unusual pieces of silver; and the sumptuous ballroom. The splendour of the house is matched by the magnificent gardens, which contain a wide variety of beautiful trees, plants and borders, along with attractive displays of flowers provided by the Victorian glasshouses, which were designed by Sir Joseph Paxton, creator of the Crystal Palace.

One of the highlights of the garden is the yew hedge maze, the work of the celebrated landscape gardener William Nesfield. It was planted in 1846, and has had visitors going round in circles ever since. Other features include some interesting statuary, the walled and sunken gardens and a 70' pergola with an unusual iron framework. A more recent attraction that appeals to all ages is a miniature railway offering fine views of the Hall and surrounding parkland.

and also built Somerleyton village, a cluster of thatched redbrick cottages. Nor was this the limit of Peto's achievements, for he ran a company which laid railways all over the world and was a Liberal MP, first for Norwich, then for Finsbury and finally for Bristol. His company foundered in 1863 and Somerleyton Hall was sold to Sir Francis Crossley, one of three brothers who made a fortune in mass-producing carpets. Crossley's son became Baron Somerleyton in 1916, and the Baron's grandson is the present Lord Somerleyton.

Herringfleet

5 miles NW of Lowestoft on the B1074

Standing above the River Waveney, the parish church of St Margaret is a charming sight with its Saxon round tower, thatched roof and lovely glass. **Herringfleet Windmill** is a beautiful black-tarred smock mill in working order, the last survivor of the Broadland wind pump, whose job was to assist in draining the marshes. This example was built in 1820 and worked regularly until the 1950s. It contains a fireplace and a wooden bench, providing a modicum of comfort for a millman on a cold night shift. To arrange a visit call 01473 583352.

Kessingland
3 miles S of Lowestoft off the A12

A small resort with a big history, Palaeolithic and Neolithic remains have come to light in Kessingland, and traces of an ancient forest have been unearthed on the sea bed. At the time of William the Conqueror, Kessingland prospered with its herring industry and was a major fishing port rivalled only by Dunwich. The estuary gradually silted up, sealing off the river with a shingle bank and cutting off the village's major source of wealth. The tower of the church of St Edmund reaches up almost 100 feet – not unusual on the coast - where it provides a conspicuous landmark for

sailors and fishermen.

Most of Kessingland's maritime trappings have now disappeared: the lighthouse on the cliffs was scrapped 100 years ago, the lifeboat lasted until 1936 (having saved 144 lives), and one of the several former coastguard stations was purchased by the writer Rider Haggard as a holiday home.

The village's major tourist attraction is the **Suffolk Wildlife Park**, 100 acres of coastal parkland that are home to a wide range of wild animals, from aardvarks to zebras by way of bats, flamingos, giraffes, meerkats and sitatunga. The flamingos have their own enclosure. Burmese pythons are used for snake-handling sessions – an experience that's definitely not for everyone!

Covehithe
7 miles S of Lowestoft off the A12

Leave the A12 at Wrentham and head for the tiny coastal village of Covehithe, remarkable for its 'church within a church'. The massive church of **St Andrew**, partly funded by the Benedictine monks at Cluniac, was left

---

to decline after being laid waste by Dowsing's men. The villagers could not afford a replacement on the same grand scale, so in 1672 it was decided to remove the roof and sell off some of the material. From what was left a small new church was built within the old walls. The original tower still stands, spared by Cromwell for use as a landmark for sailors.

Southwold
15 miles S of Lowestoft on the A1095

A town full of character and interest for the holidaymaker and for the historian. Though one of the most popular resorts on the east coast, Southwold has very little of the kiss-me-quick commercialism that spoils so many seaside towns. It's practically an island, bounded by creeks and marshes, the River Blyth and the North Sea, and has managed to retain the genteel atmosphere of the 19th century. There are some attractive buildings, from pink-washed cottages to elegant Georgian

town houses, many of t around a series of greens undeveloped to act as fir much of the town was los fire of 1659.

In a seaside town whose present a wide variety of styles, shapes and sizes, William Denny's **Buckenham House** is among the most elegant and interesting. On the face of it a classic Georgian town house, it's actually much older, dating probably from the middle of the 16th century. Richard Buckenham, a wealthy Tudor merchant, was the man who had it built and it was truly impressive in size, as can be deduced from the dimensions of the cellar (now the Coffee House). Many fine features survive, including moulded cornices, carefully restored sash windows, Tudor brickwork and heavy timbers in the ceilings.

The town, which was granted its charter by Henry VII in 1489, once prospered, like many of its neighbours, through herring fishing, and the few remaining fishermen share the harbour

Sole Bay Inn
East Green, Southwold, Suffolk IP18 6JN
Tel: 01502 723736

Located just yards from the sea near the Adnam's Brewery and in the shadow of the impressive lighthouse, **Sole Bay Inn** is a handsome pub with bags of character.

Hidden away in a maze of streets, this charming pub offers a friendly and warm welcome to all guests, and a range of excellent food and drink.

All meals are home-made; the menu is made up of traditional favourites served at lunch (12.00-14.00) in winter and from midday till 6 p.m. July to September.

River Blyth with pleasure craft. Also adding to the period atmosphere is the pier, though as a result of storm damage this is much shorter than in the days when steamers from London called in on their way up the east coast.

There are also bathing huts, and a brilliant white lighthouse that's over 100 years old. It stands 100 feet tall and its light can

Southwold Beach

be seen 17 miles out to sea. Beneath the lighthouse stands a little Victorian pub, the Sole Bay Inn, whose name recalls a battle fought off Southwold in 1672 between the British and French fleets and the Dutch. This was an episode in the Third Anglo-Dutch War, when the Duke of York, Lord High Admiral of England and later to be crowned James II, used Sutherland House in Southwold as his headquarters and launched his fleet (along with that of the French) from here. One distinguished victim of this battle was Edward Montagu, 1st Earl of Sandwich, great-grandfather of the man whose gambling mania did not allow him time for a formal meal. By inserting slices of meat between slices of bread, the 4th Earl ensured that his name would live on.

The Sole Bay Inn is one of several owned by the local brewery Adnams. One of the best known is the Lord Nelson, where traces can be seen of a smugglers' passageway leading to the cliffs. Where there were smugglers, there are usually ghosts, and here it's a man in a frock coat who disappears into the cliff face. Adnams still use horse-drawn drays for local beer deliveries.

Southwold's maritime past is recorded in the **Museum** set in a Dutch-style cottage in Victoria Street. Open daily in the summer months, it records the famous battle and also features exhibits on local archaeology, geology and natural history, and the history of the Southwold railway. The **Southwold Sailors' Reading Room** contains pictures, ship models and other items, and at Gun Hill the **Southwold Lifeboat Museum** has a small collection of RNLI-related material with particular reference to Southwold. The main attraction at Gun Hill is a set of six 18-pounder guns, captured in 1746 at the Battle of Culloden and presented to the town (hitherto more or less undefended) by the Duke of Cumberland.

No visitor to Southwold should leave without spending some time in the splendid church of **St Edmund King and Martyr**, which emerged relatively unscathed from the ravages of the Commonwealth. The lovely painted roof and wide screen are the chief glories, but the slim-stemmed 15th century pulpit and the Elizabethan Holy Table must also be seen. Inside the church there's also a splendid 'Jack o' the Clock' – a little wooden man in War of the Roses armour, holding a bell. A rope is pulled to sound the bell to mark the start of church services.

Wangford
2 miles NW of Southwold off the A12

There's some great walking in the country around Southwold, both along the coast and inland. At Wangford, a mile or so inland, **Henham Walks** are waymarked paths through Repton Park, lake and woods. A splendid place for a ramble or a picnic, or to see the wildlife, rare-breed sheep and Highland cattle,

the paths are open only on specific dates, and there's an entry fee.

Also at Wangford is the Perpendicular church of St Peter and St Paul, built on the site of a Benedictine priory. Even closer to Southwold is Reydon Wood Nature Reserve.

Blythburgh
2 miles SW of Southwold, A1095 then A12

Blythburgh's church of **Holy Trinity** is one of the wonders of Suffolk, a stirring sight as it rises from the reed beds, visible for miles around and floodlit at night to spectacular effect. This 'Cathedral of the Marshes' reflects the days when Blythburgh was a prosperous port with a bustling quayside wool trade. With the silting up of the river, trade rapidly fell off and the church fell into decay. In 1577 the steeple of the 14th century tower was struck by lightning in a severe storm; it fell into the nave, shattering the font and taking two lives. The scorch marks visible to this day on the north door are said to be the claw marks of the Devil in the guise of

hellhound Black Shuck, left as he sped towards Bungay to terrify the congregation of St Mary's.

Disaster struck again in 1644, when Dowsing and his men smashed windows, ornaments and statues, blasted the wooden angels in the roof with hundreds of bullets and used the nave as a stable, with tethering rings screwed into the pillars of the nave. Luckily, the bench-end carvings escaped the desecration, not being labelled idolatrous. These depict the Labours of the Months, and the Seven Deadly Sins. Blythburgh also has a Jack o'the Clock, a brother of the figure at Southwold, and the priest's chamber over the south porch has been lovingly restored complete with an altar made with wood from *HMS Victory*. The angels may have survived, but the font was defaced to remove the signs of the sacraments.

A mile south, at the junction of the A12 and the Walberswick road, **Toby's Walks** is an ideal place for a picnic and, like so many places in Suffolk, has its own ghost story. This concerns Tobias Gill, a dragoon drummer who murdered a local girl and was hanged here after a trial at Ipswich. His ghost is said to haunt the heath, but this should not deter picnic-makers. The **Norman Gwatkin Nature Reserve** is an area of marsh and fen with two hides, walkways and a willow coppice.

Wenhaston
5 miles W of Southwold off the A12

The church of **St Peter** is well worth a detour. Saxon stones are embedded in its walls, but the most remarkable feature is the Doom (Last Judgement scene), said to have been painted around 1500 by a monk from Blythburgh.

Walberswick
1 miles SW of Southwold on the B1387

The story is familiar: flourishing fishing port; grand church; changing of the coastline due to erosion and silting; decline of fishing and trading; no money to maintain the church; church falls into disrepair. Towards the end of the 16th century, a smaller church was built within the original St Andrew's, by then in ruins through neglect. The situation in Walberswick had also

The River Blithe, Walberswick

HUNTSMAN & HOUNDS

Stone Street, Spexhall, Halesworth,
Suffolk IP19 0RN
Tel: 01986 781341

A 15th century traditional country inn offering
a warm welcome and genuine hospitality,
Huntsman & Hounds is a family-run business
specialising in good food and real ale.
Spacious and attractive, with open log fires
adding to the cosy and comfortable ambience,
it's well worth a visit.

All food is home-cooked and uses the
freshest ingredients for lunchtime and evening
menus seven days a week. Three rooms en
suite B&B or self-catering accommodation
also available.

been exacerbated by the seizing of
church lands and revenues by the King,
and by a severe fire.

Fishing hardly exists today, and
boating in Walberswick is almost
entirely a weekend and holiday activity.
The tiny 'church within a church' is still
in use, its churchyard a nature reserve.
South of the village is the bird sanctuary
of **Walberswick & Westleton Heaths**.

For more than two centuries,
Walberswick has been a magnet for
painters, with the religious ruins, the
beach and the sea being favourite
subject for visiting artists. The tradition
continues unabated, and many
academics have also made their
homes here.

Halesworth
16 miles SW of Lowestoft on the A144

Granted a market in 1222, Halesworth
reached the peak of its trading
importance when the River Blyth was
made navigable as far as the town in
1756. A stroll around the streets reveals
several buildings of architectural
interest. The Market Place has a
handsome Elizabethan timber-framed
house, but the chief attraction for the
visitor is the **Halesworth and District
Museum** at the railway station, in
Station Road, where exhibits feature
local geology and archaeology, with
various fossils and flints on display, and

THE TRIPLE PLEA

Broadway, Halesworth, Suffolk IP19 8QW
Tel: 01986 874750
e-mail: teresa.fleming@virgin.net

The Triple Plea is an excellent country inn
dating back to the 1700s. Its name comes
from an old legend recounting the story of a
dying man whose body, money and soul are
being fought over by a doctor, lawyer and
parson respectively. Here you'll find a warm
welcome from new owners Teresa and
Michael, as well as great food, drink and

service. Open: Mon-Sat 11.00-23.00; Sun
12.00-22.30. Meals served 11.00-15.00;
18.00-23.00; bar snacks available at
other times.

there's also a fascinating account of the Halesworth witchcraft trials of 1645.

Halesworth Gallery, at Steeple End, holds a collection of contemporary paintings, sculpture and other artwork in a converted row of 17th century almshouses.

Bramfield

3 miles S of Halesworth on the A144

The massive Norman round tower of **St Andrew's** Church is separate from the main building and was built as a defensive structure, with walls over 3 feet thick. Dowsing ran riot here in 1643, destroying 24 superstitious pictures, one crucifix, a picture of Christ and 12 angels on the roof. The most important monument is one to Sir Arthur Coke, sometime Lord Chief Justice, who died in 1629, and his wife Elizabeth. Arthur is kneeling, resplendent in full armour, while Elizabeth is lying on her bed with a baby in her arms. This monument is the work of Nicholas Stone, the most important English mason and sculptor of his day. The Cokes at one time occupied Bramfield Hall, and another family, in residence for 300 years, were the Rabetts, whose coat of arms in the church punningly depicts rabbits on its shield.

Bungay

9 miles N of Halesworth on the A144

An ancient fortress town on the River Waveney, the river played an important part in Bungay's fortunes until well into the 18th century, with barges laden with coal, corn, malt and timber plying the route to the coast. The river is no longer navigable above Geldeston, but is a great attraction for anglers and yachtsmen.

Bungay is best known for its **Castle**, built in its original form by Hugh Bigod, 1st Earl of Norfolk, as a rival to Henry II's castle at Orford. In 1173 Hugh took the side of the rebellious sons of Henry, but this insurrection ended with the surrender of the castle to the King. Hugh was killed not long after this episode while on the Third Crusade; his son Roger inherited the title and the castle, but it was another Roger Bigod who came to Bungay in 1294 and built the round tower and mighty outer walls that stand today.

To the north of the castle are Bungay's two surviving churches of note (the *Domesday Book* records five). The Saxon round tower of **Holy Trinity Church** is the oldest complete structure in the town, and a brass plate on the door commemorates the church's narrow escape from the fire of 1688 that destroyed much of the town (similar disasters overtook many other towns with close-set timber-and-thatch buildings). The church of **St Mary** - now deconsecrated - was not so lucky, being more or less completely gutted. The tower survives to dominate the townscape, and points of interest in the church itself include a woodcarving of the Resurrection presented by Rider Haggard, and a monument to General

Robert Kelso, who fought in the American War of Independence.

A century before the fire, the church received a visit, during a storm, from the devilish Black Shuck, a retriever-like hound who, hot from causing severe damage at Blythburgh, raced down the nave and killed two worshippers. A weather vane in the market place puts the legend into verse:

> *All down the church in midst of fire*
> *The Hellish Monster Flew*
> *And Passing onwards to the Quire*
> *He many people slew.*

Nearby is the famous octagonal **Butter Cross**, rebuilt after the great fire of 1688 and topped by Justice with her scales and sword. This building was once used as a prison, with a dungeon below.

Earsham
1 mile SW of Bungay off the A143

All Saints Church and Earsham Hall are well worth a visit, but what brings most people here is the **Otter Trust**, on the banks of the Waveney, where the largest collection of otters in natural enclosures are bred for re-introduction into the wild. There are some lovely walks by the lakes and river.

Flixton
2 miles SW of Bungay on the B1062

Javelin, Meteor, Sea Vixen, Westland Whirlwind: names that evoke earlier days of flying, and just four of the 20 aircraft on show at The **Norfolk and**

NORFOLK & SUFFOLK AVIATION MUSEUM

The Street, Flixton, Nr. Bungay,
Suffolk NR35 1NZ Tel: 01986 896644
e-mail: nsam.flixton@virgin.net
website: www.aviationmuseum.net

Founded in 1972, the **Norfolk & Suffolk Aviation Museum** was officially opened to the public in 1976. Set in the picturesque Waveney Valley, the complex covers 7½ acres, with unique undercover exhibitions, military and civil, from the pioneer days through World War I, the inter-war years, World War II right up to the present day.

The Museum incorporates the Museums of the 446th Bomber Group, Royal Observer Corps, RAF Bomber Command, Air-Sea Rescue and Coastal Command. More than 25 historic aircraft are on display, along with engines, missiles, guns, bombs and ejector seats. Throughout the Museum there are examples of aviation art, together with themed displays, including WWII decoy sites, Civil Defence, telephones, compasses,

models and (perhaps the most fascinating of all) wreckology - the digging for the remains of aircraft in areas where they are known to have crashed.

Among the aircraft on display are an Avro Anson C19, the first aircraft acquired by the Museum; a Dassault Mystère IVA, a Vampire, a Meteor, a Javelin and two Westland helicopters. The Museum, officially recognised as East Anglia's Aviation Heritage Centre, is located on the B1062 off the A143 a mile west of Bungay. Admission is free, the Museum relying on money put in the donation boxes or spent in the shop or NAAFI.

Suffolk Aviation Museum (see panel on page 185), on the site of a USAAF Liberator base during the Second World War. There's a lot of associated material, both civil and military, covering the period from the First World War to the present day. The museum incorporates the Royal Observer Corps Museum, RAF Bomber Command Museum, and the Museum and Memorial of the 446th Bomb Group - the Bungay Buckeroos.

Mendham
6 miles SW of Bungay off the A143

This pretty little village on the Waveney was the birthplace of Sir Alfred Munnings RA, who was born at Mendham Mill, where his father was the miller. Sir Alfred's painting *Charlotte and her Pony* was the inspiration for the village sign, which was unveiled by his niece Kathleen Hadingham.

Beccles
9 miles W of Lowestoft on the A146

The largest town in the Waveney district at the southernmost point of the Broads, Beccles has in its time been home to Saxons and Vikings, and at one time the market here was a major supplier of herring (up to 60,000 a year) to the Abbey at Bury St Edmunds. At the height of its trading importance Beccles must have painted a splendidly animated picture, with wherries constantly on the move transporting goods from seaports to inland towns. The same stretch of river is still alive, but now with the yachts and pleasure boats of the holidaymakers and weekenders who fill the town in summer. The regatta in July and August is a particularly busy time.

Fire, sadly such a common part of small-town history, ravaged Beccles at various times in the 16th and 17th centuries, destroying much of the old town. For that reason the dwellings extant today are largely Georgian in origin, with handsome redbrick facades. One that is not is **Roos Hall**, a gabled building dating from 1583. Just outside the town, far enough away to escape the great fire of 1586, it was built to a Dutch design, underlining the links between East Anglia and the Low Countries forged by the wool and weaving trades.

Elizabeth I stayed at the Hall just after it was completed, when she visited Beccles to present the town's charter; the occasion is depicted in the town sign. One of the hall's owners was Sir John Suckling (later to become Controller of the Household to James I), one of whose descendants was Lord Nelson. Any old hall worth its salt has a ghost, and the Roos representative is a headless coachman who is said to appear on Christmas Eve.

The parish church of **St Michael** was built in the second half of the 14th century by the Abbot of Bury. Its tower stands separate, built in the 16th century, rising almost 100 feet and containing a peal of bells. An unusual feature at the north facade is an outside pulpit taking the form of a small balcony. The priest could enter the pulpit from inside the church and preach to lepers, who were not allowed inside. Nelson's parents, the Reverend Edmund Nelson and Catherine Suckling, were married in St Michael's, as was the great Suffolk poet George Crabbe.

Another building with Dutch-style gables houses the **Beccles and District Museum**, whose contents include 19th century toys and costume, farm implements, items from the old town gaol and memorabilia from the sailing wherries, including a wealth of old photographs. Beccles, like Bungay, is an old printing town, and has the **William Clowes Museum of Print** on the site of the Newgate works of the famed printer. Here the visitor will learn about the history of printing since the 1800s, with woodcuts, books and machinery; tours of the factory are also available.

Ringsfield
2 miles SW of Beccles off the A146

In a wooded valley away from the main village, Ringfield's parish church of All Saints has a dual appeal: the marvellous array of spring flowers in the churchyard and the story of the robins. A pair nested in the lectern 50 years ago and raised a family, an event recalled in carvings on the new lectern and on the porch gates. The original nest, in the old lectern, can still be found in the church.

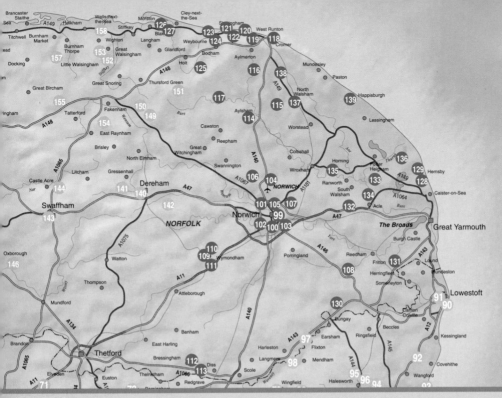

PLACES TO STAY, EAT AND DRINK

● Denotes entries in other chapters

5 Norwich and East Norfolk

'Norwich has the most Dickensian atmosphere of any city I know' declared J B Priestley in his *English Journey of 1933*. 'What a grand, higgledy-piggledy, sensible old place Norwich is!'

More than half a century later, in a European Commission study of 'most habitable' cities, Norwich topped the list of British contenders, well ahead of more favoured candidates such as Bath and York. The political, social and cultural capital of Norfolk, Norwich has

an individual charm that is difficult to define, a beguiling atmosphere created in part by its prodigal wealth of sublime buildings, and partly by its intriguing dual personality as both an old-fashioned Cathedral town and a vibrant, modern metropolis.

The central part of East Norfolk that surrounds Norwich is effectively a plateau, where the gentle contours never rise or fall more than a few metres. The valleys of the Rivers Nar and Wensum display some of the most enchanting

PLACES TO STAY, EAT AND DRINK

● Denotes entries in other chapters

Hunsett Mill, Norfolk Broads

scenery in the county, and the area boasts two of the finest Gothic parish churches in England, at Cawston and Salle. In prehistoric times, this was the most wooded part of Norfolk, and a good number of medieval natural woods still remain, a feature which adds another visual attraction to this pastoral area of the country. Dotted throughout these rural pleasures is a wealth of quiet, unspoilt villages hidden away on minor roads.

The northeast coast makes up the Highlands of Norfolk - the Cromer Ridge, which attains a modest height of 330 feet above sea level. Substantial stretches of the coast are, happily, in the care of the National Trust, but anyone in search of a beach holiday will probably want to focus attention on the coastline east of Sheringham. From this decorous resort, a broad strip of excellent sands runs almost uninterrupted past Cromer and southwards to Great Yarmouth.

Visitors who want to experience a bird's-eye view that encompasses the essence of the Norfolk Broads should climb the tower of the 'Cathedral of the Broads', the Church of St Helen's at Ranworth. Spread out beneath lies a vast panorama of glittering waterways, acres of marshland dotted with windmills, reed beds which are still harvested for thatch, grand medieval churches and farmhouses of warm, red brick.

This is Britain's finest wetland area, a National Park in all but name. Broadland covers some 220 square miles, in a rough oval to the northwest of Great Yarmouth. Three main rivers, the Ant, the Thurne and the Bure, thread their way through the marshes, providing some 120 miles of navigable

waterways. The Broads remain a refuge for many species of endangered birds and plants, and during the spring and autumn they are a favourite stopping-off place for migrating birds.

Norwich

Back in prehistoric times, there were several settlements around the confluence of the Rivers Wensum and Yare. By the late fourth century, one of them was important enough to have its own mint. This was *Northwic*. By the time of the *Domesday Book* 700 years later, Northwic/Norwich, had become the third-most populous city in England, only outnumbered by London and York. To the Norman conquerors, such a major centre of population (about 5,500 residents) needed a **Castle** to ensure

that its Saxon inhabitants could be kept in order.

The first castle structure, in wood, was replaced in the late 1100s by a mighty fortress in stone which, unlike most blank-walled castles of the period, is decorated with a rich facade of blind arcades and ornamental pilasters. This great fort never saw any military action, and as early as the 13th century was being used as the county gaol, a role it continued to fill until 1889. From its walls, in December 1549, the leader of the rebellion against land enclosures, Robert Kett, was hung in chains and left to starve to death.

The Castle is now home to the **Castle Museum and Art Gallery**, home to some of the most outstanding regional collections of fine art, archaeological

HOLLY TREE HOUSE

20 Old Library Mews, Norwich,
Norfolk NR1 1ET
Tel: 01603 270263 Fax: 01603 270597
e-mail: BrendaCMcFadyen@ aol.com
website:
www.cottageguide.co.uk/hollytreehouse

A haven of peace and relaxation in the centre of Norwich, near the riverside, **Holly Tree House** is located in a beautiful mews development of 23 town houses completed in 2001/2. Convenient for all the sights and attractions of Norwich yet hidden away in a tranquil spot, it makes an elegant base from which to explore the city.

The house sleeps four and is comfortably and tastefully furnished and decorated. Well-equipped with every amenity to provide accommodation of the highest standard of quality, it comprises a ground-floor sitting room, cloakroom with handbasin and wc, kitchen with dining area and French doors leading out to the courtyard garden and heated conservatory, and first floor with three beautiful bedrooms (one double, two singles), bathroom and en suite shower room. The kitchen boasts a dishwasher, washing machine, double oven, gas hob, microwave, fridge/freezer, food processor, toaster, iron and hairdryer. Linen, towels, heating and electricity are all included in the price. No smoking. No pets. Not suitable for children.

exhibits and natural history displays. The former dungeons contain a forbidding display of instruments of torture, along with the death masks of some of the prisoners who were executed here. Among the countless other fascinating exhibits are those devoted to Queen Boudica, which features the life of the Iceni tribe with an interactive chariot ride, the Egyptian gallery with its mummy Ankh Hor, and new and interactive displays in the Castle keep and keep basement, recently made accessible to the public.

The Art Gallery's incomparable collection of paintings by the celebrated Norwich artist, John Sell Cotman (1782-1842), and others in the group known as the Norwich School. Their subjects were mostly landscape scenes, such as John Crome's *The Poringland Oak*. Quite apart from the artistic quality of their works, they have left a fascinating pictorial record of early 19th century Norfolk.

The **Bulwer and Miller** collection of more than 2,600 English china teapots makes its home in a brand new gallery called the Twinings Gallery, while the museum's Langton collection of around 100 cats fashioned in porcelain, ivory, bronze, glass and wood, originating from anywhere between Derbyshire and China, and Margaret Elizabeth Fountaine's mind-boggling accumulation of 22,000 butterflies which she had personally netted during her travels around the world, are available to view by appointment at the Shirehall Study Centre, next door to the Royal Norfolk Regimental Museum on Market Avenue.

The great open space of the Market Square, where every weekday a colourful jumble of traders' stalls can be found, offers just about every conceivable item for sale. Dominating the western side of

THE PLANTATION GARDEN

4 Earlham Road, Norwich, Norfolk
Tel: 01603 621868
e-mail: chair@plantationgarden.co.uk
website: www.plantationgarden.co.uk

The Plantation Garden is a hidden treasure of Norwich, a green oasis just a few minutes walk from the city centre. It was created in the 19th century by Henry Trevor, a Norwich business man, who transformed an old chalk quarry into a most unusual and delightful garden. It fell into disrepair in the mid 20th century and was discovered overgrown in 1980. The Plantation Garden Preservation trust was formed to restore it.

Within its 3 acres can be found a 'Gothic' fountain, Italianate terraces, 'medieval' terrace walls, woodland walkways and a rustic bridge as well as mature trees, flower beds and lawns. It is a haven of peace and

tranquility and a glimpse into a bygone age.

This Grade II English Heritage registered garden is open all year round. The modest entry fee is placed in the honesty box if the garden is unattended. Teas are served on the lawn on Sundays during the summer. Wheelchair access is possible to many areas of the garden but not the WC. No dogs allowed. For further information contact as above.

the Market Square is **City Hall**, modelled on Stockholm City Hall and opened by King George VI in 1938. Opinions differ about its architectural merits, but there are no such doubts about the nearby **Guildhall**, a fine example of 15th century flintwork that now houses a tea room.

Around the corner from London Street, in Bridewell Alley, is the **Bridewell Museum**, a late 14th century merchant's house now dedicated to Norfolk's crafts and industries. Another museum/shop, this one located in the **Royal Arcade**, a tiled riot of Art Nouveau fantasy, celebrates the county's great contribution to world cuisine: mustard. Back in the early 1800s, Jeremiah Colman perfected his blend of

Norwich Cathedral

mustard flours and spice to produce a condiment that was smooth in texture and tart in flavour. Together with his nephew James he founded J & J Colman in 1823; 150 years later **The Mustard**

THE BEECHES HOTEL

2/6 Earlham Road, Norwich,
Norfolk NR2 3DB
Tel: 01603 621167 Fax: 01603 620151
e-mail: reception@beeches.co.uk
website: www. beeches.co.uk

Just minutes from Norwich city centre, **The Beeches Hotel** boasts 36 comfortable and welcoming en suite non-smoking guest bedrooms. This excellent accommodation is provided in one of three Victorian buildings – *Plantation House*, built in 1856 by a wealthy Norwich businessman, with views of the garden and Cathedral, and an exlusive four-bedroom apartment, *Governors House*, built around 1827 as a residence for the Governor of Norwich City Gaol, and *Beeches House*, which includes the hotel's Lounge Bar, Restaurant, and a modern extension with 10 bedrooms. All three have been carefully restored while retaining many charming and gracious original features, and offer the highest standard of comfort and quality. Together with The Abbey Hotel, this fine hotel is owned and run by a dedicated and professional team who provide excellent service and hospitality.

Shop was established to commemorate the company's history. The shop has an appropriately late-Victorian atmosphere and a fascinating display of vintage containers and advertisements, some of them from 'Mustard Club' featuring such characters as Lord Bacon of Cookham and Miss Di Gester, created by no less distinguished a writer than Dorothy L Sayers. All in all, a most appetising exhibition.

Millennium Plain just off Theatre Street is where visitors will find **The Forum**, an architecturally stunning new building designed by Sir Michael Hopkins. Combining a unique horseshoe shape with an all-glass façade, this spectacular structure has, at its heart, the **Atrium** and **Bridge**, meeting places where you can enjoy a meal or drink anytime through to midnight, seven days a week. At the **Origins Visitor Centre**, an attractive multi-media display on three floors affords the opportunity to experience the life and times of Norwich and the wider Norfolk region. Here can also be found the Tourist Information Centre. The new **Norfolk & Norwich Millennium Library** houses 120,000 books and offers the best in information and communication technology.

The Assembly House in Theatre Street is one of the city's finest historical houses and also a leading venue for the arts. With two concert halls, three galleries featuring changing exhibitions and a restaurant and tea rooms, this magnificent Georgian home must be included in any visit to the city.

While the Castle has been used for many purposes over the years, the **Cathedral** remains what it has always been: the focus of ecclesiastical life in the county. It's even older than the castle, its service of consecration taking place over 900 years ago, in 1101. This peerless building, its flint walls clad in creamy-white stone from Caen is, after Durham, the most completely Norman cathedral in England, its appeal enhanced by later Gothic features such as the flying buttresses. The Norman cloisters are the largest in the country and notable for the 400 coloured and gilded bosses depicting scenes from medieval life. Another 1,200 of these wondrous carvings decorate the glorious vaulted roof of the nave.

DRAGON HALL

115-123 King Street, Norwich NR1 1QE
Tel: 01603 663922

Dragon Hall is a magnificent medieval merchant's hall with an outstanding timber-framed structure. The 15th century Great Hall has a crown post roof with an intricately carved and painted dragon.

Opening times: 2nd January to 31st March, Monday to Friday 10am-4pm; 1st April to 31st October, Monday to Saturday 10am-4pm; 1st November to 20th December, Monday to Friday 10am-4pm. Closed 21st December to 1st January and Bank Holidays.

Admission prices and further information can be obtained from the telephone number above.

It's impossible to list all the Cathedral's treasures here, but do seek out the **Saxon Bishop's Throne** in the Presbytery, the lovely 14th century altar painting in St Luke's Chapel, and the richly carved canopies in the Choir.

Outside, beneath the slender 315-foot spire soaring heavenwards, the **Cathedral Close** is timeless in its sense of peace. There are some 80 houses inside the Close, some medieval, many Georgian, their residents enjoying an idyllic refuge free from cars. At peace here lie the remains of Nurse Edith Cavell. A daughter of the rector of Swardeston, a few miles south of Norwich, Nurse Cavell worked at a Red Cross hospital in occupied Brussels during the First World War. She helped some 200 Allied soldiers to escape to neutral Holland before being detected and court-martialled by the Germans. As she faced execution by firing squad on 12 October 1915, she spoke her own resonant epitaph: 'Standing as I do, in the view of God and eternity, I realise that patriotism is not enough. I must have no hatred or bitterness towards anyone.'

A stroll around the Close will take you to **Pull's Ferry** with its picturesque flint gateway fronting the River Wensum. In medieval times a canal ran inland from here so that provisions, goods and, in the earliest days, building materials, could be moved direct to the Cathedral. A short stroll along the riverside walk will bring you to **Cow**

Pull's Ferry, Norwich

Tower, built around 1378 and the most massive of the old city towers.

At the western end of the Cathedral Close is the magnificent **Erpingham Gate**, presented to the city in 1420 by a hero of the Battle of Agincourt, Sir Thomas Erpingham.

Beyond this gate, in Tombland (originally Toom- or wasteland), is **Samson and Hercules House**, its entrance flanked by two 1674 carvings of these giants. Diagonally opposite stands the 15th century Maid's Head Hotel.

Norwich is home to some 32 medieval churches in all, every one of them worth attention, although many are now used for purposes other than worship. Outstanding among them are **St Peter Mancroft**, a masterpiece of Gothic architecture built between 1430-55 (and the largest church in Norwich), and **St Peter Hungate**, a handsome 15th century church standing at the top of

Elm Hill, Norwich

Elm Hill, a narrow, unbelievably picturesque lane where in medieval times the city's wool merchants built their homes, close to their warehouses beside the River Wensum.

St Gregory's Church in Pottergate is another Norwich church to have been deconsecrated, and its fate might well have been a sad one. Happily, it is now the home to an arts centre where local artists, actors, musicians, dancers and other arts groups stage a variety of performances and exhibitions throughout the year.

When the basic structure of the present St Gregory's was built in the late 14th century, the general rule seems to have been that any parish of around 1,000 people would have its own place

CITY OF NORWICH AVIATION MUSEUM

Old Norwich Road, Horsham St Faiths,
Norwich, Norfolk NR10 3JF
Tel: 01603 893080

Follow the brown tourist signs from the A140 Norwich-Cromer road to find the **City of Norwich Aviation Museum**, a museum dedicated to keeping Norfolk's aviation heritage alive. Dominating the museum's collection is a massive Avro Vulcan bomber, a veteran of the Falklands War of 1982.

Eight other military and civilian aircraft are on show, and although they are the main

attraction for many visitors, the most fascinating feature is the display within the main exhibition building showing the development of aviation in Norfolk. From the pioneering days of aviation to present-day civilian and military operations, every aspect is covered in a number of displays that are constantly being revised and expanded. The major roles played by Norfolk-based aircraft during the great air battles of World War II are remembered by exhibitions on the USAAF 8th Air Force and the role of the Royal Air Force in this conflict.

A special section is dedicated to the operations of RAF Bomber Command's 100 Group which flew on electronic counter measure, deception and night intruder missions from a number of Norfolk airfields

of worship. St Gregory's was founded on the site of a Saxon church in 1210 and rebuilt in its present form in 1394. The church takes it name from Gregory the Great, the 6th century Pope best known for his campaign to convert the heathen Anglo-Saxons of 'Angle-land' to Christianity, despatching a party of 40 monks to Angle-land in AD596, led by Augustine, whom the Pope consecrated as the first Archbishop of Canterbury.

The **Inspire** Discovery Centre, housed in the medieval church of St Michael in Coslany Street, just across the Wensum northeast of the city centre, is full of exciting hands-on displays and activities that make scientific enquiry come to life.

There are also a large number of beautiful and well-maintained parks in the city, some of which offer chess, lawn tennis and hard tennis courts, bowls, pitch and putt, rowing and more, together with a programme of entertainments ranging from theatre to concerts. One worth particular mention is The Plantation Garden in Earlham Road, three acres of Victorian plantings restored after having fallen into

disrepair, and thought to be the only one in the nation with a Grade II listing.

On the western edge of the city stands the **University of East Anglia**. It's well worth making your way here to visit the **Sainsbury Centre for Visual Arts**. Housed in a huge hall of aluminium and glass designed by Norman Foster, the Centre contains the eclectic collection of a 'passionate acquirer' of art, Sir Robert Sainsbury. For more than 50 years, Sir Robert purchased whatever works of art took his fancy, ignoring fashionable trends. Thus the visitor finds sculptures and pictures by Henry Moore, Bacon and Giacometti, along with African and pre-Columbian artefacts, Egyptian, Etruscan and Roman bronzes, works by Native Americans and Inuit Eskimos, and sculptures from the Cyclades, the South Seas, the Orient and medieval Europe. This extraordinary collection was donated to the University by Sir Robert and Lady Lisa Sainsbury in 1973; their son David complemented his parents' generosity by paying for the building in which it is housed.

To the south of Norwich in the village of Caistor St Edmund are the remains of

HAYNFORD LODGE

Hall Road, Haynford, Norwich,
Norfolk NR10 3LX
Tel: 01603 898844 Fax: 01603 710056
e-mail: john@jchamberlin.freeserve.co.uk

A truly rural and rustic retreat, **Haynford Lodge** is a delightful guest house dating back in parts to 1540. Set in two acres of gardens, including a small outdoor pool, it boasts three handsome and comfortable guest bedrooms.

There's also a lovely beamed dining room with open inglenook fire overlooking the garden, and an attractive guests' lounge. Just

four miles from the Broads, and eight miles from Norwich, it makes an excellent base from which to explore the region.

BECKLANDS GUEST HOUSE

105 Holt Road, Horsford, Norwich,
Norfolk NR10 3AB
Tel: 01603 898582 Fax: 01603 754223

Set in a handsome village off the B1149 not far from Norwich and Cromer, **Becklands Guest House** has been offering hospitality and great accommodation to guests for many years. Conveniently located for access to Aylsham, the Horse Sanctuary at Caldicott, Blickling Hall and Felbrigg Hall National Trust properties, the coast and other sights and attractions of the region, this superior

establishment has nine gracious and attractive guest bedrooms.

Tastefully and comfortably decorated and furnished, all rooms are welcoming, warm, quiet and lovely. All boast every amenity, and in addition there's a charming and spacious guests' lounge. The delicious and hearty breakfast is served in the elegant dining room. Owner Angela Magnus offers all her guests a warm welcome and a high standard of quality and attentive service. 3 Diamonds ETC.

DRIFTWOOD LODGE

102 Wroxham Road, Sprowston, Norwich,
Norfolk NR7 8EX
Tel: 01603 444908
e-mail: john.brown6080@ntlworld.com
website: www.driftwoodlodge.co.uk

The personal touch makes all the difference at **Driftwood Lodge**, a handsome 1930s detached house set in beautiful landscaped gardens located along the A1151 Wroxham Road to Wroxham and Cromer, just two miles from Norwich city centre.

All the comforts of home await guests here, including good home cooking and a warm and friendly welcome. There are three guest bedrooms (one single, two doubles/twins, large enough to accommodate families), all located on the first floor. All the rooms are tastefully and comfortably furnished, with every amenity guests have come to expect and some luxurious extras — dressing gowns are provided, for example. The dining room, on the ground floor, doubles as a guests' lounge with television, games, books and other diversions. Proprietors John and Kate Brown are friendly and welcoming hosts, who conscientiously attend to guests' every need and ensure that all their guests have a relaxing and enjoyable stay. No smoking.

Venta Icenorum, the Roman town established here after Boudica's rebellion in AD61. Unusually, this extensive site has not been disturbed by later developments, so archaeologists have been able to identify the full scale of the original settlement. Sadly very little remains above ground, although in dry summers the grid pattern of the streets show up as brown lines in the grass. Most of the finds discovered during excavations in the 1920s and 1930s are now in **Norwich Castle Museum**, but the riverside site still merits a visit.

Around Norwich

Poringland
6 miles SE of Norwich on the B1332

The name of this sizable village will be familiar to those who love the paintings of the Norwich artist John Crome (1794-1842) whose arcadian painting of *The Poringland Oak* hangs in the Tate Gallery.

To the southwest of Poringland is **The Playbarn**, an indoor and outdoor adventure centre specially designed for the under-sevens. All the play equipment is based on a farmyard theme, with a miniature farm, bouncy tractors, soft play sheep pens, and donkey rides among the attractions. Refreshments and light lunches are available, or you can bring along your own picnic.

Wymondham
9 miles SW of Norwich off the A11

The exterior of **Wymondham Abbey** presents one of the oddest ecclesiastical

DILRAJ

23 Bridge Street, Loddon, Norfolk
Tel: 01508 522042
Fax: 01508 522041

Authentic Bangladeshi cuisine awaits diners at **Dilraj**, an attractive family-run restaurant run by four partners, all from Bangladesh and who grew up together, and all with a wealth of experience in cookery and catering. Bright and warm with an intimate atmosphere, this 44-cover restaurant is comfortable and welcoming.

All food on the extensive menu is expertly prepared and presented by the talented chefs. Bangladesh, of course, is lush river delta country, producing herbs, spices, fruits, vegetables, rice and fish in abundance. All these ingredients and more are blended to create mouth-watering dishes in traditional ways.

Among the culinary delights on offer are Shatkora dishes – Shatkora is a citrus fruit which grows in only a small area of

Bangladesh – Tok Tamarind dishes prepared with tangy tamarind and coriander, and Roshun Naga dishes – hot and spicy, made with fresh green chillies and garlic.

A take-away service is also available, with a 10% discount off menu prices.

WYMONDHAM CONSORT HOTEL AND SEASONS RESTAURANT

28 Market Street, Wymondham,
Norfolk NR18 0BB
Tel: 01953 606721 Fax: 01953 601361
e-mail: wymondham@bestwestern.co.uk
website: www.hotelnet.co.uk/wymondham

Wymondham Consort Hotel is a privately-owned hotel located in the centre of this historic Norfolk market town. Built in the 18th century, it is gracious and elegant, with 20 handsome and comfortable ensuite guest bedrooms ranging from singles to family-sized rooms.

Decorated and furnished in tasteful and traditional town house style, this marvellous hotel boasts welcoming guest lounges (one non-smoking) and an attractive Bar with a good range of real ales, liqueurs, wines and spirits.

The Lemon Tree Café is the perfect place for delicious snacks and meals throughout the day. It opens out onto a lovely garden where meals can be taken on fine days.

At the **Seasons** restaurant, residents and non-residents alike can enjoy excellent dishes created by the talented and innovative chefs who use the best local produce to produce menus offering everything from fresh fish and seafood to vegetarian dishes, steaks, chicken, lamb and more, as well as mouth-watering desserts.

THE GREEN DRAGON

Church Street, Wymondham,
Norfolk NR18 0PH
Tel: 01953 607907 Fax: 01953 600605

The Green Dragon is a delightful Tudor inn that narrowly averted destruction in a fire of 1615 that destroyed 300 houses in the town. One of Wymondham's oldest gems, this fine inn boasts original features such as the dark solid beams and panelling, and a Tudor mantelpiece in the cosy snug. It's believed that a tunnel once ran from the cellar to the Benedictine Priory, and that the inn served as a hostelry for visitors to Wymondham Abbey.

The accent at this fine inn is firmly on the delicious food, with menus and daily specials featuring home-cooked and freshly prepared beef, chicken and seafood dishes as well as a superb selection of vegetarian meals, to tempt every palate.

To drink, there's a choice of real ales and a good complement of lagers, cider, stout, wines, spirits and soft drinks.

With five guest bedrooms, this charming establishment makes an excellent base from which to explore Wymondham and the surrounding area.

buildings in the county; the interior reveals one of the most glorious. The Abbey was founded in 1107 by the Benedictines - or Black Monks, as they were known because of the colour of their habits. The richest and most aristocratic of the monastic orders, the Black Monks apparently experienced some difficulty in respecting their solemn

Wymondham Abbey

vows of poverty and humility. Especially the latter. Constantly in dispute with the people of Wymondham, the dissension between them grew so bitter that in 1249 Pope Innocent IV himself attempted to reconcile their differences. When his efforts failed, a wall was built across the interior of the Abbey, dividing it into an area for the monks and another for the parishioners. Even this drastic measure failed to bring peace, however. Both parties wanted to ring their own bells, so each built a tower. The villagers erected a stately rectangular tower at the west end; the monks an octagonal one over the crossing, thus creating the Abbey's curious exterior appearance.

Step inside and you find a magnificent Norman nave, 112 feet long. (It was originally twice as long, but the eastern end, along with most of the Abbey buildings, was demolished after the Dissolution of the Monasteries.) The superb hammerbeam roof is supported by 76 beautifully carved angels. There's also an interesting 16th century tomb, of the last Abbot, in delicate terracotta work, and a striking modern memorial: a gilded and coloured reredos and tester commemorating the local men who lost their lives in the First World War.

The rectangular western tower of the Abbey was the setting for one of the last acts in the ill-fated Kett's Rebellion of 1549. From its walls, William Kett was hung in chains and left to die: his brother Robert, the leading figure in the uprising, suffered the same fate at Norwich Castle.

Although many of Wymondham's oldest houses were lost in the fire of 1615, when some 300 dwellings were destroyed, there are still some attractive Elizabethan buildings in the heart of the town. The **Market Place** (Friday is market day, and on the first Friday of every month there's an antiques and collectors' fair held in Central Hall) is given dignity by the picturesque octagonal Market Cross, rebuilt two years after the fire. Crowned by a pyramid roof, this appealing timber-framed building is open on all sides on the ground floor, and its upper floor is reached by an outside stairway. Also of interest is **Becket's Chapel**, founded in 1174 and restored in 1559. In its long history it has served as a pilgrim's chapel, grammar school, and coal store. Currently, it houses the town library. **The Bridewell**, or House of Correction, in Bridewell Street was built as a model prison in 1785 along lines recommended by the prison reformer, John Howard, who had condemned the earlier gaol on the site as 'one of the vilest in the country'. Wymondham's Bridewell is said to have served as a model for the penitentiaries established in the United States. Now owned by the town's

Heritage Society, Bridewell is home to several community projects, including the **Wymondham Heritage Museum**.

Railway buffs will also want to visit the historic **Railway Station**, built in 1845 on the Great Eastern's Norwich-Ely line. At its peak, the station and its section employed over 100 people. Still providing a rail link to Norwich, London and the Midlands, the station has been restored, and its buildings house a railway museum, restaurant and tea room, and a piano showroom.

Attleborough
8 miles SW of Wymondham off the A11

The greatest glory of this pleasant market town is to be found in its church

THE ABBEY HOTEL

10 Church Street, Wymondham, Norfolk
NR18 0PH
Tel: 01953 602148 Fax: 01953 606247
e-mail: info@abbeyhotels.co.uk
website: www.abbeyhotels.co.uk

With 20 attractive and comfortable guest bedrooms, **The Abbey Hotel** in Wymondham makes a welcoming base from which to explore this part of the country. Church Street remains as much as it was in 1680, as

proven by drawings done at the time, and in 1880 a private house was transformed into a gracious hotel. Over the ensuing years, the cottages adjacent were purchased and added to the accommodation. Dating back to the early 1500s, these cottages had made up a timber-framed baronial hall, as can be witnessed by their charming winding corridors and exposed beams. The façade is Georgian. All rooms are en suite and non-smoking, and boast new beds with pocket-sprung mattresses, lovely furnishings and every home comfort. Together with The Beeches Hotel in Norwich, this fine hotel is owned and run by a dedicated and professional team who provide excellent service and hospitality.

of **St Mary**. Here, a remarkable 15th century chancel screen stretches the width of the church and is beautifully embellished with the arms of the 24 bishoprics into which England was divided at that time. The screen is generally reckoned to be one of the most outstanding in the country, a remarkable survivor of the Reformation purging of such beautiful creations from churches across the land.

Collectors of curiosities will be interested in a strange memorial in the churchyard. It takes the form of a pyramid, about 6 feet high, and was erected in 1929 to mark the grave of a local solicitor with the rather splendid name of Melancthon William Henry Brooke, or 'Lawyer' Brooke as he was more familiarly known. Melancthon was an amateur Egyptologist who became convinced by his studies of the Pharoahs' tombs that the only way to ensure an agreeable after-life was to be buried beneath a pyramid, precisely placed and of the correct physical dimensions. Several years before his death, he gave the most punctilious instructions as to how this assurance of his immortal existence should be constructed and located.

A couple of miles west of Attleborough, the **Tropical Butterfly Gardens and Bird Park** is set in 2,400 square feet of landscaped tropical gardens and provides a congenial home for hundreds of exotic tropical butterflies. There's also a Falconry Centre with flying displays twice daily,

one and a half miles of paths and a waterside walk, a two-acre garden centre with more than 2,000 plant varieties on offer, a gift shop, coffee shop and tea gardens.

Banham
7 miles S of Attleborough on the B1114

Banham Zoo provides the opportunity to come face to face with some of the world's rarest wildlife - many of the animals who find a home here otherwise face extinction. The Zoo is particularly concerned with monkeys and apes, but in the 25 acres of landscaped gardens you'll also come across tigers, cheetahs, lemurs, penguins and many other species. There are educational talks and displays, a children's play area, Shire Horse dray rides, and a restaurant.

Bressingham
5 miles S of Banham off the A1066

Bressingham Gardens and Steam Museum boasts one of the world's finest collections of British and Continental locomotives, amongst them the famous 'Royal Scot'. A number of the locomotives on display here are on loan from the National Railway Museum at York. All are housed under cover in the museum's extensive locomotive sheds, which also contain many steam-driven industrial engines, traction engines, and **The Fire Museum**, whose collection of fire engines and fire-fighting equipment could form a complete museum in its

BRESSINGHAM GARDENS

Bressingham, Norfolk IP22 2AB
Tel: 01379 688585 Fax: 01379 688490
website: www.blooms-online.com/about/
bressingham.php

A day to remember is guaranteed at Bressingham, where gardeners will be in paradise and children past and present can experience the thrill of the golden age of steam. Alan Bloom, one of the most respected plantsmen of his age, created the Dell Garden and its famous Island Beds between 1955 and 1962, and his garden is now world-renowned for its collection of nearly five thousand species and varieties of hardy perennials. The Garden Centre has a comprehensive collection of hardy perennials

including the Blooms Heritage Collection, plus plants for the house and conservatory and all sorts of gardening gifts and accessories, as well as a café and bookshop.

Alan's son-in-law Jaime Blake carries on the family tradition as Curator of Dell Garden, while son Adrian has created a garden for all seasons at nearby Foggy Bottom, where trees, conifers and shrubs provide a backdrop which is enhanced by plantings of perennials and ornamental grasses. The two gardens are open from April to October, the Garden Centre and Steam Experience all year round. There's a full programme of special events, lectures, talks and demonstrations. This really is a place to linger, and Alan Bloom offers B&B accommodation at his Georgian home, Bressingham Hall.

own right. Visitors can view the interior of the Royal Coach and ride along five miles of track through the woods and gardens. The six acres of landscaped grounds are notable in themselves, since they are planted with more than 5,000 alpine and other types of plants. A two-acre plant centre adjoins the gardens and here there are thousands of plant specimens, many of them rare, available for purchase. Bressingham is renowned for its special 'Steam Days' when the engines can be seen in full steam on the three narrow-gauge lines, and talks and footplate rides are given on the standard-gauge locomotives.

Diss

4 miles E of Bressingham on the A1066/A140

The late Poet Laureate, John Betjeman, voted Diss his favourite Norfolk town, and it's easy to understand his enthusiasm. The River Waveney running alongside forms the boundary between Norfolk and Suffolk, but this attractive old market town – winner of Best Kept Market Town in Norfolk, whose town centre is now a designated conservation area - keeps itself firmly on the northern bank of the river. The town is a pleasing mixture of Tudor, Georgian and

Victorian houses grouped around **The Mere**, which gives the town its name, derived from the Anglo-Saxon word for 'standing water'.

The old town grew up on the hill above The Mere, perhaps because, as an 18th century resident observed, 'all the filth of the town centring in the Mere, beside the many conveniences that are placed over it, make the water very bad and altogether useless ... it stinks exceedingly, and sometimes the fish rise in great numbers, so thick that they are easily taken; they are chiefly roach and eels.' A proper sewerage system was finally installed in 1851.

There's a public park beside the six-acre Mere, and from it a narrow street leads to the small **Market Place**. This

The Mere, Diss

former poultry market is dominated by the somewhat over-restored **St Mary's** church. The oldest parts date back some 700 years, and the St Nicholas Chapel is

particularly enjoyable with its wonderful corbels, angels in the roof, and gargoyles. In the early 1500s, the Rector here was John Skelton, Court poet and tutor to Prince Henry, later Henry VIII. A bitter, quarrelsome man, Skelton was appointed Poet Laureate through the patronage of Cardinal Wolsey, despite the fact that most of Skelton's output has been described as 'breathless doggerel'. Appointed Rector of Diss in 1502, he appears to have been suspended nine years later for having a concubine. Not far from his church is the delightful Victorian **Shambles** with a cast-iron veranda and a small museum inside.

Scole
2 miles E of Diss on the A140

Scole's history goes back to Roman times, since it grew up alongside the Imperial highway from Ipswich to Norwich at the point where it bridged the River Waveney. Traffic on this road (the A140) became unbearable in the 1980s, but a bypass has now mercifully restored some peace to the village. There are two hostelries of note: a coaching inn of 1655, built in an extravagant style of Dutch gables, giant pilasters and towering chimney stacks, and the Crossways Inn, which must have a good claim to being the prettiest pub in the county.

Langmere
6 miles NE of Diss on minor road off the A140 (through Dickleburgh)

Veterans of the Second World War and their families and friends will be interested in the **100th Bomb Group Memorial Museum**, a small museum on the edge of Dickleburgh Airfield (now disused). The Museum is a tribute to the U S 8th Air Force which was stationed here during the war, and includes displays of USAAF decorations and uniforms, equipment, combat records and other memorabilia. Facilities include refreshments, a museum shop, visitor centre and a picnic area.

Harleston
7 miles NE of Diss off the A143

This pretty market town with some

River Waveney, Scole

notable half-timbered and Georgian houses, and a splendid 12th century coaching inn, was a favourite of the renowned architectural authority, Nikolaus Pevsner, who particularly admired the early Georgian Candlers House at the northern end of the town. Another writer has described the area around the marketplace as 'the finest street scene in East Anglia'. The town lies in the heart of the Waveney Valley, a lovely area which inspired many paintings by the locally-born artist, Sir Alfred Munnings.

Great Witchingham

11 miles NW of Norwich off the A1067

Norfolk Wildlife Centre & Country Park is home to an interesting collection of rare, or ancient, breeds of farm livestock such as white-faced woodland and Shetland sheep, pygmy goats and Exmoor ponies. Set in 40 acres of peaceful parkland, the Centre also has reindeer, otters and badgers, pools teeming with wildfowl and a huge colony of wild herons nesting in the trees. There are also 'Commando' and Adventure Play Areas, one of the finest collection of trees and flowering shrubs in the county, a cafe and gift shop. The Centre is also home to **Wings Raptor**, the most spectacular birds-of-prey flying display in Norfolk.

A little further southeast, the **Dinosaur Adventure Park** near Lenwade doesn't have any living creatures, but as you wander through the woods here you will come across some startlingly convincing life-size models of dinosaurs. One of them, the 'Climb-a-Saurus', is a children's activity centre. A woodland maze, picnic area with gas-fired barbecues, a play area for toddlers, a restaurant and a 'Dinostore' offering a wide variety of dinosaur models, books and gifts are among the park's other attractions.

Anyone who has ever read Parson Woodforde's enchanting *Diary of a Country Parson* will want to make a short diversion to the tiny village of **Weston Longville**, a mile or so south of the Dinosaur Park. The Revd James Woodforde was vicar of this remote parish from 1774 until his death in 1803, and throughout that time he conscientiously maintained a daily diary detailing a wonderful mixture of the momentous and the trivial. 'Very great Rebellion in France' he notes when, 10 days after the Fall of the Bastille, the dramatic news eventually arrived at Weston Longville. More often he records his copious meals ('We had for dinner a Calf's head, boiled Fowl and Tongue, a saddle of Mutton roasted on the side table, and a fine Swan roasted with Currant Jelly Sauce for the first Course. The Second Course a couple of Wild Fowl, Larks, Blamange, Tarts etc. etc.'), the weather (during the winter of 1785, for example, the frost was so severe that it froze the chamberpots under the beds), and his frequent dealings with the smuggler Andrews, who kept the good parson well-supplied with contraband tea, gin and cognac. Inside the simple village church there's a portrait of Parson Woodforde, painted by his nephew, and across the road the inn has been named after this beguiling character.

Swannington
11 miles NW of Norwich off the A1067/B1149

The gardens of **Swannington Manor** are famous for the 300-year-old yew and box topiary hedge. Other features of this small town are the 13th century St Margaret's church, Swannington Hall – where can be seen the remains of the former moat – and the charming thatched village water pump.

Swannington's Ketts Lane was named for Robert Kett, leader of the peasants' revolt, who reputedly was captured in a barn nearby.

Reepham
12 miles NW of Norwich on the B1145

Reepham is an attractive town set in the rich countryside between the Wensum and Bure Valleys. Lovely 18th century houses border the Market Place, and there is delightful walking along the Marriott's Way cycle path. Market day is Wednesdays, and regular antiques fairs are held at the Old Reepham Brewery.

Cawston
12 miles NW of Norwich on the B1145

'Lovers of the Norfolk churches can never agree which is the best,' wrote Sir John Betjeman. 'I have heard it said that you are either a Salle man or a Cawston man.' In this county so rich in exceptionally beautiful churches, Salle and Cawston are indeed in a class of their own. **St Agnes Church** in Cawston, among many other treasures, boasts a magnificent double hammerbeam roof, where angels with protective wings 8 feet across float serenely from the roof, and a gorgeous 15th century rood screen embellished with lovely painted panels of saints and Fathers of the Church. The two churches are just a couple of miles apart, so you can easily decide for yourself whether you are 'a Salle man or a Cawston man'. Surprisingly for such a genial character, Sir John seems to have overlooked the possibility that other visitors to these two remarkable churches might define themselves as either 'a Salle woman or a Cawston woman'.

On the edge of Cawston village is **Broadland Wineries**, a family-owned business established in 1965, which moved to this 4.5 acre site in 1971.

Aylsham
14 miles N of Norwich on the A140

The attractive little town of Aylsham is set beside the River Bure, the northern terminus of the **Bure Valley Railway**. It has an unspoilt **Market Place**, surrounded by late 17th and early 18th century houses, reflecting the prosperity the town enjoyed in those years from the

BURE VALLEY RAILWAY

Aylsham Station, Norwich Road, Aylsham, Norfolk NR11 6BW
Tel: 01263 7338585 Fax: 01263 733814
e-mail: info@bvr.co.uk
website: www.bvrw.co.uk

Norfolk's longest narrow gauge heritage railway is a 15" gauge line operating between the old market town of Aylsham and Wroxham, a distance of nine miles. The line was built in 1989-1990 on the track bed of the former East Norfolk Railway, which opened in 1880. **The Bure Valley Narrow Gauge Railway** was opened in July 1990 with new station buildings and workshops at Aylsham and a new station adjacent to Hoveton and Wroxham station. Unstaffed stations are at Coltishall (the famous RAF Battle of Britain station), Buxton and Brampton. The railway is operated primarily by steam locomotives, of which there are four. Passengers are carried in 22 fully enclosed and luxuriously upholstered coaches. During 1998 two new wheelchair accessible coaches were completed at Aylsham. These can each carry four wheelchairs with their carers. The journey time is 45 minutes.

At Aylsham the workshops are usually open to visitors; on site are a small museum and model railway, a well-stocked gift shop and the Whistlestop Restaurant open for full English breakfasts, lunch and high tea. A shop selling confectionery and drinks is located at Wroxham station. There is ample free car and coach parking at both stations, with fully equipped facilities for disabled visitors.

The Bure Valley Railway specialises in joint operations with other attractions. There is a regular boat train facility from Aylsham connecting with cruises on the Broads from Wroxham. In off-peak periods the Railway operates Steam Locomotive Driving Courses for beginners and the more experienced.

The Bure Valley Railway operates regular services from April to October, Santa Specials towards Christmas and Day out with Thomas the Tank Engine events in May and September.

---

cloth trade, and a 14th/15th century church, St Michael's, said to have been built by John O'Gaunt. In the churchyard is the tomb of one of the greatest of the 18th century landscape gardeners, Humphrey Repton, the creator of some 200 parks and gardens around the country.

One of Repton's many commissions was to landscape the grounds of **Blickling Hall** (National Trust), a 'dream of architectural beauty' which stands a mile or so outside Aylsham. Many visitors have marvelled at their first sight of the great Hall built for Sir Henry Hobart in the 1620s. 'No-one is prepared on coming downhill past the church into the village, to find the main front of this finest of Jacobean mansions, actually looking upon the road, unobstructedly, from behind its velvet lawns' enthused Charles Harper in 1904. 'No theatrical manager cunning in all the artful accessories of the stage could devise anything more dramatic.'

From the outside, Sir Henry's house fully satisfied the contemporary architectural vogue for perfect symmetry.

Four towers topped with lead-covered turret-caps rise at each corner, there are lines of matching Dutch gables and mullioned windows, and even the chimneys were placed in corresponding groups of twos, threes or fours.

Blickling Hall

Inside, the most spectacular feature is the Long Gallery, which extends for 135 feet and originally provided space for indoor exercise in bad weather. Its glory is the plaster ceiling, an intricately patterned expanse of heraldic panels bearing the Hobart arms, along with others displaying bizarre and inscrutable emblems such as a naked lady riding a two-legged dragon.

Other treasures at Blickling include a dramatic double-flight carved oak staircase, the Chinese Bedroom lined with 18th century hand-painted wallpaper, and the dazzling Peter the Great Room. A descendant of Sir Henry Hobart, the 2nd Earl of Buckinghamshire, was appointed Ambassador to Russia in 1746, and he returned from that posting with a magnificent tapestry, the gift of Empress Catherine the Great. This room was redesigned so as to display the Earl's sumptuous souvenir to its full effect, and portraits of himself and his Countess by Gainsborough were added later.

The Earl was a martyr to gout, and his death in 1793 at the age of 50 occurred when, finding the pain unbearable, he thrust his bloated foot into a bucket of icy water, and suffered a heart attack.

POPLAR FARM

Banningham, Norwich, Norfolk NR11 7DS
Tel: 01263 732680
e-mail: g.harvey@tiscali.co.uk

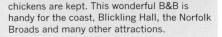

Poplar Farm, with its relaxed atmosphere, is a delightful place offering excellent bed and breakfast accommodation. There are three guest bedrooms, all of them extremely comfortable and attractive, one on the ground floor and all overlooking the garden. The delicious breakfasts feature home-made breads, preserves and free-range eggs. The conservatory looks out onto a large garden and pond. Hens, sheep, ducks, turkeys and chickens are kept. This wonderful B&B is handy for the coast, Blickling Hall, the Norfolk Broads and many other attractions.

He was buried beneath the idiosyncratic Egyptian Pyramid in the grounds, a 45-foot high structure designed by Ignatius Bonomi that combines Egyptian and classical elements to create a mausoleum which, if nothing else, is certainly distinctive.

Blickling also offers its visitors miles of footpaths through lovely grounds, a plant centre, picnic area, restaurant and shop.

Within a few miles of Blickling Hall are two other stately homes, both the properties of Lord and Lady Walpole. **Mannington** Gardens and Countryside are set around a medieval moated manor house and feature a wide variety of plants, trees and shrubs, including thousands of roses, and particularly classic varieties. The Heritage Rose Garden and Twentieth century Rose Garden are set in small gardens reflecting their period of origin. There are also Garden Shops, with plants, souvenirs and crafts, and tea rooms. The Hall itself is open by appointment, while the grounds are open Sundays May-September and also Weds-Fri June-August.

Wolterton Park, the stately 18th century Hall built for Horatio Walpole, brother of Sir Robert, England's first Prime Minister, stands in grounds landscaped by Humphrey Repton. Here can be found walks and trails, orienteering, an adventure playground and various special events are held throughout the year. The Hall is open

---

BUTTERFLY COTTAGE

The Green, Aldborough, Norwich,
Norfolk NR11 7AA
Tel/Fax: 01263 768198
e-mail: butterflycottage@btopenworld.com
website: www.butterflycottage.com

At **Butterfly Cottage**, Peter and Janet Davison offer both bed and breakfast and self-catering accommodation. Overlooking the village green, this handsome setting within easy reach of Cromer, Sheringham, Holt, Alysham and Wroxham makes an excellent touring base.

The National Trust properties of Blickling Hall and Felbrigg Hall are also nearby, and Norwich and Great Yarmouth are not far afield.

The superior accommodation comprises **The Garden Annexe**, accessible by its own private entrance and suitable for longer stay, self-catering holidays, with a double bedroom, second bedroom with bunk beds and well-equipped kitchen.

Spacious and light, it also offer private parking and a patio garden. Well behaved pets are accepted in the Annexe.

The **Butterfly Rooms** are three newly converted self-contained first-floor rooms. *Swallowtail* and *Red Admiral* overlook the village green, while *Peacock* is at the rear of the property. Cot available in all rooms.

The delicious and hearty breakfast is served in the conservatory of Butterfly Cottage.

Open all year round, this excellent establishment has been awarded 3 Diamonds by the English Tourism Council.

THE WALPOLE ARMS

The Common, Itteringham, Norwich,
Norfolk NR11 7AR
Tel: 01263 587258 Fax: 01263 587074
e-mail: goodfood@thewalpolearms.co.uk
website: www.thewalpolearms.co.uk

seasonal dishes. The range of tempting seafood, game, organic meats, fruits and vegetables are always freshly bought from suppliers who offer produce grown and selected with genuine care. These basic elements are then used and blended with expertise and style to create delicious dishes that will tempt every palate.

The Walpole Arms is a treat to be discovered, a gracious and attractive restaurant serving up excellent food and wine. More than just another pub restaurant, this traditional village pub has been lauded in The Observer, Norfolk Lifestyle Magazine and the Eastern Daily Press for its superb menus and ambience. Voted Country Pub of the Year 2001 in the Norfolk Food Awards, guests come from far and wide

to enjoy a pint of locally brewed ale in the 18th century bar with its attractive exposed oak beamwork or, when the weather is fine, in the lovely garden. The dining room has its own private bar, and seats 40. Tasteful and distinctive, the décor and furnishings are attractive and comfortable, enhancing the restaurant's relaxed and welcoming ambience.

The freshest ingredients are expertly prepared and presented for local and

The dedicated team of chefs, headed by Andy Parle – undoubtedly one of the region's finest chefs – offer guests a passion and commitment that shows in everything they do. Owners Richard Bryan – producer of the BBC's Masterchef – and Keith Reeves – a highly respected wine merchant · have brought together their talents and passion for great food and drink to provide a superbly varied and unfailingly impressive menu of delights. Keith's knowledge and flair have gone into creating a comprehensive and distinguished wine list to complement the fine food.

Located just a few miles northwest of Blickling Hall and Aylsham, off the B1354, The Walpole Arms is well worth seeking out for a highly enjoyable and memorable dining experience.

for tours every Friday from April.

Over 20 miles of waymarked public footpaths and permissive paths around Mannington and Wolterton link into the Weavers Way long-distance footpath and Holt circular walk.

Just north of Mannington Hall stands the village of **Little Barningham**, where St Mary's Church is a magnet for collectors of ecclesiastical curiosities. Inside, perched on the corner of an ancient box pew, stands a remarkable wood-carved skeletal figure of the Grim Reaper. Its fleshless skull stares hollow-eyed at visitors with a defiant, mirthless grin: a scythe gripped in one clutch of bones, and an hour-glass in the other, symbolise the inescapable fate that awaits us all. This gruesomely powerful *memento mori* was donated to the church in 1640 by one Stephen Crosbie who, for good measure, added the inscription: 'As you are now, even so was I, Remember death for ye must dye.' Those words were a conventional enough adjuration at that time, but what is one supposed to make of Stephen's postscript inscribed on the back of the pew: 'For couples joined in wedlock this seat I did intend'?

Cromer and The Northeast Coast

Cromer
25 miles N of Norwich on the A149

As you enter a seaside town, what more reassuring sight could there be than to see the pier still standing? **Cromer Pier** is the genuine article, complete with Lifeboat Station and the Pavilion Theatre, which still stages traditional end-of-the-pier shows. The Pier's survival is all the more impressive since it was badly damaged in 1953 and 1989, and in 1993 sliced in two by a drilling rig which had broken adrift in a storm.

Cromer has been a significant resort since the late 1700s and in its early days even received an unsolicited testimonial from Jane Austen. In her novel *Emma* (1816), a character declares that 'Perry was a week at Cromer once, and he holds it to be the best of all the sea-bathing places.' A succession of celebrities, ranging from Lord Tennyson and Oscar Wilde to Winston Churchill and the German Kaiser, all came to see for themselves. The inviting sandy

Cromer Beach

THE KNOLL GUEST HOUSE

23 Alfred Road, Cromer, Norfolk NR29 9AN
Tel: 01263 512753
e-mail: ian@knollguesthouse.co.uk
website: www.knollguesthouse.co.uk

The Knoll is a charming licensed guest house with five comfortable, clean and attractive bedrooms and a homely and welcoming ambience.

Located in the heart of Cromer on a quiet lane, with great walking, cycling and horse riding nearby, and close to Cromer's Blue Flag beaches, it is the perfect place to enjoy a

relaxing break at any time of year. Breakfasts are hearty and delicious; evening meals by prior arrangement. No smoking.

beach remains much as they saw it (horse-drawn bathing machines aside), as does the Church of **St Peter & St Paul**, which boasts the tallest tower in Norfolk, 160 feet high. And then as now, Cromer Crabs were reckoned to be the most succulent in England. During the season, between April and September, crab-boats are launched from the shore (there's no harbour here), sail out to the crab banks about 3 miles offshore, and there the two-man teams on each boat deal with some 200 pots.

The **Lifeboat Museum**, however, is a fairly recent addition. Housed in the former Lifeboat Station, it tells the dramatic story of the courageous men who manned the town's rescue service. Pre-eminent among them was Harry Blogg who was coxswain of the lifeboat for 37 years, from 1910 to 1947. During those years his boat, the *H F Bailey*, was called out 128 times and saved 518 lives. In 1991, the H F Bailey was purchased by Peter Cadbury of the chocolate manufacturing family and presented to the Museum as its prime exhibit.

Also well worth visiting is the **Cromer Museum**, housed in a row of restored fishermen's cottages near the church, where you can follow the story of Cromer from the days of the dinosaurs, some of whose bones were found nearby, up to the present, and access the computer for thousands of pictures and facts about this attractive town.

Aylmerton
3 miles W of Cromer on minor road off the A148

Aylmerton is home to one of Norfolk's grandest houses, **Felbrigg Hall** (National Trust). Thomas Windham began rebuilding the old manor house at Felbrigg in the 1620s, erecting in its place a grand Jacobean mansion with huge mullioned windows, pillared porch, and at roof-level a dedication in openwork stone: *Gloria Deo in Excelsis*, 'Glory to God in the Highest'. Later that century, Thomas' grandson William Windham I married a wealthy heiress and added the beautifully proportioned Carolean West Wing, where visitors can

Felbrigg Hall

see portraits of the happily married couple painted by Sir Peter Lely. Their son, William Windham II, returning from his four-year-long Grand Tour, filled the house with treasures he had collected - so many of them that he had to extend the Hall yet again. The Windham family's ownership of Felbrigg Hall came to a tragi-comic end in the 1860s when William Frederick Windham inherited the estate. William was one of the great English eccentrics. He loved uniforms. Accoutred in the Felbrigg blue and red livery, he would insist on serving at table; in guard's uniform he caused chaos on the local railway with his arbitrary whistle-blasts;

dressed as a policeman, he sternly rounded up the ladies of easy virtue patrolling London's Haymarket. Inevitably, 'Mad' Windham fell prey to a pretty fortune-hunter and Felbrigg was only saved from complete bankruptcy by his death at the age of 26.

The Hall was acquired by the National Trust in 1969, complete with its 18th century furnishings, collection of paintings by artists such as Kneller and van der Velde, and a wonderful Gothic library. There are extensive grounds which include a Walled Garden containing an elegant octagonal dove-house, an Orangery of 1707 sheltering an outstanding collection of camellias, many woodland and lakeside walks, and a restaurant, tea room and shop.

West Runton
3 miles W of Cromer on the A149

The parish of West Runton can boast that within its boundaries lies the

MIRABELLE RESTAURANT & BISTRO

Station Road, West Runton, Cromer, Norfolk NR27 9QD
Tel: 01263 837396

Manfred Hollwoger is the Austrian-born chef and proprietor who for some 30 years has been settled at the distinguished **Mirabelle Restaurant & Bistro**. Food lovers from all over Norfolk and beyond come to sample the delights of the fine menu and excellent choice of wines. Only the freshest, best ingredients –

including locally caught seafood – are used to create delicious dishes that are prepared and presented with flair.

THE NORFOLK SHIRE HORSE CENTRE

West Runton, Cromer, Norfolk NR27 9QH
Tel: 01263 837339 Fax: 01263 837132
e-mail: bakewekk@norfolkshirehorse.fsnet.co.uk
website: www.norfolk-shirehorse-centre.co.uk

Shires, Suffolk Punches and Clydesdales are among the stars of the show at the **Norfolk Shire Horse Centre**, and visitors can meet these wonderful, gentle giants at close quarters in the front yard stables. Two large museum sheds contain a video room and an indoor demonstration area, and also on show are carts, coaches, gypsy caravans and farm machinery of yesteryear. Next to the museum is a children's play area.

A short walk through a meadow brings visitors to the area where the small animals are kept in their sheds and pens and aviaries. This really is a paradise for animal lovers: native pony mares with their foals, donkeys, Dexter cows, pigs, goats, lambs, guinea pigs, rabbits, chipmunks, chinchillas, cage birds. The ducks and geese have a great time in their own little pond. Twice a day the centre's proprietor, David Blakewell, accompanies demonstrations with a friendly, informative talk about the heavy horses; themes include harnessing and working the horses with the old machinery. Children can have a ride in a cart and join in the feeding of small animals. Numerous specials events are held throughout the summer, including foal days, blacksmiths days, sheepdog days, plough days and harvesting with the heavy horses. Dogs are welcome on leads; the site has a two-acre car park, a café and a gift shop.

Next to the centre, in the same ownership, West Runton Riding Stables offer instruction and accompanied rides for both novice and more experienced riders. The Stables are open throughout the year, the Shire Horse Centre from April to October. Follow the brown tourist signs off the A149 Cromer-Sheringham road or the A148 Cromer-Holt road.

highest point in Norfolk - **Beacon Hill**. This eminence is 330 feet high, so you won't be needing any oxygen equipment to reach the summit, but there are some excellent views. Nearby is the Roman Camp (National Trust), a misleading name since there's no evidence that the Romans ever occupied this 70 acres of heathland. Excavations have shown, however, that in Saxon and medieval times this was an iron-working settlement.

West Runton's major tourist attraction is undoubtedly the **Norfolk Shire Horse Centre** (see above) where twice a day, during the season, these noble beasts are harnessed up and give a half-hour demonstration of the important role they played in agricultural life right up until the 1930s. They are the largest (19 hands/6 feet 4 inches high) and heaviest horses in the world, weighing more than a ton, and for generations were highly valued both as war-horses and draught animals. Several other heavy breeds, such as the Suffolk Punch, Clydesdale and Percheron, also have their home here, along with no fewer than nine different breeds of pony. The Centre also has a video room showing a 30-minute film, a small animals' enclosure and an adventure playground for children, a cafe and gift shop. A horse-drawn cart will transport you around the village and at the West Runton Riding School (on site) you can hire riding horses by the hour.

Sheringham

5 miles W of Cromer on the A149

Sheringham has made the transition from fishing village to popular seaside resort with grace and style. There are plenty of activities on offer, yet Sheringham has managed to avoid the brasher excesses of many English seaside

Sheringham Beach

towns. The beach here is among the cleanest in England, and markedly different from the shingle beaches elsewhere on this part of the coast. Consisting mainly of gently sloping sand, it is excellent for bathing and the team of lifeguards makes it ideal for families with children. Rainfall at Sheringham is one of the lowest in the county, and the bracing air has also recommended the town to sufferers from rheumatism and respiratory problems.

A small fleet of fishing boats still operates from here, mostly concentrating on crabs and lobsters, but also bringing in catches of cod, skate, plaice, mackerel and herring. Several original fishermen's cottages remain, some with lofts where the nets were mended. Sheringham has never had a harbour, so boats are launched from the shore where stacks of creels stand as they have for generations. A 'golden lobster' in the town's coat of arms celebrates this traditional industry.

Like so many other former fishing villages in England, Sheringham owes its transformation into a resort to the arrival of the railway. During the Edwardian peak years of rail travel, some 64 trains a day steamed into the station

THE DUNSTABLE ARMS

27 Cromer Road, Sheringham, Norfolk NR26 8AB
Tel: 01263 824825 Fax: 01263 826076

For over 140 years, **The Dunstable Arms** in Sheringham has been providing warm hospitality and great food and drink to locals and weary travellers alike. This absolutely lovely pub has a friendly staff and atmosphere, and cosy traditional features such as the oak beamed ceiling and large open fire. Charming and welcoming, the pub serves up a range of quality ales, lagers, wines, spirits and soft drinks, and good, hearty meals every day at lunch and dinner. A

further enhancement to this delightful pub is it's Large Family Beer Garden & Children's Play Area's which has an under 5's Enclosed Kiddies Corner & for over 5's, Climbing Frame, Table Tennis, Outdoor Bowlero Lane & Kids Pool Table. It also has Live Entertainment most Weekends.

SHERINGHAM MUSEUM

Station Road, Sheringham, Norfolk NR26 8RE
Tel: 01263 821871

Sheringham is the only place in the world to possess four of its original lifeboats. The **Sheringham Museum** Trust owns three of these and two are currently on display.

A new museum is planned to house all three historic boats plus the existing social history museum. The latter has wealth of interesting displays, from boat building, lifeboats, fishing and fishermen, to the war years, a local Roman kiln, beach finds and the Weybourne Elephant, dating back over one and a half million years.

New displays include one on golf · the first course was made in 1892 and had a cricket pitch in the middle! · and one tracing the relationship between the local squires and the town. The museum is open Easter to October Tuesday to Saturday 10am-4pm and Sundays 2pm-4pm. Please phone the above number for more information and admission prices.

SHERINGHAM
TWIXT SEA AND PINE
Guide free from Town Clerk, Sheringham, Norfolk
Train services and fares from BRITISH RAILWAYS stations offices and agencies

but the line became yet another victim of the Beeching closures of the 1960s. Devotees of steam trains joined together and, by dint of great effort and enthusiasm, managed to re-open the line in 1975 as the **North Norfolk Railway**, better known as The Poppy Line.

The name refers to 'Poppyland", a term given to the area by the Victorian journalist Clement Scott who visited in pre-herbicide days when the summer fields were ablaze with poppies. In 1883, Scott travelled to Cromer on the newly-opened Great Eastern Railway's extension from Norwich. Walking out of the town, he was entranced by the tranquillity of the countryside. In his dispatch to the *Daily Telegraph* he wrote: 'It is difficult to convey an idea of the silence of the fields through which I

passed, or the beauty of the prospect that surrounded me - a blue sky without a cloud across it, a sea sparkling under a haze of heat, wild flowers in profusion around me, poppies predominating everywhere ...' Spurred by Scott's enthusiasm, a succession of notable Victorians made their way here - painters, writers, actors, even a youthful Winston Churchill. Later, during the Second World War, Churchill returned to the area, staying at Pear Tree Cottage in Mundesley.

Although greatly diminished in number, plenty of brilliant poppies can still be seen as you travel the scenic five-mile journey from Sheringham to Holt. The railway operates up to eight trains daily in each direction during the season, March to October, and there are special Saturday evening and Sunday lunchtime services when you can dine in style in one of the Pullman coaches from the old 'Brighton Belle'.

Just to the west of the town, at Upper Sheringham, footpaths lead to the lovely grounds of **Sheringham Park** (National Trust). The Park was landscaped by Humphrey Repton, who declared it to be his 'favourite and darling child in Norfolk'. There are grand views along the coast, dense growths of oak, beech and fir trees and banks of rhododendrons which are at their most dazzling in late May and June.

There's yet more grand scenery at the aptly-named **Pretty Corner**, just to the east of the A1082 at its junction with the A148. This is a particularly beautiful area of woodland and also offers superb views over the surrounding countryside.

Bodham
9 miles W of Cromer off the A148

About midway between Bodham and Weybourne, in the grounds of the Kelling Park Hotel, is the **East Anglian Falconry Centre** which, in addition to having daily flying displays, is also the largest sanctuary in the country for injured owls and birds of prey. The centre keeps and cares for over 200 birds, among them kestrels and sparrowhawks, as well as a number of rarer birds such as goshawks, peregrine falcons, harriers and redtail hawks, eagles and snowy owls.

Weybourne
9 miles W of Cromer on the A149

Here, the shingle beach known as **Weybourne Hope** (or Hoop) slopes so steeply that an invading fleet could bring its ships right up to the shore. Which is exactly what the Danes did many times during the 9th and 10th centuries. A local adage states that 'He who would Old England win, Must at Weybourne Hoop begin,' and over the centuries care has been taken to protect this stretch of the coast. A map dated 1st May 1588 clearly shows 'Waborne Fort', and Holt's Parish Register for that year of the Armada notes that *'in this yeare was the town of Waborne fortified with a continuall garrison of men bothe of*

horse and foote with sconces (earthworks) ordinaunce and all manner of appoyntment to defend the Spannyards landing theare.'

As it turned out, the 'Spannyards' never got close, but during both World Wars the same concern was shown for defending this vulnerable beach. The garrison then became the Anti-Aircraft Permanent Range and Radar Training Wing, providing instruction for National Servicemen until the camp finally closed in 1959. It was reckoned that by then some 1,500,000 shells had been fired out to sea. The site has since been returned to agricultural use, but the original NAAFI building remains and now houses **The Muckleburgh Collection**, a fascinating museum of military vehicles, weapons and equipment, most of which

have seen action in battlefields all over the world. All of the tanks, armoured cars and amphibious vehicles on display can be inspected at close quarters, and there are regular tank demonstrations. Meals and snacks are available - served in a NAAFI-style canteen.

Incidentally, despite Weybourne's exposed position, it has in fact only been attacked once, by the Luftwaffe on 11th July 1940. A stick of bombs landed in the main street and badly damaged two cottages.

Holt

10 miles W of Cromer on the A148

A perennial finalist in the 'Anglia in Bloom' competition, Holt's town centre always looks a picture, with hanging

---

THE SHIP INN

The Street, Weybourne, Holt,
Norfolk NR25 7SZ
Tel: 01263 588721
e-mail: shipweybourne@aol.com

A real gem of Olde Worlde Charm, **The Ship Inn** stands right on the North Norfolk coast road. Warm, comfortable and friendly, this cosy pub which features in the Camra guide, offers a good range of drinks, including several real ales and a large range of soft

drinks. Home-cooked meals range from traditional Steak & Kidney Pudding to the more adventurous such as Curries and Oriental dishes. Vegetatians are particularly well catered for, and for those with a sweet tooth the comments book states that the White Chocolate and Cherry Bread and Butter Pudding is to die for. It is advisable to book on busy weekends and for the very popular Sunday lunch. Wendy and Eddie Williams and their attentive staff cheerfully provide guests with everything they need. With occasional live music and regular quiz nights, this convivial pub with its pretty, sunny garden is well worth a visit.

THE HARE & HOUNDS

Holt Road, Hempstead, Holt, Norfolk
Tel: 01263 712329
Fax: 01263 711962

Tucked away in this small village off the A148, **The Hare & Hounds** is a charming inn dating back to 1640. Once the farm estate house, this delightful pub is a food-lover's paradise, with a vast range of delicious dishes freshly prepared for lunch and dinner.

Without doubt one of the cosiest pubs in

Norfolk, this hidden place is well worth seeking out. Booking is advised at weekends.

baskets and flowers everywhere. Back in 1892, a guide-book to the county described Holt as 'A clean and very prettily situated market town, being planted in a well undulating and very woody neighbourhood.' More than a century later, one can't quarrel with that characterisation.

The worst day in the town's history was May 1st, 1708, when a raging fire consumed most of the town's ancient houses. The consequent rebuilding replaced them with some elegant Georgian houses, gracious buildings which played a large part in earning the town its designation as a Conservation Area.

The town's most famous building, **Gresham's School**, somehow escaped the disastrous conflagration of 1708. Founded in 1555 by Sir John Gresham, the school began as an altruistic educational establishment, its pupils accepted solely on the basis of their academic promise. Since then, the school has abandoned both its town centre location and its founder's commitment to educating, free, those bright children who could not otherwise

afford it. Placing your child here, today, will drain more than £15,000 each year from your income. Solace yourself with the thought that among the school's many distinguished alumni are the dour creator of the BBC, Lord Reith, the poets W H Auden and Stephen Spender, and the composer Benjamin Britten.

Look out for one of Holt's most unusual buildings, **Home Place**. Designed and built in 1903-5 by E S Prior, an architect follower of the Arts & Crafts movement, the exterior of the house is completely covered with an ingeniously contrived cladding of local pebbles.

Cley-next-the-Sea
12 miles W of Cromer on the A149

Cley's name is no longer appropriate. Cley-a-mile-away-from-the-Sea would be more truthful. But in early medieval times, Cley (pronounced Cly, and meaning clay) was a more important port than King's Lynn, with a busy trade exporting wool to the Netherlands. In return, Cley imported a predilection for houses with curved gables, Flemish

Cley Mill

most northerly extremity of East Anglia. This spit of land that stretches three miles out into the sea is a twitcher's paradise. Some 256 species of birds have been spotted here, and the variety of flora is scarcely less impressive: almost 200 flowering species have been recorded.

Glandford

12 miles W of Cromer off the B1156

Near this delightful village, the **Natural Surroundings Wild Flower Centre** is dedicated to gardening with a strong ecological emphasis. There are wild flower meadows and gardens, organic vegetable and herb gardens, nurseries, a nature trail alongside the unspoilt River Glaven, and the Centre also organises a wide range of events with a conservation theme. A short walk down the valley from the Centre is the **Glandford Shell Museum**, a lovely Dutch-style building which houses the private collection of Sir Alfred Jodrell, a unique accumulation of sea shells gathered from beaches all around the world, together with a fascinating variety of artefacts made from them.

A couple of miles south of Glandford you'll find a building of 1802 which, year after year, has been awarded the title of 'Top Tourist Attraction in North Norfolk'. **Letheringsett Watermill** stands on the site of an earlier mill

bricks and pantiles. The windmill overlooking the harbour adds to the sense that a little piece of Holland has strayed across the North Sea. This is the famous **Cley Mill**, the subject of thousands of paintings. Built in 1713 and in use until 1921, the Mill is open to visitors during the season (afternoons only), and also offers bed and breakfast.

The village's prosperity in the past is reflected in the enormous scale of its 14th/15th century parish church, **St Mary's**, whose south porch is particularly notable for its fine stonework and 16 armorial crests. The gorgeous fan-vaulted roof is decorated with bosses carved with angels, flowers, and a lively scene of an old woman throwing her distaff at a fox running away with her chickens.

From Cley it's possible to walk along the shoreline to **Blakeney Point**, the

Letheringsett Watermill

recorded in the *Doomsday Book*, and was rescued from near-dereliction in the 1980s. This fully functional, water-powered mill produces 100% wholewheat flour from locally grown wheat; there are regular demonstrations of the milling process, with a running commentary from the miller; and the end product can be purchased in the gift shop.

Morston
13 miles W of Cromer on the A149

Great stretches of salt marshes and mud flats lie between this pleasant village and the sea, which is reached by way of a tidal creek that almost disappears at low tide. Morston is a particularly pleasing village with quiet lanes and clusters of cottages built from local flint cobbles. If the church tower looks rather patched-up, that's because it was struck

by lightning in 1743. It's said that local people took this as a sign that the Second Coming of Christ was imminent, and that repairing their church was therefore pointless. It was many years before restoration work was finally undertaken, by which time the fabric of the tower had deteriorated even further.

Langham
14 miles W of Cromer off the A149/A148

The minor road leading south from Morston will bring you, after a mile or so, to **Langham Glass & Rural Crafts** where, in a wonderful collection of restored 18th century barn workshops, you watch a variety of craftspeople exercising their traditional skills. In addition to the now famous Langham Glass works where a master glass-maker will give a running commentary, there's a pyrographer, wood-turner, stained glass maker, and glass engraver. The Factory Gift Shop is well stocked with their creations, the Antiques & Collectibles Shop offers a wide variety of items from Victorian china to Lalique, and there's also a walled garden, seven-acre maize maze, adventure playground and restaurant.

Blakeney
14 miles W of Cromer on the A149

One of the most enchanting of the North Norfolk coastal villages, Blakeney

BLAKENEY COTTAGE COMPANY

5 Westgate Street, Blakeney,
North Norfolk NR25 7NQ
Tel: 01263 741777 Fax: 01263 741666
e-mail: susie@blakeneycottagecompany.co.uk
website: www.blakeneycottagecompany.co.uk

With an accent on 'pure indulgence' the **Blakeney Cottage Company** has an outstanding range of 30 stunning holiday retreats from traditional beamed cottages to superb coastal houses. Supreme comfort is

guaranteed - imagine, four poster beds, crisp cotton sheets and roaring log fires. Blakeney is North Norfolks 'jewel in the crown' a haven for wildlife, boats bobbing in the harbour and local Inns offering mouthwatering seafood. You are in safe hands with us so, treat yourselves... you deserve it.

HOLLY COTTAGE

52, The High Street, Blakeney, Norfolk
Tel: 01328 862172 Fax: 01328 863916
e-mail: thecrown@paston.co.uk

Located just off the High Street and close to the quayside, **Holly Cottage** is a delightful period cottage offering self-catering accommodation. This picturesque country cottage sleeps up to five, with a bright and cheerful living room/dining area and a fully equipped kitchen. Open all year round, it makes a charming base from which to explore

the North Norfolk Coast, and is close to several pubs and restaurants.

was a commercial port until the beginning of the 20th century, when silting up of the estuary prevented all

Blakeney Harbour

but pleasure craft from gaining access. The silting has left a fascinating landscape of serpentine creeks and channels twisting their way through mud banks and sand hills. In a side street off the quay is the 14th century **Guildhall** (English Heritage), which was probably a private house and contains an interesting undercroft, or cellar, which is notable as an early example of a brick-built vaulted ceiling.

The beautifully restored Church of St Nicholas, set on a hill overlooking village and marshland, offers the visitor a lovely Early English chancel, built in 1220, and the magnificent west tower, 100 feet high, a landmark for miles around. In a small turret on the northeast corner of the chancel a light would once burn as a beacon to guide ships safely into Blakeney Harbour.

Stiffkey

16 miles W of Cromer on the A149

Regarded as one of the prettiest villages in the county, Stiffkey lies beside the little river of the same name. Pronounced 'Stewkey', the name means 'island of tree stumps' and is most likely derived from the marshy river valley of reed beds and fallen trees, which indeed gives the village the appearance of an island. At the east end of the village is the church of St John the Baptist; from the churchyard there are fine views of the river and of Stiffkey Hall to the south. All that now remains of this once-impressive building, built by the Bacon family in 1578, are the towers, one wing of the house, and the 17th century gatehouse. The stately ruins of the great hall have been transformed into a rose terrace and sunken garden and are open to the public.

The former Rectory is a grand Georgian building, famous as the residence of the Revd Harold Davidson, Rector of Stiffkey during the 1920s and 1930s. Rather like the central character in Michael Palin's film *The Missionary*, Harold launched a personal crusade to save the fallen women of London, and caused much gossip and scandal by doing so. Despite the fact that his notoriety regularly filled the church to capacity, he constantly fell foul of the ecclesiastical authorities and eventually lost his living. There is a rather bizarre ending to his story. After handing over the keys of Stiffkey Rectory, Harold joined a travelling show and was later killed by a lion whose cage he was sharing.

To the north of the village are the **Stiffkey Salt Marshes**, a National Trust nature reserve which turns a delicate shade of purple in July when the sea lavender is in bloom. Here on the sandflats can be found the famous 'Stewkey blues' - cockles which are highly regarded as a delicacy by connoisseurs of succulent bivalve molluscs.

A couple of miles south of Stiffkey stand the picturesque ruins of **Binham Priory** (English Heritage), its magnificent nave still serving as the parish church. This represents only about one-sixth of the original Priory, founded in 1091 by a nephew of William the Conqueror. The church is well worth a visit to see its unusually lofty interior with a Monk's Walk at roof level, its Seven Sacraments font, and noble west front.

Great Yarmouth

The topography of Great Yarmouth is rather curious. Back in Saxon times, it was actually an island, a large sandbank dotted with fishermen's cottages. Later, the narrow estuary of the River Bure at the northern end was blocked off, causing it to flow down the western side of the town. It runs parallel to the sea for two miles before joining the larger River Yare, and then their united waters

Great Yarmouth Harbour

in miniature, which are illuminated at dusk, and the **Pleasure Beach**, featuring over 70 rides and attractions combining all the thrills of modern high-tech amusement park rides with the fun of traditional fairground attractions.

For heritage enthusiasts, Great Yarmouth has a rich and proud maritime history. The **Norfolk Nelson Museum** on South Quay features displays, paintings and contemporary memorabilia relating to the life and times of Horatio Lord Nelson. Also on South Quay is the **Elizabethan House Museum**, built by a wealthy merchant and now a museum of domestic life, with 16th century panelled rooms and a functional Victorian kitchen. In Row 117, South Quay, the **Old Merchant's House** is an excellent example of a 17th century dwelling and a showplace for local wood and metalwork. Nearby is **The Tollhouse**, originally built in 1262 as a gaol and later used as a courthouse. It is now a museum with original dungeons.

At South Denes the 144-foot high **Nelson's Monument** crowned by a statue, not of Norfolk's most famous son, but of Britannia.

Most of Yarmouth's older buildings are concentrated in the western, or riverside, part of the town. Here you will find **The Quay**, which moved Daniel Defoe, in 1724, to describe it as 'the finest quay in England, if not Europe'. It

curve around the southern edge of the town for another three miles before finally entering the sea.

So Yarmouth is now a promontory, its eastern and western sides displaying markedly different characters. The seaward side is a 5-mile stretch of sandy beaches, tourist attractions and countless amusements, with a breezy promenade from which one can watch the constant traffic of ships in Yarmouth Roads. There are two fine old traditional piers, the Britannia (810 feet long) and the Wellington (600 feet long), as well as The Jetty, first built in the 16th century for landing goods and passengers. A host of activities are on offer for families: **The Sealife Centre** with many kinds of marine life including octopus and seahorses, and an underwater viewing channel passing through shark-infested 'oceans'; **Amazonia**, an indoor tropical paradise featuring the largest collection of reptiles in Britain; **Merrivale Model Village** which offers an acre of attractive landscaped gardens with over 200 realistic models of town and country is more than a mile long and in places 150 yards wide. The **Town Hall** is well known for its grand staircase, Court Room and Assembly Room; the building itself is in use by the Local Authority. **The Rows**, a medieval network of tiny courtyards and narrow alleys, are a mere 2 feet wide in places. Badly damaged during a bombing raid in

Great Yarmouth Beach

1942, enough remains to show their unique character. There were originally 145 of these rows, about 7 miles in total, all of them built at right angles to the sea and therefore freely ventilated by onshore breezes which, given the urban sanitary conditions of those times, must have been extremely welcome.

The bombing raid of 1942 also completely destroyed the interior of **St Nicholas'** church, but left its walls standing. Between 1957 and 1960 this huge building - the largest parish church in England - was completely restored and furnished in traditional style largely by using pieces garnered from redundant churches and other sources. The partly Norman font, for example, came from Highway church in Wiltshire, the organ from St Mary-the-Boltons in Kensington.

Just south of the church, off the Market Place, is the half-timbered **Anna Sewell House**, built in 1641, in which the author of *Black Beauty* lived. Sewell was born in the town in 1820, but it was only when she was in her late fifties that

she transmuted her concern for the more humane treatment of horses into a classic and seemingly timeless novel. Anna was paid just £20 for the rights to a book which, in the five months that elapsed between its publication and her death in 1878, had already sold an incredible 100,000 copies.

Another famous author associated with the town is Charles Dickens, who stayed at the Royal Hotel on Marine Parade in 1847-48 while writing *David Copperfield*. Dickens had visited the town as a child and had actually seen an upturned boat on the beach being used as a dwelling, complete with a chimney emerging from its keel. In his novel, this becomes Peggotty's house to which young Copperfield is brought following the death of his mother. 'One thing I particularly noticed in this delightful house,' he writes, 'was the smell of fish; which was so searching, that when I took out my pocket-handkerchief to wipe my nose, I found it smelt exactly as if it had wrapped up a lobster.'

In fact, the whole town at that time

was pervaded with the aroma of smoked herring, the silvery fish that were the basis of Yarmouth's prosperity. Around the time of Dickens' stay here, the author of the town's directory tried to pre-empt any discouraging effect this might have on visitors by claiming that 'The wholesome exhalations arising from the fish during the operation of curing are said to have a tendency to dissipate contagious disorders, and to be generally beneficial to the human constitution which is here sometimes preserved to extreme longevity.'

Across the town, some 60 curing houses were busy gutting, salting and spicing herrings to produce Yarmouth's great contribution to the English breakfast, the kipper. The process had been invented by a Yarmouth man, John Woodger: a rival of his, a Mr Bishop, developed a different method which left the fish wonderfully moist and flavoursome, and so created the famous Yarmouth bloater.

For centuries, incredible quantities of herring were landed, nearly a billion in 1913 alone. In earlier years the trade had involved so many fishermen that there were more boats (1,123) registered at Yarmouth than at London. But the scale of the over-fishing produced the inevitable result: within the space of two decades Yarmouth's herring industry foundered, and by the late 1960s found itself dead in the water. Luckily, the end of that historic trade coincided with the beginning of North Sea oil and gas exploitation, a business which has kept the town in reasonably good economic health up to the present day.

In and Around Great Yarmouth

Burgh Castle
4 miles W of Great Yarmouth off the A12 or A143

When the Romans established their fortress of *Garionnonum*, now known as Burgh Castle, the surrounding marshes were still under water. The fort then stood on one bank of a vast estuary, commanding a strategic position at the head of an important waterway running into the heart of East Anglia. The ruins are impressive, with walls of alternating

THE ROYAL OAK

Ormesby, Great Yarmouth, Norfolk NR29 3JT
Tel: 01493 384144 Fax: 01493 731063
e-mail: janeeread@aol.com

Overlooking the Ormesby village green, **The Royal Oak** is an impressive and handsome inn offering great food and drink and comfortable accommodation. This Grade II listed building has ample room for guests to enjoy the many fine ales, lagers, wines, spirits and soft drinks on offer, together with the hearty freshly cooked meals and convivial atmosphere.

There are eight comfortable and welcoming guest bedrooms.

flint and brick layers rising 15 feet high in places, and spreading more than 11 feet wide at their base. The Romans abandoned Garionnonum around AD 408 and some two centuries later the Irish missionary St Fursey (or Fursa) founded a monastery within its walls. Later generations cannibalised both his building, and much of the crumbling Roman castle, as materials for their own churches and houses.

Caister-on-Sea

3 miles N of Great Yarmouth off the A149

In Boudica's time, this modern holiday resort with its stretch of fine sands was an important fishing port for her people, the Iceni. After the Romans had vanquished her unruly tribe, they settled here sometime in the 2nd century and built a *castra*, or castle, or Caister, of which only a few foundations and remains have yet been found. **Caister Castle**, which stands in a picturesque setting about a mile to the west of the town, is a much later construction, built in 1432-5 by the legendary Sir John Fastolf with his spoils from the French wars in which he had served, very profitably, as Governor of Normandy and also distinguished himself leading the English bowmen at the Battle of Agincourt. Academics have enjoyed themselves for centuries disputing whether this Sir John was the model for Shakespeare's immortal rogue, Falstaff. Certainly the real Sir John was a larger-than-life character, but there's no evidence that he shared Falstaff's other characteristics of cowardliness, boastfulness or general over-indulgence.

Caister Castle was the first in England to be built of brick, and is in fact one of the earliest brick buildings in the county. The 90-foot tower remains, together with much of the moated wall and gatehouse, now lapped by still waters and with ivy relentlessly encroaching. The castle is open daily from May to September and, as an additional attraction, there is a Car Collection in the grounds which features an impressive collection of veteran, Edwardian and vintage cars, an antique fire engine, and the original car used in the film of Ian Fleming's *Chitty Chitty Bang Bang*.

THE BELL INN

Hemsby, Great Yarmouth, Norfolk RN29 4EU
Tel/Fax: 01493 730291

Dating back to the late 1800s, **The Bell Inn** is a spacious and welcoming inn that is tastefully and comfortably decorated and furnished. Here guests can choose from a wide range of beers, lager, wines, spirits and soft drinks, and savour a menu of English and Asian cuisine. The 70-cover restaurant is gracious and attractive, just the place to enjoy the freshly prepared food served every day at

lunch (12.00-14.00) and dinner (19.00-21.00)

About three miles west of Caister Castle, the pleasantly landscaped grounds surrounding an 1876 Victorian mansion have been transformed into the **Thrigby Hall Wildlife Gardens**, home for a renowned collection of Asian mammals, birds and reptiles. There are snow leopards and rare tigers; gibbons and crocodiles; deer and otters; and other attractions include a tropical house, aviaries, waterfowl lake, willow pattern garden, gift shop and cafe. The Gardens are open every day, all year round.

St Benets Abbey, River Bure

Fritton

6 miles SW of Great Yarmouth off the A143

At **Fritton Lake Countryworld** (see panel opposite), visitors will find a large undercover falconry centre with birds-of-prey flying displays twice daily. There are also heavy horse stables and a children's farm, 9-hole golf and 18-hole putting courses, lakeside gardens, boating and a large adventure playground. Open end-March to end-September every day, and weekends and half-term in October.

The Norfolk Broads

Reedham

8 miles SW of Great Yarmouth off the B1140

Here in Reedham is the single remaining car and passenger ferry in the Broads. There's also an interesting craft showroom at the Old Brewery, and a great pub in The Reedham Ferry Inn.

THE OLIVE TREE

Yarmouth Road, Ellingham, Great Yarmouth, Norfolk NR35 2PN
Tel: 01508 518147
e-mail: gtevola@hotmail.com

Fresh fish is a speciality at **The Olive Tree** in Ellingham, an award-winning restaurant featuring home-cooked Italian food at its finest. Spacious and comfortable, the interior has a warm and welcoming ambience. The menu (lunch Weds-Fri 12.00-14.00; dinner Tues-Sat 18.30 till late) offers up an excellent range of beef, lamb, veal, chicken and pasta

dishes, expertly prepared and presented. Advance booking recommended.

FRITTON LAKE COUNTRYWORLD

Church Lane, Fritton, Great Yarmouth,
Norfolk NR31 9HA
Tel: 01493 488288/488208
Fax: 01493 488355
website: www.frittonlake.co.uk

For an enjoyable day out in the country,
Fritton Lake Countryworld has few rivals. The
beautiful grounds offer a splendid contrast
between natural woodland and formal

Victorian gardens, and Fritton Lake, with
fishing and boating both available, is one of
the loveliest stretches of water in East Anglia.
A miniature railway runs by the lake, and
among the many new attractions introduced
since 2001 are a family cycle trail, an
orienteering course and giant outdoor board
games. Also on site are a 9 hole par 3 golf
course and an 18-hole putting green, displays
of falconry and basket-making, a growing
collection of waterfowl, a children's farm and
a heavy horse centre with working Suffolk
Punches and Shires.

Acle

*10 miles W of Great Yarmouth off
the A47*

A thousand years ago, this small market
town, now 10 miles inland, was a small
fishing port on the coast. Gradually,
land has been reclaimed from the
estuaries of the Rivers Bure, Waveney
and Yare, so that today large expanses of
flat land stretch away from Acle towards
the sea. The town's importance as a
boating centre began in the 19th
century with boat-building yards
springing up beside the bridge. When
Acle's first Regatta was held in 1890,
some 150 yachts took part. The town
became known as the 'Gateway to the
Broads' and also as the gateway to
'Windmill Land', a picturesque stretch of
the River Bure dotted with windmills.
The medieval bridge that formerly
crossed the Bure at Acle has less
agreeable associations, since it was used
for numerous executions with the
unfortunate victims left to dangle
over the river.

Acle was granted permission for a
market in 1272, and it's still held every
Thursday, attracting visitors from miles
around. Others come to see the unusual
church of **St Edmund** with its Saxon
round tower, built some time around AD
900, crowned with a 15th century belfry
from which eight carved figures look
down on the beautifully thatched roof of
the nave. The treasures inside include a
superbly carved font, 6 feet high, and
inscribed with the date 1410, and a fine
15th century screen.

THE KING'S HEAD

24 Station Road, Lingwood, Norwich,
Norfolk NR13 4AZ
Tel: 01603 713168

Comfortable and cosy, **The King's Head** is a spacious and very pleasant inn with superb food, a variety of real ales, and a relaxed atmosphere. Situated next to Lingwood Railway Station (on the Norwich-Great Yarmouth line), this charming pub offers menus packed with delicious meals, to be enjoyed in the bar, separate restaurant overlooking the large and lovely garden, or in the garden itself when the weather is fine.

Thursday night is Curry Night at this superior inn – booking is advised. There's also a take-away service.

CLIPPESBY HALL

Clippesby, Great Yarmouth,
Norfolk NR29 3BL   Tel: 01493 367800
e-mail: holidays@clippesby.com
website: www.clippesby.com

Clippesby Hall encompasses beautiful holiday lodges, cottages and a touring park for caravans. Located off the B1152 not far from Acle, Norwich and Great Yarmouth, this superb, award-winning site lies in the heart of the Broads National Park, in a charming countryside setting with pine woods, heated outdoor swimming pool, café and shop, family golf course, pub, tennis court, football pitch, treehouse and play area – everything required for a memorable, fun and relaxing holiday.

South Walsham

9 miles E of Norwich on the B1140

This small village is notable for having two parish churches built within yards of each other. Just to the north of the village is the **Fairhaven Woodland and Water Garden**, an expanse of delightful water gardens lying beside the private **South Walsham Inner Broad**. Its centrepiece is the 900-year-old King Oak, lording it over the surrounding displays of rare shrubs and plants, native wildflowers, rhododendrons and giant lilies. There are tree-lined walks, a bird sanctuary, plants for sale, and a

restaurant. A vintage-style riverboat runs trips every half-hour around the Broad.

The best way to see the remains of **St Benet's Abbey** is from a boat along the River Bure (indeed, it's quite difficult to reach it any other way). Rebuilt in 1020 by King Canute, after the Vikings had destroyed an earlier Saxon building, St Benet's became one of the richest abbeys in East Anglia. When Henry VIII closed it down in 1536 he made an unusual deal with its last Abbot. In return for creating the Abbot Bishop of Norwich, the Cathedral estates were to be handed over to the King, but St Benet's properties could remain in the Abbot/

THE WHITE HORSE

Chapel Road, Upton, Norfolk NR13 6BT
Tel/Fax: 01493 750696
website: www.whitehorseupton.com

More like a large and attractive house than a pub, **The White Horse** in Upton is run by Ray Norman, who gained his first licence in October 1972, making him one of the longest-serving landlords in the county. Locals and visitors alike have been enjoying the delights on offer here since 1844, when the pub was converted from three cottages built in 1817. This wonderful traditional pub has many original features such as the wooden bar, quarry-tiled flooring and inglenook fires. Memorabilia collected over the years adorns the walls and includes an eclectic collection of clocks and photos of the village cricket and football teams across the generations.

The great food and drink on offer can be enjoyed in the main bar, the snug, small dining area/restaurant, the conservatory dining room or the lovely enclosed lawn garden, which also boasts a mini-aviary with cockatoo, budgies and a miniature parrot.

Bishop's possession. Even today, the Bishop of Norwich retains the additional title of Abbot of St Benet's, and on the first Sunday in August each year travels the last part of the journey by boat to hold an open-air service near the stately ruins of the Abbey gatehouse.

clear day, the spire of Norwich Cathedral. Inside, the church houses one of Norfolk's greatest ecclesiastical treasures, a breathtaking early 15th century Gothic choir screen, the most beautiful and the best preserved in the county. In glowing reds, greens and

Ranworth

14 miles NW of Great Yarmouth off the B1140

This beautiful Broadland village is famous for its church and its position on Ranworth Broad. From the tower of **St Helen's** church it is possible to see five Norfolk Broads, Horsey Mill, the sea at Great Yarmouth and, on a

Reed Cutting, Ranworth

TaPs Restaurant

25 Lower Street, Horning, Norwich,
Norfolk NR12 8AA
Tel: 01692 630219 Fax: 01692 631565
e-mail: terrywestall@lineone.net

Gracious and elegant, **TaPs Restaurant** in Horning is well worth seeking out. The brick-and-whitewashed exterior presents a pleasant and welcoming face to the world, with the restaurant on the ground floor and private accommodation in the gabled end above. Opposite the flowing River Bure, its exterior is adorned with lovely hanging baskets in summer.

Inside, all is comfortable and intimate. The cosy reception/lounge area offers a sample of the delightful dining experience to come. Candlelit and tastefully decorated, with sparkling silver and glassware, this 40-cover restaurant is further enhanced by the helpful and friendly service. Subdued and subtle lighting increases the warm and relaxed ambience.

Open for lunch and dinner Tuesday through Saturday, this excellent restaurant boasts meticulously prepared menus. All meals are freshly prepared to order using local and seasonal meats and produce. Winner of AA Rosette awards for 2001, 2002 and 2003, Michelin recommended and voted Restaurant of the Year (2001) by the Journal Publishing Company, the dishes are best described as modern with a classic twist,

blending the best of traditional and more innovative ingredients to create tempting dishes to suit every palate.

Co-owner and head chef Terry Westall brings a wealth of experience in cookery and catering to creating everything on the menu, and also bakes his own bread and makes all the ice-cream, biscuits and pastries. Together with his wife Angela, daughter Leah and chef Jack Thompson, he has established

an enviable reputation for quality and service. Opened in 1999, this fine restaurant attracts diners from far and wide keen to savour dishes such as roast loin of venison, duck breast, fillet of beef, loin of lamb, fillet of salmon and vegetarian choices. The wine list is superb.

golds, gifted medieval artists painted a gallery of more than 30 saints and martyrs, inserting tiny cameos of such everyday scenes as falcons seizing hares, dogs chasing ducks and, oddly for Norfolk, lions. Cromwell's men, offended by such idolatrous images, smothered them with brown paint - an ideal preservative for these wonderful paintings, as became apparent when they were once again revealed during the course of a 19th century restoration of the church.

Just to the north of the village is the **Broadland Conservation Centre** (Norfolk Naturalists Trust), a thatched building floating on pontoons at the edge of Ranworth Broad. It houses an informative exhibition on the history of the Broads, and there's also an interesting Nature Trail which shows how these wetlands gradually developed over the centuries.

Horning
12 miles NW of Great Yarmouth off the A1062

The travel writer Arthur Mee described Horning as 'Venice in Broadland', where 'waterways wandering from the river into the gardens are crossed by tiny bridges.' With its pretty reed-thatched cottages lining the bank of the River Bure and its position in the heart of the Broads, there are few more attractive places from which to explore this magical area.

Potter Heigham
13 miles NW of Great Yarmouth off the A149

Modern Potter Heigham has sprung up around the medieval bridge over the River Thurne, a low-arched structure with a clearance of only 7 feet at its highest, a notorious test for novice sailors. The Thurne is a major artery through the Broads, linking them in a continuous waterway from Horsey Mere in the east to Wroxham Broad in the west. Generally regarded as one of the liveliest of the Broadland boating centres, Potter Heigham is also home to the **Museum of the Broads**, located in boat sheds in the historic Herbert Woods boat yard. Among the museum's many intriguing exhibits are the only concrete dinghy ever constructed, an ice yacht, tools from traditional Broads

KINGS ARMS

15 The Green, Martham, Great Yarmouth, Norfolk NR29 4PL
Tel: 01493 740204

Impressive inside and out, the **Kings Arms** in the quiet village of Martham overlooks the village green and duck pond. In this traditional countryside setting, the pub meets up to expectations, providing warm hospitality in cosy and comfortable surroundings. The food on offer ranges from light snacks to a la carte, and comprises a good selection of home-

made dishes all freshly prepared to order and served at lunch and dinner.

industries such as eel catching, gun punts for duck-shooting (complete with incredibly long guns), and a display featuring one of Broadland's most destructive pests, the coypu.

A pleasant excursion from Potter Heigham is a visit to **Horsey Mere**, about six miles to the east, and **Horsey Windpump** (both National Trust). From this early 20th century drainage mill, now restored and fully working, there are lovely views across the Mere. A circular walk follows the north side of Horsey Mere, passes another windmill, and returns through the village. There's a small shop at the Windpump, and light refreshments are available.

Wroxham Broad

Wroxham

8 miles NE of Norwich on the A1151

This riverside village, linked to its twin, Hoveton, by a hump-backed bridge over the River Bure, is the self-styled 'capital' of the Norfolk Broads and as such gets extremely busy during the season. The banks of the river are chock-a-block with boatyards full of cruisers of all shapes and sizes, there's a constant traffic of boats making their way to the open spaces of **Wroxham Broad**, and in July the scene becomes even more hectic when the annual Regatta is under way.

Wroxham is also the southern terminus of the **Bure Valley Railway**, a nine-mile long, narrow-gauge (15-inch) steam train service that closely follows the course of the River Bure through lovely countryside to the market town of Aylsham. It runs along the trackbed of the old East Norfolk Railway, has two half-scale locomotives, and specially constructed passenger coaches with large windows to provide the best possible views. In the high season there are half a dozen trains each day, in both directions, and throughout the year there are special events such as the 'Friends of Thomas the Tank Engine' days and 'Santa Specials'. And if you still cherish that childhood ambition of becoming a train driver, the BVR also runs one- or two- day steam-driving courses, framed to suit anyone from the absolute beginner upwards.

A couple of miles north of Wroxham is **Wroxham Barns**, a delightful collection of beautifully restored 18th century barns set in 10 acres of countryside, and housing a community of craftspeople. There are 13 workshops, producing between them a wide range of crafts, from stained glass to woodturning, stitchcraft to handmade children's clothes, pottery to floral artistry, and much more. The complex also includes a cider-pressing centre, a junior farm with lots of hands-on activities, a traditional Family Fair (with individually priced rides), a gift and craft shop, and a tearoom.

A mile or so east of Wroxham Barns, **Hoveton Hall Gardens** offer visitors a splendid combination of plants, shrubs and trees, with rare rhododendrons, azaleas, water plants and dazzling herbaceous borders within a walled garden. There are woodland and lakeside walks, plant sales, gardening books and a tearoom.

Anyone interested in dried flower arrangements should make their way to the tiny hamlet of **Cangate**, another couple of miles to the east, where **Willow Farm Flowers** provides an opportunity of seeing the whole process, from the flowers in the field to the final colourful displays. The farm shop has an abundance of dried, silk, parchment and wooden flowers, beautifully arranged, and more than 50 varieties of dried flowers are available in bunches or made into arrangements of all shapes and sizes, or to special order. Willow Farm also has a picnic and play area, a guided farm walk, lays on flower arranging demonstrations and also runs one day classes.

Coltishall
8 miles N of Norwich on the B1150/B1354

This charming village beside the River Bure captivates visitors with its riverside setting, leafy lanes, elegant Dutch-gabled houses, village green and thatched church. Coltishall has a good claim to its title of 'Gateway to Broadland', since for most cruisers this is the beginning of the navigable portion of the Bure. Anyone interested in Norfolk's industrial heritage will want to seek out the **Ancient Lime Kiln**, next door to the Railway Tavern in Station Road. Lime, formerly an important part of Norfolk's rural economy, is obtained by heating chalk to a very high temperature in a kiln. Most of the county sits on a bed of chalk, but in the area around Coltishall and Horstead it is of a particularly high quality. The kiln at Coltishall, one of the few surviving in the country, is a listed building of finely finished brickwork, built in a style unique to Norfolk.

The top of the tapered kiln pot is level with the ground, and down below a vaulted walkway allowed access to the grills through which the lime was raked out. This was uncomfortable and even dangerous work since fresh lime, when it comes into contact with a moist surface, such as a human body, becomes burning hot. The lime had to be slaked with water before it could be used as a fertiliser, for mortar or as whitewash. Access to the kiln is by way of the

Railway Tavern, but during the months from October to March you may find that the building has been taken over by a colony of hibernating bats which, by law, may not be disturbed.

A couple of miles south of Coltishall, on the B1150, is another animal refuge, the **Redwings Horse Sanctuary**, founded in 1984 to provide a caring and permanent home for horses, ponies, donkeys and mules rescued from neglect and slaughter. The Sanctuary cares for more than 1,000 animals at any one time, and there are no indications that this number is likely to diminish. Even with the help of many volunteers, the work is expensive. To raise funds, the Sanctuary holds regular Open Days, has a gift shop with many horse-related items on sale, and also runs an Adopt-a-Horse scheme.

Worstead

12 miles NE of Norwich off the A149 or B1150

Hard to imagine now, but Worstead was a busy little industrial centre in the Middle Ages. The village lent its name to the hard-wearing cloth produced in the region, and many of the original weavers' cottages can still be seen in the narrow side-streets. Worsted cloth, woven from tightly-twisted yarn, was introduced by Flemish immigrants and became popular throughout England from the 13th century onwards. The Flemish weavers settled happily into the East Anglian way of life and seem to have influenced its architecture almost

as strongly as its weaving industry.

The lovely 14th century church of **St Mary** provides ample evidence of Worstead's former prosperity. Its many treasures include a fine hammerbeam roof, a chancel screen with a remarkable painted dado, and a magnificent traceried font complete with cover. The village stages an annual weekend of events in July to raise money for the restoration of the church. The festival started up some 35 years ago, attracting more than 35,000 visitors in 1999. The memory of Worstead's days of glory is kept alive by a still-functioning Guild of Weavers. The Guild has placed looms in the north aisle of St Mary's, and from time to time there are demonstrations of the ancient skill of weaving.

North Walsham

This busy country town with its attractive **Market Cross** of 1600 has some interesting historical associations. Back in 1381, despite its remoteness from London, North Walsham became the focus of an uprising in support of Wat Tyler's Peasants' Rebellion. These North Norfolk rebels were led by John Litester, a local dyer, and their object was the abolition of serfdom. Their actions were mainly symbolic: invading manor houses, monasteries and town halls and burning the documents that recorded their subservient status. In a mass demonstration they gathered on Mousehold Heath outside Norwich, presented a petition to the King, and then retreated to North Walsham to

THE WHITE SWAN

Church Street, North Walsham,
Norfolk NR28 9DR
Tel/Fax: 01692 402354

A happy blend of old and new, with a stylish contemporary restaurant and a traditional pub, **The White Swan** is a cosy and comfortable place to enjoy great food, drink and hospitality.

Near the town centre and close to the ancient church, the simple exterior belies the handsome and welcoming décor and furnishings inside. The menu boasts a range of traditional and more innovative snacks and main courses, served every day from midday until 8 p.m.

await his answer. It came in the form of the sanguinary Bishop of Norwich, Henry Despenser, who, as his admiring biographer recorded, led an assault on the rebels, 'grinding his teeth like a wild boar, and sparing neither himself nor his enemies ... stabbing some, unhorsing others, hacking and hewing'. John Litester was captured, summarily executed and, on the orders of the Bishop, 'divided into four parts, and sent throughout the country to Norwich, Yarmouth, Lynn and to the site of his own house.'

A more glorious fate awaited the town's most famous resident, Horatio Nelson, who came to the Paston School here in 1768 as a boy of ten. Horatio was already dreaming of a naval career and, three years later when he read in the county newspaper that his Uncle Maurice had been appointed commander of a warship, he prevailed on his father to let him join the *Raisonnable*.

The **Paston School** had been founded in 1606 by Sir William Paston. His ancestors were the writers of the extraordinary collection of more than a thousand letters, written between 1422 and 1509, which present an astonishingly vivid picture of East Anglian life at the end of the turbulent Middle Ages. Sir William himself is buried in the parish church where he personally supervised (and paid for) the construction of the impressive marble and alabaster monument he desired to be erected in his memory.

About four miles east of North Walsham, near the village of Erpingham

The Paston School, North Walsham

THORPEWOOD COTTAGES

Nursery Farm, Cromer Road, Thorpe Market,
Norfolk NR11 8TU
Tel/Fax: 01263 834493
mobile: 07775 646527
e-mail: davidhowarth@thorpegate.fsnet.co.uk
website: www.thorpewoodcottages.co.uk

Enjoying a lovely location only 5 miles from
the beach, and once forming part of the
historic Gunton Hall Estate,**Thorpewood
Cottages** are set in the grounds of
Nursery Farm which include 8 acres
of woodland that guests are free to
explore.

Thorpegate Cottage is a one-
bedroom barn conversion that
sleeps two. All of its rooms boast
attractive beamed and vaulted
ceilings. *Pinewood Cottage* also
sleeps two. New for 2003,
Tanglewood Cottage is a single-
storey brick and flint former barn
that sleeps four.

Each of these three superb

cottages is tastefully and comfortably
furnished and decorated, has excellent
kitchen facilities, its own terraced garden
area and all the amenities that will make your
stay here a pleasant and comfortable one.
The cottages open all year round are non
smoking and pets cannot be accommodated.

Thorpe Market, as well as being within
easy reach of the many sights and attractions
of North Norfolk, is a very pretty village
offering an excellent local farm shop, pubs
and restaurants.

Tanglewood

THE HILL HOUSE

Happisburgh, Norfolk NR12 0PW
Tel/Fax: 01692 650004
e-mail: sue.clivehillhouse@amserve.com

The Hill House in Happisburgh (pronouced
Haze-borough) is an excellent traditional
coaching inn located next to the 12th century
parish church of St Mary. This family-friendly
Free House is run by Sue and Clive Stockton,
who are welcoming and
attentive hosts. This
attractive pub and guest
house offers an excellent
range of food and drink, to
be enjoyed in the warm glow
of the open fires in the main
bar, the handsome
restaurant, the spacious
family room or the lovely
beer garden. Parts of this
distinctive coaching inn date
back to Tudor times, and it
was a favourite haunt of Sir
Arthur Conan Doyle, who

penned the Sherlock Holmes' story *The
Dancing Men* while staying at the pub in
1903. The accommodation consists of three
attractive and comfortable guest bedrooms.

Every summer solstice the pub hosts a
marvellous beer festival featuring 40 different
beers and ciders, along with music and other
entertainments.

Theme Nights are also regular events at
The Hill House, featuring Greek, Indian,
Mexican, Thai and other exotic cuisines.

on the A140, **Alby Crafts & Gardens** has a Crafts Gallery promoting the excellence of mainly East Anglian and British craftsmanship - lacework, woodturning, jewellery, canework and much more. The 'Plantsman's Garden' displays a fine collection of unusual shrubs, plants and bulbs in a 4-acre site; there are also workshops where you can watch craftsmen at work, a Bottle Museum (small charge for admission) and a tearoom.

Around North Walsham

Mundesley

2 miles NE of North Walsham on the B1159

'The finest air in the kingdom has been wasted for centuries,' said a speaker celebrating the arrival of the railway at Mundesley in 1898, 'because nobody had the courage to bring the people to the district.' The railway has been and gone, but the fresh breezes off the North Sea remain as invigorating as ever.

After the hazards of the coastline immediately to the north where cliffs, fields and houses have all been eroded by the relentless sea, it's a pleasure to arrive at this unassuming holiday resort with its superb sandy beach, considered by many the very best in Norfolk. Mundesley village is quite small (appropriately, its Maritime Museum is believed to the smallest museum in the country), but it provides all the facilities conducive to a relaxing family holiday.

Best of all, there is safe swimming in the sea, and when the tide is out children can spend many a happy hour exploring the many 'lowes', or shallow lagoons, left behind.

Paston

2 miles NE of North Walsham on the B1159

It was in this small village that the Paston family entered historical record. The vivid collection of letters they wrote to each other during the years that England was being wracked by the Wars of the Roses has already been mentioned, and the village boasts another magnificent legacy from this remarkable family. In 1581, Sir William Paston built a cavernous tithe-barn here with flint walls and a thatched roof. It still stands, its roof still thatched: 160 feet long, almost 60 feet high - the longest, most imposing barn in Norfolk. In the nearby church, the most striking of the family memorials is the one dedicated to Katherine Paston. Sculpted in alabaster by Nicholas Stone in 1628, Katherine lies dressed to kill in her Jacobean finery of starched ruff, embroidered bodice, puffed sleeves and pearl necklaces. The monument cost £340, a staggering sum of money at that time.

Happisburgh

4 miles E of North Walsham on the B1159

The coastal waters off Happisburgh (or 'Hazeborough', to give the village its correct pronunciation), have seen many a shipwreck over the centuries, and the victims lie buried in the graveyard of **St Mary's** church. The large grassy mound on the north side of the church contains the bodies of the ill-fated crew of HMS *Invincible*, wrecked on the treacherous sandbanks here in 1801. The ship was on its way to join up with Nelson's fleet at Copenhagen when the tragedy occurred, resulting in the deaths of 119 sailors. Happisburgh's distinctive Lighthouse, built in 1791 and striped like a barber's pole, certainly proved ineffectual on that occasion; as did the soaring 110-foot tower of the church itself, which could normally be relied on as a 'back-up' warning to mariners.

Inside the Church is a splendid 15th century octagonal font carved with the figures of lions, satyrs and 'wild men'; embedded in the pillars along the aisle are the marks left by shrapnel from German bombs dropped on the village in 1940.

Lessingham
5 miles SE of North Walsham off the B1159

From this small village a lane winds down through spectacular dunes to the sands at Eccles Beach and, a little further north, to Cart Gap with its gently sloping beach and colourful lines of beach huts.

About four miles south of Lessingham stands a windmill that is not just the tallest in Norfolk, but in the whole of England. Eighty feet high, **Sutton Windmill** was built in the year of the French Revolution, 1789, and its millstones only finally ground to a halt in 1940.

Chris Nunn bought the mill in 1976, and since then he has devoted himself to renovating this glorious nine-storey building with the ultimate aim of restoring it to working order. During those years, Chris and his family have also built up a fascinating private collection of artefacts which reflect the social history of Norfolk over the past 150 years or so. These are on display in the family's privately-owned **Broadlands Museum**, a magpie's nest in which you'll find anything from vintage kitchen and veterinary tools to a reconstructed Pharmacy Shop of the 1880s, complete with a fine collection of patent medicines, ointments and pills.

6 King's Lynn and West Norfolk

Breckland, which extends for more than 360 square miles in southwest Norfolk and northwest Suffolk, is underlain by chalk with only a light covering of soil. The name 'Breckland' comes from the dialect word *breck*, meaning an area of land which has been cultivated for a while and then allowed to revert to heath after the soil has become exhausted. This quiet corner of the county is bounded by the Rivers Little Ouse and Waveney, which separate Norfolk from Suffolk.

It's surprising to find that one of England's most important ports in medieval times, King's Lynn, sat at the southern end of an underwater maze of sandbanks in The Wash. Keels were shallower then, of course, but without such modern aids as echo-sounders it must still have taken sailing skills of a high order to navigate one's way into the safety of King's Lynn harbour.

Along most of The Wash's 50-mile shoreline there is no human habitation: good news for the more than 160,000 wading birds and 51,000 wild ducks who have claimed the coast for themselves.

South of King's Lynn the countryside never quite decides whether it belongs to the Cambridgeshire fenland, with its bread-board level contours and over-arching skyscapes, or to the subtly-rounded undulations of central Norfolk where each twist of the road reveals yet another unblemished rural scene.

Within a radius of a few miles from the small town of Fakenham can be found a remarkable variety of places of interest. To the north, in the valley of the River Stiffkey, the Shrine of Our Lady of Walsingham was in medieval times second only to that of Thomas à Becket at Canterbury as a pilgrim

Holkham Hall

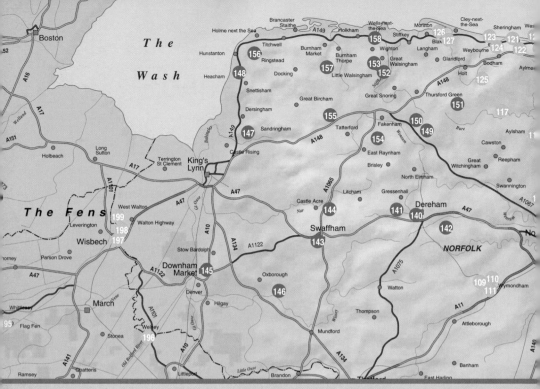

PLACES TO STAY, EAT AND DRINK

● Denotes entries in other chapters

destination. To the northeast, the Thursford Collection is home to an astonishing gathering of steam-powered engines of every description, including a monumental Wurlitzer organ. On the eastern outskirts of the town you can visit the premier collection of endangered and exotic waterbirds to be found in Europe, and over to the west stands the Marquess of Cholmondely's majestic home, Houghton Hall.

The shoreline along Norfolk's northwest coast changes from the perfect sands at Hunstanton to salt marshes threaded by winding creeks, and windswept dunes barely held in place by marram grass. It's an exhilarating coast, with huge skies, ozone-tangy breezes sweeping in from the North Sea, and an abundance of wildlife. There are three separate Nature Reserves within an eight-mile stretch, including the huge National Trust-owned bird sanctuary of Scolt Head Island. An admirable way to experience the area to the full is to walk all or part of the Coastal Footpath which begins at Holme next the Sea and follows the coastline for some 36 miles eastwards to Cromer, for most of its route well away from any roads.

Thetford

Some 2,000 years ago, Thetford may well have been the site of **Boudica's Palace**. In the 1980s, excavations for building development at Gallows Hill, north of the town, revealed an Iron Age enclosure. It is so extensive it may well have been the capital of the Iceni tribe which gave the Romans so much trouble. Certainly, the town's strategic location at the meeting of the Rivers Thet and Little Ouse made it an important settlement for centuries. At the time of the *Domesday Book*, 1086, Thetford was the sixth-largest town in the country and the seat of the Bishop of East Anglia, with its own castle, mint and pottery.

Of the **Castle**, only the 80-foot motte remains, but it's worth climbing to the top of this mighty mound for the views across the town. An early Victorian traveller described Thetford as '*An ancient and princely little town … one of the most charming country towns in England.*'

Binham Abbey

St Peters Church, Thetford

Despite major development all around, the heart of the town still fits that description, with a goodly number of medieval and Georgian houses presenting an attractive medley of flint and half-timbered buildings. Perhaps the most striking is the **Ancient House** Museum in White Hart Street, a magnificent 15th century timber-framed house with superb carved oak ceilings. It houses the Tourist Information Centre and a museum where some of the most interesting exhibits are replicas of the Thetford Treasure, a 4th century hoard of gold and silver jewellery discovered as recently as 1979 by an amateur archaeologist with a metal detector. The originals of these sumptuous artefacts are housed in the British Museum in London.

Even older than the Ancient House is the 12th century **Cluniac Priory** (English Heritage), now mostly in ruins but with an impressive 14th century gatehouse still standing. During the Middle Ages, Thetford could boast 24 churches; today, only three remain.

Thetford's industrial heritage is vividly displayed in the **Burrell Steam Museum**, in Minstergate, which has full-size steam engines regularly 'in steam', re-created workshops and many examples of vintage agricultural machinery. The Museum tells the story of the Burrell Steam Company, which formed the backbone of the town's

Thomas Paine Statue

industry from the late 18th to the early 20th centuries, their sturdy machines famous around the world.

In King Street, the **Thomas Paine Statue** commemorates the town's most famous son, born here in 1737. The revolutionary philosopher, and author of *The Rights of Man* emigrated to America in 1774, where he helped formulate the American Bill of Rights. Paine's democratic views were so detested in England that even ten years after his death in New York,

Euston Hall, Thetford

the authorities refused permission for his admirer, William Cobbett, to have the remains buried in his home country. And it wasn't until the 1950s that Thetford finally got around to erecting a statue in his honour. Ironically for such a robust democrat, his statue stands in King Street and opposite **The King's House**, named after James I, who was a frequent visitor here between 1608 and 1618. At the Thomas Paine Hotel in White Hart Street, the room in which it is believed that Paine was born is now the Honeymoon Suite, complete with four-poster bed.

To the west of the town stretch the 90 square miles of **Thetford Forest**, the most extensive lowland forest in Britain. The Forestry Commission began planting in 1922, and although the woodland is largely given over to conifers, with Scots and Corsican Pine and Douglas Fir predominating, oak, sycamore and beech can also be seen throughout. There is a particularly varied trail leading from the Forestry Commission Information Centre which has detailed information about this and other walks through the area.

On the edge of the forest, about two miles west of Thetford, are the ruins of **Thetford Warren Lodge**, built around 1400. At that time a huge area here was preserved for farming rabbits, a major element of the medieval diet. The vast warren was owned by the Abbot of Thetford Priory, and it was he who built the Lodge for his gamekeeper.

Still in the forest, reached by a footpath from the village of Santon Downham, are **Grimes Graves** (English Heritage), the earliest major industrial site to be discovered in Europe. At these unique Neolithic flint mines, Stone Age labourers extracted the materials for their sharp-edged axes and knives. It's a strange experience entering these 4,000 year old shafts which descend some 30 feet to an underground chamber. (The experience is even better if you bring your own high-powered torch.)

Around Thetford

East Harling
8 miles E of Thetford on the B1111

This attractive little town boasts a beautiful 15th century church in a pastoral location beside the River Thet. Inside, a magnificent hammerbeam roof crowns the lofty nave, there's some outstanding 15th century glass and, in the Harling Chapel, the fine marble **Tomb of Robert Harling**. Harling was one of Henry V's knights, who met his death at the siege of Paris in 1435. Since this was long before the days of refrigeration, the knight's body was instead stewed, then stuffed into a barrel and brought back to East Harling for a ceremonious burial.

The church houses another equally sumptuous memorial, the **Tomb of Sir Thomas Lovell**. Sculpted in alabaster, Sir Thomas is an imposing figure, clad in armour with a long sword, his head resting on a helmet, his feet on a spray of peacock's feathers. He and his wife lie beneath a wondrously ornamented canopy, decorated with multi-coloured shields and pinnacles.

Mundford
8 miles NW of Thetford on the A1065/A134

Mundford is a large Breckland village of flint-built cottages, set on the northern edge of Thetford Forest and with the River Wissey running by. If you ever watch television, you've almost certainly seen Lynford Hall, a mile or so northwest of Mundford. It has provided an impressive location for scenes in *Dad's Army, Allo, Allo, You Rang My Lord?* and *Love on a Branch Line*, as well as featuring in numerous television commercials. The Hall is a superb Grade II listed mansion, built for the Lyne-Stevens family in 1885 (as a hunting-lodge, incredibly) and designed in the Jacobean Renaissance style by William Burn.

Thompson
10 miles NE of Thetford on minor road off the A1075

This is a quiet village with a marshy man-made lake, **Thompson Water**, and a wild common. **The Peddars Way** long-distance footpath passes about a mile to the west and, about the same distance to the northeast, the Church is a splendid early 14th century building notable for its fine carved screen and choice 17th century fittings.

Watton
14 miles NE of Thetford on the A1075

Watton's striking town sign depicts the 'Babes in the Wood' of the famous nursery story. The story, which was already current hereabouts in the 1500s, relates that as Arthur Truelove lay dying he decided that the only hope for his two children was to leave them in the care of their uncle. Unfortunately, the uncle decided to help himself to their inheritance and paid two men to take the children into nearby **Wayland Wood** and kill them. In a moment of unexpected compassion, one of the men decided that he could not commit the dastardly act. He disposed of his accomplice instead, and abandoned the children in the wood to suffer whatever fate might befall them. Sadly, unlike the nursery tale in which the children find their way back home and live happily ever after, this unfortunate brother and sister perished. Their ghosts are said to wander hand in hand through the woods to this day.

Wayland Wood is now owned by the Norfolk Naturalist Trust, and is believed to be one of the oldest in England; **Griston Hall** (private), half a mile south of the wood, is a Grade II listed building, reputedly once the home of the 'Wicked Uncle' in the real-life Babes in the Wood story.

Watton itself boasts an unusual **Clock Tower**, dated 1679, standing at the centre of its long main street.

Dereham

One of the most ancient towns in the county, Dereham has a recorded history stretching back to AD 654 when St Withburga founded a Nunnery here. Her

---

THE GEMINI PUB & RESTAURANT

Sandy Lane, Dereham, Norfolk NR19 2EA
Tel: 01362 698841 Fax: 01362 699543
e-mail: thegeminipub@aol.com

Just outside the centre of Dereham on the old A47, **The Gemini Pub & Restaurant** is a modern pub built in the 1960s and featuring an attractive dining area with large windows and comfortable seating. All the food is freshly prepared and home-cooked, locally sourced and cooked to order. The menus and daily specials feature such favourites as gammon steak, steak and kidney or chicken and ham pie, vegetarian lasagne and chilli con carne.

Real ales on tap include Greene King IPA and a changing guest ale, together with Budweiser on tap, cider, stout, wines, spirits and soft drinks. The one-third of an acre garden boasts a barbecue and children's play area. Live entertainment is featured every weekend at this friendly and welcoming pub, where the service, atmosphere and hospitality are second to none.

THE WHITE HORSE AT LONGHAM

Wendling Road, Longham, Dereham,
Norfolk NR19 2RD
Tel: 01362 687464 Fax: 01362 687484

Excellent, affordable home-cooked food, a range of real ales, wines and spirits, and superb accommodation await guests at **The White Horse at Longham**.

For over 350 years, this fine establishment has been providing genuine hospitality to guests from far and near. Family run for over 80 years, proprietor Barry White and his capable, friendly staff ensure that every guest has an enjoyable and relaxing time while here, whether for a drink, meal or several nights' stay.

This quintessentially English inn has all the features that make for a

wonderful dining experience: tasteful and comfortable seating in the spacious lounge bar or beer garden, a handsome wood and brick bar, cheery wood-burning stove and attractive décor. Real ales on tap at this Free House include Woodfords and two changing guest ales. There's also a good range of lagers, wines, spirits, scrumpy cider and soft drinks.

There are two restaurant areas (both non-smoking), including a delightful conservatory area

overlooking the lawned garden. The home-cooked, tempting dishes are freshly prepared and served at lunch (Tues-Sun) and dinner (seven days a week), with specialities such as fresh fish on Fridays and Saturdays and a separate vegetarian menu.

The seasonal menus make use of the freshest local ingredients to create beef, chicken, lamb, pork, seafood and other dishes that will tempt every palate. And it's always a good idea to leave room for one of the mouth-watering desserts!

The first-class accommodation comprises five charming ensuite guest bedrooms. All rooms are equipped with every modern amenity, and boast supremely comfortable furnishings and a warm and welcoming ambience. Ideally located for exploring this part of Norfolk — Dereham, Swaffham, King's Lynn and the Northwest Norfolk coast – or just for enjoying the pampering and quality hospitality on hand here, The White Horse is well worth seeking out.

name lives on at St Withburga's Well, just to the west of the church. This is where she was laid to rest but, some 300 years later, the Abbot and monks of Ely robbed her grave and ensconced the precious, fundraising relic in their own Cathedral. In the saint's desecrated grave a spring suddenly bubbled forth, its waters possessed of miraculous healing properties, and St Withburga's shrine attracted even more pilgrims than before. Some still come.

In the church of St Nicholas, the second largest in Norfolk, there are features from every century from the 12th to the 16th: a magnificent lantern tower, a lofty Bell Tower, painted roofs, and a Seven Sacrament Font. This is the largest of these notable fonts, of which only 30 have survived - 28 of them in Norfolk and Suffolk.

In the northeast transept is buried a poet, some of whose lines have become embedded in the language:

> "Variety's the very spice of life, the
> monarch of all I survey
> God made the country and man
> made the town."

They all came from the pen of William Cowper who, despite being the author of such cheery poems as 'John Gilpin', suffered grievously from depression, a condition not improved by his association with John Newton, a former slave-trader who had repented and become 'a man of gloomy piety'. The two men collaborated on a book of hymns that included such perennial favourites as 'Oh! for a closer walk with God', 'Hark, my soul, it is the Lord' and 'God moves in a mysterious way'. Cowper spent the last four years of his life at Dereham, veering in and out of madness. In a late-flowering romance he had married the widow Mary Unwin, but the strain of caring for the deranged poet drove her in turn to insanity and death. She, too, is buried in the church.

William Cowper died four years after Mary, in 1800. Three years later, another celebrated writer was born at the quaintly named hamlet of **Dumpling Green** on the edge of the town. George Borrow was to become one of the great English travel writers, producing books full of character and colour such as *Wild*

Wales and *The Bible in Spain*. In his autobiographical novel *Lavengro* he begins with a warm recollection of the town where he was born: '*I love to think on thee, pretty, quiet D[ereham], thou pattern of an English market town, with thy clean but narrow streets branching out from thy modest market place, with thine old-fashioned houses, with here and there a roof of venerable thatch.*' The house in which George Borrow was born, Borrow's Hall, still stands in Dumpling Green.

A much less attractive character connected with Dereham is Bishop Bonner, the enthusiastic arsonist of Protestant 'heretics' during the unhappy reign of Mary Tudor. He was rector of the town before being appointed Bishop of London, and he lived in the exquisite thatched terrace now called **Bishop Bonner's Cottages**. The exterior is ornamented with delightful pargetting, a frieze of flower and fruit designs below the eaves, a form of decoration which is very unusual in Norfolk. The cottages now house a small museum.

Around Dereham

Gressenhall
3 miles NW of Dereham off the B1146

The **Roots of Norfolk at Gressenhall** collection is housed in an impressive late 18th century former workhouse built in rose-red brick. Gressenhall Workhouse was designed to accommodate some 700 unfortunates, so it was built on a very grand scale indeed.

Now one of the UK's leading rural life museums and among Norfolk's top family attractions, there's ample room for the many exhibits illuminating the working and domestic life of Norfolk people over the last 150 years. Farming the old-fashioned way is there to be discovered on Union Farm, where heavy animals still work the fields. A stroll along the 1930s village high street takes in the grocer's, post office and schoolroom. The surrounding 50 acres of unspoilt countryside are perfect for walking. The site hosts numerous special events during the season, ranging from Steam Days to an international folk dance festival with more than 200 dancers taking part.

A mile or so south of Gressenhall, the tiny community of **Dillington** has great difficulty in getting itself noticed on even the most large-scale of maps. This very Hidden Place is worth seeking out for **Norfolk Herbs at Blackberry Farm**, a specialist herb farm located in a beautiful wooded valley. Visitors are invited to browse through a vast collection of aromatic, culinary and medicinal herb plants, and to learn all about growing and using herbs.

North Elmham
6 miles N of Dereham off the B1110

Near the village of North Elmham stand the sparse remains of a Saxon Cathedral. North Elmham was the seat of the Bishops of East Anglia until 1071, when they removed to Thetford (and then, 20 years later, to Norwich). Although there had been a cathedral here since the late 7th century, what has survived is mostly from the 11th century. Despite its grand title, the T-shaped ground plan reveals that the cathedral was no larger than a small parish church.

Brisley

7 miles N of Dereham on the B1145

Brisley village is well known to local historians and naturalists for its huge expanse of heathland, some 170 acres of it. It's reckoned to be the best example of unspoilt common in Norfolk, and at its centre are scores of pits that were dug out in medieval times to provide clay for the wattle-and-daub houses of the period. Another feature of interest in the village is Gately Manor (private), an Elizabethan manor house standing within the remains of a medieval moat, and yet another moated house at Old Hall Farm in the southwest corner of the green.

Swaffham

Swaffham's one-time claim to be the 'Montpellier of England' was justified by the abundance of handsome Georgian houses that used to surround the large, wedge-shaped market place. A good number still survive, along with the **Assembly Room** of 1817 where the quality would foregather for concerts, balls and soirees. The central focus of the market square is the elegant **Butter**

Cross, presented to the town by the Earl of Orford in 1783. It's not a cross at all, but a classical lead-covered dome standing on eight columns and surmounted by a life-size statue of Ceres, the Roman goddess of agriculture - an appropriate symbol for this busy market town, from which ten roads radiate out across the county.

From the market place an avenue of limes leads to the quite outstanding Church of **St Peter & St Paul**, a 15th century masterpiece with one of the very best double hammerbeam roofs in the county, strikingly embellished with a host of angels, their wings widespread. The unknown mason who devised the church's harmonious proportions made it 51 feet wide, 51 feet high and 102 feet long. Carved on a bench-end here is a man in medieval dress accompanied by a dog on a chain. The same two figures are incorporated in the town's coat of arms, and also appear in the elegantly designed town sign just beyond the market place. The man is 'The Pedlar of Swaffham', a certain John Chapman who, according to legend, dreamed that if he made his way to London Bridge he would meet a stranger who would make him rich. The pedlar and his dog set off for London, and on the bridge he was eventually accosted by a stranger who asked him what he was doing there. John recounted his dream. Scoffingly, the stranger said 'If I were a dreamer, I should go to Swaffham. Recently I dreamt that in Swaffham lived a man named Chapman, and in his garden,

Swaffham Museum

Town Hall, 4 London Street, Swaffham,
Norfolk PE37 7DQ
Tel: 01760 721230 Fax: 01760 720469
e-mail: swaffhammuseum@ic24.net
website: www.aboutswaffham.co.uk

Swaffham's Town Hall, a handsome redbrick building in the heart of the market place, is the setting for the excellent **Swaffham Museum**. The building itself has an interesting history: originally the home of 18th century brewer John Morse, it became the home of Swaffham Urban District Council in 1955; the Museum has been here since it opened in 1986. The Museum focuses on the social history of the town and the surrounding villages, and the collections cover many aspects of life including trade, industry and domestic life from prehistoric times to the present. This 'house of mystery and discovery' has many individual

attractions. One of the highlights is the DM Symonds Collection of handmade figurines, donated by Mrs Ann Peal in memory of her father Derrick Maurice Symonds (1922-1993), author, teacher, artist and craftsman. The collection consists of 66 hand-crafted figures or groups based on characters taken from the works of Tolkien, Dickens, Shakespeare and the Commedia dell'Arte. All the costumes were designed and made by Mr Symonds over a period of years.

One of the town's best-known stories, illustrated in the Museum, concerns John Chapman, 'ye pedlar of Swaffham who did by a dream find a great treasure'. John had a recurring dream that he would find his fortune in London and, with his dog, his staff and his pedlar's pack, set out on his search

for gold. On London Bridge he met a man who heard his story and declared that he, too, had a dream - but his was about a pot of gold buried under a tree in the garden of a John Chapman, a pedlar of Swaffham. Back went John to Swaffham, where he did indeed find pots of gold, which meant wealth and comfort for him and his family. They moved to a grand house and became respected citizens; John was appointed a churchwarden and was a generous benefactor of the parish church. John Chapman is perhaps a figure of legend, but two who were very much real-life sons of Swaffham were Captain William Earl Johns, author of the Biggles stories, and Howard Carter, the Egyptologist who discovered the tomb of Tutankhamun in the Valley of the Kings at Luxor in 1922. His mummy was a Swaffham girl, the daughter of a builder, while his father was a fairly successful artist. The fascinating stories of Captain Johns and Howard Carter are told in the Museum, and one of the other major attractions is the splendid Sporle Collection of locally-found artefacts.

Swaffham Museum offers excellent research and education facilities through a library of pictures, photographs, press cuttings and other documents, and staff are on hand to help with family trees or identifying objects found by visitors. The Museum and its souvenir shop are open Tuesday to Sunday from April to October.

buried under a tree, lay a treasure.' John hastily returned home, uprooted the only tree in his garden, and unearthed two jugs full of gold coins.

There was indeed a John Chapman who contributed generously to the building of the parish church in the late 1400s. Cynics claim that he was a wealthy merchant, and that similar tales occur in the folklore of most European countries. Whatever the truth, there's no doubt that the people of Swaffham took the story to their hearts.

John Chapman may be Swaffham's best-known character locally, but internationally the name of Howard Carter, the discoverer of Tutankhamen's tomb, is much better known. Carter was born at Swaffham in 1874; his death in 1939 was attributed by the popular press to 'the Curse of Tutankhamen'. If so, it must have been an extremely sluggish curse. Some 17 years had elapsed since Carter had knelt by a dark, underground opening, swivelled his torch and found himself the first human being in centuries to gaze upon the astonishing treasures buried in the tomb of the teenage Pharaoh.

Swaffham Museum (see panel opposite) in the Town Hall is the setting for the story of the town's past. Visitors can follow Howard Carter's road to the Valley of the Kings, see the Symonds Collection of handmade figurines, and admire the Sporle collection of locally-found artefacts.

Move on some 1,400 years from the death of Tutankhamen to Norfolk in the 1st century AD. Before a battle,

members of the Iceni tribe, led by Boudica, would squeeze the blue sap of the woad plant onto their faces in the hope of frightening the Roman invaders (or any other of their many enemies). At **Cockley Cley Iceni Village and Museums**, three miles southwest of Swaffham off the A1065, archaeologists have reconstructed a village of Boudica's time, complete with wooden huts, moat, drawbridge and palisades.
Reconstruction though it is, the village is remarkably effective in evoking a sense of what daily life entailed more than 1,900 years ago.

A more recent addition to Swaffham's attractions is the **EcoTech Discovery Centre**, opened in 1998. Through intriguing interactive displays and hands-on demonstrations, visitors can discover what startling innovations current, and possible, technology may have in store for us during the next millennium.

Around Swaffham

Castle Acre
4 miles N of Swaffham off the A1065

Set on a hill surrounded by water meadows, Castle Acre seems still to linger in the Middle Ages. William de Warenne, William the Conqueror's son-in-law, came here very soon after the Conquest and built a Castle that was one of the first, and largest, in the country to be built by the Normans. Of that vast fortress, little remains apart

Castle Acre

in some comfort, judging by the well-preserved Prior's House, which has its own bath and built-in wash-basin. The Priory lay on the main route to the famous Shrine at Walsingham, with which it tried to compete by offering pilgrims a rival attraction in the form of an arm of St Philip.

from the gargantuan earthworks and a squat 13th century, gateway.

Much more has survived of **Castle Acre Priory**, founded in 1090 and set in fields beside the River Nar. Its glorious West Front gives a powerful indication of how majestic a triumph of late Norman architecture the complete Priory must have been. With five apses and twin towers, the ground plan was modelled on the Cluniac mother church in Burgundy, where William de Warenne had stayed while making a pilgrimage to Rome. Despite the Priory's great size, it appears that perhaps as few as 25 monks lived here during the Middle Ages - and

Today the noble ruins of the Priory are powerfully atmospheric, a brooding scene skilfully exploited by Roger Corman when he filmed here for his screen version of Edgar Allan Poe's ghostly story, *The Tomb of Ligeia*.

Castle Acre village is extremely picturesque, the first place in Norfolk to be designated a Conservation Area, in 1971. Most of the village, including the 15th century parish church, is built in traditional flint, with a few later houses of brick blending in remarkably happily.

THE GEORGE & DRAGON

Newton by Castle Acre, King's Lynn,
Norfolk PE23 2BX
Tel/Fax: 01760 755046

The George & Dragon is a distinctive and distinguished inn offering great real ales and an impressive menu. Attractively and comfortably furnished and decorated with traditional features, there are two split-level dining areas (both non-smoking), an intimate bar area and an additional dining area where smoking is permitted. Fresh, local meats,

seafood and produce are used to create delicious meals; the home-made puddings are a real treat.

Litcham

11 miles NE of Swaffham on the B1145

Small though it is, this village strung alongside the infant River Nar can boast an intriguing **Village Museum**, with displays of local artefacts from Roman times to the present, an extensive collection of photographs, some of which date back to 1865, and an underground lime kiln.

King's Lynn

In the opinion of James Lee-Milne, the National Trust's architectural authority, 'The finest old streets anywhere in England' are to be found at King's Lynn. Tudor, Jacobean and Flemish houses mingle harmoniously with grand medieval churches and stately civic buildings. It's not surprising that the BBC chose the town to represent early 19th century London in their production of *Martin Chuzzlewit*. It seems, though, that word of this ancient sea-port's many treasures has not yet been widely broadcast, so most visitors to the area tend to stay on the King's Lynn bypass while making their way to the better-known attractions of the north Norfolk coast. They are missing a lot.

The best place to start an exploration of the town is at the beautiful church of **St Margaret**, founded in 1101 and with a remarkable leaning arch of that original building still intact. The architecture is impressive, but the church is especially famous for its two outstanding 14th century brasses, generally reckoned to be the two largest and most monumental in the kingdom. Richly engraved, one shows workers in a vineyard, the other, commemorating Robert Braunche, represents the great feast which Robert hosted at King's Lynn for Edward III in 1364.

Marks on the tower doorway indicate the church's, and the town's, vulnerability to the waters of the Wash and the River Great Ouse. They show the high-water levels reached during the great floods of 11 March 1883 (the lowest), 31 January 1953 and 11 January, 1978.

The organist at St Margaret's in the mid 18th century was the celebrated

Customs House, King's Lynn

writer on music, Dr Charles Burney, but his daughter Fanny was perhaps even more interesting. She wrote a best-selling novel, *Evelina*, at the age of 25, became a leading light of London society, a close friend of Dr Johnson and Sir Joshua Reynolds, and at the age of 59 underwent an operation for breast cancer without anaesthetic. She only fainted once during the 20-minute operation, and went on to continue her active social life until her death at the ripe old age of 87.

Alongside the north wall of St Margaret's is the **Saturday Market Place**, one of the town's two market places, where visitors can explore The Old Gaol House, an experience complete with the sights and sounds of the ancient cells. A few steps further is one of the most striking sights in the town, the **Guildhall of the Holy Trinity** with its distinctive chequerboard design of black flint and white stone. The Guildhall was built in 1421, extended in Elizabethan times, and its Great Hall is still used today for wedding ceremonies and various civic events.

Next door to the Guildhall is the Town Hall of 1895, which in a good-neighbourly way is constructed in the same flint-and-stone pattern. The Town Hall also houses the **Museum of Lynn Life** where, along with displays telling the story of the town's 900 years, you can also admire the municipal regalia. The greatest treasure in this collection is King John's Cup, a dazzling piece of medieval workmanship with coloured enamel scenes set in gold. The Cup was supposed to be part of King John's treasure which had been lost in 1215 when his overburdened baggage train was crossing the Nene Estuary and sank into the treacherous quicksands. This venerable legend is sadly undermined by the fact that the Cup was not made until 1340, more than a century after John's death.

A short distance from the Town Hall, standing proudly by itself on the banks of the River Purfleet, is the handsome **Custom House** of 1683, designed by the celebrated local architect Henry Bell.

There's not enough space here to list all of the town's many other important buildings, but mention must be made of the **Hanseatic Warehouse** (1428), the **South Gate** (1440), the **Greenland Fishery Building** (1605), and the **Guildhall of St George**, built around 1406 and reputedly the oldest civic hall in England. The Hall was from time to time also used as a theatre; it's known that Shakespeare's travelling company played here, and it is considered highly likely that the Bard himself trod the boards. If true, his appearance would be very appropriate, since the Guildhall is now home to the **King's Lynn Arts Centre**, active all year round with events and exhibitions and since 1951 the force behind an annual Arts Festival in July with concerts, theatre and a composer in residence. Some of the concerts are held in St Nicholas' Chapel, a medieval building whose acoustics outmatch those of many a modern concert hall.

At **Caithness Crystal** Visitor Centre, you can watch craftsmen at close quarters as they shape and manipulate glass into beautiful objets d'art.

Around King's Lynn

Terrington St Clement

6 miles W of King's Lynn off the A17

Terrington St Clement is a sizable village notable for the **'Cathedral of the Marshland'**, a 14th century Gothic masterwork more properly known as St Clement's church, and for the **African Violet Centre**, where some quarter of a million violets are grown each year, in a wide range of colour and species.

Stow Bardolph

8 miles S of King's Lynn off the A10

Holy Trinity church at Stow Bardolph houses one of the oddest memorials in the country. Before her death in 1744, Sarah Hare, youngest daughter of the Lord of the Manor, Sir Thomas Hare, arranged for a life-sized effigy of herself to be made in wax. It was said to be an exceptionally good likeness: if so, Sarah appears to have been a rather uncomely maiden, and afflicted with boils to boot. Her death was attributed to blood poisoning after she had pricked her finger with a needle, an act of Divine retribution, apparently, for her sin of sewing on a Sunday. Sarah was then attired in a dress she had chosen herself, placed in a windowed mahogany cabinet, and the monument set up in the Hare family's chapel, a grandiose structure which is larger than the chancel of the church itself.

Downham Market

10 miles S of King's Lynn off the A10/A1122

Once the site for a major horse fair, this compact little market town stands at the very edge of the Fens, with the River Great Ouse and the New Bedford Drain running side by side at its western edge. Many of its houses are built in the distinctive brick and carrstone style of the area. One of the finest examples of this traditional use of local materials can be seen at Dial House in Railway Road, built in the late 1600s.

The parish church has managed to find a small hill on which to perch. It's an unassuming building with a rather incongruously splendid glass chandelier from the 1730s. Another feature of the town, much loved by postcard manufacturers, is the elegant, riotously decorated cast-iron **Clock Tower** in the market place. This was erected in 1878 at a cost of £450. The tower's backdrop of attractive cottages provides a charming setting for a holiday snap.

Two great names are associated with this small town: Charles I, disguised as a clergyman, stayed at Downham Market for a night during his flight after the Battle of Naseby, and Horatio (later Lord) Nelson, son of the parson of Burnham Thorpe, was sent to the little school here.

THE CASTLE HOTEL

High Street, Downham Market,
Norfolk PE38 9HF
Tel/Fax: 01366 384311
e-mail: castle@castle-hotel.com
website: www.castle-hotel.com

The Castle Hotel has a centuries-old history of providing excellent accommodation and a warm welcome to all visitors. Dating back to the early 18th century, this gracious and impressive hotel has 12 charming and comfortable ensuite guest bedrooms, all twins and doubles with every amenity and facility guests could expect. Three rooms have four-poster beds; two feature a jacuzzi bath. All are tastefully decorated and furnished.

Helen and Howard Fradley and their team of conscientious and friendly staff provide superb personal service to ensure that all their guests have a pleasant, relaxing stay. The bar and restaurant, open to residents and non-residents alike, are attractive and welcoming. The restaurant serves both a la carte and table d'hote menus, with a range of delicious dishes and an extensive wine list. Special mini-break offers make this a particularly good choice as a base from which to explore Downham Market and the surrounding region. The hotel also boasts superior conference and banqueting facilities. AA/RAC/ETB 2 Stars Recommended.

Near Downham Bridge on the A1122 you will find Collectors World and the Magical Dickens World. The first boasts a plethora of farming and household memorabilia, carts, carriages, radios, cameras, antique and collectible dolls, Armstrong Siddeley cars and much more, with rooms dedicated to Barbara Cartland, Horatio Nelson, the 1960s and more. Dickens World offers visitors a chance to step back in time into a maze of late 19th century streets, shops, sights and sounds.

Denver

2 miles S of Downham Market off the A10/A1122

Denver Sluice was originally built in 1651 by the Dutch engineer, Cornelius Vermuyden, as part of a scheme to drain 20,000 acres of land owned by the Duke of Bedford. Various modifications were made to the system over the years, but the principle remains the same, and the oldest surviving sluice, built in 1834, is still in use today. Running parallel with it is the modern **Great Denver Sluice**, opened in 1964; together these two sluices control the flow of a large complex of rivers and drainage channels, and are able to divert floodwaters into the Flood Relief Channel that runs alongside the Great Ouse.

The two great drainage cuts constructed by Vermuyden are known as the Old and New Bedford rivers, and the strip of land between them, never more than 1,000 yards wide, is called the Ouse

Washes. This is deliberately allowed to flood during the winter months so that the fields on either side remain dry. The drains run side by side for more than 13 miles, to Earith in Cambridgeshire, and this has become a favourite route for walkers, with a rich variety of bird, animal and insect life to be seen along the way.

Denver Windmill, built in 1835 but put out of commission in 1941, when the sails were struck by lightning, re-opened in 2000. This wonderful working mill set on the edge of the Fens has been carefully restored. On-site attractions include a visitor centre, craft workshops, bakery and tea shop. Holiday accommodation is also available.

Hilgay
3 miles S of Downham Market off the A10

When the *Domesday Book* was written, Hilgay was recorded as one of only two settlements in the Norfolk fens. It was then an island, its few houses planted on a low hill rising from the surrounding marshland. The village is scarcely any larger today, and collectors of unusual gravestones make their way to its churchyard seeking the last resting place of George William Manby. During the Napoleonic wars,

Manby invented a rocket-powered life-line that could be fired to ships in distress. His gravestone is carved with a ship, an anchor, a depiction of his rocket device and an inscription that ends with the reproachful words, 'The public should have paid this tribute.'

Oxborough
10 miles SE of Downham Market off the A134

How many hamlets in the country, one wonders, can boast two such different buildings of note as those to be seen at Oxborough? First there's the church of **St John the Evangelist**, remarkable for its rare brass eagle lectern of 1498 and its glorious Bedingfeld Chapel of 1525, sheltering twin monuments to Sir Edmund Bedingfeld and his wife fashioned in the then newly popular material of terracotta.

It was Sir Edmund who built **Oxburgh Hall** (National Trust), a breathtakingly lovely moated house built of pale-rose

Oxburgh Hall

brick and white stone. Sir Edmund's descendants still live in what a later architect, Pugin, described as 'one of the noblest specimens of domestic architecture of the 15th century.' Henry VII and his Queen, Elizabeth of York, visited in 1497 and lodged in the splendid State Apartments which form a bridge between the lofty gatehouse towers, and which ever since have been known as the King's Room and the Queen's Room. On display here is the original Charter of 1482, affixed with Edward IV's Great Seal of England, granting Sir Edmund permission to build with 'stone, lime and sand', and to fortify the building with battlements. These rooms also house some magnificent period furniture, a collection of royal letters to the Bedingfelds, and the huge Sheldon Tapestry Map of 1647 showing Oxfordshire and Berkshire. Another more poignant tapestry, known as the Marian Needlework, was the joint handiwork of Elizabeth, Countess of Shrewsbury, and Mary, Queen of Scots,

during the latter's captivity here in 1570. The Bedingfelds seemed always to draw the short straw when the Tudors needed someone to discharge an unpleasant or difficult task. It was an earlier Sir Edmund who was charged with the care of Henry VIII's discarded wife, Catherine of Aragon; Edmund's son, Sir Henry, was given the even more onerous task of looking after the King's official bastard, the Princess Elizabeth. After Elizabeth's accession as Queen, Sir Henry presented himself at Court, no doubt with some misgivings. Elizabeth received him civilly but, as he was leaving, tartly observed that 'if we have any prisoner whom we would have hardlie and strictly kept, we will send him to you.'

As staunch Catholics, the Bedingfelds were, for the next two and a half centuries, consigned to the margins of English political life. Their estates dwindled as portions were sold to meet the punitive taxes imposed on adherents of the Old Faith. By the middle of the 20th century, the Bedingfelds' long

THE WHITE HART INN

White Hart Street, Foulden, Thetford, Norfolk IP26 5AW
Tel: 01366 328638 Fax: 01366 328060
e-mail: mosses@talk21.com

A traditional country inn with home-cooked food, great drink and luxurious accommodation, **The White Hart Inn** in Foulden – off the B1112/B1106/B1386 southeast of Downham Market and Swaffham, on the edge of the Thetford Forest – is well worth seeking out. Real ales include Greene King IPA and Abbot, while the delicious food makes the most of locally-grown vegetables

and locally-reared beef and other fresh ingredients in a range of traditional and exotic (Thai, Chinese, Italian) specials. Booking advised at weekends.

tenure of Oxburgh was drawing to a close. In 1951 the 9th Baronet, another Sir Edmund, sold Oxburgh to a builder, who promptly announced his intention of demolishing the house. Sir Edmund's mother,

Castle Rising

the Dowager Lady Sybil, was shocked by such vandalism and used her considerable powers of persuasion to raise sufficient funds to buy back the house. She then conveyed it into the safe keeping of the National Trust.

The grounds at Oxburgh provide the perfect foil for the mellow old building, reflected in its broad moat. There's a wonderfully formal and colourful French garden, a walled kitchen garden, and woodland walks.

Castle Rising
5 miles NE of King's Lynn off the A148/A149

As the bells ring for Sunday morning service at Castle Rising, a group of elderly ladies leave the mellow redbrick Bede House and walk in procession to the church. They are all dressed in long scarlet cloaks, emblazoned on the left breast with a badge of the Howard family arms. Once a year, on Founder's Day, they add to their regular Sunday costume a tall-crowned hat typical of the Jacobean period, just like those worn in stereotypical pictures of broomstick-flying witches.

These ladies are the residents of the almshouses founded by Henry Howard, Earl of Northampton in 1614, and their regular Sunday attendance at church was one of the conditions he imposed on the original 11 needy spinsters who were to enjoy his beneficence. Howard also required that each inmate of his 'Hospital of the Holy and Undivided Trinity' must also 'be able to read, if such a one may be had, single, 56 at least, no common beggar, harlot, scold, drunkard, haunter of taverns, inns or alehouses'.

The weekly *tableau vivant* of this procession to the church seems completely in keeping with this picturesque village, which rates high on any 'not to be missed' list of places to visit in Norfolk. The church to which the women make their way, St

Lawrence's, is an outstanding example of Norman and Early English work, even though much of it has been reconstructed. But overshadowing everything else in this pretty village is the massive **Castle Keep** (English Heritage), its well-preserved walls rising 50 feet high, and pierced by a single entrance. The Keep's towering presence is made even more formidable by the huge earthworks on which it stands. The Castle was built in 1150, guarding what was then the sea approach to the River Ouse. (The marshy shore is now some three miles distant and still retreating.)

Despite its fortress-like appearance, Castle Rising was much more of a residential building than a defensive one. In 1331, when Edward III found it necessary to banish his ferocious French-born mother, Isabella, to some reasonably comfortable place of safety, he chose this far-from-London castle. She was to spend some 27 years here before her death in 1358, never seeing her son again during that time. How could Edward treat his own mother in such a way? Her crime, in his view, was that the 'She-Wolf of France', as all her enemies and many of her friends called Isabella, had joined forces with her lover Mortimer against her homosexual husband Edward II (young Edward's father) and later colluded in the king's grisly murder at Berkeley Castle. A red-hot poker, inserted anally, was the instrument of his death. For three years after that loathsome assassination, Isabella and Mortimer ruled England as Regents. The moment Edward III achieved his majority, he had Mortimer hung, drawn and quartered. His mother he despatched to a lonely retirement at Castle Rising.

Six and a half centuries later, the spacious grounds around the castle provide an appropriate backdrop for an annual display by members of the White Society. Caparisoned in colourful medieval garments and armed with more-or-less authentic replicas of swords and halberds, these modern White Knights stage a battle for control of the castle.

Sandringham
8 miles NE of King's Lynn off the A149/B1140

A couple of miles north of Castle Rising is the entrance to **Sandringham Country Park** and **Sandringham House** (see panel below), the royal family's country retreat. Unlike the State Rooms at Windsor Castle and Buckingham Palace, where visitors marvel at the awesome trappings of majesty, at Sandringham they can savour the atmosphere of a family home. The rooms the visitor sees at Sandringham are those used by the royal family when in residence, complete with family portraits and photographs, and comfy armchairs. Successive royal owners have furnished the house with an intriguing medley of the grand, the domestic and the unusual. Entering the principal reception room, The Saloon, for example, you pass a weighing-machine with a leather-covered seat, apparently a common amenity in great houses of the 19th century. In the same room, with its attractively carved Minstrels' Gallery, hangs a fine family portrait by one of Queen Victoria's favourite artists, Heinrich von Angeli. It shows the Prince of Wales (later Edward VII), his wife Alexandra and two of their children, with Sandringham in the background.

The Prince first saw Sandringham on 4th February 1862. At Victoria's instigation, the 20-year-old heir to the throne had been searching for some time for a country property, a refuge of the kind his parents already enjoyed at Balmoral and Osborne. A courtier accompanying the Prince reported back that although the outside of house was ugly, it was pleasant and convenient within, and set in pretty grounds. The surrounding countryside was plain, he went on, but the property was in excellent order and the opportunity of securing it should not be missed. Within days, the purchase was completed.

Most of the 'ugly' house disappeared a few years later when the Prince rebuilt the main residence; the 'pretty grounds' have matured into one of the most beautiful landscaped areas in the country. And the 'plain' countryside around - open heath and grassland

SANDRINGHAM HOUSE

Sandringham, Norfolk PE35 6EN
Tel: 01553 772675 Fax: 01553 541571
e-mail: enquiries@sandringhamestate.co.uk

Sandringham House is the charming country retreat of Her Majesty The Queen hidden in the heart of 60 acres of beautiful wooded gardens. Still maintained in the style of Edward and Alexandra, Prince and Princess of Wales (later King Edward VII and Queen Alexandra), all the main ground-floor rooms used by the Royal Family, full of their treasured ornaments, portraits and furniture, are open to the public. More family possessions are displayed in the Museum

housed in the old stable and coach houses; these include vehicles ranging in date from the first car owned by a British monarch, a 1900 Daimler, to a half-scale Aston Martin used by Princes William and Harry. A new display tells the mysterious tale of the Sandringham Company, who fought and died at Gallipoli in 1915, recently the subject of a television film *All the King's Men*. A free Land Train from within the entrance will carry passengers less able to walk through the grounds to the House and back.

overrun by rabbits - has been transformed into a wooded country park, part of the coastal Area of Outstanding Natural Beauty.

One of the additions the Prince made to the house in 1883 was a Ballroom, much to the relief of Princess Alexandra. 'It is beautiful I think & a great success.' she wrote, '& avoids pulling the hall to pieces each time there is a ball or anything'. This attractive room is now used for cinema shows and the estate workers' Christmas party. Displayed on the walls is a remarkable collection of Indian weapons, presented to the Prince during his state visit in 1875-6; hidden away in a recess are the two flags planted at the South Pole by the Shackleton expedition.

Just across from the house, the old coach-houses and stables have been converted into a fascinating museum. There are some truly splendid royal vehicles here, including the first car bought by a member of the royal family - a 1900 Daimler - and an evocative series of old photographs depicting the life of the royal family at Sandringham from 1862 until Christmas 1951. Other attractions at Sandringham include a visitors centre, adventure playground, nature walks, souvenir shop, restaurant and tearoom.

Dersingham
9 miles NE of King's Lynn off the A149

This large village just north of

Sandringham was actually the source of the latter's name: in the *Domesday Book*, the manor was inscribed as 'Sant-Dersingham'. Norfolk tongues found 'Sandringham' much easier to get around. Dersingham village has expanded greatly in recent years and modern housing has claimed much of Dersingham Common, although there are still many pleasant walks here through **Dersingham Wood** and the adjoining Sandringham Country Park.

Snettisham
11 miles N of King's Lynn off the A149

Snettisham is best known nowadays for its spacious, sandy beaches and the **RSPB Bird Sanctuary**, both about two miles west of the village itself. But for centuries Snettisham was much more famous as a prime quarry for carrstone, an attractive soft-red building-block that provided the 'light relief' for the walls of thousands of Georgian houses around the country, and for nearby Sandringham House. The carrstone quarry is still working, its product now destined mainly for 'goldfish ponds and the entrance-banks of the more pretentious types of bungalow'. Unfortunately, one has to go to the British Museum in London to see Snettisham's greatest gift to the national heritage: an opulent collection of gold and silver ornaments from the 1st century AD, the largest hoard of treasure trove ever found in Britain, discovered here in 1991.

Heacham

13 miles N of King's Lynn off the A149

Norfolk Lavender, Heacham

Heacham Park Fishery on Pocahontas Lake is set within the original boundary of Heacham Hall. This three-and-a-half acre freshwater lake was re-established in 1996. Spring 1997 saw the introduction to the lake of specimen carp, to be followed in 1998 by rudd, bream, perch and roach. The lake takes its name from the renowned Native American princess, who married into the Rolfe family, owners of Heacham Hall, and lived here in the 1600s.

Just outside this charming village is the famous **Norfolk Lavender**, the largest lavender-growing and distilling operation in the country. Established in 1932, it is also the oldest. The information point at the western entrance is sited in an attractive listed building which has become something of a Norfolk landmark. On entering the site, visitors instinctively breathe in, savouring the unmistakable aroma that fills the air. Guided tours of the grounds run throughout the day from the Spring Bank Holiday until the end of September, and during the lavender harvest, visitors can tour the distillery and see how the wonderful fragrance is made.

As well as being a working farm, this is also the home of the National Collection of Lavenders, a living botanical dictionary which displays the many different colours, sizes and smells of this lovely plant. Amongst other

THE COTTAGE PANTRY

28 High Street, Heacham, King's Lynn, Norfolk PE31 7EP
Tel: 01485 572220

Set in a small terraced house, **The Cottage Pantry** is a traditional English tearoom in the best sense of the word.

Excellent meals at very modest prices are the order of the day here, with home-cooked, freshly prepared pies, roasts, casseroles and more, together with a superb range of delicious puddings, baked sponges, fruit pies, crumbles, cheesecake and treacle tarts. Open Mon-Sat 9-5.30 (10-4 in winter).

TYLERS BARN

Wood Norton Road, Stibbard, Norfolk
NR21 0EX
Tel/Fax: 01328 829260
e-mail: allanurquhart@freenet.co.uk

The gracious elegance of a bygone past awaits visitors to **Tylers Barn**, a superb residence that began life as a barn back in the 18th century, and has been converted to an extremely high standard to provide excellent bed and breakfast accommodation, with private sitting room, gallery bedroom, twin room overlooking the terrace and garden, and single room. Also on-site is a

charming self-contained cottage with one single and one double bedroom. Each of the bedrooms in both the barn and the cottage is individually designed (and owner Allan Urquhart is an interior designer, so guests can expect a superior standard of comfort, taste and quality), and each has its own private bathroom. Floor-to-ceiling windows grace the loft suite with gallery bedroom. Exquisitely furnished and decorated, the rugs, books, a piano and other charming accoutrements add to the homely and graceful ambience.

Set in two acres of lovely gardens, with a walled garden with pond and fountain and surrounding gardens where guests are welcome to sit and relax, and (weather permitting) take their meals on the terrace, this beautiful place combines the luxury of a first-class hotel with the warm ambience and conviviality of a good B&B. Guests are received by Allan with tea and home-made scones. As a trained chef, Allan's breakfasts are a truly special treat, featuring home-made breads and preserves, fresh stewed fruits, local eggs and kippers. Dinner is also available by prior arrangement.

Located just five miles from Fakenham, and handy for the North Norfolk Coast, the handsome Georgian town of Holt and many other sights and attractions of the region, this wonderful establishment makes an excellent touring base and is well worth seeking out. No smoking.

attractions at Norfolk Lavender are a Fragrant Meadow Garden, Fragrant Plant Centre, Herb Garden, a gift shop selling a wide variety of products, and a tearoom serving cream teas and even lavender-and-lemon scones!

Fakenham

Fakenham is a busy and prosperous-looking market town, famous for its National Hunt Racecourse, antique & bric-a-brac markets and auctions, and as a major agricultural centre for the region. Straddling the River Wensum, this attractive country town has a number of fine late18th and early 19th century brick buildings in and around the Market Place. And it must surely be one of the few towns in England where the former gasworks (still intact) have been turned into a **Museum of Gas & Local History**, housing an impressive historical display of domestic gas appliances of every kind. Fakenham Church also has an unusual feature, a powder room - a room over the large porch, built in 1497, used for storing gunpowder. Even older than the church is the 700-year-old hunting lodge, built for the Duchy of Lancaster, which is now part of the Crown Hotel. As an antidote to the idea that Norfolk is unremittingly flat, take the B1105 north out of Fakenham and after about half a mile take the first minor road to the left. This quiet road loops over and around the rolling hills, a 10-mile drive of wonderfully soothing countryside that ends at Wells-next-the-Sea.

Around Fakenham

Southeast of Fakenham, off the A1067, **Pensthorpe Waterfowl Park** (see panel on page 270) is home to Europe's best collection of endangered and exotic waterbirds. Over 120 species of waterfowl can be seen here in their natural surroundings, a wonderful avian refuge where you may come across anything from a scarlet ibis to the more familiar oystercatcher, along with avocets and ruff. The spacious walk-through enclosures offer close contact with shy wading birds, and in the Dulverton Aviary elegant spoonbills and bearded tits vie for your attention. There are good facilities for children and visitors with disabilities, a Wildlife Brass Rubbing Centre, nature trails through 200 acres of the Wensum Valley countryside, and a restaurant and a shop.

Thursford Green
4 miles NE of Fakenham off the A148

About two minutes' walk from Thursford Green stands what is perhaps the most unusual museum in Norfolk, **The Thursford Collection Sight and Sound Spectacular**. George Cushing began this extraordinary collection of steam-powered traction engines, fairground organs and carousels back in 1946 when 'one ton of tractor cost £1'. Perhaps the most astonishing exhibit is a 1931 Wurlitzer organ whose 1,339 pipes can produce an amazing repertoire of sounds - horses' hooves, fire engine sirens, claps of thunder, waves crashing on sand, and

PENSTHORPE WATERFOWL PARK & NATURE RESERVE

Pensthorpe, Fakenham, Norfolk NR21 0LN
Tel: 01328 851465 Fax: 01328 855905

Southeast of Fakenham, off the A1067, the **Pensthorpe Waterfowl Park & Nature Reserve** is a 200-acre site with a world-renowned collection of waterfowl. As well as familiar native breeds, birds from all over the world are represented, including king eiders and harlequins from the Arctic; diminutive pygmy geese from tropical Africa; the Javan tree duck; and the sacred, glossy and scarlet ibises. The flock of endangered red-breasted geese, native to northern Siberia, is a special attraction, as is the unusual oldsquaw (long-tailed duck) that is the symbol of the Pensthorpe Waterfowl Trust. Walk-through aviaries, bird hides and strategically sited feeding stations around the lakes allow close contact

with the birds, and access to all areas is easy thanks to specially built colour-coded paths. Animal life as well as bird life abounds here, including otters, voles, red squirrels and the secretive, humble slow worm, and there is also a wide range of insect and plant life to be discovered. Among other attractions within the site are a children's adventure playground, exhibition centre, wildlife gift shop and licensed restaurant.

Pensthorpe Waterfowl Trust is a charitable trust whose aims are to protect waterfowl and wetland habitats; to encourage public appreciation of the importance of wetlands for wildlife; to work with young people and schools to develop a sense of enjoyment of the natural world and an appreciation of the need for wildlife conservation; and to provide facilities to promote the enjoyment of waterfowl and other wildlife on the Pensthorpe Reserve.

the toot-toot of an old railway engine are just some of the Wurlitzer's marvellous effects. There are regular live music shows when the Wurlitzer displays its virtuosity. Other attractions include a steam-powered Venetian Gondola ride, shops selling a wide variety of goods, many of them locally made, and a tearoom.

A mile or so north of the Thursford museum, in the village of Hindringham, Mill Farm Rare Breeds is home to dozens of cattle, sheep, pigs, goats, ponies, poultry and waterfowl which were once commonplace but are now very rare. These intriguing creatures have some 30 acres of lovely countryside to roam

around. Children are encouraged to feed the animals and there's also an adventure playground, crazy golf course, craft & gift shop, picnic area and tearoom.

Great Snoring
5 miles NE of Fakenham off the A148

The names of the twin villages, Great and Little Snoring, are such a perennial source of amusement to visitors it seems almost churlish to explain that they are derived from a Saxon family called Snear. At Great Snoring the main street rises from a bridge over the River Stiffkey and climbs up to St Mary's Church.

Little Walsingham

5 miles N of Fakenham on the B1105

Every year, some half a million pilgrims make their way to this little village of just over 500 souls, noted for its impressive timber-framed buildings and fine Georgian facades, to worship at the **Shrine of Our Lady of Walsingham**. In 1061 the Lady of the Manor of Walsingham, Lady Richeldis de Faverches, had a vision of the Holy Virgin in which she was instructed to build a replica of the Holy House in Nazareth, the house in which the Archangel Gabriel had told Mary that she would be the mother of Christ. Archaeologists have located the original house erected by Lady Richeldis. It was just 13 feet by 23 feet and made of wood, later to be enclosed in stone.

These were the years of the Crusades, and the **Holy House** at Walsingham soon became a major centre of pilgrimage, because it was regarded by the pious as an authentic piece of the Holy Land. Around 1153, an **Augustinian Priory** was established to protect the shrine, now encrusted with jewels, gold and silver, and to provide accommodation for the pilgrims. The Priory is in ruins now but the largest surviving part, a stately Gatehouse on the east side of the High Street is very impressive.

For almost 500 years, Walsingham prospered. Erasmus of Rotterdam visited in 1511 and was critical of the rampant commercialisation of the Shrine with its

THE JOHN H STRACEY

West End, Briston, Melton Constable, Norfolk NR24 2JA
Tel: 01263 860891 Fax: 01263 862984
e-mail: johnstracey@btinternet.com

Located on the B1354 Aylsham-to-Fakenham Road, **The John H Stracey** in Briston is a great pub named for the boxer of the same name, who re-opened the pub about 30 years ago – though the inn dates back to the 1500s – as the then-owner was Stracey's sparring partner. This popular coaching inn was a stop enroute from Wells to Norwich, and has been offering great food, drink and hospitality for centuries. Today's owners, Ray and Hilary Fox, provide friendly service and attention to all their guests. This characterful inn boasts a real log fire with lustrous copper canopy, exposed oak-beamed ceilings and other original features that add to the warm ambience.

Famed for its food, the menus and daily specials offer a range of steaks, home-made pies, fish, lasagne and many other dishes, together with beverages ranging from real ales to wines, spirits and soft drinks. Themed food evenings are regular events, and accommodation is available in two attractive and comfortable guest bedrooms. 3 Diamonds ETC.

plethora of bogus relics and religious souvenirs for sale. He was shown a gigantic bone, 'the finger-joint of St Peter' no less, and in return for a small piece of translation was presented with a highly aromatic fragment of wood - a sliver of a bench on which the Virgin had once seated herself.

In the same year that Erasmus visited, Henry VIII also made the pilgrimage that all his royal predecessors since Richard I had undertaken. He stayed overnight at the enchanting early-Tudor mansion, **East Barsham Hall**, a glorious medley of mullioned windows, towers, turrets, and a group of 10 chimneys, each one individually carved with an amazing variety of styles. Since the King's visit the Hall has had a succession of owners over the years, among them a Hapsburg Duke who entertained his neighbours in truly Imperial style before disappearing, leaving behind some truly imperial debts, and the brothers Gibb of the pop group the Bee Gees. The Hall is today owned by a London businessman and is not open to the public, but it stands for all to see as they enter the village.

Shrine of Our Lady of Walsingham

After his overnight stay at East Barsham Hall, Henry VIII, like most other pilgrims, went first to the **Slipper Chapel**, a beautiful 14th century building about a mile away in Houghton St Giles. Here he removed his shoes and completed the last stretch on foot. Despite this show of piety, some 25 years

PILGRIMS' REST BED & BREAKFAST

61 High Street, Little Walsingham, Norfolk NR22 6BZ
Tel: 01328 820043

Believed to be over 600 years old, the **Pilgrims' Rest Bed & Breakfast** began life as a nunnery, and is set in the centre of this lovely village. Each of the three guest bedrooms is light and airy, with attractive furnishings and tasteful décor. The guests' lounge is a lovely place to relax at the end of a day spent visiting the many sights and

attractions of the region. This comfortable family home is set in a beautiful enclosed garden with private parking.

WALSINGHAM SHIREHALL MUSEUM & ABBEY GROUNDS

Common Place, Little Walsingham,
Norfolk NR22 6BP
Tel: 01328 820510/820259
Fax: 01328 820098
e-mail: walsingham.museum@farmline.com

Set in the picturesque village of Little Walsingham, the early 16th century building that now houses the **Walsingham Shirehall Museum** was used as a hostel for important visitors as it was only 80 feet away from the Priory Church. In the 1770s it was converted into the shirehall for the quarter sessions, which were held here until 1861; the petty sessions continued until 1971.

The courtroom has survived unaltered since it was last used and is now part of the 'hands-on' museum, which includes a comprehensive display on Walsingham as a place of pilgrimage since 1061, as well as local artefacts and photographs. The building also houses local tourist information and a well-stocked gift shop, and is the entrance to the historic Abbey grounds, which contain the remains of the Augustinian Priory and the site of the original shrine and holy house.

later Henry had no hesitation in closing the Priory along with all the other monastic institutions in his realm, seizing its treasures and endowments, and having its image of the Virgin publicly burnt at Chelsea.

Little Walsingham itself is an exceptionally attractive village, set in the midst of parks and woodlands, with the interesting 16th century octagonal **Clink in Common Place**, used in medieval times as a lock-up for petty offenders, the scanty ruins of Walsingham's **Franciscan Friary** of 1347, and the former **Shire Hall** (see panel above), which is now a museum and tourist information centre.

Great Walsingham
5 miles N of Fakenham on the B1388

English place names observe a logic of their own, so Great Walsingham is of course smaller than Little Walsingham. The two villages are very different in atmosphere and appearance, Great Walsingham displaying the typical layout of a rural Norfolk settlement, with attractive cottages set around a green watered by the River Stiffkey, and dominated by a fine 14th century church, **St Peter's**, noted for its superb window tracery, wondrously carved Norman font, and perfectly preserved 15th century carved benches.

Wighton
7 miles N of Fakenham, on the B1105

Wighton Post Office must be one of very few in the country where you can buy a postal order and a pint at the same time. This happy state of affairs has come about because the post office desk is located in the bar of the village pub,

The Carpenters Arms. The desk is open two days a week and provides all the normal post office services apart from passports and Road Tax licences. This unusual arrangement has been featured on the TV programme *Country File*.

Just outside the village, the Wells—Walsingham Light Railway trundles its way between Little Walsingham and Wells-next-the-Sea. The longest 10¼-inch narrow-gauge steam railway in the world, it runs throughout the summer along a 20-minute scenic journey through the North Norfolk countryside.

Tatterford
5 miles SW of Fakenham off the A148 or A1065

This tiny village is well known to botanists for **Tatterford Common**, an unspoilt tract of rough heathland with tiny ponds, some wild apple trees and the River Tat running through it to join the River Wensum about a mile away.

About four miles west of Tatterford stands **Houghton Hall**, home of the Marquess of Cholmondely and one of Norfolk's most magnificent buildings. This glorious demi-palace was built in the Palladian style during the 1720s by Sir Robert Walpole, England's first Prime Minister. The Walpoles had been gentlemen of substance here since the 14th century. With his family revenues augmented by the considerable profits Sir Robert extracted from his political office, he was in a position to spend lavishly and ostentatiously on his new

THE COLKIRK CROWN

Crown Road, Colkirk, Fakenham,
Norfolk NR21 7AA
Tel: 01328 862172 Fax: 01328 863916
e-mail: thecrown@paston.co.uk

Combining traditional features with modern comforts, **The Colkirk Crown** in the peaceful village of Colkirk is warm and welcoming. There has been an inn on this spot for over 300 years, and proprietors Roger and Bridget Savell are happy to maintain the pub's reputation for quality, service and hospitality. Food is served every day at lunch (Mon-Sat 12.00-13.45; Sun 12.00-13.30) and dinner (Mon-Sat 18.30-21.30; Sun 19.00-21.00), with menus and daily specials offering up a range of home-cooked starters, main courses and desserts.

Guests can enjoy their food and drink in either of the two bars or in the non-smoking restaurant – or, on fine days, in the patio area and garden to the rear of the pub. Open Mon-Sat 11.00-14.30 and 18.00-23.00, Sundays 12.00-15.00 and 19.00-22.30, this excellent pub is well worth seeking out.

house. The first step was to destroy completely the village of Houghton (it spoilt the view), and re-house the villagers a mile away at New Houghton.

Although Sir Robert deliberately cultivated the manner of a bluff, down-to-earth Norfolk squire, the personal decisions he made regarding the design and furnishings of the house reveal a man of deep culture and refined tastes. It was he who insisted that the Hall could not be built in homely Norfolk brick, and took the expensive decision to use the exceptionally durable stone quarried at Aislaby in North Yorkshire and transport it by sea from Whitby to King's Lynn. More than two and a half centuries later, the Aislaby stone is still flawless, the only sign of its age a slight weathering that has softened its colour to a creamy gold.

To decorate the interior and design the furniture, Sir Robert commissioned the versatile William Kent. Kent was at the peak of his powers - just look at the decoration in the Stone Hall, the exquisite canopied bed in the Green Velvet Bedchamber, and the finely-carved woodwork throughout which made impressive use of the newly-discovered hardwood called mahogany. And then there were the paintings, an incomparable collection of Old Masters personally selected by Sir Robert. Sadly, many of them are now in the Hermitage Museum in St Petersburg, sold by his wastrel grandson to the Empress Catherine of Russia.

TATT VALLEY HOLIDAY COTTAGES

Lower Farm, Tattersett, King's Lynn, Norfolk PE31 8RT
Tel: 01485 528506
e-mail: enquiries@norfolkholidayhomes.co.uk
website: www.norfolkholidayhomes.co.uk

The small hamlet of Tattersett is home to Tatt Valley Holiday Cottages, situated within a working farm and providing the highest standard of comfortable accommodation. Four cottages sleep up to four, one sleeps six. Each of the five cottages retains its own character while offering every modern amenity. They all have beautiful exposed beams, wooden floors, excellent furnishings and other cosy and homely traditional country house features.

Each of these lovely cottages has its own walled garden with barbecue and garden furniture; the five cottages share a safe children's play area and large games barn with snooker table, pool table, table football and other diversions. Cottages are bookable from Sat to Sat throughout the year. Prices include electricity and heating. This haven of rural tranquillity is handy for day trips to the coast, Sandringham, Holkham and many other sights and attractions of this lovely part of Norfolk.

This grandson, George, 3rd Earl of Orford, succeeded to the title at the age of 21 and spent the next 40 years dissipating his enormous inheritance. When his uncle Horace (the 4th Earl, better known as Horace Walpole, novelist, MP and inveterate gossip) succeeded to the title he found 'Houghton half a ruin ... the two great staircases exposed to all weathers; every room in the wings rotting with wet; the park half-covered with nettles and weeds; mortgages swallowing the estate, and a debt of above £40,000.'

Houghton's decline was arrested when the Hall passed by marriage to the Marquess of Cholmondely, Lord Great Chamberlain, in 1797. But it wasn't until 1913, when George, later the 5th Marquess, moved into the house with his new wife, Sybil Sassoon, that Houghton was fully restored to its former state of grace. The depleted collection of paintings was augmented with fine works by Sir Joshua Reynolds and others from Cholmondely Castle in Cheshire, and the Marchioness introduced new collections of exquisite French furniture and porcelain.

One of the 6th Marquess' interests was military history, and in 1928 he began the astonishing Model Soldiers Collection now on display at Houghton. More than 20,000 perfectly preserved models are deployed in meticulous reconstructions of battles such as Culloden and Waterloo, and in one exhibit, recreating the Grand Review of the British Army in 1895, no fewer than 3,000 figures are on parade.

East Raynham

3 miles SW of Fakenham, on the A1065

Raynham Hall is another superb Palladian mansion, designed by Inigo Jones and with magnificent rooms created a century later by William Kent. The house is only open to the public by appointment since it is the private residence of the 7th Marquess of Townshend. It was his 18th century ancestor, the 2nd Viscount (better known as 'Turnip' Townshend), who revolutionised English agriculture by promoting the humble turnip as an effective means of reclaiming untended land for feeding cattle in winter, and along with wheat, barley and clover, as part of the four-year rotation of crops that provided a cycle of essential nutrients for the soil. The Townshend family have owned extensive estates in this area for centuries, and in St Mary's Church there are some fine monuments to their ancestors, the oldest and most sumptuous of which commemorates Sir Roger, who died in 1493.

The Northwest Coast

Although the whole of Norfolk lies on a foundation of chalk, 1,000 feet deep in places, it is only in this northwest corner that it lies close enough to the surface to have been used as a building material. Once exposed to the air, the chalk, or 'clunch' as it's known, becomes a surprisingly durable material. It was widely used in medieval buildings and can still be found in many barns, farmhouses and cottages in the area. Chalk was also quarried and then burnt to produce lime, prodigious quantities of which were used in building the sublime churches of the Middle Ages.

Hunstanton

16 miles N of King's Lynn on the A149

The busy seaside resort of Hunstanton can boast two unique features: one, it has the only cliffs in England made up of colourful levels of red, white and brown strata, and two, it is the only east coast resort that faces west, looking across The Wash to the Lincolnshire coast and the unmistakeable tower of the 272-foot high

Hunstanton Cliffs and Beach

Boston Stump (more properly described as the Church of St Botolph).

Hunstanton town is a comparative newcomer, developed in the 1860s by Mr Hamon L'Estrange of nearby Hunstanton Hall to take advantage of the arrival of the railway here, and to exploit the natural appeal of its broad, sandy beaches. The centre is well-planned with mock-Tudor houses grouped around a green that falls away to the shore.

Hunstanton's social standing was assured after the Prince of Wales, later Edward VII, came here to recover from typhoid fever. He stayed at the Sandringham Hotel which, sadly, has since been demolished, along with the grand Victorian pier and the railway. But Hunston, as locals call the town, still has a distinct 19th century charm about it and plenty to entertain visitors.

The huge stretches of sandy beach, framed by those multi-coloured cliffs, are just heaven for children who will also be fascinated by the **Sea Life Sanctuary**, on Southern Promenade, where an underwater glass tunnel provides a fascinating opportunity to watch the varied and often weird forms of marine life that inhabit Britain's waters. A popular excursion from Hunstanton is the boat trip to Seal Island, a sandbank in The Wash where seals can indeed often be seen sunbathing at low tide.

Holme next the Sea

3 miles NE of Hunstanton, off the A149

This otherwise unremarkable village is

THE GIN TRAP INN

6 High Street, Ringstead,
Norfolk PE36 5JU
Tel: 01485 525264 Fax: 01485 525321
e-mail: info@gintrap.co.uk
website: www.gintrap.co.uk

A haven of rural peace and tranquillity, the delightfully-named **Gin Trap Inn** is a lovely country inn with rooms. This welcoming 17th century coaching inn is located in a quiet village on the Peddars Way and near the scenic North West Norfolk coast. The bar area is warm and friendly, with an open stove

and pew bench seating. The ceilings are beamed and traditional farm implements adorn the beams. The separate non-smoking dining room is elegant and comfortable. This Free House serves a range of Woodfords cask ales and Adnams ales, as well as 'own label' Gin Trap bitter and there is also an extensive wine list. The menus are changed weekly and always feature a selection of delicious, freshly prepared home-cooked meals, using seasonal produce. The accommodation comprises three spacious ensuite double rooms as well as charming self-catering cottages that sleep up to six.

These delightful cottages have been carefully converted from old farm buildings and are surrounded by beautiful countryside. The two cottages have a 5 Key rating from the English Tourist Board and

boast beautiful interiors, with highly comfortable beds, sofas and armchairs, attractive prints, lamps, curtains and everything that will enhance visitors' enjoyment while staying in this cosy and homely environment. Both have garden furniture and access to nearly an acre of garden.

Adjacent to the inn and cottages, owners Margaret and Don Greer are also proprietors of **The Ringstead Gallery**, housed in a lovely old whitewashed stable building. With an upstairs gallery and display areas downstairs, this is a showcase for paintings by artists such as Lawrie Williamson, Jeremy Barlow, Phillip Gardner, Rosemary Cook, Sue Riley and many more, whose works capture the beguiling Norfolk landscape. The gallery also features an exciting range of striking bronzes and a good selection of limited editions. From the fine turned wood and oak furniture to the sculpture and paintings, all the work exhibited bear testimony to a high standard of artistry and craftsmanship. Exhibitions are held throughout the year, either mixed or one-artist shows. Open Monday-Saturday 10-5.

notable as the northern end of the **Peddar's Way**, the 50-mile pedestrian trail that starts at the Suffolk border near Thetford and, almost arrow-straight for much of its length, slices across northwest Norfolk to Holme, with only an occasional deviation to negotiate a necessary ford or bridge. This determinedly straight route was already long-trodden for centuries before the Romans arrived, but they incorporated long stretches of it into their own network of roads. It was from the Latin word *pedester* that the route takes its name. With few gradients of any consequence to negotiate, the Peddar's Way is ideal for the casual walker. At Holme, the Peddar's Way meets with the Norfolk Coastal Footpath, a much more recent creation. Starting at Hunstanton, it closely follows the coastline all the way to Cromer.

Holme-next-the-Sea is of course famous in part as the site of 'Sea Henge', a 4,500-year-old Bronze Age tree circle discovered on Holme Beach. This early religious monument was removed by English Heritage for study and preservation to Flag Fen, Peterborough, though after its restoration it is hoped that it will be returned to Holme.

Ringstead
3 miles E of Hunstanton off the A149

Another appealing village, with pink and white-washed cottages built in wonderfully decorative Norfolk carrstone. A rare Norman round tower,

all that survives of St Peter's church, stands in the grounds of the former Rectory and adds to the visual charm.

In a region well-provided with excellent nature reserves, the one on **Ringstead Downs** is particularly attractive, and popular with picnickers. The chalky soil of the valley provides a perfect habitat for the plants that thrive here and for the exquisitely marked butterflies they attract.

Docking
9 miles SE of Hunstanton, on the B1454 & B1153

One of the larger inland villages, Docking was at one time called Dry Docking because, perched on a hilltop 300 feet above sea level, it had no water supply of its own. The nearest permanent stream was at Fring, almost three miles away, so in 1760 the villagers began boring for a well. They had to dig some 230 feet down before they finally struck water, which was then sold at a farthing (0.1p) per bucket. A pump was installed in 1928, but a mains supply didn't reach Docking until the 1930s.

Great Bircham
7 miles SE of Hunstanton off the B1153

A couple of miles south of Docking stands the five-storey **Great Bircham Windmill**, one of the few in Norfolk to have found a hill to perch on, and it's still working. If you arrive on a day when there's a stiff breeze blowing, the

Great Bircham Windmill

important RSPB reserve comprising some 420 acres of shingle beach, reed beds, freshwater and salt-marsh. These different habitats encourage a wide variety of birds to visit the area throughout the year, and many of them breed on or around the reserve. Brent geese, ringed plovers, marsh harriers, terns, waders and shore larks may all be seen, and two of the three hides available are accessible to wheelchairs.

Brancaster Staithe
9 miles NE of Hunstanton, on the A149

In Roman times a castle was built near Brancaster to try and control the Iceni, Boudica's turbulent tribe. Nothing of it remains, although a Romano-British cemetery was discovered nearby in 1960. In the 18th century, this delightful village was a port of some standing, hence the 'Staithe', or quay, in its name. The waterborne traffic in the harbour is now almost exclusively pleasure craft, although whelks are still dredged from the sea bed, 15 miles out, and mussels are farmed in the harbour itself.

From the harbour a short boat trip will take you to Scolt Head Island (National Trust), a three-and-a-half mile sand and shingle bar separated from the mainland by a narrow tidal creek. It was originally much smaller, but over the centuries deposits of silt and sand have steadily

windmill's great arms will be groaning around; on calm days, content yourself with tea and home-made cakes in the tearoom, and take home some bread baked at the Mill's own bakery.

Titchwell
7 miles E of Hunstanton, on the A149

Perhaps in keeping with the village's name, the church of **St Mary** at Titchwell is quite tiny - and very pretty indeed. Its circular, probably Norman tower is topped by a little 'whisker' of a spire, and inside is some fine late 19th century glass.

Just to the west of the village is a path leading to **Titchwell Marsh**, a nationally increased its size, and continue to do so. Scolt Head is home to England's largest colony of Sandwich terns, who flock here to breed during May, June and July.

Burnham Market

9 miles E of Hunstanton, on the B1155

There are seven Burnhams in all, strung along the valley of the little River Burn. Burnham Market is the largest of them, its past importance reflected in the wealth of Georgian buildings surrounding the green and the two churches that lie at each end of its broad main street, just 600 yards apart. In the opinion of many, Burnham Market has the best collection of small Georgian houses in Norfolk, and it's a delight to wander through the yards and alleys that link the town's three east—west streets.

Burnham Market also boasts two excellent bookshops and probably the best hat shop in the county. Auctions are held on the village green every other Monday in summer.

Burnham Thorpe

11 miles E of Hunstanton off the B1355

From the tower of All Saints' Church, the White Ensign flaps in the breeze; the only pub in the village is the *Lord Nelson*; and the shop next door to it is called the Trafalgar Stores. No prizes for deducing that Burnham Thorpe was the birthplace of Horatio Nelson. His father, the Revd Edmund Nelson, was the Rector here for 46 years; Horatio was

Nelson's Medicine Chest, Burnham Thorpe

the sixth of his eleven children.

Parsonage House, where Horatio was born seven weeks' premature in 1758, was demolished during his lifetime, but the pub (one of more than 200 hostelries across the country bearing the hero's name) has become a kind of shrine to Nelson's memory, its walls covered with portraits, battle scenes and other marine paintings.

There's more Nelson memorabilia in the church, among it a crucifix and lectern made with wood from HMS *Victory*, a great chest from the pulpit used by the Revd Nelson, and two flags from HMS *Nelson*. Every year on Trafalgar Day, October 21st, members of the Nelson Society gather at this riverside church for a service in commemoration of the man who had specified in his will that he wanted to be buried in its country graveyard 'unless the King decrees otherwise'. George III did indeed decree otherwise, and the great hero was

THE JOLLY FARMERS

1 Burnham Road, North Creake,
Norfolk NR21 9JW
Tel: 01328 738185

Built in the early 1800s, **The Jolly Farmers** is a large and welcoming traditional inn with great food, drink and hospitality. The exterior is painted a bright sunny yellow. Inside, all is warm woods and enormous open hearths, with a homely feel provided by the way the pub is divided into smaller rooms, with book shelves and intimate corners.

Convivial, tasteful and relaxed, the atmosphere is always welcoming. The main bar area has walls painted a pale yellow, a large open fire, wooden bar, quarry tiled floor and scrubbed pine tables. There's

also a smaller bar area with pool table, log stove and pew-style benches. Guests can eat anywhere in the pub, but the 'red room' (named for the vivid colour of the walls) is a non-smoking dining area.

The excellent menu and specials board offer up a range of superb food such as game and fish (in season), beef, chicken, vegetarian dishes, salads, sandwiches and more, all home-cooked to order and created with the freshest local produce – no frozen ingredients allowed!

Run by Adrian Sanders and his wife Heather (who is the creative force behind most of the delicious food), real ales at this delightful Free House include Woodfords and Wherry straight from the cask, plus a changing guest ale.

On fine days, the handsome beer garden is just the place to enjoy the great food and drink available.

Adrian, Heather and their friendly, helpful staff offer a warm welcome and excellent service to all their customers.

Popular with locals and visitors exploring the cycle and walking routes that pass by, this superior inn is open at lunch Weds-Sun and for dinner/evenings Tues-Sun.

interred in St Paul's Cathedral.

A little over a mile to the south of Burnham Thorpe stand the picturesque ruins of **Creake Abbey** (English Heritage, free), an Augustinian monastery founded in 1206. The Abbey's working life came to an abrupt end in 1504 when, within a single week, every one of the monks died of the plague.

Holkham
16 miles E of Hunstanton, on the A149

If the concept of the Grand Tour ever needed any justification, **Holkham Hall** amply provides it (see panel below). For six years, from 1712 to 1718, young Thomas Coke (pronounced Cook) travelled extensively in Italy, France and Germany, studying and absorbing at first hand the glories of European civilisation. And, wherever possible, buying them. When he returned to England, Coke realised that his family's modest Elizabethan manor could not possibly house the collection of treasures he had amassed. The manor would have to be demolished and a more worthy building erected in its place.

During his travels in Italy, Coke had been deeply impressed by the cool, classical lines favoured by the Renaissance architect Andrea Palladio. Working with his friend Lord Burlington - another fervent admirer of Palladio - and the architect William Kent, Coke's monumental project slowly took shape. Building began in 1734 but was not completed until 1762, three years after Coke's death.

HOLKHAM HALL & BYGONES MUSEUM

Wells-next-the-Sea, Norfolk NR23 1AB
Tel: 01328 710227 Fax: 01328 711707
website: www.holkham.co.uk

In a lakeside deer park on the beautiful North Norfolk coast stands **Holkham Hall**, one of Britain's most majestic stately homes, seat of seven generations of the Earls of Leicester. This classic 18th century mansion in Palladian style is a veritable treasure house of artistic and architectural history, and each part has its separate character and appeal, from the

stunning grandeur of the Marble Hall and the magnificence of the State Rooms to the old kitchen with its original pots and pans and the elegant formal gardens. In addition to the superb house and gardens there are other attractions at Holkham, including a Bygones Museum crammed with over 4,000 domestic and agricultural artefacts, nursery gardens, a pottery shop, restaurant and tearooms.

The completed building, its classical balance and restraint emphasised by the pale honey local brick used throughout, has been described as 'the ultimate achievement of the English Palladian movement'. As you step into the stunning entrance hall, the tone is set for the rest of the house. Modelled on a Roman Temple of Justice, the lofty coved ceiling is supported by 18 huge fluted columns of pink Derbyshire alabaster, transported to nearby Wells by river and sea.

Historically the most important room at Holkham is the Statue Gallery, which contains one of the finest collections of classical sculpture still in private ownership. In this sparsely furnished room there is nothing to distract one's attention from the sublime statuary that has survived for millennia, among it a bust of Thucydides (one of the earliest portrayals of man) and a statue of Diana, both of which have been dated to 4BC.

Each room reveals new treasures: Rubens and Van Dyck in the Saloon (the principal reception room), the Landscape Room with its incomparable collection of paintings by Lorrain, Poussin and other masters, the Brussels tapestries in the State Sitting Room and, on a more domestic note, the vast, high-ceilinged kitchen which remained in use until 1939 and still displays the original pots and pans.

Astonishingly, the interior of the house remains almost exactly as Thomas Coke planned it, his descendants having respected the integrity of his vision.

They concentrated their reforming zeal on improving the enormous estate. It was Coke's great-nephew, Thomas William Coke (1754-1842), in particular who was responsible for the elegant layout of the 3,000-acre park visitors see today. Universally known as 'Coke of Norfolk', Thomas was a pioneer of the Agricultural Revolution, best known for introducing the idea of a four-crop rotation.

As well as the Pottery in the former brickworks and its associated shop, Holkham's other attractions include an 18th century walled garden, a fascinating bygones museum, a garden centre, gift shop and tearoom.

Wells-next-the-Sea
17 miles E of Hunstanton, on the A149

There's no doubt about the appeal of Wells' picturesque quayside, narrow streets and ancient houses. Wells has been a working port since at least the 13th century, but over the years the town's full name of Wells-next-the-Sea has become increasingly inapt - its harbour now stands more than a mile from the sea. In 1859, to prevent the harbour silting up altogether, Lord Leicester of Holkham Hall built an Embankment cutting off some 600 acres of marshland. This now provides a pleasant walk down to the sea.

The Embankment gave no protection, however, against the great floods of 1953 and 1978. On the 11th January 1978 the sea rose 16 feet 1 inch above high tide, a

Wells-next-the-Sea

narrow-gauge railway is operated by the same company as the **Wells— Walsingham Light Railway** which carries passengers on a particularly lovely ride along the route of the former Great Eastern Railway to Little Walsingham. The four-mile journey takes about 20 minutes with stops at Warham St Mary and Wighton. Both the WWR and the Harbour Railway services are seasonal.

In a curious change of function, the former GER station at Wells is now home to the well-known **Burnham Pottery**, the former signal box is now the station, while the old station at Walsingham is now a church!

few inches less than the 16 feet 10 inches recorded on the 31st January 1953 when the flood-waters lifted a ship on to the quay. A silo on the harbour is marked with these abnormal levels.

Running alongside the Embankment is the **Harbour Railway**, which trundles from the small museum on the quay to the lifeboat station by the beach. This

PLACES TO STAY, EAT AND DRINK

● Denotes entries in other chapters

7 Cambridgeshire

Far removed from the hustle and bustle of modern life, the Fens are like a breath of fresh air. Extending over much of Cambridgeshire from the Wash, these flat, fenland fields contain some of the richest soil in England. Villages such as Fordham and small towns like Ely rise out of the landscape on low hills.

Before the Fens were drained, this was a land of mist, marshes and bogs, of small islands inhabited by independent folk, their livelihood the fish and waterfowl of this eerie, watery place. The region is full of legends of web-footed people, ghosts and witchcraft.

Today's landscape is the result of human ingenuity, with its constant desire to tame the wilderness and create farmland. This fascinating story spans the centuries from the earliest Roman and Anglo-Saxon times, when the first embankments and drains were constructed to lessen the frequency of

PLACES TO STAY, EAT AND DRINK

Denotes entries in other chapters

Bridge of Sighs, Cambridge

and visitors with an interest in wildlife will be in their element.

Southeastern Cambridgeshire covers the area around the city of Cambridge and is rich in history, with a host of archaeological sites and monuments to visit, as well as many important museums.

The area is fairly flat, so it makes for great walking and cycling tours, and offers a surprising variety of landscapes. The Romans planted vines here, and to this day the region is among the main producers of British wines.

At the heart of it all is Cambridge itself, one of the leading academic centres in the world and a city which deserves plenty of time to explore - on foot, by bicycle or by the gentler, more romantic option of a punt.

The old county of Huntingdonshire is the heartland of the rural heritage of Cambridgeshire. Here, the home of Oliver Cromwell beckons with a wealth of history and pleasing landscapes. Many motorists follow the Cromwell Trail, which guides tourists around the legacy of buildings and places in the area associated with the man. The natural start of the Trail is Huntingdon itself, where he was born the son of a country gentleman. Other main stopping places are covered in this chapter.

The Ouse Valley Way (26 miles long) follows the course of the Great Ouse

flooding. Throughout the Middle Ages large areas were reclaimed, with much of the work being undertaken by the monasteries. The first straight cut bypassed the Great Ouse, allowing the water to run out to sea more quickly. After the Civil War, the New Bedford River was cut parallel to the first. These two still provide the basic drainage for much of Fenland.

The significant influence of the Dutch lives on in some of the architecture and place names of the Fens. Over the years it became necessary to pump rainwater from the fields up into the rivers and, as in the Netherlands, windmills took on this task. They could not always cope with the height of the lift required, but fortunately the steam engine came along, to be replaced eventually by the electric pumps that can raise thousands of gallons of water a second to protect the land from the ever-present threat of rain and tide.

The Fens offer unlimited opportunities for exploring on foot, by car, bicycle or by boat. Anglers are well catered for, through pretty villages and a variety of natural attractions. A gentle cruise along this area can fill a lazy day to perfection, but for those who prefer something more energetic on the water there are excellent, versatile facilities at Grafham Water.

The Nene-Ouse Navigation Link, part of the Fenland Waterway, provides the

Sunset at Ely

opportunity for a relaxed look at a lovely part of the region. It travels from Stanground Lock near Peterborough to a lock at the small village of Salters Lode in the east, and the 28-mile journey passes through several Fenland towns and a rich variety of wildlife habitats.

Ely

Ely is the jewel in the crown of the Fens, in whose history the majestic **Cathedral** and the Fens themselves have played major roles. The Fens' influence is apparent even in the name: Ely was once known as Elge or Elig ('eel island')

because of the large number of eels which lived in the surrounding fenland.

Ely owes its existence to St Etheldreda, Queen of Northumbria, who in AD 673 founded a monastery on the 'Isle of Ely', where she remained as abbess until her death in AD 679. It was not until 1081 that work started on the present Cathedral, and in 1189 this remarkable example of Romanesque architecture was completed. The most outstanding feature in terms of both scale and beauty is the Octagon, built to replace the original Norman tower, which collapsed in 1322.

STEEPLEGATE TEA ROOMS AND CRAFTS

16/18 High Street, Ely,
Cambridgeshire CB7 4JU
Tel: 01353 664731

Steeplegate Tea Rooms and Crafts occupies a delightful 15th century cottage. The tea rooms on the first floor serve a superb selection of light lunches, savoury snacks and home-made cakes, while the ground floor is home to a wonderful mix of craftware and objets d'art. In the cellar's finely preserved medieval vaulted chamber, original paintings

and locally crafted wood-turned pieces are for sale. Open 9.00-17.00 (17.30 in summer) Mon-Sat.

Ely Cathedral

Alan of Walsingham was the inspired architect of this massive work, which took 30 years to complete and whose framework weighs an estimated 400 tons. Many other notable components include the 14th century Lady Chapel, the largest in England, the Prior's Door, the painted nave ceiling and St Ovin's cross, the only piece of Saxon stonework in the building.

The Cathedral is set within the walls of the monastery, and many of the ancient buildings still stand as a tribute to the incredible skill and craftsmanship of their designers and builders. Particularly worth visiting among these are the monastic buildings in the College, the Great Hall and Queens Hall.

Just beside the Cathedral is the Almonry, in whose 12th century vaulted undercroft visitors can take coffee, lunch or tea - outside in the garden if the weather permits. Two other attractions that should not be missed are the **Brass Rubbing Centre**, where visitors can make their own rubbings from replica brasses, and the **Museum of Stained Glass**. The latter, housed in the south Triforium of the Cathedral, is the only museum of stained glass in the country and contains over 100 original panels from every period, tracing the complete history of stained glass.

No 11 Chapel Street

11, Chapel Street, Ely,
Cambridgeshire CB6 1AD
Tel: 01353 668768

With two charming and comfortable guest bedrooms, **No 11 Chapel Street** is a distinguished and gracious cottage dating back some 1,000 years.

This Grade II listed building, has medieval foundations of ancient stone; is quietly located very close to the cathedral, places of historical interest and the river Great Ouse. There is a restful secluded courtyard garden and lovely conservatory for guests. You are assured of warm hospitality and relaxation. No smoking.

Ely Tourist Information Centre

Ely's **Tourist Information Centre** is itself a tourist attraction, since it is housed in a pretty black-and-white timbered building that was once the home of Oliver Cromwell. It is the only remaining house, apart from Hampton Court, where Oliver Cromwell and his family are known to have lived; parts of it trace back to the 13th century, and its varied history includes periods when it was used as a public house and, more recently, a vicarage. There are eight period rooms, exhibitions and videos to enjoy.

The Old Gaol, in Market Street, houses **Ely Museum**, with nine galleries telling the Ely story from the Ice Age to modern times. The tableaux of the condemned and debtors' cells are particularly fascinating and poignant.

Ely is not just the past, and its fine architecture and sense of history blend well with the bustle of the streets and shops and the riverside. That bustle is at its most fervent on Thursdays, when the largest general market in the area is held. Every Saturday there's a craft and collectibles market, and on the second and fourth Saturdays of the month Ely hosts a Farmers' Market.

At **Babylon Gallery** on Ely's Waterside, in a converted 18th century brewery warehouse, visitors will find an exciting collection of contemporary arts and crafts, in a programme of changing local and international exhibitions.

Cambridgeshire

KINGS ARMS

St Mary Street, Ely, Cambridgeshire CB7 4ES
Tel: 01353 668582
e-mail: graham.young13@btopenworld.co.uk

Ely's oldest pub, **Kings Arms** dates back to 1805 and boasts a laid-back and friendly staff. A real pub-lover's pub, the ales here are justly renowned and the atmosphere always welcoming.

Open Mon-Weds 11.00-16.00, 19.00-23.00; Thurs-Sat 11.00-23.00 and Sun 12.00-22.30, food is served Mon-Sat 12.00-15.00 and Sunday lunchtime all year round.

Located in the shadow of the cathedral, it makes an excellent place to stop for a refreshing drink.

OLD EGREMONT HOUSE

31 Egremont Street, Ely,
Cambridgeshire   CB6 1AE
Tel: 01353 663118 Fax: 01353 614516

Just a short walk from the magnificent Ely
Cathedral, **Old Egremont House** is a 16th
century house with superb mature gardens
extending over one acre. This splendid
residence offers two beautiful and comfortable
guest bedrooms (one en suite, the other with
private bath). Both rooms are south facing
and have fine views of the Cathedral. Booking
is required for accommodation at this

superior house, where every room is exquisite
and an air of peace and tranquillity pervades
every space.

Around Ely

Prickwillow
4 miles NE of Ely on the B1382

On the village's main street is the
Prickwillow Drainage Engine Museum,
which houses a unique collection of
large engines associated with the
drainage of the Fens. The site had been
in continuous use as a pumping station
since 1831, and apart from the engines
there are displays charting the history of
Fens drainage, the effects on land levels
and the workings of the modern
drainage system.

Littleport
6 miles N of Ely on the A10

St George's Church, with its very tall
15th century tower, is a notable landmark
here in Littleport. Of particular interest
are two stained-glass windows depicting
St George slaying the dragon. Littleport
was the scene of riots in 1861, when
labourers from Ely and Littleport, faced
with unemployment or low wages, and
soaring food prices, attacked houses and

people in this area, causing several
deaths. Five of the rioters were hanged
and buried in a common grave at St
Mary's church. A plaque commemorating
the event is attached to a wall at the
back of the church.

Little Downham
3 miles N of Ely off the A10

Little Downham's church of St Leonard
shows the change from Norman to
Gothic in church building at the turn of
the 13th century. The oldest parts are
the Norman tower and the elaborately
carved south door. Interior treasures
include what is probably the largest
royal coat of arms in the country. At the
other end of the village are the remains
(mainly the gatehouse and kitchen) of a
15th century palace built by a Bishop of
Ely. The property is in private hands and
part of it is an antiques centre.

Coveney
3 miles W of Ely off the A10/A142

A Fenland hamlet on the Bedford Level
just above West Fen, Coveney's church
of St Peter-ad-Vincula has several

interesting features, including a colourful German screen dating from around 1500 and a painted Danish pulpit. Unusual figures on the bench ends and a fine brass chandelier add to the opulent feel of this atmospheric little church.

Sutton
6 miles W of Ely off the A142/ B1381

A very splendid 'pepperpot' tower with octagons, pinnacles and spire tops marks out Sutton's grand church of St Andrew. Inside, take time to look at the 15th century font and a fine modern stained-glass window.

The reconstruction of the church was largely the work of two Bishops of Ely, whose arms appear on the roof bosses. One of the Bishops was Thomas Arundel, appointed at the age of 21.

A mile further west, there's a great family attraction in the **Mepal Outdoor Centre**, an outdoor leisure centre with a children's playpark, an adventure play area and boat hire.

Haddenham
5 miles SW of Ely on the A1123

More industrial splendour: **Haddenham Great Mill**, built in 1803 for a certain Daniel Cockle, is a glorious sight, and one definitely not to be missed. It has four sails and three sets of grinding stones, one of which is working. The mill last worked commercially in 1946 and was restored between 1992 and 1998. Open on the first Sunday of each month and by appointment.

The Church of St Andrew stands on a hillside in Haddenham. Look for the stained-glass window depicting two souls entering Heaven, and the memorial (perhaps the work of Grinling Gibbons) to Christopher Wren's sister, Anne Brunsell.

Stretham
5 miles S of Ely off A10/A1123

The **Stretham Old Engine**, a fine example of a land-drainage steam engine, is housed in a restored, tall-chimneyed brick engine house. Dating from 1831, it

be let with the flat. Both the private patio garden and the flat boast panoramic views. No smoking; no pets or children under 12.

BRIDGE HOUSE

Green End, Stretham, nr Ely,
Cambridgeshire CB6 3LF
Tel/Fax: 01353 649212

Set in 13 acres with the River Ouse running through the land, **Bridge House** is a very comfortable, large house found at the end of a long lane. Well worth seeking out, this wonderful establishment offers three comfortable and attractive guest bedrooms. There's private river-fishing for guests, and all the amenities and facilities guests could wish for. A true home from home, it makes an

excellent base from which to explore Ely, Cambridge and the surrounding area.

is one of 90 steam pumping engines installed throughout the Fens to replace some 800 windmills. It is the last to survive, having worked until 1925 and still under restoration. During the great floods of 1919 it really earned its keep by working non-stop for 47 days and nights.

This unique insight into Fenland history and industrial archaeology is open to the public on summer weekends, and on certain dates the engine and its wooden scoop-wheel are rotated (by electricity, alas!). The adjacent stoker's cottage contains period furniture and photographs of fen drainage down the years.

Wicken
9 miles S of Ely off the A1123

Owned by the National Trust, **Wicken Fen** is the oldest nature reserve in the country, 600 acres of undrained fenland famous for its rich plant, insect and bird life and a delight for both naturalists and ramblers. Features include boardwalk and nature trails, hides and watchtowers, a cottage with 1930s furnishings, a working wind pump (the

oldest in the country), a visitor centre and a shop. Open daily, dawn to dusk.

St Lawrence's Church is well worth a visit, small and secluded among trees. In the churchyard are buried Oliver Cromwell and several members of his family. One of Cromwell's many nicknames was 'Lord of the Fens': he defended the rights of the Fenmen against those who wanted to drain the land without providing adequate compensation.

Wicken Windmill is a fine and impressive smock windmill restored back to working order. One of only four smock windmills making flour by windmill in the UK, it is open the first weekend of every month and every Bank Holiday (except Christmas and Good Friday) from 11 a.m. until 5 p.m., and also over the National Mills Weekend, the second week in May.

Soham
6 miles SE of Ely off the A142

Downfield Windmill was built in 1726 as a smock mill, destroyed by gales and rebuilt in 1890 as an octagonal tower

Saucy Megs

Soham, Cambridgeshire CB7 5HA
Tel: 01353 720843

Just off the High Street and opposite the village war memorial, **Saucy Megs** is a jolly and welcoming place, with a warm and convivial atmosphere. This Grade II listed wooden building serves up bistro-style meals and snacks, including all-day breakfasts and an enormous range of ice-creams. Freshness is the by word here, and the superb range of dishes are created using local ingredients

wherever possible. Food is served Mon-Sat 9.30-16.00 (17.00 in summer), and Sundays 12.00-16.00

mill. It still grinds corn and produces a range of flours and breads for sale (open Sundays and Bank Holidays).

St Andrew's church is a fine example of the Perpendicular style of English Gothic architecture. Very grand and elaborate, it was built on the site of a 7th century cathedral founded by St Felix of Burgundy. The 15th century west tower has an ornate parapet and two medieval porches. Note, too, the chancel with its panelling and stained glass.

A plaque in Soham commemorates engine driver Ben Gimbert and fireman James Nightall, who were taking an ammunition train through the town when a wagon caught fire. They uncoupled it and began to haul it into open country. The wagon exploded, killing the fireman and a signalman.

Isleham
10 miles SE of Ely off the B1104

The remains of a Benedictine priory, with a lovely Norman chapel under the care of English Heritage, are a great draw here in Isleham. Also well worth a visit is the church of St Andrew, a 14th century cruciform building entered by a very fine lychgate. The 17th century eagle lectern is the original of a similar lectern in Ely Cathedral.

Fordham
10 miles SE of Ely off the A142

A small village on the **Newmarket Cycle Way**, the poet James Withers

Sunningdale

10 Collins Hill, Fordham, Ely,
Cambridgeshire CB7 5PA
Tel: 01638 721769 Fax: 01638 721293
website: www.dial-m.co.uk

Sunningdale Lodge is the name given to this handsome detached house set in large landscaped gardens. Here guests can enjoy friendly hospitality and charming and comfortable accommodation. There are two lovely groundfloor guest bedrooms (no smoking), which are both elegant and homely,

and Fordham makes a perfect base from which to explore the many historic and National Trust sights and attractions in the region.

THE CHEQUERS

Carter Street, Fordham, nr Ely,
Cambridgeshire CB7 5JS
Tel: 01638 720808

The Chequers is an 18th century traditional village pub with charming original features such as the oak-beamed ceilings. The intimate restaurant area is a relaxing and lovely place to enjoy the good range of home-made dishes (12.00-14.30 and 19.00-22.00 every day) created using local produce whenever possible. To drink, there's an excellent range of real ales, lagers, cider, stout, wines, spirits and soft drinks, to suit every palate. Open Mon-Sat 12.00-14.30 and 18.00-23.00; Sun 12.00-23.00

spent most of his life in Fordham and is buried in the churchyard. A stained-glass window in the church is inscribed in his memory.

Snailwell

12 miles SE of Ely off the A142

Snailwell's pretty, mainly 14th century church of St Peter on the banks of the River Snail boasts a 13th century chancel, a hammerbeam and tie beam nave roof, a 600-year-old font, pews with poppy heads and two medieval oak screens. The Norman round tower is unusual for Cambridgeshire.

Cambridge

There are nearly 30 Cambridges spread around the globe, but this, the original, is the one that the whole world knows as one of the leading university cities. Cambridge was an important town many centuries before the scholars arrived, standing at the point where forest met fen, at the lowest fording point of the river. The Romans took over a site previously settled by an Iron Age Belgic tribe, to be followed in turn by the Saxons and the Normans. Soon after the Norman Conquest, William I built a wooden motte-and-bailey castle; Edward I built a stone replacement: a mound still marks the spot. The town flourished as a market and river trading centre, and in 1209 a group of students fleeing the Oxford riots arrived.

The first College was **Peterhouse**, founded by the Bishop of Ely in 1284, and in the next century Clare, Pembroke, Gonville & Caius, Trinity

Kings College Chapel

Hall and Corpus Christi followed. The total is now 31, the latest being **Robinson College**, the gift of self-made millionaire David Robinson. The Colleges represent various architectural styles, the grandest and most beautiful being King's. Robinson has the look of a fortress; its concrete structure covered with a 'skin' of a million and a quarter hand-made red Dorset bricks.

The Colleges are all well worth a visit, but places that simply must not be missed include **King's College Chapel** with its breathtaking fan vaulting, glorious stained glass and Peter Paul Rubens' *Adoration of the Magi*; **Pepys Library**, including his diaries, in Magdalene College; and Trinity's wonderful **Great Court**. A trip by punt along the 'Backs' of the Cam brings a unique view of many of the Colleges and passes under six bridges, including the **Bridge of Sighs** (St John's) and the extraordinary wooden **Mathematical Bridge** at Queens'.

Cambridge has nurtured more Nobel Prize winners than most countries - 32 from Trinity alone - and the list of celebrated alumni covers every sphere of human endeavour and achievement: Byron, Tennyson, Milton and Wordsworth; Marlowe and Bacon; Samuel Pepys; Sir Isaac Newton and Charles Darwin; Charles Babbage, Bertrand Russell and Ludwig Wittgenstein; actors Sir Ian McKellen,

Sir Derek Jacobi and Stephen Fry; Lord Burghley; Harold Abrahams, who ran for England in the Olympics; and Burgess, Maclean, Philby and Blunt, who spied for Russia.

The Colleges apart, Cambridge is packed with interest for the visitor, with a wealth of grand buildings both religious and secular, and some of the country's leading

Trinity College Great Court

museums, many of them run by the University. The **Fitzwilliam Museum** is renowned for its art collection, which includes works by Titian, Rembrandt, Gainsborough, Hogarth, Turner, Renoir, Picasso and Cezanne, and for its antiquities from Egypt, Greece and Rome. **Kettle's Yard** has a permanent display of 20th century art in a house maintained just as it was when the Ede family donated it, with the collection, to the University in 1967. The **Museum of Classical Archaeology** has 500 plaster casts of Greek and Roman statues, and the **University Museum of Archaeology and Anthropology** covers worldwide prehistoric archaeology with special displays relating to Oceania and to the Cambridge area. The **Museum of Technology**, housed in a Victorian sewage pumping station, features an impressive collection of steam, gas and electric pumping engines and examples, great and small, of local industrial technology. Anyone with an interest in fossils should make tracks for the **Sedgwick Museum of**

CAMBRIDGE & COUNTY FOLK MUSEUM

2-3 Castle Street, Cambridge,
Cambridgeshire CB3 0AQ
Tel: 01223 355159
website: www.folkmuseum.org.uk

Housed in a late 15th century timber-framed building that was formerly the White Horse Inn, the **Cambridge & County Folk Museum** takes a nostalgic, warm-hearted look at the everyday lives of people from Cambridge and the surrounding area from 1700 onwards. Topics include Crafts & Trades, Town & Gown, Witchbottles, Skating and Eels, and throughout the year themed talks and exhibitions take place. The Museum Shop stocks an interesting range of games and puzzles, books and many other items that make ideal Christmas stocking fillers, all with a nostalgic feel.

Earth Sciences, while in the same street (Downing) the **Museum of Zoology** offers a comprehensive and spectacular survey of the animal kingdom. The **Whipple Museum of the History of Science** tells about science through instruments; the **Scott Polar Research Institute** has fascinating, often poignant exhibits relating to Arctic and Antarctic exploration; and the **University Botanic Garden** boasts a plant collection that rivals those of Kew Gardens and Edinburgh.

The work and life of the people of Cambridge and the surrounding area are the subject of the **Cambridge and County Folk Museum** (see panel above), housed in a 16th century building that for 300 years was the White Horse Inn. One of the city's greatest treasures is the **University Library**, one of the world's great research libraries with 6 million books, a million maps and 350,000 manuscripts.

Cambridge also has many fine churches, some of them used by the Colleges before they built their own chapels. Among the most notable are **St Andrew the Great** (note the memorial to Captain Cook); **St Andrew the Less**; **St Benet's** (its 11th century tower is the oldest in the county); **St Mary the Great**, a marvellous example of Late Perpendicular Gothic; and **St Peter Castle Hill**. This last is one of the smallest churches in the country, with a nave measuring just 25 feet by 16 feet.

Punting on the River Cam

Originally much larger, the church was largely demolished in 1781 and rebuilt in its present diminished state using the old materials, including flint rubble and Roman bricks. The Church of the Holy Sepulchre, always known as the **Round Church**, is one of only four surviving circular churches in England.

Around Cambridge

Bottisham

5 miles E of Cambridge on the A1303

John Betjeman ventured that Bottisham's Holy Trinity Church was 'perhaps the best in the county', so time should certainly be made for a visit. Among the many interesting features are the 13th century porch, an 18th century monument to Sir Roger Jenyns and some exceptionally fine modern woodwork in Georgian style.

Swaffham Prior

8 miles NE of Cambridge on the B1102.

Swaffham Prior gives double value to the visitor, with two churches in the same churchyard and two fine old windmills. The churches of St Mary and St Cyriac stand side by side, a remarkable and dramatic sight in the steeply rising churchyard. One of the mills, a restored

THE RED LION

The Street, Kirtling, Newmarket,
Suffolk CB8 9PD
Tel: 01638 731976
website: downourlocal.com/redlionkirtling

About six miles southeast of Newmarket, **The Red Lion** in Kirtling is an exquisite little village pub changed only slightly since it was built in 1723. The cosy and lovely public bar has a roaring 'stove'-type fire, while the restaurant is plush and comfortable, and the menu simply a joy: freshly cooked fish is just one

speciality among game dishes, steaks, pies and more, served Tues-Sun 12.00-14.00 and 19.00-21.30.

THE THREE BLACKBIRDS

36 Ditton Green, Woodditton,
Suffolk CB8 9SQ
Tel: 01638 730811 Fax: 01638 730162

Set among a bevy of stud farms in the wonderful little village of Woodditton, near Newmarket, **The Three Blackbirds** is a charming thatched inn dating back to 1642, which has made a name for itself providing excellent food and drink to the racing set elite. Owner Paul Lange is an experienced chef with a passion for food that shows in the superb menu. The wine lists are

comprehensive and a delightful complement to the delicious food.

SYCAMORE HOUSE

56 High Street, Great Wilbraham,
nr Newmarket, Cambridgeshire CB1 5JD
Tel/Fax: 01223 880751
e-mail: barry@thesycamorehouse.co.uk
website: www.thesycamorehouse.co.uk

Sycamore House is a pleasant detached house in a small village with a shop and pub, close to good local restaurants.Its large gardens extend to over an acre, with a conservatory in which to relax and enjoy the superb breakfasts. Only 7 miles from Cambridge and Newmarket, close to Duxford War Museum, Anglesey Abbey (with its beautiful winter walk) and other N.T.properties, it is ideally situated for touring, racing and golf.

1850s tower mill, still produces flour and can be visited by appointment.

At **Swaffham Bulbeck**, a little way to the south, stands another church of St Mary, with a 13th century tower and 14th century arcades and chancel. Look for the fascinating carvings on the wooden benches and a 15th century cedarwood chest decorated with biblical scenes.

Lode
6 miles NE of Cambridge on the B1102

Anglesey Abbey dates from 1600 and was built on the site of an Augustinian priory, but the house and the 100-acre garden came together as a unit thanks to the vision of the 1st Lord Fairhaven. The garden, created in its present form from the 1930s, is a wonderful place for a stroll, with 98 acres of landscaped gardens including wide grassy walks, open lawns, a riverside walk, a working water mill and one of the finest collections of garden statuary in the country. There's also a plant centre, shop and restaurant. In the house itself is Lord Fairhaven's magnificent collection of paintings, sumptuous furnishings, tapestries and clocks.

Swaffham Prior Windmill

Burwell

10 miles NE of Cambridge on the B1102

Burwell is a village of many attractions with a history going back to Saxon times. **Burwell Museum** reflects many aspects of a village on the edge of the Fens up to the middle of the 20th century. A general store, model farm, local industries and children's toys are among the displays. Next to the museum is the famous **Stephens Windmill**, built in 1820 and extensively restored.

The man who designed parts of King's College Chapel, Reginald Ely, is thought to have been responsible for the beautiful St Mary's church, which is built of locally quarried clunch stone

and is one of the finest examples of the Perpendicular style. Notable internal features include a 15th century font, a medieval wall painting of St Christopher and roof carvings of elephants, while in the churchyard a gravestone marks the terrible night in 1727 when 78 Burwell folk died in a barn fire while watching a travelling Punch & Judy show.

Behind the church are the remains of Burwell Castle, started in the 12th century but never properly completed.

The Devil's Dyke runs through Burwell on its path from Reach to Woodditton. This amazing dyke, 30 yards wide, was built, it is thought, to halt Danish invaders.

Reach

8 miles NE of Cambridge off the A4280

The charming village of Reach is home to the oldest fair in England, which celebrated its 800th anniversary on 1st May, 2000.

Waterbeach

5 miles N of Cambridge off the A10

Denny Abbey, easily accessible on the A10, is an English Heritage Grade I listed Abbey with ancient earthworks. On the same site, and run as a joint attraction, is the **Farmland Museum** (see panel opposite). The history of Denny Abbey runs from the 12th century, when it was a Benedictine monastery. It was later home to the Knights Templar, Franciscan nuns and the Countess of Pembroke, and from the 16th century was

Stephens Windmill, Burwell

FARMLAND MUSEUM & DENNY ABBEY

Ely Road, Waterbeach,
Cambridgeshire CB5 9PQ
Tel/Fax: 01223 860489
e-mail: f.m.denny@tesco.net
website: www.dennyfarmlandmuseum.org.uk

Two thousand years of history are brought fascinatingly to life in a lovely rural setting on the A10 six miles north of Cambridge. The stone-built farmhouse at the heart of the site is actually the remains of a 12th century Benedictine Abbey which at different times was home to Benedictine monks, the Knights Templar and nuns of the Franciscan order, the Poor Clares. The superb Norman interior has been beautifully preserved and restored, and visitors can see the nuns' refectory and the rooms converted for their founder, the Countess of Pembrokeshire. Displays and children's activities tell the story of how Denny has evolved down the centuries.

On the same site, and run by English Heritage as a joint attraction, is the Farmland Museum. Old farm buildings have been splendidly renovated and converted to tell visitors about the rural history of Cambridgeshire from early days to modern times. The Museum is ideal for family visits, with specially designed activities for children, and among the top displays are a village shop, agricultural machinery, a magnificent 17th century stone barn, a traditional farmworker's cottage and the workshops, which include a basket maker and a blacksmith. Special weekend events, from buttermaking demonstrations to traditional building methods, are held regularly at the Museum, which is open from noon to 5pm April to October.

a farmhouse. The old farm buildings have been splendidly renovated and converted to tell the story of village life and Cambridgeshire farming up to modern times. The museum is ideal for family outings, with plenty of hands-on activities for children and a play area, gift shop and weekend tearoom.

Milton

3 miles N of Cambridge off the A10

Milton Country Park offers fine walking and exploring among acres of parkland, lakes and woods. There's a visitor centre, a picnic area and a place serving light refreshments.

LION & LAMB

High Street, Milton, Cambridgeshire CB4 6DF
Tel: 01223 860202
e-mail: flik@declancity.fsnet.co.uk

Just off the A10 about 2 miles north of Cambridge city centre, in the quiet village of Milton, **Lion & Lamb** is a superb pub dating back to the 1600s and recently rebuilt with taste and a careful eye towards retaining the inn's charming original features and style. There's a great range of ales, lagers, cider, stout, wines, spirits and soft drinks at this

convivial and welcoming pub, which also serves hearty and delicious lunchtime meals.

THE CHEQUERS

297 High Street, Cottenham,
Cambridgeshire CB4
Tel: 01954 250307

Dating back to the 16th century, **The Chequers** is a Cottenham landmark. This pristine example of a rural Cambridgeshire pub is open Mon-Sat 12.00-23.00; Sun 12.00-22.30 and serves up a good range of ales, lagers, wines, spirits and soft drinks, as well as sandwiches and snacks at lunchtime every day. James Hutchinson and his friendly,

helpful staff take pride in ensuring that all their guests get great service and hospitality.

Cottenham

5 miles NW of Cambridge on the B1049

At nearby Cottenham, All Saints Church has an unusual tower of yellow and pink Jacobean brick topped with four pinnacles that look like pineapples. The original tower fell down in a gale, and its replacement was partially funded by former US President Calvin Coolidge, one of whose ancestors had lived in the village at the time when the tower fell down.

Rampton

6 miles N of Cambridge off the B1050/B1049

A charming village in its own right, with a tree-fringed village green, Rampton is also the site of one of the many archaeological sites in the area. This is **Giant's Hill**, a motte castle with part of an earlier medieval settlement.

Girton

3 miles NW of Cambridge off the A14

The first Cambridge College for women was founded in 1869 in Hitchin, by Emily Davies. It moved here to Girton in 1873, to be *'near enough for male lecturers to visit but far enough away to discourage male students from doing the same'*. The problem went away when Girton became a mixed College in 1983.

Madingley

4 miles W of Cambridge on the A428

The **American Cemetery** is one of the loveliest, most peaceful and most moving places in the region, a place of pilgrimage for the families of the American servicemen who operated from the many wartime bases in the county. The cemetery commemorates 3,811 dead and 5,125 missing in action in the Second World War.

Caxton

6 miles W of Cambridge off the A12198/A428

Caxton is home to Britain's oldest surviving postmill, and at **Little Gransden**, a couple of miles further southwest on the B1046, another venerable mill has been restored. A scheduled ancient monument, it dates from the early 17th century and was worked well into the early years of the 20th century.

Barton

3 miles SW of Cambridge off the A603/B1046

Looking south from this pleasant village you can see the impressive array of radio telescopes that are part of Cambridge University's Mullard Radio Astronomy Observatory.

Grantchester

2 miles SW of Cambridge off the A603

A pleasant walk by the Cam, or a punt on it, brings visitors from the bustle of Cambridge to the famous village of Grantchester, where Rupert Brooke lived and Byron swam. The walk passes through **Paradise Nature Reserve**.

> 'Stands the church clock at ten to three
> And is there honey still for tea?'

The Orchard, with its Brooke connections, is known the world over. Brooke spent two happy years in Grantchester, and immortalised afternoon tea in The Orchard in a poem he wrote while homesick in Berlin. Time should also be allowed for a look at the church of St Andrew and St Mary, in which the remains of a Norman church have been incorporated into the 1870s main structure.

Arrington

11 miles SW of Cambridge off the A603/A1198

Arrington's 18th century **Wimpole Hall**, owned by the National Trust, is probably the most spectacular country mansion in the whole county, and certainly the largest 18th century country house in Cambridgeshire. The lovely interiors are the work of several celebrated architects, and there's a fine collection of furniture and pictures. The magnificent formally laid-out grounds include a Victorian parterre, a rose garden and a walled garden.

THE BARN TEAROOMS

Burwash Manor Farm, New Road, Barton, Cambridgeshire CB3 7BD
Tel: 01223 264821

Morning coffee, luncheon, afternoon tea – all can be enjoyed at **The Barn Tearooms**, part of the selection of shops and amenities at Burwash Manor Farm. There's an excellent choice of delicious home-cooked meals, snacks, cakes and savouries served here. Parties welcome.

Outside catering provided for dinner parties, children's parties and corporate hospitality. These cosy and attractive tea rooms are open every day from 10 a.m. (11 a.m. Sun) until 4.30 (Mon-Fri; 5 p.m. Sat-Sun).

Chapel in the Hall, Wimpole

A brilliant attraction for all the family is **Wimpole Home Farm**, a working farm that is the largest rare breeds centre in East Anglia. The animals include Bagot goats, Tamworth pigs, Soay sheep and Longhorn cattle, and there's also a pets corner and horse-drawn wagon ride. Children can spend hours with the animals or in the adventure playground.

Landscaped **Wimpole Park**, with hills, woodland, lakes and a Chinese bridge, provides miles of wonderful walking and is perfect for anything from a gentle stroll to a strenuous hike.

Shepreth
8 miles S of Cambridge off A10

A paradise for lovers of nature and gardens and a great starting point for

THE KINGS HEAD

High Street, Sawston, nr Cambridge, Cambridgeshire
Tel/Fax: 01223 833541
e-mail: kaywheeler25@excite.com

Just 6 miles south of Cambridge off the A1307, **The Kings Head** is the preferred pub (and this small village has six of them!) of locals, and is well worth seeking out. Open Mon-Sat 11.00-23.00, Sunday 12.00-22.30, it has a full complement of ales, lagers, cider, stout, wines, spirits and soft drinks, to be enjoyed in the cosy surroundings or in the attractive beer garden. There are also four comfortable en suite guest bedrooms.

THE GREYHOUND

2 High Street, Sawston,
Cambridgeshire CB2 4BG
Tel: 01223 832260
e-mail: roz.clarke@virgin.net

The Greyhound is a distinctive old coaching inn dating back to the 16th century. Spacious and welcoming, many original features grace this charming and comfortable inn, which serves up a good range of beers, wines and spirits. Home-cooked food is served at lunch and dinner (every night but Sunday), and themed nights include tapas Mon-Fri, pasta Tuesday, pie night Wednesday, 'Big' steaks on Thursdays, and Sunday lunch carvery, in addition to the range of good value, tasty dishes on the menu. Open 12.00-15.00, 17.00-23.00 (Sun 12.00-15.00, 19.00-22.30).

country walks, **Shepreth L Moor Nature Reserve** is an L-shaped area of wet meadowland - now a rarity - that is home to birds and many rare plants. The nearby **Shepreth Wildlife Park** is a haven in natural surroundings to a wide variety of animals, which visitors can touch and feed. The 18th century **Docwra's Manor** is a series of enclosed gardens with multifarious plants that is worth a visit at any time of year. Fowlmere, on the other side of the A10, is another important nature reserve, with hides and trails for the serious bird-watcher.

Duxford

8 miles S of Cambridge off A505 by J10 of M11

Part of the **Imperial War Museum** (see panel below), Duxford Aviation Museum is probably the leader in its field in Europe, with an outstanding collection of over 150 historic aircraft from biplanes through Spitfires to supersonic jets. The American Air Museum, where aircraft are suspended as if in flight, is part of this terrific place, which was built on a former RAF and US fighter base. Major air shows take place several times a year, and among the permanent features are a reconstructed wartime operations room, a hands-on exhibition for children and a dramatic land warfare hall with tanks, military vehicles and artillery. Everyone should take time to see this marvellous show - and it should be much more than a flying visit!

At nearby **Hinxton**, a few miles further south, is another mill: a 17th century water mill that is grinding once more.

IMPERIAL WAR MUSEUM DUXFORD

Duxford, Cambridgeshire CB2 4QR
Tel: 01223 835000 Fax: 01223 837267

A branch of the **Imperial War Museum**, Duxford is Europe's premier aviation museum. It was built on a former RAF and USAF fighter base that saw that service throughout the Second World War, and the preserved hangars, a control tower and operations room retain a period atmosphere and from the historic heart of the 85-acre complex.

Over 400,000 visitors come to Duxford each year to see the biplanes and the Spitfires, the Concorde and the Gulf War jets that are among the 180 historic aircraft on show. A major exhibition on the Battle of Britain charts events of 1940, giving an insight into life at the time, and features an RAF Hurricane and a Luftwaffe Messerschmitt 109 that saw action in the Battle. An award-winning modern building designed by Lord Foster houses the American Air Museum with

aircraft both on the ground and suspended from the roof as though in flight. Exhibits here range from a U2 Spyplane to a T-10 Tankbuster and the mighty B-52 Stratofortress. Tanks and artillery are on show in the exciting Land Warfare Hall, which houses 50 military vehicles and artillery pieces in a series of realistic and authentic battlefield scenes.

This wonderful museum, which lies south of Cambridge at Junction 10 of the M11, is open throughout the year apart from three days at Christmas.

Linton

10 miles SE of Cambridge on the B1052

The village is best known for its zoo, but visitors will also find many handsome old buildings and the church of St Mary the Virgin, built mainly in Early English style.

A world of wildlife set in 16 acres of spectacular gardens, **Linton Zoo** is a major wildlife breeding centre and part of the inter-zoo breeding programme for endangered species. Collections include wild cats, birds, snakes and insects. For children there is a play area and, in summer, pony rides and a bouncy castle.

Chilford Hall Vineyard, on the B1052 between Linton and Balsham, comprises 18 acres of vines, with tours and wine-tastings available.

Some two miles further off the A1307, **Bartlow Hills** are the site of the largest Roman burial site to be unearthed in Europe.

Huntingdon

The former county town of Huntingdonshire is an ancient place first settled by the Romans. It boasts many grand Georgian buildings, including the handsome three-storeyed Town Hall.

Oliver Cromwell was born in

SPRINGFIELD HOUSE

14-16 Horn Lane, Linton,
Cambridgeshire CB1 6HT
Tel: 01223 891383 Fax: 01223 890335
website: www.smoothhound.co.uk/hotels/
springf2.html

Set on a vast expanse of lawn with a gravel drive, **Springfield House** is an elegant double-fronted and gabled period house with conservatory, and grounds stretching down to the River Granta, provides genteel relaxation and is open all year round. The guests' lounge, dining room and two en suite double

rooms are tastefully decorated and comfortable, with views of the garden, river and church. 4 Stars ETB.

DOG AND DUCK

63 High Street, Linton,
Cambridgeshire CB1 6HS
Tel/Fax: 01223 891257
e-mail: doganduck@hotmail.com
website: www.dogandducklinton.co.uk

Set in the conservation area of this historic village, **Dog & Duck** is a traditional thatched inn dating back to the 1500s. A pub since the 1850s, the long bar has handsome oak beams, stone floors and large open fireplace; the River Granta flows by the garden. A good selection of real ales and delicious freshly cooked meals

from the superb menus (Tues-Sat 12.00-14.15, 18.30-21.30; Sun 12.00-14.00, 19.00-21.00) await you at this lovely inn.

Huntingdon in 1599 and attended Huntingdon Grammar School. The schoolhouse was originally part of the Hospital of St John the Baptist, founded during the reign of Henry II by David, Earl of Huntingdon. Samuel Pepys was also a pupil here.

Cromwell was MP for Huntingdon in the Parliament of 1629, was made a JP in 1630 and moved to St Ives in the following year. Rising to power as an extremely able military commander in the Civil War, he raised troops from the region and made his headquarters in the Falcon Inn.

Appointed Lord Protector in 1653, Cromwell was ruler of the country until his death in 1658. The school he attended is now the **Cromwell Museum**, located on Huntingdon High Street, housing the only public collection relating specifically to him, with exhibits that reflect many aspects of his political, social and religious life. The museum's exhibits include an extensive collection of Cromwell family portraits and personal objects, among them a hat and seal, contemporary coins and medals, an impressive Florentine cabinet - the gift of the Grand Duke of Tuscany - and a surgeon's chest made by Kolb of Augsburg. This fine collection helps visitors interpret the life and legacy of Cromwell and the

Republican movement.

All Saints Church, opposite the Cromwell Museum, displays many architectural styles, from medieval to Victorian. One of the two surviving parish churches of Huntingdon, All Saints was considered to be the church of the Hinchingbrooke part of the Cromwell family, though no memorials survive to attest to this. The Cromwell family burial vault is contained within the church, however, and it is here that Oliver's father Robert and his grandfather Sir Henry are buried. The church has a fine chancel roof, a very lovely organ chamber, a truly impressive stained glass window and the font in which Cromwell was baptised, as it's the old font from the destroyed St John's church, discovered in a local garden in 1927!

All Saints, Huntingdon

Huntingdon's other church, **St Mary's**, dates from Norman times but was almost completely rebuilt in the 1400s. It boasts a fine Perpendicular west tower, which partially collapsed in 1607. The damage was extensive, and the tower was not completely repaired until 1621. Oliver Cromwell's father Robert contributed to the cost of the repairs, as recorded on the stone plaque fixed to the east wall on the nave, north of the chancel arch.

Cowper House (No 29 High Street) has an impressive early 18th century frontage. A plaque commemorates the fact that the poet William Cowper (pronounced 'Cooper') lived here between 1765 and 1767.

Among Huntingdon's many fine former coaching inns is **The George Hotel**. Although badly damaged by fire in 1865, the north and west wings of the 17th century courtyard remain intact, as does its very rare wooden gallery. The inn was one of the most famous of all the posting houses on the old Great North Run. It is reputed that Dick Turpin used one of the rooms here. The medieval courtyard, gallery and open staircase are the scene of annual productions of Shakespeare.

Along the south side of the Market Square, the **Falcon Inn** dates back in parts to the 1500s. Oliver Cromwell is said to have used this as his headquarters during the Civil War.

About half a mile southwest of town stands **Hinchingbrooke House**, which today is a school but which has its origins in the Middle Ages, when it was a nunnery (ghostly nuns are said to haunt the building to this day). The remains of the Benedictine nunnery can still be seen. It was given to the Cromwell family by Henry VIII in 1538. Converted by the Cromwell family in the 16th century and later extended by the Earls of Sandwich, today's visitors can see examples of every period of English architecture from the 12th to early 20th centuries. King James I was a regular visitor, and Oliver Cromwell spent part of his childhood here. The 1st Earl of Sandwich was a central figure in the Civil War and subsequent Restoration, while the 4th Earl (inventor of the lunchtime favourite that bears his name) was one of the most flamboyant politicians of the 18th century. The House is open for guided tours, including lovely cream teas served in the Tudor kitchens.

Hinchingbrooke Country Park covers 180 acres of grassy meadows, mature woodland, ponds and lakes. There is a wide variety of wildlife including woodpeckers, herons, kestrels, butterflies and foxes. The network of paths makes exploring the park easy, and battery-powered wheelchairs are provided for less able visitors. The Visitors Centre serves refreshments at peak times.

Half a mile north, **Spring Common** offers another chance to enjoy some marvellous Cambridgeshire countryside. Covering 13 acres, its name comes from the natural spring that runs constantly and has long been a gathering place. The town developed around rather than within this area of rural tranquillity, which boasts a range of diverse habitats including marsh, grassland, scrub and streams. Plant life abounds, providing food and shelter for a variety of animals, amphibians, birds and invertebrates.

Around Huntingdon

Hartford
½ mile N of Huntington off the B1514

At just half a mile from Hartford Marina, this lovely village offers plenty of excellent riverside walks.

Alconbury
3 miles NW of Huntingdon off the A1

Fenland walks can be interspersed with pauses at the local inns and a look at the church of St Peter and St Paul, whose steeple and chancel are particularly noteworthy. This long village has a large green, an ancient village pump and a 15th century bridge crossing the brook that runs through Alconbury.

Barham
6 miles W of Huntingdon off the A1/A14

This delightful hamlet boasts 12 houses, 30 people and an ancient church with box pews, surrounded by undulating farmland. Nearby attractions include angling and sailing on Grafham Water, go-karting at Kimbolton and National Hunt racing at Huntingdon.

Ramsey
9 miles NE of Huntingdon on the B1040

A pleasant market town with a broad main street down which a river once ran, Ramsey is home to the medieval Ramsey Abbey, founded in AD 969 by Earl Ailwyn as a Benedictine monastery. The Abbey became one of the most important in England in the 12th and 13th centuries, and as it prospered, so did Ramsey, so that by the 13th century it had become a town with a weekly market and an annual three-day festival at the time of the feast of St Benedict.

(just a mile away) and several good pubs, restaurants and other amenities.

After the Dissolution of the Monasteries in 1539, the Abbey and its lands were sold to Sir Richard Williams, great-grandfather of Oliver Cromwell. Most of the buildings were then demolished, the stones being used to build Caius, King's and Trinity Colleges at Cambridge, the towers of Ramsey, Godmanchester and Holywell churches, the gate at Hinchingbrooke House and several local properties. In 1938 the house was converted for use as a school, which it remains to this day.

To the northwest are the ruins of the once magnificent stone gatehouse of the late 15th century - only the porter's lodge remains, but inside can be seen an unusual large carved effigy made of Purbeck marble and dating back to the 14th century. It is said to represent Earl Ailwyn, founder of the Abbey. The gatehouse, now in the care of the National Trust, can be visited daily from April to October.

The church of **St Thomas à Becket of Canterbury** forms an impressive vista at the end of the High Street. Dating back to about 1180, it is thought to have been built as a hospital or guesthouse for the Abbey. It was converted to a church to accommodate the many pilgrims who flocked to Ramsey in the 13th century. The church has what is reputed to be the finest nave in Huntingdonshire, dating back to the 12th century and consisting of seven bays. The church's other treasure is a 15th century carved oak lectern, thought to have come from the Abbey.

Most of **Ramsey Rural Museum** is housed in an 18th century farm building and several barns set in open countryside. Among the many fascinating things to see are a Victorian home and school, a village store, and restored farm equipment, machinery, carts and wagons. The wealth of traditional implements used by local craftsmen such as the farrier, wheelwright, thatcher, dairyman, animal husbandman and cobbler offer an insight into bygone days.

The unusual Ramsey War Memorial is a listed Grade II memorial consisting of a fine bronze statue of St George slaying the dragon atop a tall, octagonal pillar crafted of Portland stone.

Upwood
8 miles NE of Huntingdon off the B1040

Upwood is a pleasant, scattered village in a very tranquil and picturesque setting. **Woodwalton Fen** nature reserve is a couple of minutes' drive to the west.

Sawtry
8 miles NW of Huntingdon on the A1

The main point of interest here has no point! All Saints Church, built in 1880, lacks both tower and steeple, and is topped instead by a bellcote. Inside the church are marvellous brasses and pieces from ancient Sawtry Abbey.

Just south of Sawtry, **Aversley Wood** is a conservation area with abundant birdlife and plants.

Hamerton

9 miles NW of Huntingdon off the A1

Hamerton Zoological Park has hundreds of animals from tortoises to tigers. Speically designed enclosures make for unrivalled views of the animals, and the park features meerkats, marmosets and mongooses, lemurs, gibbons, possums and sloths, snakes and even creepy-crawlies such as cockroaches!

Great Gidding

10 miles NW of Huntingdon off the B660

Stained-glass windows are a notable feature of **St Michael's** church in this, the largest of the three Giddings. A fire ravaged the village in the 1860s and the church was one of the few buildings to survive. Today the church is the atmospheric setting for concerts and plays.

Stilton

12 miles NW of Huntingdon off the A1

Stilton has an interesting high street with many fine buildings, and is a good choice for the hungry or thirsty visitor, as it has been since the heyday of horse-drawn travel. Journeys were a little more dangerous then, and Dick Turpin is said to have hidden at the Bell Inn. The famous cheese is still produced and sold here.

Ellington

4 miles W of Huntingdon off the A14

Ellington is a quiet village just south of the A14 and about a mile north of Grafham Water. Both Cromwell and Pepys visited, having relatives living in the village, and it was in Ellington that Pepys' sister Paulina found a husband, much to the relief of the diarist, who had written: *'We must find her one, for she grows old and ugly.'* All Saints church is magnificent, like so many in the area, and among its many fine features are the 15th century oak roof and the rich carvings in the nave and the aisles. The church and its tower were built independently.

Spaldwick

6 miles W of Huntingdon off the A14

A sizable village that was once the site of the Bishop of Lincoln's manor house, Spaldwick boasts the grand church of St James, which dates from the 12th century and has seen restoration in most centuries, including the 20th, when the spire had to be partly rebuilt after being struck by lightning.

Two miles further west, Catworth is another charming village, regularly voted Best Kept Village in Cambridgeshire and well worth exploring.

Keyston

12 miles W of Huntingdon off the A14

A delightful village with a pedigree that

Cambridgeshire

can be traced back to the days of the Vikings, Keyston has major attractions both sacred and secular: the **Church of St John the Baptist** is impressive in its almost cathedral-like proportions, with one of the most magnificent spires in the whole county.

Brampton

2 miles SW of Huntingdon off the A1

Brampton is where Huntingdon racecourse is situated. An average of 18 meetings (all jumping) are scheduled every year, including Bank Holiday fixtures (extra-special deals for families). In November, the Grade II Peterborough Chase is the feature race.

Brampton's less speculative attractions include the 13th century church of St Mary, and Pepys House, the home of Samuel's uncle who was a cousin of Lord Sandwich's and who got Samuel his job at the Admiralty.

Grafham

5 miles SW of Huntingdon on the B661

Created in the mid-1960s as a reservoir,

Grafham Water offers a wide range of outdoor activities for visitors of all ages, with 1,500 acres of beautiful countryside, including the lake itself. The ten-mile perimeter track is great for jogging or cycling, and there's excellent sailing, windsurfing and fly-fishing. The area is a Site of Special Scientific Interest, and an ample nature reserve at the western edge is run jointly by Anglian Water and the Wildlife Trust. There are nature trails, information boards, a wildlife garden and a dragonfly pond. Bird-watchers have the use of six hides, three of them accessible to wheelchairs. An exhibition centre has displays and video presentations of the reservoir's history, a gift shop and a café.

Kimbolton

8 miles SW of Huntingdon on the B645

History aplenty here, and a lengthy pause is in order to look at all the interesting buildings. St Andrew's Church would head the list were it not for **Kimbolton Castle** which, along with its gatehouse, dominates the village. Parts of the original Tudor building are

THE GRANGE HOTEL

115 High Street, Brampton, Cambridgeshire PE28 4RA
Tel: 01480 459516 Fax: 01480 459 391
e-mail: nsteiger@grangehotelbrampton.com
website: www.grangehotelbrampton.co.uk

The Grange Hotel dates back to 1773, and has in its time served as a girls' school, a private house and headquarters for the American Air Force and the RAF. With seven en suite guest bedrooms, this spacious and elegant hotel also

boasts an excellent licensed restaurant and bar, serving a menu of Modern English dishes at luncheon (12.00-14.00) and evenings (18.30-21.30) amid gracious surroundings.

still to be seen, but the appearance of the castle today owes much to the major remodelling carried out by Vanbrugh and Nicholas Hawksmoor in the first decade of the 18th century. The gatehouse was added by Robert Adam in 1764. Henry VIII's first wife Catherine of Aragon spent the last 18 months

Riverside Walk, St Neots

of her life imprisoned here, where she died in 1536. The castle is now a school, but can be visited on certain days in the summer (don't miss the Pellegrini murals).

Buckden

4 miles SW of Huntingdon on the A1

This historic village was an important coaching stop on the old Great North Road. It is known particularly as the site of **Buckden Towers**, the great palace built for the Bishops of Lincoln. In the splendid grounds are the 15th century gatehouse and the tower where Henry VIII imprisoned his first wife, Catherine of Aragon, in 1533 (open only on certain days of the year).

St Neots

10 miles SW of Huntingdon off the A1

St Neots dates back to the founding of a Saxon Priory, built on the outskirts of Eynesbury in AD 974. Partially destroyed by the Danes in 1010, it was re-established as a Benedictine Priory in about 1081 by St Anselm, Abbot of Bec and later Archbishop of Canterbury. For the next two centuries the Priory flourished. Charters were granted by Henry I to hold fairs and markets. The first bridge over the Great Ouse, comprising 73 timber arches, was built in 1180. The name of the town comes from the Cornish saint whose remains were interred in the Priory some time before the Norman Conquest. With the Dissolution of the Monasteries, the Priory was demolished. In the early 17th century the old bridge was replaced by a stone one. This was then the site of a battle between the Royalists and Roundheads in 1648 - an event sometimes re-enacted by Sealed Knot societies.

St Neots repays a visit on foot, since there are many interesting sites and old buildings tucked away. The famous Market Square is one of the largest and most ancient in the country. A market has been held here every Thursday since the 12th century. The magnificent parish church of St Mary the Virgin is a very fine edifice, known locally as the Cathedral of Huntingdonshire. It is an outstanding example of Late Medieval architecture. The gracious interior complements the 130-foot Somerset-style tower, with a finely carved oak alter, excellent Victorian stained glass and a Holdich organ, built in 1855.

St Neots Museum - opened in 1995 - tells the story of the town and the surrounding area. Housed in the former magistrates' court and police station, it still has the original cells. Eye-catching displays trace local history from prehistoric times to the present day. Open Tuesday to Saturday.

Little Paxton

2½ miles N of St Neots off the A1/ A428

Fewer than three miles north of St Neots at Little Paxton is **Paxton Pits Nature Reserve**. Created alongside gravel workings, the Reserve attracts thousands of water birds for visitors to observe from hides. The wealth of wildlife means that the area is an SSSI (Site of Special Scientific Interest) and ensures a plethora of colour and activity all year round. The site also features nature trails and a visitors' centre. It has thousands of visiting waterfowl, including one of the largest colonies of cormorants, and is particularly noted for its wintering wildfowl, nightingales in late spring and kingfishers. There are about four miles of walks, some suitable for wheelchairs. Spring and summer also bring a feast of wildflowers, butterflies and dragonflies.

Eynesbury

1 mile S of St Neots on the A428

Eynesbury is actually part of St Neots, with only a little stream separating the two. Note the 12th century church of St Mary with its Norman tower. Rebuilt in the Early English period, it retains some well-preserved locally sculpted 14th century oak benches.

History has touched this quiet and

ARDLE HOUSE

4 Berkley Street, Eynesbury, St Neots, Cambridgeshire PE19 2NB
Tel: 01480 474226
e-mail: olivia.brennan@ntlworld.com

Situated just off the A114/A428, **Ardle House** is a quiet and relaxed guest house with four attractive and comfortable guest bedrooms (one twin, one double/family room and two singles).

The guests' lounge and dining room are beautifully furnished and decorated. This gracious home from home exudes an air of comfort and quality throughout.

Owner Olivia Brennan is everything guests

could wish for in her welcoming demeanour and attentive service.

Cambridgeshire

lovely village from time to time: it was the home of the famous giant James Toller, who died in 1818 and is buried in the middle aisle of the church. Only 21 when he died, he measured some 8 feet tall - it is said he was buried here to escape the attention of body-snatchers, whose activities were widespread at the time. Eynesbury was also the birthplace of the Miles' Quads, the first-ever surviving quadruplets in Britain.

Bushmead
4 miles W of St Neots off the B660

The remains of **Bushmead Abbey**, once a thriving Augustinian community, are well worth a detour. The garden setting is delightful, and the surviving artefacts include some interesting stained glass. Open weekends in July and August.

Godmanchester
2 miles SW of Huntingdon off the A1

Godmanchester is linked to Huntingdon by a 14th century bridge across the River Ouse. It was a Roman settlement and one that continued in importance down the years, as the number of handsome buildings testifies. One such is **Island Hall**, a mid-18th century mansion built for John Jackson, the Receiver General for Huntingdon; it contains many interesting pieces. This family home has lovely Georgian rooms, with fine period detail and fascinating possessions relating to the owners' ancestors since their first occupation of the house in 1800. The tranquil riverside setting and

formal gardens add to the peace and splendour - the house takes its name from the ornamental island that forms part of the grounds. Octavia Hill was sometimes a guest, and wrote effusively to her sister that Island Hall was 'the loveliest, dearest old house, I never was in such a one before.' Open only to pre-booked groups.

Wood Green Animal Shelter at Kings Bush Farm, Godmanchester is a purpose-built, 50-acre centre open to the public all year round. Cats, dogs, horses, donkeys, farm animals, guinea pigs, rabbits, llamas, wildfowl and pot-bellied pigs are among the many creatures for visitors to see, and there is a specially adapted nature trail and restaurant.

A footpath leads from the famous Chinese Bridge (1827) to **Port Holme Meadow**, at 225 acres one of the largest in England and the site of Roman remains. It is a Site of Special Scientific Interest, with a huge diversity of botanical and bird species. Huntingdon racecourse was once situated here, and it was a training airfield during the First World War. Another site of considerable natural activity is **Godmanchester Pits**, accessed along the Ouse Valley Way and home to a great diversity of flora and fauna.

Papworth Everard
6 miles S of Huntingdon on the A1198

One of the most recent of the region's churches, St Peter's dates mainly from the mid-19th century. Neighbouring

Papworth St Agnes has an older church in St John's, though parts of that, too, are Victorian. Just up the road at **Hilton** is the famous **Hilton Turf Maze**, cut in 1660 to a popular medieval design.

Boxworth

7 miles SE of Huntingdon off the A14

A village almost equidistant from Huntingdon and Cambridge, and a pleasant base for touring the area, Boxworth's church of St Peter is unusual in being constructed of pebble rubble.

A mile south of Boxworth is **Overhall Grove**, one of the largest elm woods in the country and home to a variety of wildlife.

The Great Ouse Valley

Hemingford Abbots

3 miles SE of Huntingdon off the A14

Once part of the Ramsey Abbey Estate, Hemingford Abbots is set around the 13th century church of St Margaret, along the banks of the Great Ouse. Opportunities for angling and boating facilities, including rowing boats for hire, as well as swimming, country walks, golf and a recreation centre are all within a couple of miles. The village hosts a flower festival every two years.

Just to the east is **Hemingford Grey**,

HOUGHTON MILL

Houghton, Huntingdon,
Cambridgeshire PE28 2AZ
Tel: 01480 301494 Fax: 01480 469641
website: www.nationaltrust.org.uk/
   houghtonmill

The National Trust-owned **Houghton Mill** deserves its reputation as a popular tourist attraction. There has been a mill on this site for some 1,000 years. The present mill dates from the 18th century. This impressive five-story brick and clapboard structure stands on a tributary of the River Ouse midway between Huntingdon and St Ives.

The mill is one of the last and the most complete to survive in the area. As such it is the most important of the very few remaining mills. It has recently had its wheel restored, as part of a 1.2 million pound restoration project and is fully operational. This has provided improved facilities for visitors. Open days during the summer months offer visitors the chance to see the mill in action, and to appreciate the different forms of sustainable energy - a water turbine which generates electricity for the site and for other National Trust properties, and the waterwheel at work to produce stoneground flour. Milling takes place on Sundays and Bank Holiday Mondays, and the site also contains an art gallery, miniature millstones to turn by hand, and a tea room. In addition, the area to the north of the mill is an unusual survival of undeveloped Ouse riverbank, which the Trust intends to protect for its ecological interest and landscape value as an appropriate setting for this fine mill.

with its church on the banks of the Ouse. The manor at Hemingford Grey is reputedly the oldest continuously inhabited house in England, built around 1130. Visits (by appointment only) will reveal all the treasures in the house and garden.

Fenstanton

7 miles SE of Huntingdon off the A14 bypass

Capability Brown was Lord of the Manor from 1768, and he, his wife and his son are buried in the medieval church. Any visit here should also take in the 17th century manor house and the red-brick Clock Tower.

Swavesey

10 miles SE of Huntingdon off the A14

Look for the large 14th century church and the windmill a little way west, on the way to Fen Drayton, whose church is built of pebble rubble.

Wyton

2 miles E of Huntington off the A1123

Wyton is mentioned in the *Domesday Book*, and is thought to have been founded in the 8th century. It is a popular tourist destination thanks to its proximity to **Houghton Mill** (see panel opposite) and opportunities for riverside walks, as well as its charming thatched buildings and shops.

Houghton

5 miles E of Huntingdon on the A1123

Houghton Meadows is a Site of Special Scientific Interest with an abundance of hay meadow species. One of the most popular walks in the whole area links Houghton with St Ives.

St Ives

6 miles E of Huntingdon off the A1123

This is an ancient town on the banks of the Great Ouse which once held a huge annual fair and is named after St Ivo, said to be a Persian bishop who came here in the Dark Ages to spread a little light. In the Middle Ages, kings bought cloth for their households at the village's great wool fairs and markets, and a market is still held every Monday. The Bank Holiday Monday markets are particularly lively affairs, and the Michaelmas fair fills the town centre for three days.

Seagoing barges once navigated up to the famous six-arched bridge that was built in the 15th century and has a most unusual two-storey chapel in its middle. Oliver Cromwell lived in St Ives in the 1630s; the statue of him on Market Hill, with its splendid hat, is one of the village's most familiar landmarks. It was made in bronze, with a Portland stone base, and was erected in 1901. It was originally designed for Huntingdon, but they wouldn't accept it!

The beautiful parish church in its churchyard beside the river is well worth a visit. The quayside provides a tranquil mooring for holidaymakers and there are wonderful walks by the riverside.

Clive Sinclair developed his tiny TVs and pocket calculators in the town, and another famous son of St Ives was the great Victorian rower John Goldie, whose name is remembered each year by the second Cambridge boat in the Boat Race.

The **Norris Museum**, in a delightful setting by the river, tells the story of Huntingdonshire for the past 175 million years or so, with everything from fossils, mammoth tusks and models of the great historic reptiles through flint tools, Roman artefacts and Civil War armour to lace-making and ice-skating displays, and contemporary works of art. A truly fascinating place that is open throughout the year, admission is free. Exhibitions include a life-size replica of a 160-million-year-old ichthyosaur. There are remains of woolly mammoths

from the Ice Ages, tools and pottery from the Stone Age to Roman times and relics from the medieval castles and abbeys. Also on show are toys and models made by prisoners of the Napoleonic Wars.

*'As I was going to St Ives I met a man with seven wives.
Each wife had seven sacks,
each sack had seven cats,
each cat had seven kits.
Kits, cats, sacks and wives,
how many were going to St Ives?'*

- None, of course, but today's visitors are certain to have a good time while they are here.

Just outside St Ives are **Wilthorn Meadow**, a Site of Natural History Interest where Canada geese are often to be seen, and **Holt Island Nature Reserve**, where high-quality willow is being grown to reintroduce the traditional craft of basket-making. Take some time for spotting the butterflies, dragonflies and kingfishers.

Earith
4 miles E of St Ives on the A1123

The **Ouse Washes**, a special protection area, runs northeast from the village to Earith Pits, a well-known habitat for birds and crawling creatures; some of the pits are used for fishing. The Washes

St Ives Bridge and River Ouse

Green Man

East Street, Colne, Cambridgeshire PE28 3LZ
Tel: 01487 840368
e-mail: philspub@supanet.com

Standing proudly in the centre of the village, **Green Man** is a convivial and welcoming traditional pub. Warm hospitality awaits all visitors. The food and drink are excellent at this handsome pub, which dates back to 1707 with more modern additions to make it both cosy and comfortable. Open Mon-Fri 12.00-15.00, 18.00-23.00; Sat 11.00-23.00; Sun 12.00-22.30. Food is served 12.00-14.00 and 19.00-21.30 Mon-Fri, and all day at weekends. Live music Sat and Sun eves.

are a wetland of major international importance supporting such birds as ruffs, Bewick and Whooper swans, and hen harriers. The average bird population is around 20,000. Some of the meadows flood in winter, and ice-skating is popular when the temperature really drops. There's a great tradition of ice-skating in the Fens, and Fenmen were the national champions until the 1930s.

Somersham

4 miles NE of St Ives on the B1040/B1060

The **Raptor Foundation** is found here, a major attraction where owls and other birds of prey find refuge. There are regular flying displays and falconry shows. Somersham once had a palace for the Bishops of Ely, and its splendid church of St John would have done them proud.

Peterborough

The second city of Cambridgeshire has a long and interesting history that can be traced back to the Bronze Age, as can be seen in the archaeological site at Flag Fen. Although a cathedral city, it is also a New Town (designated in 1967), so modern development and expansion have vastly increased its facilities while retaining the quality of its historic heart.

Peterborough's crowning glory is, of course, the Norman **Cathedral**, built in

Rose and Crown

99 High Street, Somersham, Cambridgeshire PE28 3EE
Tel: 01487 840228

Rose & Crown in Somersham is a Grade I listed 17th century building with many charming original features such as the huge central open fireplace, oak floors and stone walls. The atmosphere is always welcoming at this friendly traditional coaching inn. Home-made dishes make up the menu and tempting daily specials. Open Mon-Thurs 12.00-23.00; Fri-Sat 12.00-0.00; Sun 12.00-22.30. Live music Fri and Sat eves.

the 12th and 13th centuries on a site that had seen Christian worship since AD 655. Henry VIII made the church a cathedral, and his first queen, Catherine of Aragon, is buried here, as for a while was Mary Queen of Scots after her execution at Fotheringay. Features to note are the huge (85-foot) arches of the West Front, the unique

River Nene, Peterborough

painted wooden nave ceiling, some exquisite late15th century fan vaulting, and the tomb of Catherine.

Though the best-known of the city's landmarks, the Cathedral is by no means the only one. The **Peterborough Museum and Art Gallery** covers all

Peterborough Cathedral

aspects of the history of Peterborough from the Jurassic period to Victorian times.

The Gildenburgh Gallery at 44 Broadway boasts a good collection of fine art from the 20th and 21st centuries and a design-led craft shop. The views of Peterborough to be had from the gallery are panoramic and impressive.

There are twin attractions for railway enthusiasts in the shape of **Railworld**, a hands-on exhibition dealing with modern rail travel, and the wonderful **Nene Valley Railway**, which operates 15-mile steam-hauled trips between Peterborough and its HQ and museum at Wansford. A feature on the main railway line at Peterborough is the historic Iron Bridge, part of the old Great Northern Railway and still virtually as built by Lewis Cubitt in 1852.

Just outside the city, by the river Nene, is **Thorpe Meadows Sculpture Park**, one of several open spaces in and around the city with absorbing collections of modern sculpture.

BLUE BELL

6 The Green, Werrington,
Peterborough PE4 6RU
Tel: 01733 571264

Close to the A47 but in a quiet location, the welcoming **Blue Bell** is a spacious and attractive pub and restaurant with an elegant dining room, comfortable public bar and quiet lounge brimming with character.

Good food, ale and the friendly staff make this fine pub well worth seeking out. The

menu offers delicious Anglo/French cuisine at lunch and dinner seven days a week.

Around Peterborough

Longthorpe

2 miles W of Peterborough off the A47

Longthorpe Tower, part of a fortified manor house, is graced by some of the very finest 14th century domestic wall paintings in Europe, featuring scenes both sacred and secular: the Nativity, the Wheel of Life, King David, the Labours of the Months. The paintings were discovered during renovations after the Second World War.

Elton

6 miles SW of Peterborough on the B671

Elton is a lovely village on the river Nene, with stone-built houses and thatched roofs. **Elton Hall** is a mixture of styles, with a 15th century tower and chapel, and a major Gothic influence. The grandeur is slightly deceptive, as some of the battlements and turrets were built of wood to save money. The hall's sumptuous rooms are filled with art treasures (Gainsborough, Reynolds, Constable) and the library has a wonderful collection of antique tomes.

Thornhaugh

8 miles NW of Peterborough off the A1/A47

Hidden away in a quiet valley is **Sacrewell Farm and Country Centre**, whose centrepiece is a working watermill. All kinds of farming

THE MILL

Barnwell Road, Oundle, nr Peterborough, Northamptonshire PE8 5PB
Tel: 01832 272621 Fax: 01832 272221

On the banks of the River Nene, **The Mill** is the gracious and beautiful setting for two excellent restaurants – The Trattoria on the first floor and The Granary on the top floor - and a Waterside Bar. Solid oak beams, thick stone walls and other original features grace this fabulous venue, mentioned in records dating back to AD875. The menus boast

delectable dishes from all points of the globe.

equipment are on display, and there's a collection of farm animals, along with gardens, nature trails and general interest trails, play areas, a gift shop and a restaurant serving light refreshments.

Peakirk

7 miles N of Peterborough off the A15

Peakirk boasts a village church of Norman origin that is the only one in the country dedicated to St Pega, the remains of whose hermit cell can still be seen.

Crowland

10 miles NE of Peterborough off the A1073

It is hard to imagine that this whole area was once entirely wetland and marshland, dotted with inhospitable islands. Crowland was one such island, then known as Croyland, and on it was established a small church and hermitage back in the 7th century, which was later to become one of the nation's most important monasteries. The town's impressive parish church was just part of the great edifice which once stood on the site. A wonderful exhibition can be found in the **Abbey** at Crowland, open all year round. The remains cover a third of the Abbey's original extent.

Crowland's second gem is the unique **Trinity Bridge** - set in the centre of town on dry land! Built in the 14th century, it has three arches built over

THE ABBEY HOTEL

East Street, Crowland, nr Peterborough,
Lincolnshire PE6 0EN
Tel: 01733 210200

Built in the late 1800s, **The Abbey Hotel** is a
tranquil and welcoming establishment just a
stone's throw from the ancient church in the
quiet and scenic village of Crowland. Fresh,
good-value dishes are served at lunch and
dinner (Mon-Sun 12.00-14.30; Mon-Sat 18.00-
21.00) and the hotel bar is open Mon-Thurs
12.00-15.00, 17.00-23.00 and all day Fri-Sun.

The 12 guest bedrooms are bright,
comfortable and fitted with every amenity.

one over-arching structure. Before the
draining of the Fens, this bridge crossed
the point where the River Welland
divided into two streams.

Thorney

*8 miles E of Peterborough on the
A47*

Thorney Abbey, the church of St Mary
and St Botolph, is the dominating
presence even though what now stands
is but a small part of what was once one
of the greatest of the Benedictine
abbeys. Gravestones in the churchyard
are evidence of a Huguenot colony that
settled here after fleeing France in the
wake of the St Bartholomew's Day
massacre of 1572.

The **Thorney Heritage Museum** is a
small, independently-run museum of
great fascination, describing the
development of the village from a Saxon
monastery, via Benedictine Abbey to a
model village built in the 19th century
by the Dukes of Bedford. The main
innovation was a 10,000-gallon water
tank that supplied the whole village;
other villages had to use unfiltered
river water.

Whittlesey

*5 miles E of Peterborough off the
A605*

The market town of Whittlesey lies
close to the western edge of the Fens
and is part of one of the last tracts to be
drained. Brick-making was a local
speciality, and 180-foot brick chimneys
stand as a reminder of that once-
flourishing industry. The church of **St
Andrew** is mainly 14th century, with a
16th century tower; the chancel,
chancel chapels and naves still have
their original roofs.

A walk round this charming town
reveals an interesting variety of
buildings: brick, of course, and also some
stone, thatch on timber frames, and rare
thatched mud boundary walls.

The **Whittlesey Museum**, housed in
the grand 19th century Town Hall in
Market Street, features an archive of
displays on local archaeology,
agriculture, geology, brick-making and
more. Reconstructions include a 1950s
corner shop and post office, blacksmith's
forge and wheelwright's bench.

A highlight of Whittlesey's year is the

Cambridgeshire

THE GREYHOUND

41 Crowland Road, Eye Green,
nr Peterborough, Cambridgeshire
Tel: 01733 222487 Fax: 01733 223518
e-mail: kenpmurphy@aol.com

Just off the A47 towards Wisbech, Eye Green is home to **The Greyhound**, a distinctive pub that manages to be spacious and cosy at the same time. Decorated and furnished with taste and comfort in mind, it is homely and welcoming. Renowned for its excellent home-cooked food – served every day 12.00-15.00 and 18.00-21.30 – this charming pub also boasts a superb wine list and a good selection of ales, lagers, cider, stout, spirits and soft drinks. Open all day Fri, Sat & Sun during the summer months.

Straw Bear procession that is part of a four-day January festival. A man clad in a suit of straw dances and prances through the streets, calling at houses and pubs to entertain the townspeople. The origins are obscure: perhaps it stems from pagan times when corn gods were invoked to produce a good harvest; perhaps it is linked with the wicker idols used by the Druids; perhaps it derives from the performing bears which toured the villages until the 17th century. What is certain is that at the end of the jollities the straw suit is ceremoniously burned.

Whittlesey was the birthplace of the

FLAG FEN

Britain's Bronze Age Centre, The Droveway,
Northey Road, Peterborough PE6 7QJ
Tel: 91733 313414 Fax: 01733 349957
e-mail: office@flagfen.freeserve.co.uk
website: www.flagfen.com

Flag Fen is one of Europe's most important Bronze Age sites; this archaeological jewel is situated on the outskirts of the Cathedral City of Peterborough. This Bronze Age religious site pre dates the Cathedral by nearly 2000 years. The Museum of the Bronze Age contains artefacts found on the site over the last 20 years of excavating.

The park is entered through a uniquely designed 21st Century roundhouse; this visitor centre is your portal to the past, with information boards, and pictures. Once out on the park you will be stepping back into the past, and have the chance to see how your ancestors used to live, as you explore the Bronze Age and Iron Age roundhouses in their landscape setting.

The Preservation Hall contains undercover archaeology, along with a 60 metre mural painting depicting life in the Bronze Age in the Fens. During the summer months, archaeologist's can often be seen at work, uncovering Peterborough's past.

Workshops and Lectures are among our full programme of events, which include Sword and Bronze Casting, Flint Knapping, Theatre in the Park, and our Annual big event, which attracts visitors from across the country. If you would like details please contact us.

writer L P Hartley (*The Go-Between*) and of General Sir Harry Smith, hero of many 19th century campaigns in India. He died in 1860, and the south chapel off **St Mary's** church (note the beautiful spire) was restored and named after him.

Flag Fen
6 miles E of Peterborough signposted from the A47 and A1139

Flag Fen Bronze Age Centre (see panel opposite) comprises massive 3,000-year-old timbers that were part of a major settlement and have been preserved in peaty mud. The site includes a Roman road with its original surface, the oldest wheel in England, re-creations of a Bronze Age settlement, a museum of artefacts, rare breed animals, and a visitor centre with a shop and restaurant. Ongoing excavations, open to the public, make this one of the most important and exciting sites of its kind.

March
14 miles E of Peterborough off the A141

March once occupied the second-largest 'island' in the great level of Fens. As the land was drained the town grew as a trading and religious centre, and in more recent times as a market town and major railway hub. **March and District Museum**, in the High Street, tells the story of the people and the history of March and the surrounding area, and includes a working forge and a

reconstruction of a turn-of-the-century home.

St Wendreda's uniquely dedicated church, at Town End, is notable for its magnificent timber roof, a double hammerbeam with 120 carved angels, a fine font and some impressive gargoyles. John Betjeman declared the church to be 'worth cycling 40 miles into a headwind to see'.

The **Nene—Ouse Navigation Link** runs through the town, affording many attractive riverside walks and, just outside the town off the B1099, **Dunhams Wood** comprises four acres of woodland set among the fens. The site contains an enormous variety of trees, along with sculptures and a miniature railway.

St Wendreda's Church, March

Chatteris

8 miles S of March off the A141

A friendly little market town, the **Chatteris Museum and Council Chamber** features a series of interesting displays on Fenland life and the development of the town. Themes include education, agriculture, transport and local trades, along with temporary exhibitions and local photographs, all housed in five galleries.

The church of St Peter and St Paul has some 14th century features but is mostly more modern in appearance, having been substantially restored in 1909.

Stonea

3 miles SE of March off the B1098

Stonea Camp is the lowest 'hill'-fort in Britain. Built in the Iron Age, it proved unsuccessful against the Romans. A listed ancient monument whose banks and ditches were restored after excavations in 1991, the site is also an increasingly important habitat for wildlife.

Welney

4 miles SE of March off the A1101

The **Wildfowl & Wetlands Trust** (see panel below) in Welney is a nature reserve that attracts large numbers of swans and ducks in winter. Special floodlit 'swan evenings' are held, and there is also a wide range of wild plants and butterflies to be enjoyed.

Wisbech

One of the largest of the Fenland towns, a port in medieval times and still enjoying shipping trade with Europe, Wisbech is at the centre of a thriving

THE WILDFOWL & WETLANDS TRUST

Hundred Foot Bank, Welney, Wisbech, Cambridgeshire PE14 9TN
Tel/Fax: 01353 860711
e-mail: welney@wwt.org.uk
website: wwt.org.uk

The Wildfowl & Wetlands Trust Welney is a wetland paradise of international importance with something to offer whatever the season. In winter, enjoy the magic of hundreds of Whooper and Bewick's Swans accompanied by flocks of thousands of ducks. During the day, carpets of Wigeon graze this precious wetland, while flocks of Pintail, Teal, Gadwall and Shoveler dabble in the pools and lagoons. Late afternoon is a special time as flocks of swans flight-in to claim their night roosting sites. Summer brings an atmosphere of peace and tranquillity broken only by the piping calls of waders, drumming Snipe and the chatter of warblers. Lush meadows are bordered by a dazzling display of Purple Loosestrife, Great Willowherb and Marsh Woundwort. Visitors can stroll along the boardwalks through rustling reedbeds, and spend a while pond-dipping for water beasts. The Visitor Centre houses displays, educational facilities and a well-stocked gift shop. WWT Welney also runs a packed programme of special events throughout the year.

WEST END INN

Levington Road, Wisbech,
Cambridgeshire PE13 1PJ
Tel: 01945 584407 Fax: 01945 467276
e-mail: pwestend@oal.com

Set alongside the river, the **West End Inn** is a cosy little pub which serves up excellent home-cooked food and quality real ales. Charming and comfortable, the large conservatory restaurant boasts a range of traditional English dishes and a very good wine list. Open Mon-Sat 12.00-15.00, 18.00-23.00; Sun 12.00-15.00, 19.00-22.30, food is served every day between 12.00-14.30 and 18.00-21.30. For genuine hospitality and great food and drink, this pub is well worth seeking

agricultural region. The 18th century in particular saw the building of rows of handsome houses, notably in North Brink and South Brink, which face each other across the river. The finest of all the properties is undoubtedly **Peckover House**, built in 1722 and bought at the end of the 18th century by Jonathan Peckover, a member of the Quaker banking family. The family gave the building to the National Trust in 1948. Behind its elegant facade are splendid panelled rooms, Georgian fireplaces with richly carved overmantels, and ornate plaster decorations. At the back of the house is a beautiful walled garden with summerhouses and an orangery.

No 1 South Brink Place is the birthplace of Octavia Hill (1838-1912), co-founder of the National Trust and a tireless worker for the cause of the poor, particularly in the sphere of housing. The house is now the **Octavia Hill Museum** with displays and exhibits commemorating her work.

More Georgian splendour is evident in the area where the Norman castle once stood. The castle was replaced by a bishop's palace in 1478, and in the 17th century by a mansion built for Cromwell's Secretary of State, John Thurloe. Local builder Joseph Medworth built the present Regency villa in 1816; of the Thurloe mansion, only the gate piers remain.

The **Wisbech and Fenland Museum** is one of the oldest purpose-built museums in the country,

Georgian Crescent, Wisbech

ELGOOD'S BREWERY & GARDENS

North Brink, Wisbech,
Cambridgeshire PE12 1LN
Tel: 01945 583160
Fax: 01945 587711

Elgood's Brewery is a 200-year-old classic Georgian brewery situated on the bank of the River Nene. This friendly and relaxing place is set amid true rural splendour.

The brewery was established in 1795, and was one of the first in this style to be built outside London. It is a lively and welcoming establishment, the perfect setting in which to savour a pint of one of their famous award-winning ales, enjoy a range of delicious snacks and home-made cakes in the cafe, or stroll around the gardens. Visitors can also enjoy observing traditional brewing methods, which use original open copper vessels · and can then sample a selection of real ales.

Famous locally and further afield for its welcoming hospitality and classic ales, Elgood's is not just for real ale enthusiasts · though there's plenty here to delight them as well. Behind the brewery is a four-acre garden with 150-year-old specimen trees, herbaceous borders, a lake, rockery, water features, exotics house, rose and herb gardens, and boasting many original Georgian and Victorian features. Beyond the walled gardens, there are lawns leading to the Millennium Maze, planted in the winter of 1992/93 · photographs of its progress are in the Visitors' Centre. The resident team of gardeners are happy to answer any questions. There is no 'formal route' to follow; visitors are welcome to roam at will, enjoying this marvellous garden, as have the Elgoods for many years.

This family-owned business is still run by the Elgoods: Nigel, his wife Anne and their three daughters. Belinda Sutton and Jennifer Everall are responsible for the Brewery and Claire Simpson, who is qualified in garden design, has re-landscaped and planted the garden. Other amenities and attractions to delight the visitor include the café and

licensed bar, gift and plant shop. The staff are helpful and friendly; in the garden shop they are happy to offer advice.

Gardens open: May to September, Wednesday to Friday, Sundays and Bank Holiday Mondays 1 pm · 5 pm; brewery tours Wednesday to Friday 2 pm. Please phone for more details.

and in charming Victorian surroundings visitors can view displays of porcelain, coins, rare geological specimens, Egyptian tomb treasures and several items of national importance, including the manuscript of Charles Dickens' *Great Expectations*, Napoleon's Sèvres breakfast set captured at Waterloo, and an ivory chess set that belonged to Louis XIV.

Museum Square, Wisbech

Wisbech is the stage for East Anglia's premier church flower festival, with flowers in four churches, strawberry teas, crafts, bric-a-brac, plants and a parade of floats. The event takes place at the beginning of July. The most important of the churches is the church of St Peter and St Paul, with two naves under one roof and an independent tower with a peal of ten bells. Note the royal arms of James I and the 17th century wall monuments in the chancel.

Other sights to see in Wisbech include **Elgoods Brewery** (see panel oppose) on North Brink and the impressive 68-foot limestone memorial to Thomas Clarkson, one of the earliest leaders of the abolitionist movement. The monument was designed by Sir George Gilbert Scott in Gothic style.

Still a lively commercial port, Wisbech boasts a restored **Marina** and new facilities for small craft that include floating pontoons with berths for 75 yachts. River trips are available from the yacht harbour.

The Angles Theatre – the third-oldest working theatre in Britain – is a vibrant centre for the arts located in a Georgian building with a history stretching back over 200 years. Some of the best talent in the nation, from poets and musicians to dance, comedy and theatrical troupes – come to perform in the intimate 112-seat auditorium.

Wisbech's **Lilian Ream Photographic Gallery** is named for a daughter of Wisbech born in the late 19th century who at the time of her death in 1961 had amassed a collection of over 1,000 photographs of Wisbech people, places and events, making for a unique and fascinating insight into the history and culture of the town. The gallery is housed in the Tourist Information Centre in Bridge Street, and offers changing exhibitions from this treasure trove of pictorial memorabilia.

Cambridgeshire

KING OF HEARTS

School Road, West Walton, Wisbech,
Cambridgeshire PE14 7ES
Tel/Fax: 01945 584785

Enjoying a well-deserved reputation for quality food, **King of Hearts** serves up a wide range of tempting dishes Tues-Sat 12.00-14.00 and 19.00-21.30; Sundays 12.00-21.00. The décor and surroundings are tasteful and comfortable. Guests from all over the region and beyond come to sample the delights of the menu. *Hidden Places* readers qualify for

10% off if they bring along a copy of this book!

Around Wisbech

West Walton and Walton Highway
3 miles NE of Wisbech off the A47/B198

Several attractions can be found here, notably the Church of St Mary the Virgin in West Walton with its magnificent 13th century detached tower that dominates the landscape. Walton Highway is home to the **Fenland and West Norfolk Aviation Museum**, whose exhibits include Rolls-Royce Merlin engines, a Lightning jet, a Vampire and a Jumbo jet cockpit simulator. The museum is open weekends in summer.

Leverington
1 mile NW of Wisbech off the A1101

The tower and spire of the church of St Leonard date from the 13th and 14th centuries. The most exceptional feature of an exceptionally interesting church is the 15th century stained-glass Jesse window in the north aisle. There are many fine memorials in the churchyard. Oliver Goldsmith wrote *She Stoops to Conquer* while staying in Leverington.

Parson Drove
6 miles W of Wisbech on the B1187

Parson Drove is a Fenland village which Samuel Pepys visited in 1663. He stayed at the village's **Swan Inn**, and mentions it in his diaries, though he was not complimentary. It was a centre of the woad industry until 1914, when the last remaining woad mill was demolished. Parson Drove is most certainly not the *'heathen place'* once described by Pepys!

The Parson Drove Visitors Centre is set in the old Victorian lock-up on the village green, a building with an unusual 170-year history. Photographs and documents trace the story of this lovely Fens village.

TOURIST INFORMATION CENTRES

CAMBRIDGESHIRE

CAMBRIDGE

Wheeler Street
Cambridge
Cambridgeshire
CB2 3QB
Tel: 0906 5862526 (premium rate number,
calls charged at 60p per min)
e-mail: tourism@cambridge.gov.uk
website: www.tourismcambridge.com

ELY

Oliver Cromwell's House
29 St Mary's Street
Ely
Cambridgeshire
CB7 4HF
Tel: 01353 662062
Fax: 01353 668518
e-mail: tic@eastcambs.gov.uk

HUNTINGDON

The Library
Princes Street
Huntingdon
Cambridgeshire
PE29 3PH
Tel: 01480 388588
Fax: 01480 388591
e-mail: hunts.tic@huntsdc.gov.uk
website: www.huntsdc.gov.uk

PETERBOROUGH

3-5 Minster Precincts
Peterborough
Cambridgeshire
PE1 1XS
Tel: 01733 452336
Fax: 01733 452353
e-mail: tic@peterborough.gov.uk

ST NEOTS

The Old Court
8 New Street
St Neots
Cambridgeshire
PE19 1AE
Tel: 01480 388788
Fax: 01480 388791
e-mail: stneots.tic@huntsdc.gov.uk
website: www.huntsdc.gov.uk

WISBECH

2-3 Bridge Street
Wisbech
Cambridgeshire
PE13 1EW
Tel: 01945 583263
Fax: 01945 463078
website: www.fenland.gov.uk

ESSEX

BRAINTREE

Tourist Information Centre
Town Hall Centre
Market Place
Braintree
Essex
CM7 3YG
Tel: 01376 550066
Fax:01376 344345
e-mail: tic@bdctourism.demon.co.uk

BRENTWOOD

Tourist Information Centre
44 High St
Brentwood
Essex
CM14 4AJ
Tel: 01277 200300
Fax: 01277 202375

CHELMSFORD

Tourist Information Centre
County Hall
Market Road
Chelmsford
Essex
CM1 1GG
Tel: 01245 283400
Fax: 01245 430705
e-mail: chelmtic@essexcc.gov.uk

CLACTON-ON-SEA

Tourist Information Centre
23 Pier Avenue
Clacton-on-Sea
Essex
CO15 1QD
Tel: 01255 423400
Fax: 01255 430906
e-mail: emorgan@tendringdc.gov.uk

COLCHESTER
Visitor Information Centre
1 Queen Street
Colchester
Essex
CO1 2PG
Tel: 01206 282920
Fax: 01206 282924

FLATFORD
Flatford Lane
Flatford, East Bergholt
Colchester
Essex
CO7 6UL
Tel 01206 299460
e-mail: flatfordvic@babergh.gov.uk

HARWICH
Tourist information Centre
Iconfield Park
Parkeston
Harwich
Essex
CO12 4EN
Tel: 01255 506139
Fax: 01255 240570
e-mail:
harwich@touristinformation.fsnet.co.uk

MALDON
Tourist Information Centre
Coach Lane
Maldon
Essex
CM9 4UH
Tel: 01621 856503
Fax: 01621 875873
e-mail: tic@maldon.gov.uk

SAFFRON WALDEN
Tourist Information Centre
1 Market Place
Saffron Walden
Essex
CBIO 1HR
Tel: 01799 510444
Fax: 01799 510445
e-mail: tourism@uttlesford.gov.uk

SOUTHEND
Tourist Information Centre
19 High Street
Southend-on-Sea
Essex
SS1 IJE
Tel: 01702 215120
Fax: 01702 431449
e-mail: shop@sbctic3.fsnet.co.uk

THURROCK
Tourist Information Centre
Granada Motorway Service Area
M25 Thurrock
Grays
Essex
RM16 3BG
Tel 01708 863733
Fax: 01708 862440
e-mail: kwillson.tc@gtnet.gov.uk

WALTHAM ABBEY
Tourist Information Centre
Unit B
2-4 Highbridge Street
Waltham Abbey
Essex
EN9 1DG
Tel 01992 652295
Fax: 01992 716234
e-mail: townclerk@walthamabbey.org.uk

NORFOLK

AYLSHAM
Bure Valley Railway Station
Norwich Road
Aylsham
Norfolk
NR11 6BW
Tel: 01263 733903
Fax: 01263 733814
e-mail: aylsham.tic@broadland.gov.uk

CROMER
Prince of Wales Road
Cromer
Norfolk
NR27 9HS
Tel: 01263 512497
Fax: 01263 513613
e-mail: jn@north-norfolk.gov.uk

DISS
Meres Mouth
Mere Street
Diss
Norfolk
IP22 3AG
Tel: 01379 650523
Fax: 01379 650838
e-mail: disstic@dial.pipex.com

DOWNHAM MARKET

The Priory Centre
78 Priory Road
Downham Market
Norfolk PE38 9JS
Tel: 01366 387440
Fax: 01366 385 042
e-mail: downham-market.tic@west-norfolk.gov.uk

GREAT YARMOUTH

Marine Parade
Great Yarmouth
Norfolk
NR31 8NE
Tel: 01493 842195
Fax: 01493 858588
e-mail: tourism@great-yarmouth.gov.uk

HOVETON

Station Road
Hoveton
Norfolk
NR12 8UR
Tel: 01603 782281
Fax: 01603 782281

HUNSTANTON

Town Hall
The Green
Hunstanton
Norfolk
PE36 6BQ
Tel: 01485 532610
Fax: 01485 533972
e-mail: hunstanton.tic@west-norfolk.gov.uk

KING'S LYNN

The Custom House
Purfleet Quay
King's Lynn
Norfolk
PE30 1HP
Tel: 01553 763044
Fax: 01553 819441
e-mail: kings-lynn.tic@west-norfolk.gov.uk

MUNDESLEY

2 Station Road
Mundesley
Norfolk
NR11 8JH
Tel: 01263 721070
Fax: 01263 722796
e-mail: jn@north-norfolk.gov.uk

NORWICH

The Guildhall
Gaol Hill
Norwich
Norfolk
NR2 1NF
Tel: 01603 666071
Fax: 01603 765389
e-mail: tourism.norwich@gtnet.gov.uk

SHERINGHAM

Station Approach
Sheringham
Norfolk
NR26 8RA
Tel: 01263 824329
Fax: 01263 821668
e-mail: jn@north-norfolk.gov.uk

WELLS-NEXT-THE-SEA

Staithe Street
Wells-next-the-Sea
Norfolk
NR23 1AN
Tel: 01328 710885
Fax: 01328 711405
e-mail: jn@north-norfolk.gov.uk

SUFFOLK

ALDEBURGH

152 High Street
Aldeburgh
Suffolk
IP15 5AQ
Tel: 01728 453637
Fax: 01728 453637
e-mail: atic@suffolkcoastal.gov.uk

BECCLES

The Quay
Fen Lane
Beccles
Suffolk
NR34 9BH
Tel: 01502 713196
Fax: 01502 713196

BURY ST EDMUNDS

6 Angel Hill
Bury St Edmunds
Suffolk
IP33 1UZ
Tel: 01284 764667
Fax: 01284 757084
e-mail: tic@stedsbc.gov.uk

FELIXSTOWE

The Seafront
Felixstowe
Suffolk
IP11 2AE
Tel: 01394 276770
Fax: 01394 277456
e-mail: tic@suffolkcoastal.gov.uk

IPSWICH

St Stephens Church
St Stephens Lane
Ipswich
Suffolk
IP1 1DP
Tel: 01473 258070
Fax: 01473 432017
e-mail: tourist@ipswich.gov.uk

LAVENHAM

Lady Street
Lavenham
Suffolk
CO10 9RA
Tel: 01787 248207
Fax: 01787 249459
e-mail: lavenhamtic@babergh.gov.uk

LOWESTOFT

East Point Pavilion
Royal Plain
Lowestoft
Suffolk
NR33 OAP
Tel: 01502 533600
Fax: 01502 539023
e-mail: touristinfo@waveney.gov.uk

NEWMARKET

Palace House
Palace Street
Newmarket
Suffolk
CB8 8EP
Tel: 01638 667200
Fax: 01638 660394
e-mail: newmarket.tic@forest-heath-dc.demon.co.uk

SOUTHWOLD

69 High Street
Southwold
Suffolk
IP18 6DS
Tel: 01502 724729
Fax: 01502 722978
e-mail: southwoldtic@waveney.gov.uk

STOWMARKET

Wilkes Way
Stowmarket
Suffolk
IP14 1DE
Tel: 01449 676800
Fax: 01449 614691
e-mail: info@tic.keme.co.uk

SUDBURY

Town Hall
Market Hill
Sudbury
Suffolk
CO10 1TL
Tel: 01787 881320
Fax: 01787 242129
e-mail: sudburytic@babergh.gov.uk

WOODBRIDGE

Station Buildings
Woodbridge
Suffolk
IP12 4AJ
Tel: 01394 382240
Fax: 01394 386337
e-mail: wtic@suffolkcoastal.gov.uk

LIST OF ADVERTISERS

H

I

J

K

L

M

N

INDEX OF TOWNS, VILLAGES AND PLACES OF INTEREST

HIDDEN PLACES ORDER FORM

To order any of our publications just fill in the payment details below and complete the order form. For orders of less than 4 copies please add £1 per book for postage and packing. Orders over 4 copies are P & P free.

Please Complete Either:

I enclose a cheque for £ [   ] made payable to Travel Publishing Ltd

Or:

Card No: [   ]   Expiry Date: [   ]

Signature: [   ]

Name: [   ]

Address: [   ]

Tel no: [   ]

Please either send, telephone, fax or e-mail your order to:

Travel Publishing Ltd, 7a Apollo House, Calleva Park, Aldermaston, Berkshire RG7 8TN

Tel: 0118 981 7777   Fax: 0118 982 0077   e-mail: karen@travelpublishing.co.uk

	PRICE	QUANTITY		PRICE	QUANTITY
HIDDEN PLACES REGIONAL TITLES			**HIDDEN INNS TITLES**		
Cambs & Lincolnshire	£7.99	....	East Anglia	£5.99	....
Chilterns	£7.99	....	Heart of England	£5.99	....
Cornwall	£8.99	....	Lancashire & Cheshire	£5.99	....
Derbyshire	£8.99	....	North of England	£5.99	....
Devon	£8.99	....	South	£5.99	....
Dorset, Hants & Isle of Wight	£8.99	....	South East	£7.99	....
East Anglia	£8.99	....	South and Central Scotland	£5.99	....
Gloucs, Wiltshire & Somerset	£8.99	....	Wales	£7.99	....
Heart of England	£7.99	....	Welsh Borders	£5.99	....
Hereford, Worcs & Shropshire	£7.99	....	West Country	£7.99	....
Highlands & Islands	£7.99	....	Yorkshire	£5.99	....
Kent	£8.99	....	**COUNTRY LIVING RURAL GUIDES**		
Lake District & Cumbria	£8.99	....	East Anglia	£9.99	....
Lancashire & Cheshire	£8.99	....	Heart of England	£9.99	....
Lincolnshire & Notts	£8.99	....	Ireland	£10.99	....
Northumberland & Durham	£8.99	....	Scotland	£10.99	....
Sussex	£8.99	....	South of England	£9.99	....
Yorkshire	£8.99	....	South East of England	£9.99	....
HIDDEN PLACES NATIONAL TITLES			Wales	£10.99	....
England	£10.99	....	West Country	£9.99	....
Ireland	£10.99	....			
Scotland	£10.99	....			
Wales	£9.99	....	**Total Quantity**	[ ]	

Post & Packing [   ]   **Total Value** [   ]

Easy-to-use, Informative
Travel Guides on the British Isles

READER REACTION FORM

The *Travel Publishing* research team would like to receive reader's comments on any visitor attractions or places reviewed in the book and also recommendations for suitab le entries to be included in the next edition. This will help ensure that the *Country Living series of Rural Guides* continues to provide its readers with useful information on the more interesting, unusual or unique features of each attraction or place ensuring that their visit to the local area is an enjoyable and stimulating experience. To provide your comments or recommendations would you please complete the forms below and overleaf as indicated and send to:

The Research Department, Travel Publishing Ltd,
7a Apollo House, Calleva Park, Aldermaston, Reading, RG7 8TN.

Your Name:

Your Address:

Your Telephone Number:

Please tick as appropriate:

    Comments ☐   Recommendation ☐

Name of Establishment:

Address:

Telephone Number:

Name of Contact:

READER REACTION FORM

Comment or Reason for Recommendation:

READER REACTION FORM

The *Travel Publishing* research team would like to receive reader's comments on any visitor attractions or places reviewed in the book and also recommendations for suitab le entries to be included in the next edition. This will help ensure that the *Country Living series of Rural Guides* continues to provide its readers with useful information on the more interesting, unusual or unique features of each attraction or place ensuring that their visit to the local area is an enjoyable and stimulating experience. To provide your comments or recommendations would you please complete the forms below and overleaf as indicated and send to:

**The Research Department, Travel Publishing Ltd,
7a Apollo House, Calleva Park, Aldermaston, Reading, RG7 8TN.**

Your Name:

Your Address:

Your Telephone Number:

Please tick as appropriate:

Comments ☐   Recommendation ☐

Name of Establishment:

Address:

Telephone Number:

Name of Contact:

READER REACTION FORM

Comment or Reason for Recommendation:

READER REACTION FORM

The *Travel Publishing* research team would like to receive reader's comments on any visitor attractions or places reviewed in the book and also recommendations for suitab le entries to be included in the next edition. This will help ensure that the *Country Living series of Rural Guides* continues to provide its readers with useful information on the more interesting, unusual or unique features of each attraction or place ensuring that their visit to the local area is an enjoyable and stimulating experience. To provide your comments or recommendations would you please complete the forms below and overleaf as indicated and send to:

**The Research Department, Travel Publishing Ltd,
7a Apollo House, Calleva Park, Aldermaston, Reading, RG7 8TN.**

Your Name:

Your Address:

Your Telephone Number:

Please tick as appropriate:

Comments ☐   Recommendation ☐

Name of Establishment:

Address:

Telephone Number:

Name of Contact:

READER REACTION FORM

Comment or Reason for Recommendation:

READER REACTION FORM

The *Travel Publishing* research team would like to receive reader's comments on any visitor attractions or places reviewed in the book and also recommendations for suitab le entries to be included in the next edition. This will help ensure that the *Country Living series of Rural Guides* continues to provide its readers with useful information on the more interesting, unusual or unique features of each attraction or place ensuring that their visit to the local area is an enjoyable and stimulating experience. To provide your comments or recommendations would you please complete the forms below and overleaf as indicated and send to:

**The Research Department, Travel Publishing Ltd,
7a Apollo House, Calleva Park, Aldermaston, Reading, RG7 8TN.**

Your Name:

Your Address:

Your Telephone Number:

Please tick as appropriate:

Comments ☐   Recommendation ☐

Name of Establishment:

Address:

Telephone Number:

Name of Contact:

READER REACTION FORM

Comment or Reason for Recommendation: